CONTROVERSIAL ISSUES

IN SOCIAL WORK

CONTROVERSIAL ISSUES IN SOCIAL WORK

Edited by

Eileen Gambrill

Robert Pruger

University of California, Berkeley

ALLYN AND BACON
Boston London Toronto Sydney Tokyo Singapore

Series Editor: Karen Hanson
Series Editorial Assistant: Laura Lynch
Production Administrator: Susan McIntyre
Editorial-Production Service: Ruttle, Shaw & Wetherill, Inc.
Text Designer: Anne Marie Fleming
Cover Administrator: Linda Dickinson
Cover Designer: Suzanne Harbison
Manufacturing Buyer: Louise Richardson

Copyright © 1992 by Allyn and Bacon
A Division of Simon & Schuster, Inc.
160 Gould Street
Needham Heights, MA 02194

ISBN 0–205–12902–1

Printed in the United States of America

10   9   8   7   6   5   97

Contents

II. Debates about Social Work Knowledge

III. Debates about Social Work Practice

IV. Debates about Special Client Populations

Preface

    This book has four major purposes: (1) to present different perspectives on a number of current issues related to social work; (2) to demonstrate the value of presenting different positions concerning an issue in a debate format; (3) to demonstrate that controversy can be carried out in a constructive manner that highlights (rather than mutes) issues involved in each topic; and (4) to offer readers some guidelines and practice opportunities to enhance their skills in identifying and countering tendencies and fallacies that result in the evasion, distortion, or confusion of issues.

    Controversial Issues in Social Work is for social work educators as well as social work practitioners and students of social work. It is for readers who wish to deepen their understanding of issues of concern to social work by considering opposing viewpoints on these issues. It is for use both within and outside of formal educational programs. It could be used as a text in courses on the field of social work or social work practice to highlight points that should be considered when discussing or thinking about important issues or it could be used to supplement a main text.

    A representative set of issues was selected that concern a broad array of professional interests, levels of practice, client populations, and problems. Criteria for selection included a decision that any issue was a proper professional matter, had a genuinely controversial content, and that there were well informed, willing and fairly matched opponents. Twenty-four different issues are discussed in this book. We selected some issues that are often avoided, such as "Should social workers blow the whistle on incompetent colleagues?" Although the code of ethics of the National Association of

Social Workers says that social workers have an obligation to offer competent services to their clients, many (if not most) social workers do not blow the whistle on incompetent colleagues (although they complain often about them). Our selection of issues reveals that we are not persuaded that because something is, it ought to be. This can be seen by inclusion of questions "Should social workers work for for-profit firms?" and "Should social workers be licensed?" Each discussant prepared a position statement arguing for or against a position and, in addition, prepared a rebuttal to the opposite side. This format allows for an engaging exchange that offers readers an opportunity to consider the relevance of rejoinder points that are made. Questions can be raised such as: Does the reply address points raised in the opposing statements? Are the replies persuasive? Is any evidence presented to support claims made? Have relevant facts been cited?

The issues discussed are clustered into four parts. Debates about social work as a profession are included in Part I, such as: "Are union membership and professional social work incompatible?" Understanding issues that confront the profession as a whole will help social workers to be more informed about factors that influence their day-by-day practice with clients and will be helpful in identifying options for enhancing the quality of practice and job satisfaction. The issues in Part II all relate to the knowledge base of social work; what knowledge should be drawn on in offering services to clients? Examples include: "Should all social workers be well trained in behavioral principles?"; "Should social workers accept a disease model of substance abuse?" There is a notable lack of agreement about what criteria to use in selecting knowledge. That is, there is little agreement about what social workers who offer certain kinds of services should know (content knowledge) and what skills they should possess. What appears to be agreement when knowledge or skills are described in a vague manner often vanishes when concrete descriptions are given. Nor does agreement, even on a concrete level, mean that social workers use knowledge and skills agreed on as desirable. For example, most social workers (if not all) would agree that child welfare workers should know the grounds on which parental rights can be terminated in their state. However, agreement does not mean that child welfare workers indeed possess and make use of this information. Even when there is agreement on knowledge and skills of value, there may not be agreement on ensuring that these are used in practice as can be seen in the discussion of the question "Should part of social workers' salaries be contingent on outcomes achieved with clients?" in Part III. Debates about social work practice are included in this third part. Other examples include: "Should social workers use written service agreements with clients?" and "Should community organization be based on a grassroots strategy?" Debates about special client populations are contained in Part IV. Here readers will find five questions that relate to different fields of practice such as "Should maternal preference govern child custody cases?" and "Should welfare clients be required to work?"

The very selection of issues reflects certain beliefs and biases. Take for example the question "Should social workers be licensed?" When we asked a person who has argued publicly for the licensing of social workers, he refused on the grounds that the question was no longer important, that everyone agreed that social workers should be licensed. This reflects a common tendency (unless we develop skills for avoiding it) to think that what we believe and what most people believe is the best position. We do not believe that a policy or position is necessarily the best one because most people happen to believe it or because it is "in place" as an accepted practice. That is, we are not persuaded that consensus is necessarily a sound basis for acceptance of a point of view. Too many widely accepted positions have been found to be inaccurate (Gardner, 1957). In fact, we hope that one effect of this book will be to encourage readers to question what is widely accepted as well as what is new and innovative. There is a special need to question widely accepted views that work against the best interests of clients rather than for them.

Ideas, not persons, are the central element of a debate. Thus, it is not surprising that many of our opposing debaters have ongoing personal and collegial relationships with each other, or at least they worked cooperatively to produce useful debates. For example, several contributors agreed to argue positions that went beyond their own beliefs in order to make their presentation more interesting and useful and because they thought there would be some fun in taking on such a challenge. Some discussants reviewed each other's statements or outlines to suggest how opposing views might be strengthened and to ensure that the two statements addressed as many of the same points as possible. One debate takes place between a husband and wife; one between a former husband and wife. Several take place between friends or members of the same faculty. When one of the original debaters had to drop out of the international social work debate, the remaining one agreed to write both sides. (A pseudonym is used here to meet the formal debate requisite of two sides.) Nevertheless, the debate is a lively one precisely because the author, although he does have a personal conviction about the issue, has a good grasp of both sides of the argument. Are criticisms of positions accurate? (See introduction.)

Some people we approached said they would argue a controversial question only if they could argue both sides of the issue; they said they did not want to have their name associated with one side of a controversial issue although this reflected their true position. There is indeed evidence that people who argue a position are associated with believing it even when listeners are told that positions were assigned on a random basis (Nisbett and Ross, 1980). We had trouble finding anyone who would argue some positions. For example, many people refused to argue that "Social workers are well trained" although the first author was prepared to argue the position that social workers are *not* well trained.

Preparing this book highlights the existence of a substantial realm of controversy in social work that should be clarified and communicated to students rather than glossed over. No single work could capture all significant issues. It is hoped that other works will continue the task of identifying, organizing, and discussing controversial topics in the field. Possible issues for future attention include the following:

- Should family responsibility laws be enforced?
- Are clinical social workers well trained?
- Are social workers well trained for administrative responsibilities?
- Should interracial adoptions (adoptions by gays) be permitted?
- Should social workers accept gifts offered by clients?
- Can social workers be generalists?
- Should a social worker terminate a case against a client's wish to do so?
- Can a social worker promise confidentiality?
- Should there be a voucher for social services?
- Do parents have a right to know about problems revealed by children in therapy?

We hope that social workers of many different persuasions will find the dialogues interesting and useful in sharpening their understanding of issues that influence their everyday practice. Simply reading the list of issues can reveal what "side you are on." Reading the debates in this book can help readers to sharpen their clear thinking skills. Tendencies that are likely to result in errors such as the tendency to search only for evidence that confirms favored positions as well as fallacies that evade, obscure, or distort positions are described in the introduction and in Appendix A. Familiarity with these tendencies and fallacies as well as with methods to avoid and counter them will enhance critical thinking skills that will be useful whether working with clients, reading the professional literature, or thinking by oneself. Readers can sharpen their skills in recognizing and countering fallacies that get in the way of arriving at informed positions by using material in the introduction and Appendix A as well as other sources such as *Straight and Crooked Thinking* (Thouless, 1974) when reviewing statements. For example, does an author "beg the question" (assume what he or she is trying to support)? Do authors distort a position? Are key data omitted? That is, is information suppressed? Is emotional language used that influences but does not inform?

There are two ways to read this book. One is to read only statements that support preferred positions. This approach will result in the least benefit for readers; readers who do this will essentially have their biases confirmed. Another way to read this book (which we would recommend) is to read both statements and rebuttals on an issue, paying special attention to arguments against favored positions. Only in this way are readers likely to avoid the confirmation bias, the tendency to see and recall only points that favor preferred positions. We did not prepare this book to offer readers an opportunity to solidify biased positions on an issue. We prepared this book so that readers could become more informed about the many factors that should be considered in arriving at an informed position on each question.

We hope our readers will enjoy the discussions in the book and that reading arguments on both sides of issues will deepen understanding and appreciation of factors related to the questions addressed and provide an opportunity to enhance critical thinking skills. In the course of preparing this book we discovered many other books that are arranged in a debate format. Greenhaven Press has an opposing viewpoint series containing well over thirty topics including poverty, social justice, death and dying, teenage sexuality, and chemical dependency. The Dushkin Publishing Group has a *Taking Sides* Series in which "clashing views" on controversial issues are presented in areas such as legal issues (Katsh, 1986), crime and criminology (Monk, 1989), and social issues (Finsterbusch & McKenna, 1986). Stone-song Press has published *Pro and Con* (Isaacson, 1983) in which fifty-three topics are discussed including psychiatry, lying, capital punishment, the equal rights amendment, and religious cults.

We wish to thank our contributors for preparing statements and replies and for their enthusiastic reactions to the format of this book. We invite readers to share their reactions to both the format of this book and content of the discussions and to suggest topics for discussion. Readers will no doubt have their own views on the topics discussed in this book. Whether these are influenced by reading the debates will depend on many factors including the cogency of individual statements and rebuttals, the transparency of weak appeals that do not foster careful consideration of issues (such as use of emotional language), the reader's skill in detecting and countering fallacies in thinking, the reader's knowledge of content related to each topic, and attitudes that affect clear thinking, such as curiosity and openness to exploring opposing viewpoints.

WORKS CITED

Gardner, M. (1957). *Fads and fallacies in the name of science.* New York: Dover.

Nisbitt, R., & Ross, L. (1980). *Human inference: Strategies and shortcomings of social judgment.* Englewood Cliffs, N.J.: Prentice-Hall.

Thouless, R.H. (1974). *Straight and crooked thinking.* London: Pan.

CONTROVERSIAL ISSUES
IN SOCIAL WORK

Introduction

Controversy is often downplayed and discouraged in social work. Rarely do we see a position statement followed by a number of invited responses to this position. Too rarely are panel discussions offered at conferences in which different perspectives on an issue or case are presented together with rebuttals to each view. Students at the School of Social Welfare at the University of California at Berkeley tried for years to interest faculty with different practice perspectives to discuss a case in a panel presentation. Most of the individuals approached refused on the grounds that this would be divisive. Proposal of a presentation of different views seemed to trigger words such as argumentative, rather than informative, provocative, useful. Thus, too rarely do students read or hear models of constructive controversy. Reasons include a confusion between arguments and debate, a reluctance to think more deeply and expose what one thinks, and an acceptance by many practitioners and authors of unsupported pronouncements rather than carefully reasoned arguments or empirical evidence.

Controversy in which different positions on a question are offered and considered in an open, inquiring manner should be a hallmark of quality professional education and practice. There are many positive functions of controversy. Discussion of questions within a framework that highlights the value of considering both sides encourages exploration of alternative positions. Errors are more likely to be spotted and valuable options are more likely to be identified if opposing views are considered. This will enhance the quality of services provided to clients. Research on human inferences shows that we selectively search for evidence that supports preferred beliefs and tend to ignore evidence that contradicts favored assumptions (Nisbett & Ross, 1980; Snyder & Thomsen, 1988). These tendencies encourage us to overlook limitations of favored positions; they often occur with little awareness on our part. This confirmation bias may result in selection of inferior options. For example, if a clinical social worker assumes that a client's depression is related to her abuse as a child and does not examine other possibilities such as environmental or physiological factors, inappropriate treatment methods may be recommended that may exacerbate client distress (Mays & Franks, 1985).

A reluctance to discuss differences of opinion because of fear of finding errors overlooks the advantages of discovering new ways to view events (Kottler & Blau, 1989). You cannot say you have a firm grip on your own position on an issue until you can competently state the opposite view. And you do not really understand the other side of an argument until you can state it so that those who hold that view agree you have stated it correctly. Debates that can be studied offer a route to this kind of mastery of an issue.

Styles of Controversy

The term *debate* often triggers negative reactions such as arguments, back-stabbing, and so on. This image may be encouraged by media presentations in which discussants are permitted to insult, harass, and interrupt people with different ideas. The discussion of differences does not have to be conducted in such a crude manner, as illustrated by the examples in this book.

Debates are often thought of as a form of combat. For the observer there is some innocent fun in watching two sides engage each other. Some of the appeal of the form derives from this element of conflict—of winning and losing. This book uses a debate format because it is a good way to explore issues and ideas. What matters is how the clash of ideas (rather than of persons) leads to greater clarity and understanding of an issue. A reader might conclude that one side of a debate was better argued. Nevertheless, the reader might still find issues raised in the opposing side that are useful in constructing a new view.

Evaluating Arguments

The discussions in this book present arguments for or against a position. "Argumentation" refers to the process of making claims, challenging these, backing them with reasons, (assertions), criticizing these reasons, responding to the criticism offered (Toulmin, Rieke, & Janik, 1979, p. 13). An argument in this sense refers to the claims and reasons offered for these; that is, "a set of assertions that is used to support a belief" (Nickerson, 1986.

p. 2). This term has a different meaning in everyday use in which it refers to disagreements between two people as in "They had an argument about who will go to the store."

Arguments consist of parts and they can be taken apart as well as put together. They may be strong (convincing) or weak (unconvincing), simple or complex. Assertions may involve statements of fact ("a belief for which there is enough evidence to justify a high degree of confidence," Nickerson, 1986, p. 36), assumptions, or hypotheses. The term "assumption" refers to "an assertion that we either believe to be true in spite of being unable to produce compelling evidence of its truth, or are willing to accept as true for purposes of debate or discussion" (Nickerson, 1986, p. 37). An hypothesis is an assertion that we do not know to be true but that we think is testable. Assumptions, hypotheses, or statements of fact may be used as premises in an argument, or they may serve as conclusions.

A key part of an argument is the claim, conclusion, or position that is put forward. (Excessive wordiness makes a conclusion difficult to identify.) A second critical feature of an argument is the reasons or premises offered to support the claim made. "The credibility of a conclusion can be no greater than the least credible of the premises from which it is drawn, so a conclusion cannot be considered a statement of fact unless all of the premises are statements of fact . . ." (Nickerson, 1986, p. 37). Premises can be divided into two parts—grounds and warrants. The grounds (data or evidence) must be relevant to the claim as well as sufficient to support the claim and here is where "warrants" come in. Warrants concern the inference or justification of making the connection between the grounds and the claim (Toulmin, Rieke, & Janik, 1979). Do the grounds provide support for the claim made? Warrants may involve appeals to common knowledge, empirical evidence, practice theory, and so on. So warrants purport to offer evidence for making the step from the grounds to the claim and the strength of the support offered should be evaluated. Questions of concern include: How reliably does the warrant offer such evidence? Are the grounds necessary or sufficient? These questions are of concern both when considering the merits of a social worker's assessment concerning a particular client as well as when considering broader questions (Bromley, 1986).

An argument may be unsound for one of three reasons: (1) there may be something wrong with its logical structure; (2) it may contain false premises; (3) it may be irrelevant or circular. The latter two kinds are *informal* fallacies; they have a correct logical form but are still incorrect. So informal fallacies are related to the *content* of arguments rather than to their form. In deductive arguments, if the reasoning is logically valid, the conclusion necessarily follows (although it may not be true if one or more of the premises may be false.) Deductive arguments can produce false conclusions when one of the premises is false or when one of the rules of deductive inference is violated as in the logical fallacy of affirming the consequent.

The conclusion may be true but it may be invalid because it is arrived at by an illogical inference. Seldom are the major premises as well as the conclusion clearly stated in deductive arguments; more typically, at least one premise is missing. Questions of concern in evaluating a logical argument include: (1) Is it complete? (2) Is its meaning clear? (3) Is it valid (does the conclusion follow from the premises)? (4) Do I believe the premises? (Nickerson, 1986, p. 88). An argument may be worthy of consideration even though it has some defects. The following steps are helpful in analyzing incomplete logical arguments.

- Identify the conclusion or key assertion.
- List all the other explicit assertions that make up the argument as given.
- Add any unstated assertions that are necessary to make the argument complete. (Put them in parentheses to distinguish them from assertions that are explicit in the argument as given.)
- Order the premises (or supporting assertions) and conclusion (or key assertion) so as to show the structure of the argument.'' (Nickerson, 1986, p. 87)

With plausible (inductive) arguments, there are no objective criteria; what is convincing may differ from person to person. Inductive reasoning involves generalizing from the particular to the general. It is assumed that what is true of the sample is true of all possible cases. Because plausible (inductive) arguments do not have to fit any particular form, objective evaluation is more difficult. As with logical arguments, the truth of the premises is important to assess. However, even if these are assumed to be true, people may disagree as to whether they provide evidence for a conclusion. Helpful questions when evaluating inductive arguments include the following:

- Are the facts accurate?
- Do the examples consist of isolated or universal instances?
- Do the examples used cover a significant time period?
- Are the examples given typical or atypical?
- Is the conclusion correctly stated?
- Is the argument really of concern—the "so what" and "what harm" questions. (Huber, 1962, p. 140)

There are many excellent descriptions of how to analyze arguments (Nickerson, 1986; Scriven, 1976; Toulmin, Rieke, & Janik, 1979).

Counterarguments should be considered. Are there arguments on the same issue that point to the opposite conclusion or to a somewhat different conclusion? For example, an analogy may be used to support the opposite conclusion. Key premises or conclusions may be missing, and a critical part of examining an argument is filling in these parts. Arguments should not be dismissed simply because they are presented emotionally or because a conclusion is disliked; the emotion with which a position is presented is not necessarily related to the soundness of an argument (Scriven, 1976). Many statements, written or spoken, are opinions or points of view; "they frequently don't pass the test of providing reasons for a conclusion, reasons that can be separated from a conclusion" (Scriven, 1967, p. 67). The question is, can the premises be established independently of the conclusion? Is the argument convincing?

Kinds of Arguments

Arguments occur in different contexts, including courts of law, case conferences, Joe's Bar, and the American Psychiatric Association annual convention. These different contexts influence the manner in which a topic is discussed due to different norms, values, procedures, and requirements for types of evidence that are acceptable or unacceptable (Bromley, 1986). Courts of law favor an adversarial (competitive) format in which each party tries to settle a dispute in its favor. In arbitrational arguments, there is a focus on arriving at a compromise resolution that is satisfactory to both parties. In both professional and scientific contexts, value is (or should be) placed on a "willingness and ability to be self-critical, to deal sensibly with justifiable objections and queries from others" (Bromley, 1986, p. 233).

Misunderstandings and bad feelings may result when participants in a discussion do not recognize that different kinds of arguments are being used. Lawyers and social workers often have negative views of each other due to different frameworks for argument analysis. Lawyers may view clinicians as fuzzy thinkers and clinicians may view lawyers as inhumane and legalistic in their questioning concerning the credibility of evidence.

Common Sources of Error
in Thinking about Issues

Social workers are rarely trained to identify and counter formal and informal fallacies that may get in the way of viewing issues clearly. Reading the debates in this book provides an opportunity to increase skill in recognizing fallacies. We are all guilty of using these fallacies at times, and the more skilled we are in identifying them, the easier it will be to avoid them.

Some arguments are false although they are valid. A valid argument is one whose premises, if true, offer good or sufficient grounds for accepting a conclusion. The incorrectness of premises is often overlooked resulting in poor choices. Most fallacies are *informal* ones; that is, they do not involve a formal mistake. There are many different kinds of informal fallacies (see for example, Thouless, 1974). Ad hominem arguments may be used in which the background, habits, associates, or personality of the person are criticized or appealed to rather than his or her agreement. Variants of ad hominem arguments include guilt (or credit) by association, the "bad seed fallacy," appeals of faulty motives or good intentions, "special pleading," and false claims of inconsistency. Vacuous guarantees may be offered, as when assuming that because a condition ought to be, it *is* the case without providing support for the position (see Appendix 1).

Fallacies that evade the facts, such as "begging the question," appear to address them but do not. Variants of question begging include use of alleged certainty, circular reasoning, use of unfounded generalizations to support a conclusion, complex, trick, or leading questions and ignoring the issue. Some informal fallacies overlook the facts as in the fallacy of the sweeping generalization, in which a rule or assumption that is valid in general is applied to a specific example for which it is not valid. Other informal fallacies distort facts or positions as in strawperson arguments in which a position that is similar to but significantly different from the one presented is described and attacked. The informal fallacies of false cause, forcing an extension, and inappropriate use of analogues also involve the distortion of facts or positions. Diversions may be used to direct attention away from a main point of an argument. Trivial points, irrelevant objections, or emotional appeals may be made. Some fallacies work by creating confusion such as feigned lack of understanding and excessive wordiness that obscures arguments. Knowledge of formal and informal fallacies will decrease the likelihood that judgments will be influenced by these sources of error.

Misuse of language contributes to inaccurate judgments. Careless use of language is perhaps the greatest source of error. Confusion about the different functions of language may result in muddled discussions as may confusion among different levels of abstraction. If terms are not clarified, confused discussions may result because of the assumption of one word, one meaning. Two people discussing the merits of selecting practice knowledge on empirical research may disagree because different definitions of the term *empirical research* are used; the discussions may go past each other rather than engage each other. Other examples of vague terms that may have quite different definitions include abuse, aggression, and addiction. Reification of terms (using a descriptive term as an explanatory term) offers an illusion of understanding without providing any real understanding. Technical terms may be carelessly used resulting in "bafflegarb" or "psychobabble"—words that sound informative but are empty in terms of being of use in making sound decisions. We are often unaware of the influence of emotional terms. Labels have emotional connotations which influence us in ways that do not necessarily enhance the accuracy of decisions. We are influenced by primacy effects (by what we hear first) and often misuse verbal speculation (assuming that what is can be discovered by merely thinking about it). Knowledge of fallacies related to use of language and care in using language will improve the quality of judgments whether thinking, listening, writing, or reading.

Lack of self-knowledge is an impediment to clear thinking (Nickerson, 1985). Self-knowledge includes familiarity with resources and limitations of reasoning processes in general as well as knowledge of personal strengths and limitations that influence decision making. In addition to limitations of knowledge of content related to an area, there are also attitudinal obstacles that compromise the quality of reasoning. (Knowledge of content in an area is often critical in making informed decisions, see for example Elstein et al., 1978). These include carelessness, lack of interest in having a carefully thought out position on a matter, a wish to appear decisive, and a vested interest in a certain outcome. A preference for mystery over mastery and unconstructive reactions to "mistakes" and lack of success may interfere with clear thinking as may a low tolerance for ambiguity and a desire for quick success (Gambrill, 1990). Lack of understanding of the relationship between personal preferences for certain perspectives and social and cultural values and incentives will be an obstacle to examining beliefs. Many obstacles to clear thinking such as procrastination and distractibility are related to the quality of self-management skills.

Some fallacies are related to a misunderstanding of probabilities. An example is confusion of the inverse, e.g., assuming that the probability of a disease given a symptom is the same as the probability of the symptom given the disease. There may be a confusion between facts, beliefs and opinions, or between fact and theory.

Criteria for Evaluating Data

Discussion of issues involve presentations of facts, beliefs and opinions. People differ in the criteria they use to evaluate the credibility of data. In an empirical approach, it is assumed that the credibility of an assertion is related to the uniqueness and supportive value of the predictions that have been tested. Credibility of assumptions may be assessed using quite different criteria such as authority or mysticism (Thorngate & Plouffe, 1987). Differences of opinion about the value of empirical evidence arise in a number of debates in this book. Because of misunderstanding about and frequent distortions of use of scientific criteria, it is important to clarify what this is and what it is not.

An understanding of the scientific method is not usually available to the public. "It itself is esoteric knowledge" (Stevens, 1988, p. 382). Social workers are not immune from this educational deficit which is so common and which accounts for the ready acceptance of proposed causal factors without any evidence that they are relevant. Some confuse a scientific approach with "scientism," the belief that science knows or will soon know all the answers. Science educators often emphasize deterministic models rather than the uncertainty involved in understanding the relationship between variables (Shaughnessy, 1983). This encourages a common distortion of "science" as deterministic in a dogmatic sense.

Hallmarks of a scientific approach include looking for alternative explanations, updating knowledge, and selecting methods based on what has been found to be most effective through systematic investigation rather than on appeals to authority or on what "feels right." It is assumed that there are many unsolved questions and that advances can be made by posing and exploring new questions. It is also assumed that questions cannot be answered unless they are cast in a refutable form: are theories more or less accurate in making explicit predictions compared to alternative explanations. It is assumed that nothing is ever "proven," that rather, there are increments of confirmation in terms of evaluating the accuracy of any clinical assumptions (Popper, 1963).

Falsifiability is an important characteristic of assertions. Some assertions are not falsifiable; there is no way to determine if they are false. Proof is a much stronger criterion and since a future test may show an assumption to be incorrect, even one that is strongly corroborated, no assertion can ever be proven (Popper, 1963). However, a theory can be shown to be false given that it is falsifiable. If nothing can ever be proven, the least one can do is to construct theories that are falsifiable: theories that generate specific hypotheses that can be tested. Thus, a true scientific approach is quite the opposite of the characteristics often attributed to it such as "rigid," dogmatic," "closed," "trivial." Within a scientific approach, it would be just as ill advised to claim that some people are psychic as it would be to claim that there is no such thing as "psychic abilities" without confirming evidence.

> "Science . . . is a way of thinking . . . [It] invites us to let the facts in, even when they don't conform to our preconceptions. It counsels us to carry alternative hypotheses in our heads and see which ones best match the facts. It urges on us a fine balance between no-holds-barred openness to new ideas, however heretical, and the most rigorous skeptical scrutiny of everything—new ideas *and* established wisdom" (Sagan, 1990, p. 265).

A scientific approach is often criticized on the grounds that it cannot capture the full meaning of experiences; that such accounts often are trivial, unrepresentative accounts. A trivial account, by definition, cannot account for events of interest. A scientific approach to practice requires use of a broad range of methods that faithfully represent significant aspects of the phenomena under investigation. There is no doubt that social science and professional journals are replete with research reports that are irrelevant to, or distorting of, the events under investigation. This does not mean that an empirical approach is not useful. It does indicate that, like anything else, it can be appropriately or inappropriately applied. There is good science and bad science; science that accurately reflects the events under consideration and science that distorts events. Accurate understanding of the hallmarks of the scientific method is needed to distinguish between helpful and trivializing or bogus uses of this approach. Bogus uses refer to the use of scientific ideology to reaffirm and maintain current definitions of personal and social problems and service delivery systems that may, in reality, hinder rather than facilitate offering a higher quality of life to clients.

Some Clarifications and Distinctions

It is important to distinguish between facts and beliefs. A belief can be defined as "confidence that a particular thing is true as evidenced by a willingness to act as though it were" (Nickerson, 1986, p. 2). Beliefs vary in their credibility. Most social workers believe the statement that "childhood experiences influence adult development." There would be less agreement that "childhood experiences determine adult development." Facts can be viewed as beliefs that are well supported by evidence and therefore as justifying a high degree of confidence. Facts are capable of verification; beliefs may not be. Reasons (good ones) consist of justified beliefs; that is, plausible, sound arguments can be offered for claims made. Another helpful distinction is between beliefs and opinions. Beliefs are statements that, in principle, can be shown to be true or false whereas with an opinion, it does not make sense to consider it as true or false because people differ in their preferences as in "I prefer working with middle class clients."

Reasoning involves the review of evidence against as well as evidence in favor of a position; rationalizing a belief entails a selective search for evidence in support of a belief or action that may or may not be deliberate. Reasoning does not necessarily yield the truth. "People who are considered by many of their peers to be reasonable people often do take and are able to defend quite convincingly, diametrically opposing positions on controversial matters" (Nickerson, 1986, p. 12). However, effective reasoners are more likely to generate assertions that are closer to the truth than ineffective reasoners. Some assumptions are better (closer to the truth) than are others. The accuracy of a conclusion does not necessarily indicate that the reasoning used to reach it was sound; errors in the opposite direction may have cancelled each other out.

It is helpful to distinguish among propaganda, bias, and points of view (MacLean, 1981). "Bias" refers to an emotional leaning to one side. Biased people try to persuade others but may not be aware that they are doing so. They may use propaganda tactics and faulty reasoning and offer statements in a manner designed to gain uncritical or emotional acceptance of a biased position. Personal biases may make it difficult to identify biases in a statement. Propagandists are aware of their interest and usually intentionally disguise these. Here, too, messages are couched in a way to encourage uncritical acceptance. Those with a "point of view" are also aware of their interests but sources are described and propaganda devices and faulty reasoning are avoided; statements are made in a manner that solicits critical review. Views can be examined because they are clearly stated. People with a point of view are open to clarifying their statements when asked (see Ellul, 1965, for an interesting discussion of propaganda).

Hot and cold reasons correspond to two major routes to persuasion—by reasoned argument and by affective association. Many people try to persuade others by offering reasons that play on emotions and appeal to accepted beliefs and values. Learning how to recognize and counter social psychological persuasion strategies such as attempted influence based on liking and appeals to consistency, authority, or scarcity (Cialdini, 1984) will be helpful in avoiding sources of influence that decrease accuracy. Some people confuse the use of logical principles and reasoning. Logic is concerned with the form or validity of deductive arguments. "It provides methods and rules for restating information so as to make what is implicit explicit. It has little to do with the determination of truth or "falsity" (Nickerson, 1986, p. 7). Effective reasoning requires much more than logic including skill in developing arguments and hypotheses, establishing the relevance of information to an argument, and evaluating the plausibility of assertions. That is, it requires a great deal of inventiveness. It also requires a willingness to change beliefs based on evidence gathered.

It is sometimes assumed that reasoning and creativity have little to do with each other. To the contrary, creativity and reasoning go hand-in-hand especially in areas such as clinical decision making in which needed information is often missing, and in which there is often no solution and no agreed-on criteria for evaluating success. Cognitive styles, attitudes, and strategies associated with creativity include a readiness to explore and readiness to change, attention to problem finding as well as problem solving and, immersion in a task (Greeno, 1989; Nickerson, Perkins, & Smith, 1985; Weisberg, 1985).

Distinguishing between consistency, corroboration and proof is important in assigning "proper weight" to data. We often use "consistency" in support of an assumption; for example, we search for consistent evidence. An assertion should be consistent with other beliefs that are held; that is, self-contradictory views should not knowingly be entertained. However, consistency is a weak basis in terms of offering positive evidence. Two or more assertions may be consistent with each other but yield little or no insight into the soundness of an argument.

Common Pitfalls in Reasoning

Being overly enamored of one's own opinions is perhaps the most common characteristic that gets in the way of careful consideration of alternative views. For example, we have a tendency to think of our own points of view as "common sense" and view other positions as "mere opinion" (Bender, 1984). We use different criteria to examine other points of view than to examine our own beliefs. Failing to ask "Is there an alternative account that is better?" and "What are problems with my view?" result in rationalizing favored arguments rather than exploring alternative accounts to determine the best option.

This emphasis on gathering evidence for and rationalizing one's own positions rather than on understanding alternative views gets in the way of finding the optimal position and exploring issues in their complexities and possibilities. As Bender (1984) and many others point out, we often have a goal of "enlightening others" rather than learning something new from others.

Not carefully evaluating the source of data is a common pitfall. What is fact? What is opinion? What evidence is there that a certain claim is true? Another pitfall is influence by stereotypes. For example, Skinner's behavioral approach is often misrepresented and misunderstood. It may be labeled as "mechanistic" without understanding what is being criticized (Catania & Harnad, 1988; Thompson, 1988). Failing to recognize bias related to ethnic, gender, class, cultural, sexual orientation, or age differences is another common pitfall. Our particular age, class, culture, and race influence the way we view issues and potentials.

Only by cultivating habits of thought that counter these common pitfalls are we likely to avoid them. The value of reasoning skills lies in the increased likelihood of deep understanding of issues so that optimal solutions or resolutions to personal and social problems can be discovered and implemented. Careful consideration of opposing viewpoints increases the likelihood of deep understanding of issues.

REFERENCES

Bender, D.L. (1984). Social justice: Opposing viewpoints series. In B. Szumski (Ed.), *Social Justice*. St. Paul, MN: Greenhaven Press.

Bromley, D.B. (1986). The case-study method in psychology and related disciplines. New York: Wiley.

Catania, A.C., & Harnad, S. (Eds.). *The selection of behavior: The operant behaviorism of B.F. Skinner: Comments and consequences*. New York: Columbia University Press.

Cialdini, R.B. (1984). *Influence: The new psychology of modern persuasion*. New York: Quill.

Ellul, J. (1965). *Propaganda: The formation of men's attitudes*. New York: Vintage.

Elstein, A.S., Shulman, L.S., Sprafka, S.A., et al. (1978). *Medical problem solving: An analysis of clinical reasoning*. Cambridge, MA: Harvard University Press.

Gambrill, E. (1990). *Critical thinking in clinical practice*. San Francisco: Jossey-Bass.

Greeno, J.G. (1989). A perspective on thinking. *American Psychologist, 2*, 134–141.

Huber, R.B. (1963). *Influencing through argument*. New York: David McKay.

Kottler, J.A., & Blau, D.S. (1989). *The imperfect therapist: Learning from failure in therapeutic practice*. San Francisco: Jossey-Bass.

MacLean, E. (1981). *Between the lines: How to detect bias and propaganda in the news and everyday life*. Montreal: Black Rose Books.

Mays, D.T., & Franks, C.M. (Eds.). (1985). *Negative outcome in psychotherapy and what to do about it*. New York: Springer.

Nickerson, R.S. (1986). *Reflections on reasoning*. Hillsdale, NJ: Erlbaum.

Nickerson, R.S., Perkins, D.N., & Smith, E.E. (1985). *The teaching of thinking*. Hillsdale, NJ: Erlbaum.

Nisbett, R., & Ross, L. (1980). *Human inference: Strategies and shortcomings of social judgment*. Englewood Cliffs, NJ: Prentice Hall.

Popper, K.R. (1963). *Conjectures and refutations*. New York: Harper & Row.

Sagan, C. (1990). Why we need to understand science. *Skeptical Inquirer, 14*, 263–269.

Scriven, M. (1976). *Reasoning*. New York: McGraw-Hill.

Shaughnessy, J.M. (1983). *The psychology of inference and the teaching of probability and statistics: Two sides of the same coin*. In R.W. Scholz (Ed.), Decision making under uncertainty. North-Holland: Elsevier.

Snyder, M., & Thomsen, C.J. (1988). Interactions between therapists and clients: Hypothesis testing and behavioral confirmation. In D.C. Turk & P. Salovey (Eds.), *Reasoning, inference, and judgment in clinical psychology*. New York: Free Press.

Stevens, P., Jr. (1988). The appeal of the occult: Some thoughts on history, religion and science. *Skeptical Inquirer, 12*, 376–385.

Thompson, T. (1988). Retrospective review: Benedicus behavior analysis: B.F. Skinner's magnum opus at fifty. *Contemporary Psychology, 33*, 397–402.

Thouless, R.H. (1974). *Straight and crooked thinking: Thirty-eight dishonest tricks of debate*. London: Pan Books.

Toulmin, S.E., Rieke, R., & Janik, A. (1979). *An introduction to reasoning*. New York: Macmillan.

Weisberg, R. (1986). *Creativity, genius and other myths*. New York: W.H. Freeman.

Are Union Membership and Professional Social Work Compatible?

EDITOR'S NOTE: At the beginning of this century the dominant form of organization was industrial in character: factory owners employed workers to produce standard economic goods that were to be sold at a profit. There was not even the pretense that either of these groups was motivated by anything but economic self-interest. Labor unions came into existence to equalize labor's ability to compete for its share of the profit pie. As the century advanced, the service organization, one kind of which is the major employer of human service professionals, achieved dominance. Here unionization is much more problematic.

Unions exist primarily to benefit their members; professions exist primarily to benefit their clients. That distinction is fundamental. Attempts to combine these values must generate difficult, perhaps irreconcilable, conflicts. The question, then, is obvious: Can social workers also be members of unions without seriously compromising their claim to honor the ideal of service to others above all other considerations, including even their own rights and benefits as workers and employees?

Howard Jacob Karger, Ph.D., says YES. He is an Associate Professor at the Louisiana State University School of Social Work, and the author of several articles concerned with public sector labor-management relations. He also wrote *Social Workers and Labor Unions* (New York: Greenwood Press, 1988).

Michael J. Kelly, Ph.D., says NO. He is an Associate Professor at the School of Social Work of the University of Missouri-Columbia where he teaches graduate administration and planning courses and directs the Extension program. His current research and writing interests are in microcomputer-based management and training technology.

YES

HOWARD JACOB KARGER

The early relationship between social work and the labor movement was more or less one-sided. Social work reformers, especially settlement house leaders, gave aid, comfort, and technical assistance to the burgeoning labor movement of the late 1800s and early 1900s. Reformers such as Jane Addams, Florence Kelley, Mary Kenney O'Sullivan, Ellen Gates Starr, and Mary McDowell, among others, helped to organize support for the massive strikes that marked late nineteenth and early twentieth century America (Karger, 1987). Social work reformers selflessly worked to foster the goals of the early labor movement, especially as they affected women and children workers.

The overall makeup of the profession had dramatically changed by the 1930s. The well-to-do (and often religiously oriented) social worker of the early 1900s was replaced by the professionally trained social worker who frequently came from an immigrant or working-class background. Devoid of family wealth, many of these social workers were more dependent on salaries than their predecessors.

Taking their cue from other sectors of the workforce, a number of these social workers tried unsuccessfully to organize an exclusive social work union during the middle 1930s (Fisher, 1980; Karger, 1987; Haynes, 1975). Despite this setback, social workers (particularly those in public agencies) joined existing public sector unions in large numbers. Moreover, as organized labor gained credibility during the 1940s and 1950s, the initial anti-union bias of some social workers began to dissipate. In 1959 the chairperson of the New York City chapter of NASW wrote that, "It is the stated position of the National Association of Social Workers that employees have a right to belong to a union of their choice for purposes of collective bargaining" (Rehr, 1960). In less than 50 years, the profession of social work went from supporting the labor movement for altruistic reasons to supporting it for reasons of self-interest.

Social Work Professionalism versus Unionism: Is It a Bogus Argument?

The first question is whether social work, at least as practiced in some agencies, is really a profession. One of the major characteristics of a profession is autonomy, a concept stressed throughout social work education. According to Eliot Friedson (1970), professionalism is the quality of being free, self-directed, and autonomous. Autonomy implies that professionals are inner-directed, require little or no supervision, are accountable to the ideals of altruism and client service, and are responsible for their time. In short, a professional self-directs his or her work. Given that, crude performance measures, such as the number of hours worked in a given week, are irrelevant. However, in some organizations, especially public agencies, social workers must arrive and leave at designated times (they may apply for compensatory time if they work beyond 40 hours a week), must undergo intensive supervision, and are expected to put agency goals above all else. Many social workers function in a bureaucratic context where autonomy is either devalued or nonexistent. Friedson (1970) sums up the dilemma:

> Lacking identification with the prime goals of the organization, lacking an important voice in setting the formal level and direction of work, and performing work which has been so rationalized as to become mechanical and meaningless, the worker functions as a minute segment of an intricate mosaic of specialized activities which he is in no position to perceive or understand. . . . (p. 81)

Compared to the autonomy enjoyed by physicians in private practice, many agency-based social workers are workers rather than autonomous professionals. Thus, for some social workers professionalism is more a matter of self-perception than a reality of agency life. In the end, if professionalism is not an operational concept in a human service bureaucracy, and if social workers are not viewed as autonomous professionals (professionalism cannot be operational unless acknowledged by both sides), then the debate involving the compatibility between professionalism and unionization is immaterial.

The benefits of unionization are evident even for social workers who enjoy professional status and autonomy. Because most social workers are employed in a bureaucracy, issues of job security, grievances, pay, working conditions, and client service remain important considerations. These concerns are especially salient given the recent fiscal cutbacks experienced by many private and public agencies. Like other employees, social workers need workplace protection. Because the civil service rules in many places are limited, vague, and full of loopholes, the protection offered by specific clauses in union contracts can be invaluable. Moreover, because the National Association of Social Workers (NASW) has little power within the workplace, the only real protection for social workers is through union contracts.

The growth of the for-profit human service sector represents another potential challenge for social workers. Unprotected by civil service regulations, social workers in these corporations are especially vulnerable to capricious actions by management. Because the for-profit human service sector is guided by a profit rather than a service motive, social workers in these corporations may need special protection in terms of wages, promotions, working conditions, ethical protections, and concerns regarding the quality of client services.

Anti-Unionism and Protective Labor Organizations

Beliefs regarding the incompatibility of professionalism and unionization are rooted in the anti-union bias of American culture. In many advanced industrialized countries, including Sweden, Israel, and much of Western Europe, professionals in all fields (including physicians) are unionized. If not self-employed, it is assumed that you are a worker regardless of your position or occupation. Professionalism and unionism are often considered complementary concepts in these industrialized societies.

Several myths exist in the United States about professionalism and unionization. Depending on your interpretation of union, one need only look at the American Medical Association (AMA) to see that protective labor organizations in this country can take many forms. For example, the AMA helps keep the salaries of its members high by influencing the number of students admitted into medical schools. The AMA also lobbies on a range of issues that affects the salaries and working conditions of its members. Despite these activities, there is little debate about whether professionalism is compatible with membership in the AMA. Moreover, a constant criticism leveled at labor unions is that they drive up wages and thus fuel inflation. What about the argument that membership in the AMA drives up the earnings of physicians and is therefore inflationary?

Unions are often conceived of as self-aggrandizing organizations concerned only with the limited self-interest of its members. While this may be true for some unions, notably the Teamsters Union, other unions, especially those that serve the public sector, have a progressive lobbying record equal to that of NASW. For example, the American Federation of State, County and Municipal Employees' political agenda is highly congruent with NASW's, and they collectively lobby on many issues. Moreover, unions can monitor and positively affect the quality of client services. Like most organizations, unions represent their constituency. The more social workers who are involved in union affairs, the greater the commitment of the union to social work issues. Lastly, unionization and collective bargaining represent self-determination and empowerment. Because these are two principal values of the profession, there is a natural affinity between key social work values and unionization. Furthermore, the organization of social workers into strong and viable bargaining units is a good lesson for clients in self-determination and empowerment.

The Moral Dilemma of Job Actions and Unionization

Perhaps the knottiest issue in the unionization debate centers around unionized social workers and job actions. If professionalism encompasses a commitment to altruism and client service, how can social workers justify job slowdowns or strikes? In other words, if clients' best interests are primary, how can social workers abrogate the service ideal by striking? This issue has plagued unionized social workers since the 1930s, and some critics contend that this dilemma makes unionization and professionalism inherently incompatible.

Although job actions pose a problem for all union members, teachers, nurses, law officers, and even resident physicians have struck for higher wages and better working conditions. (In many industrialized countries it is not uncommon for physician strikes to virtually paralyze the medical system.) Are we more important than these other professions? Is withholding social work services potentially more dangerous than withholding nursing services? Is it unethical to believe in a service ideal, yet also have a self-interest in higher salaries and better working conditions? Physicians do not argue that higher salaries are unprofessional because they raise the cost of health care and thus result in less access for poor clients. Lastly, the belief that unionized social workers are forced to strike is spurious. For one, the overall record of successful social work strikes is dismal. Secondly, alternative forms for resolving labor-management conflicts, such as final offer or issue-by-issue arbitration, are becoming widespread in both the public and private sectors. Thirdly, in many states public sector strikes are illegal. Given these factors, it is unlikely that most unionized social workers will ever face a strike situation. Although the issue is not simple, social workers have a right to a livable wage and good working conditions.

Conclusion

By now it is obvious that I see no incompatibility between unionization and professionalism. In fact, the belief that professionalism and unionization are antagonistic concepts acknowledges, albeit in a de facto manner, that professionalism and self-interest are also antagonistic. I know of no profession that believes that the best interests of its members are inimical to its own well-being. Thus, the artificial juxtaposition of professionalism and self-interest (i.e., unionization) is counterproductive both to individual social workers and the profession. The transformation of the service ideal into a quasi-religious symbol sets up a situation in which individual social workers are compelled to relegate their material needs to an abstraction. The ongoing denigration of social workers' personal needs is a major ingredient in the burnout syndrome. In the end, union victories that result in better salaries and working conditions benefit all social workers.

REFERENCES

Fisher, J. (1980). *The response of social work to the depression.* Boston: Schenkman.

Friedson, E. (1970). Dominant professions, bureaucracy, and client services. In W.R. Rosengren and M. Leyton (eds.), *Organizations and clients: Essays in the sociology of service.* Columbus, Ohio: Charles E. Merrill Publishing Co.

Haynes, J.E. (1975). The rank and file movement in private social work. *Labor History,* 16, 78–98.

Karger, H.J. (1988). *Social workers and labor unions.* New York: Greenwood Press.

Rehr, H. (1960). Problems for a profession in a strike situation. *Social Work,* 5, 22–28.

van Kleeck, M. (1935). The common goals of labor and social work. Proceedings of the National Conference of Social Work, 1934. Chicago: The University of Chicago Press.

ANNOTATED BIBLIOGRAPHY

Alexander, L.B. Professionalization and Unionization: Compatible After All? *Social Work,* 6, 476–482.

This article examines the view that unionization and professionalization are antagonistic. The author attempts to resolve this question by proposing a model of hybrid unionism that melds professional and union concerns.

Tambor, Milton. The Social Worker as Worker: A Union Perspective. *Administration in Social Work,* 3, 289–300.

This article examines overall social service workplace issues, including the politics of professionalism, the resistance to union organizing, issues in union organizing, and collective bargaining laws and issues.

Reamer, Frederic G. Social Workers and Unions: Ethical Dilemmas. In Howard Jacob Karger, *Social Workers and Labor Unions.* New York: Greenwood Press, 1987.

This book chapter explores the values and ethical choices that must be made by unionized social workers. The author discusses the implications of ethical choices, especially on social workers' divided loyalties to clients, employers, and the general public.

Rejoinder to Professor Karger   MICHAEL J. KELLY

Professor Karger's argument in favor of social work unionization focuses on three major points: (1) the nonprofessional status of social work in large organizations; (2) support for workers and clients by public sector unions; and (3) the failure of the service ideal to recognize legitimate self-interest. These points almost miss the predominant professional concern about trade union affiliation. But, first, comments on his argument.

Certainly the public sector unions seek national priorities common to the National Association of Social Workers. Both, for example, support welfare and health program expansion as well as the reallocation of scarce federal resources to social needs. Unfortunately, that alone is not proof of trade union altruism. Rather, it is based on self-interest, because most union members are employed by public sector programs. From a public point of view, it is as akin to the United Auto Workers lobbying for legislation to support domestic automobile sales.

Furthermore, agreement on public agendas does not guarantee support for professional social work. Arguing that the service ideal is a quasi-religious and foolish abandonment of self-interest, Karger tacitly acknowledges the critical importance of self-interest in unionization. The service ideal—the forgoing of personal interests to make the client-professional relationship effective—is at the heart of professionalism.

Karger mistakenly equates professionalism with the social work jobs available in large state organizations. Arguing that professionalism is not acknowledged by these employers, he suggests unions protect client and worker welfare. Often finding state organizations unaccommodating to themselves and their clients, many professionals have learned to successfully work within them. Guided by knowledge and values, the professional seeks the best for his or her clients and, with a broad view of human need, often clashes with managers. Many professionals recognize that individual needs can frequently be met only by exploiting the imperfections of large organizations. Professionals recognize that when represented by a union, there are two large organizations to contend with, hence further curtailing their necessary flexibility.

Karger is correct in some ways about large state agencies. State level human service quality has diminished as the federal government has forsaken—and citizens have neglected—our social concerns. Professional employment in state agencies has declined and much of their work has been bureaucratized. But many good social workers remain with the service ideal being their motivation. We should applaud this willingness to serve in keeping with the highest professional ideals.

Professionals must be apprehensive about breaching their social responsibility and denigrating the service ideal. This is the crucial issue.

NO

MICHAEL J. KELLY

Should social work professionals be members of and participate in trade unions? Can professional goals be obtained through union activity? This article examines some important contradictions between the goals and methods of trade unions and those of the social work profession. These contradictions suggest that, for other than limited purposes, professional social workers should not unionize.

With few exceptions, unions do not support the social work profession's social purpose, individual judgments, or the client-professional relationship. But most importantly, the actions necessary to build and sustain effective trade unions are incompatible with the values and service ideals of the profession.

To explain the contradictions, this statement looks first at the social role of professions and examines social work's professional status. Attention is then turned to social workers and trade unions. And, finally, the argument contrasts individual judgment and class action—a phenomenon that embodies the contradiction of professionalism and unions.

The Social Role of Professions

Professions are sanctioned by society to fill needs in which an open and confidential relationship between an individual client and a provider of specialized care is necessary. Professions serve valued ends and, in return, are given jurisdiction over the selection, education, certification, and discipline of their membership. This self-regulation insures that the trust of the public will be carried out by qualified individuals, guided by a code of ethics, who promote the social welfare through "the intimate personal relationships of free professional and client" (Stein and Cloward, 1958).

Professionals provide trained and ethical judgment in situations that are private, unique, and complex. The professional must diagnose the situation and determine the course of assistance or treatment. They are required to forgo their personal interests in order to act in the client's best interests. They may consult other professionals, but ethical provisions require that what transpires within the client-professional relationship is confidential. In the final analysis, individual practitioners are solely responsible for their actions. Their unpopular, although often correct, judgment may be supported by professional associations, but no other person can take the responsibility.

Actions in the best interests of the client are the service ideal. This ideal is vital to the social role of professions and is the highest demand placed upon the professional. Among social workers, the service ideal is particularly strong, even if it is complicated by third party payment for services. When clients are unable to pay for services the costs are supported through community or governmental programs. Interestingly, this has strengthened social work's service ideal. Most feel that their clients desperately need and deserve help. Further, they feel clients have already suffered from unequal income, stigmatization, or discrimination. Social workers are ill disposed to add to the client's burden by denying service to those unable to pay or charging large fees even when such actions would directly benefit them.

Is Social Work a Profession?

If social work is not a profession, then the questions of social role and the service ideal are moot. Social workers would then have no reason to fulfill these obligations but would be simply another type of service employee. What, then, characterizes a profession?

Professions have a set of theories that guide the accumulation of a body of knowledge, coupled with a reliable method of practice that is transmitted to selected individuals through lengthy education. Relationships with clients are governed by a code of ethics administered by an association that certifies and disciplines practitioners.

Social work is not regarded as a strong profession. There is, for instance, no governing association that can certify and discipline practitioners. Although professional control over education is extended through the Council on Social Work Education, the NASW has little authority over certification and discipline, and membership is not compulsory. Further, in many private and governmental agencies, the title social worker is not restricted solely to persons with BSW or MSW degrees. In many states, anyone employed to help people—particularly in state welfare or state-run mental health agencies—can be called social workers.

By these standards, social work has been called an emerging or semi-profession (Etizoni, 1969). But, no less a critic than Ernest Greenwood

(1957), whose discussion of professional characteristics is frequently cited, called social work a profession. It is clear that social work's professional status is constantly improving.

For many years there has been an active, if somewhat divisive, debate concerning the importance of promoting social change versus individual casework. However, this debate has dwindled in the last decade as more social workers follow careers in individual, family, or group oriented casework. Because social work's knowledge base is grounded in casework and because private practice has become an increasingly attractive employment alternative, these changes will become entrenched and further strengthen professional identity.

Social Work and Trade Unionism

The sympathy of every social worker interested in social welfare or social justice automatically swings to the trade union's efforts to improve working conditions and wages. For years unions were the only organized force working for decent and safe working conditions, job security, and fair wages. Unionism is a movement complete with heroes and villains and a folk history with songs and stories of courage and sacrifice. Social workers know that workers depend on their jobs for economic security, and many believe that a profit orientation leaves little room for considering the welfare of the workers. NASW has supported unionism both for social workers and others since the 1960s (Cole, 1977).

For the same reasons as other workers, i.e., interest in their working conditions, wages, and job security, many workers with the title social worker are also union members. In 1986 there were an estimated 360,000 social workers in the United States. Of that number, an estimated 120,000 are in unions, the majority being represented by the American Federation of State, County, and Municipal Employees (62,000 social work members). Other social workers are represented by the Service Employees International Union (40,000 members) and The National Union of Hospital and Health Care Employees (10,000 members). An uncertain but smaller number are represented by the International Brotherhood of Teamsters and The Communications Workers of America (AFL-CIO, 1987). These figures indicate that about one third of all social workers are in organized trade unions.

Despite these high numbers, only one half (180,000) of the estimated 360,000 are professional social workers (AFL-CIO, 1987). Moreover, it is uncertain how many professional social workers actually participate in trade unions. Although some obviously participate because of job related benefits, others participate in the hope of creating conditions that better meet client needs. Many unions that organize professionals recognize this and base their appeals on caseload and client need. AFSCME has stressed the similarity of its social agenda to that of NASW (Karger, 1989). Tambor (1973) contends that unions have protected social workers' autonomy against bureaucratic incursion and in some instances has kept caseloads manageable. Yet, it is unlikely that a large percentage of the 180,000 professionals are among the 125,000 unionized social workers.

Without Struggle, There Can Be No Progress

Unions are organized to represent, extend, and protect workers' interests by developing countervailing power with management. They wield the power of group action behind which lies the threat of a strike, an action that denies an organization's ability to carry on its normal activities. For business, a strike is costly and may lead to an inability to compete. In the public sector, strikes can cripple safety, health, and welfare services. Because some services are vital, such as fire and police protection, several states have made public sector strikes illegal.

Unions are primarily concerned with working conditions, wages, job security, and grievance procedures. These issues are chosen because they appeal to the largest group of workers, and a union's strength is determined by the size of its membership. Unions representing social workers often include issues related to client needs because they appeal to the service ideal.

Olson (1971) notes that coercion is necessary to fulfill the ends of large unions. Large unions desire to make union membership compulsory and whenever possible move toward the closed shop. The success of a strike, as well as the sacrifices that each worker must make, requires that a supply of strikebreakers ready to continue work is either unavailable or curtailed. Thus, compulsory membership works toward union effectiveness. Further, unions seek to federate with other labor groups to enlarge their power. In federations, local issues that attract some workers, such as client concerns and case load size, are lost to the larger concerns of wages and working conditions.

Union organizing requires that workers identify their desires and needs as separate from the goals of owners and managers. Workers are encouraged to view themselves as a working class in order to foster group solidarity. This requires a world view predicated upon a natural conflict between the interests of the working class (all workers) and owners (all managers). Although associated with socialist-oriented unions, these sentiments are also found among the conservative business unionism characteristic of the American labor movement. The slogan of one union candidate expresses it succinctly: "Without struggle there can be no progress."

The Contradictions

There are major contradictions between trade unions and professionalism. First, strikes violate the service ideal as the professional must deny services to their clients. Although strikes are rare and represent a failure of the union bargaining process, the union social workers must be ready to strike when necessary. Secondly, the actions necessary to effectively manage unions involve coercion and class conflict that are antithetical to the values of social work. Social work places great emphasis on its values, including self-determination, individuality, cooperation, and diversity. Unions must seek class consciousness and use coercion to insure a disciplined membership. Further, collective bargaining often requires abandoning the individual case—often the greatest concern of a professional—for the concerns held by the largest number of members.

Unionized professionals are predicted to be common in the postindustrial society (Schmidman, 1979). Let us hope that our future unions or collective bargaining professional associations will seek a complementary path that stresses support for professional judgment at the case level, while at the same time encouraging the participation of professionals in management decisions.

REFERENCES

AFL-CIO. (1987). Professional workers and their unions. Mimeographed.
Cole, E. (1977). Unions in social work. In *Encyclopedia of social work, 1977*. New York: National Association of Social Workers.
Etzioni, A. (ed). (1969). *The semi-professions and their organizations*. New York: The Free Press.
Greenwood, E. (1957). Attributes of a profession. *Social Work, 2*, 44–55.
Karger, H. (1989). The common and conflicting goals of labor and social work. *Administration in Social Work, 13*, 1–17.
Olson, M. (1971). *The logic of collective action*. New York: Schocken Books.
Schmidman, J. (1979). *Unions in postindustrial society*. University Park, PA: The Pennsylvania State University Press.
Stein, H. and Cloward, R. (1958). *Social perspectives on behavior*. New York: The Free Press.
Tambor, M. (July 1973). Unions and voluntary agencies. *Social Work, 18*, 41–47.

ANNOTATED BIBLIOGRAPHY

AFL-CIO. Professional Workers and their Unions. Mimeographed, 1987.

This mimeographed booklet, available from the Department for Professional Employees of the AFL-CIO, provides recent data on professional employees in trade unions and the collective bargaining units of professional associations.

Etzioni, A. (ed). *The Semi-Professions and Their Organizations.* New York: The Free Press, 1969.

Unbowed by age, this volume is a complete study of the professional status of nurses, teachers, and social workers.

Schmidman, J. *Unions in Postindustrial Society.* University Park: The Pennsylvania State University Press, 1979.

This volume is an exploration and analysis of trade union structure and function in the evolving postindustrial society and provides an excellent discussion of the role of white collar and professional unions.

Rejoinder to Professor Kelly   HOWARD JACOB KARGER

Dr. Kelly has provided a forceful, if somewhat flawed, argument regarding the compatibility of unionization and social work. Kelly argues that unionism is inherently incompatible with the professional purpose of social work, the autonomous actions required of professionals, and the development of a strong client-professional relationship. Moreover, he argues that the self-interest reflected in unionism is incongruent with the service ideal.

Kelly's strong belief in the omniscience of the service ideal is laudable, even if it is out of touch with the real conditions existing in many social service workplaces. Deep budgetary cuts in private and public social services have resulted in increased client loads, cutbacks in critical services, the demoralization of many social workers, and a general diminution in the scope and goals of social services. If public sector unions engage in limited coercion or struggle to enlarge their power through federation, it is against this dismal backdrop.

Social workers and the whole apparatus of social services are in dire need of help. Over the last eight years we have experienced an increased devolution of the welfare state. The severe cutbacks of the early 1980s, coupled with highly uneven economic growth, have resulted in a growing number of poor people eligible for services, while at the same time the growth in public and private coffers has remained relatively stagnant. Forced to work in agencies with too many clients, too little money, and too few staff, grandiose notions of professionalism seem out of place.

The belief that the profession of social work can make change acting alone is ill-founded and dangerous. With few numbers and even fewer resources, social work must turn to other groups for support. To stem the erosion in social services, social workers must coalesce with others, including public sector unions. Working together, progressive organizations like the National Association of Social Workers and public sector unions can make important changes in both the workplace and the larger society.

Should Social Workers Work for For-Profit Firms?

EDITOR'S NOTE: The welfare state of the United States originated about 60 years ago. At that time and for many years after, the response to whatever problems were taken on was similar: allocate money to the problem and create or assign a public bureaucracy to carry out the solution. During the 1960s this approach came under attack from several sources, and since then the number of ways to organize the production of social services has grown considerably. The most controversial of these innovations is the use of private, for-profit firms. They already dominate the nursing home industry and deliver a substantial proportion of other services such as day care for children and in home care for the elderly. Along with government's increasing use of market mechanisms in many areas of public enterprise, the use of for-profit producers in social welfare, too, is likely to increase. This debate, then, is timely and likely to remain so for years to come.

Dale A. Masi, DSW, LCSW, argues YES, social workers should work for profit-making firms. She is a Professor at the University of Maryland School of Social Work and Community Planning, and an adjunct professor at the College of Business and Management. Dr. Masi also consults widely about employee assistance programs. She has published over 30 articles, several monographs and four books, most of which deal with human services in industry.

Michael Reisch, Ph.D., makes the NO case. He is Director of the Department of Social Work Education and Professor of Social Work and Public Administration at San Francisco State University. Working from a background in law, history, and social work, he has written extensively on social policy, macro practice, and the history and philosophy of social welfare. He has consulted with social service agencies, community and advocacy organizations, state and local governments, and political campaigns for nearly twenty years.

YES

DALE A. MASI

It is important for the reader to understand that social workers have been working for for-profit companies for over ninety years, so this debate seems a little late in coming.

> The profession apparently owes its name to industry. The first American usage of the term "social work" in 1892 and 1893 referred to housing, canteens, health care, and other amenities provided to workers by Krupp munitions plants (among others) for the purposes of supporting and stabilizing the industrial work force. Hence **social** work complemented **industrial** work. Industry served as society's means of goal attainment, while social work served as a means of integration (Anderson and Carter, 1974).

The profession has continually supported such activity. Europe and South America have an even longer history and tradition than ours. In 1914 the first social workers in the United States worked for a for-profit corporation—Macy's Department Store (Masi, 1982). Since then, through various degrees of activity, social workers have been employed by business. Industrial social work was popular until the mid-1920s. From then until World War II social workers were interested in being private entrepreneurs through private practice. The War brought an increase of interest and demand for social workers in defense plants, helping the labor force (predominately women) adjust to wartime conditions.

The 1950s and 1960s saw less development of the industrial sector. A renewed interest in the private practice specialization as well as the Civil Rights movement sparked social workers to evolve in other directions. The 1970s and 1980s, however, because of very different circumstances, saw a tremendous growth of social workers working for for-profit corporations. The changing labor force (especially the numbers of women entering the work place), the increased awareness by business to the costs of addiction to productivity, and increased human service programs such as child care, elder are, and health promotion have contributed to this development.

Before going further in this debate it is important to define the parameters of for-profit firms. The author would define an organization as such if it turns its profits back to the owners and the organization whether they are individuals or stock holders. For-profit may be a small business, such as Masi Research Consultants Inc. where the author is principal stockholder, or a vast multinational like IBM. For-profit health care corporations, such as Hospital Corporation of America, and national or regional employee assistance contracting firms, such as Personal Performance Consultants Inc., are other examples.

Last but not least is the private social work practitioner who is clearly in the for-profit business. This latter group should be recognized as perhaps the group containing the largest number of social workers working for profit. Many are incorporated, singly or with others, and many are PCs that are individual profit entities. Too often when discussing for-profit business one thinks of large multinational companies such as General Motors and Exxon, not realizing most Americans work for small businesses. The same is true of social workers.

Organizations are neutral. Power is neutral. Money is neutral. What we do with them is different. Intrinsically a for-profit corporation is not necessarily evil. Just as a not-for-profit corporation is not necessarily good. Will any of us forget the scandalous salaries of our non-profit executives and the high administrative cost that resulted in the formation of the United Way Movement in order to monitor such abuses?

The United States of America is based on a capitalistic system that utilizes for-profit entities as the main source of economic maintenance. It is the core of American democracy. It symbolizes the opportunity for the individual entrepreneur to maximize his or her potential. This is not to say there are not problems in the system. However, the discussion of these problems is not the focus of this debate. Our purpose is to show that there is no reason why social workers cannot be interested in profits while working at their profession.

In all my years of working with for-profit corporations, designing, administering and running employee assistance programs (EAP), I have never seen one try to use the EAP against the employee. I have not seen one try to find out who was attending the EAP—if anything they have gone overboard to protect confidentiality. One EAP national provider (a for-profit provider, incidentally) goes so far as to have individual waiting rooms for each client, with separate entrances and exits so that employees do not meet each other.

What has always interested me in debating this issue has been how social workers discriminate against clients they do not want to serve. When I chaired the first national National Association of Social Work/Council on Social Work Education occupational social work committee, I was in favor of having a military social worker on the committee but I was outvoted by social work members, although the military social worker would represent one of the largest employers in the United States—the Department of Defense. The reason was that his clients were military. Similarly, at the industrial social work Wingspread Conference in 1975, one of the most prominent social work educators in the United States argued that alcoholic executives didn't need the social worker's help because they had money and could get help. He had no understanding that the addicted executive is often more isolated and alone than other employees and also able to protect his or her denial more.

Social workers are supposed to reach out to people. Most people today are in the workplace and both parents or partners are working. I would think we would be delighted to have corporations fund programs, hire social workers, and even give employees time off for appointments. If we have trouble in work settings perhaps it is our problem in dealing with clients who often make more money than we, who often are more educated than we, and who often are individually brighter than we.

The bottom line is that there is a unique opportunity for social work as a profession to grow. The challenge is ours. We pride ourselves on having a systems approach. No doubt the business for-profit provides a system to cope with that may be more than we ever imagined, because it challenges us to look at our values, political beliefs and economic motivation. I think this is not so and I trust most of my colleagues will agree and welcome the challenge.

REFERENCES

Anderson, R.E., and Carter, I. (1974). *Human behavior in the social environment: A social systems approach.* Chicago: Aldine Publishing Co.

Googins, B., and Geofrey, J. (1985). The evolution of occupational social work, *Social Work,* (September/October), 396–402.

Masi, D.A. (1982). *Human services in industry.* Lexington: Lexington Books.

Masi, D.A., and Burns, L.E. (1986). Urinalysis testing and EAPs. *EAP Digest,* September/October.

McCronskey, J. (1982). Work and families: What is the employer's responsibility? *Personnel Journal,* (January), 30–38.

Rejoinder to Professor Masi MICHAEL REISCH

For purposes of clarity, I will present my rebuttal point by point. Dr. Masi's entire case assumes that whatever exists in our environment is intended to be. The presence of social workers in for-profit firms is not a justification for their continuation. Indeed, that participation was continually criticized by such early social work leaders as Florence Kelley, Mary van Kleeck, and Bertha Reynolds. The concerns they articulated (e.g., the profit motive of corporations would corrupt service delivery and jeopardize the worker's primary concern for client well-being) are equally valid today.

Dr. Masi's essay misstates the history of social welfare in the United States. For example: (1) Social workers had worked in for-profit settings as "welfare secretaries" for nearly 40 years before Macy's employed them in 1914. (2) Few social workers moved into private practice until the 1960s, when expanded third-party payments made such work financially attractive. (3) The United Way movement emerged during and immediately after World War I as a means of consolidating the role of the business community in charitable giving and volunteering in not-for-profit social agencies, not as a result of "scandalous high salaries" among not-for-profit executives, as Masi asserts.

Dr. Masi's analysis of the development of social work is naive at best. Yes, "social work [in industry] complemented industrial work." This complementarity, however, was based on adjusting workers' behavior to the needs of the factory system and not on transforming the industrial environment to the needs of labor. In the 1920s corporations determined that the "integration" function they desired could better be served by personnel departments than welfare secretaries.

Masi's comments that organizations, power, and money are "neutral," and that "intrinsically a profit-making corporation is not necessarily evil," beg the question of this debate. Organizations whose primary goal is profits have and will subordinate the social good to sustain private gain. Their earlier resistance even to the most modest reforms (e.g., the eight-hour day, collective bargaining, reform of child labor laws) continues to the present in the widespread business opposition to occupational health and safety regulations, control of environmental pollution, pension reform, increases in the minimum wage, comparable worth, child care, just to name a few current issues.

Masi's argument that the capitalist system "is the core of American democracy" may be correct. But should the preservation of such a system through the involvement of social workers be at the core of social work practice? Capitalism may "symbolize the opportunity for the individual entrepreneur to maximize his or her potential," but at whose expense and at what individual and social cost? Masi appears to ignore the basis of profit itself, which results not from entrepreneurial creativity and initiative but rather from the expropriation of the surplus value of labor, a social act, for purposes of private gain. Certainly, social workers can and should be interested in obtaining decent salaries and working conditions. Support of for-profit endeavors, however, is not a prerequisite for the pursuit of enlightened self-interest.

Finally, Masi's assertion that, in her experience, no for-profit corporation has ever tried "to use [its] EAP against [an] employee," that "if anything, they have gone overboard to protect confidentiality," flies in the face of a volume of evidence to the contrary that both labor unions and independent researchers have accumulated.

Social work should not substitute marketplace values for a professional ethos based on social justice and human dignity. These two ideologies are fundamentally in conflict. We should channel our expertise and our energies towards the maximization of public good, not private gain. Social workers should not work in for-profit organizations.

NO

MICHAEL REISCH

There is a growing belief that marketplace solutions are preferable to public sector programs in fields as diverse as social services, health care, penology, transportation, education, and the arts. This ideological shift has helped promote the "privatization" of many human service functions without a clear understanding of either the meaning of implications of this phenomenon.

In this context, the expansion of employment opportunities for social workers in the for-profit sector is worrisome. Between 1971 and 1982, the percentage of NASW members working in for-profit settings increased from 3.3 percent to 12 percent. Recent evidence suggests that during the 1980s this trend accelerated (Stoesz, 1988).

For purposes of this discussion, "for-profit" social service settings include two kinds of organizations: (1) Organizations whose primary purpose is to generate profits through the delivery of human services that have a more or less central social service component (e.g., proprietary child care centers, mental health clinics, hospitals, and nursing homes); and (2) Organizations whose profit-making activities occur through the production of a commodity unrelated to the human services, such as automobiles, computer chips, and banking services. Here are found the many employee assistance programs that have proliferated in the past 10 to 15 years. This conception specifically excludes from the field of concern individual and group social work practices and not-for-profit organizations that devote a small portion of their energies to raising some of their revenue from for-profit sources. Social workers must resist the lure of enhanced occupational opportunities in the for-profit sector, no less reverse their expansion, for at least four reasons.

The Lessons of History

There is nothing new about efforts to deliver human services through private means or to utilize them as tools to enhance labor productivity in industrial settings. For-profit social service agencies emerged late in the nineteenth century in such diverse fields as foster care, juvenile justice, and mental health. Both the constraints of the profit motive and the absence of adequate government resources prevented them from having a significant impact on the problems caused by industrialization, urbanization, and immigration (Ehrenreich, 1985). Particularly in times of crisis, such as the 1890s and the 1930s, the solutions proferred by for-profit organizations proved woefully unable to provide comprehensive, compassionate responses to human needs.

Corporate-sponsored social services for employees also are not a novel concept. Their antecedents lie in the "welfare secretaries" introduced by major industries in the 1890s to address worker concerns that interfered with productivity and compliance to the rules of the factory system. When welfare secretaries no longer served this function adequately, they were replaced in the 1920s by personnel administrators (Wenocur and Reisch, 1989).

The important point here is that employee assistance programs, in the past and today, are primarily focused on enhancing the productivity of the for-profit enterprise; employee benefits are secondary. In addition, the corporate environment precludes social workers from addressing the occupational sources of their clients' problems, and thereby severely constrains their professional effectiveness. Social workers who accept employment in these settings are ignoring the lessons of history as to the ultimate purpose of their retention by corporate employers.

Ethical Imperatives

Their professional code of ethics obliges social workers to make clients' interests paramount. Evidence exists, however, that for-profit organizations are more likely to market their services to those clients most likely to benefit the organization rather than those clients most likely to benefit from its services. Such organizations will, therefore, tend to screen out clients who cannot afford the services they provide, who have problems that are too complex or intractable for "cost-efficient" resolution, and who have demonstrated characteristics that will probably "make extraordinary demands on program resources" (Lewis, 1988). For-profit organizations also are less likely to resist the pressure to share confidential information in order to obtain third-party reimbursement for services and to satisfy the accountability requirements of funding sources (Rosner, 1980; Jacobs, 1982–83).

Even proponents of growing social work involvement in private industry recognize the ethical dilemmas for practitioners here. Shank (1985), for example, commented that "the integration of social work values is critical [in such settings] in light of the fact that occupational social workers may experience isolation and be practicing in an adversarial setting. Potential conflict over issues of confidentiality, client self-determination and advocacy must be recognized" (p. 57). In a similar vein, the NASW (November, 1987) emphasized the importance of social workers in for-profit organizations having "a clear understanding of their own professional code of ethics as they attempt to resolve fundamental conflicts that may arise with individuals or with organizations" (p. 161).

Service Effectiveness

The basic drive of for-profit organizations to maximize the return to owners and shareholders conflicts with the social work practice imperative to maximize access to service for clients, especially those who are most often denied services by the marketplace because of their socioeconomic status, race, gender, age, or sexual orientation. In fact, as Titmuss (1958) argued decades ago, the very evolution of social services in modern society arose as a means to compensate individuals and groups for the "diswelfares" inflicted upon them by the operations of the profit-centered economic system. More recently, Lewis (1988) pointed out that the provision of fair access to services can increase an organization's operating cost to the point where it is "an unrealistic expectation that equity of access will be assured if the usual market mechanisms are allowed to determine outcomes." In their efforts to maintain high levels of profitability, for-profit organizations, therefore, are more likely to exclude persons whose needs either do not match the services they wish to provide or whose needs are too complex for the organization to respond to in a cost-efficient manner.

For-profit organizations are also more likely to equate effectiveness in service delivery with the maintenance of cost-benefit models of service "production" and "distribution." They tend "to compete only for high-pay, full-pay and contract-eligible clients, [leaving] the public agency and the private not-for-profit agency to serve the low-pay and no-pay client" (Kettner, 1989). The burden of sustained support falls to public or not-for-profit providers, adding further to the public's perception of such organizations as cost-inefficient.

Finally, the substitution of a profit incentive for altruistic motives or a sense of contribution to the communal welfare as the motivating factor behind service provision alters the character of the power relationship between the service delivery organization and the client. Instead of clients being treated out of the desire to "do good" (as in the private, not-for-profit agency) or out of a legal or political obligation to satisfy the "entitlement" of citizens (as in the public agency), their relationship to for-profit social service organizations is primarily financial. For those individuals whose lack of financial resources inhibits the choice of service providers, the absence of an altruistic motive underlying the service transaction places their well-being at the mercy of marketplace imperatives. Under such circumstances, clients are more likely to be forced to conform to organizationally dictated behavioral standards in order to receive services.

Protecting the Welfare State

During the 1980s, the privatization of social services and health care— through government "load-shedding" and the shifting of financial resources—has "strengthen[ed] the two-class welfare state and reproduce[d] inequalities that the free market inevitably creates" (Abramovitz, 1986). Social workers should resist this policy direction out of self-interest as well as concern for the well-being of clients. As private, for-profit agencies "cream off" the most lucrative and desirable clients, public and voluntary sector agencies are increasingly being asked to do more with fewer resources. Reduction in government spending for the social services, combined with growing demand for services from low-pay or no-pay clients jeopardizes the capacity of such agencies to deliver services effectively and erodes the legitimacy of their functions in the eyes of the public (Reisch and Wenocur, 1984). This growing incapacity endangers the survival of such organizations and, in turn, our society's ability to address the needs of the most disadvantaged members of our communities. As these agencies struggle to do more with less, their political support, already considerably eroded by more than a decade of conservative attacks, will diminish further. This will add yet another element to the steady decline of resources and the reduction of the scope and potential of social welfare in the United States.

As long as such issues as support for low-income families and access, quality, and cost of services are important to the social work profession, social workers must resist the temptation to define professional and organizational success in terms of profit rather than in meeting individual or community need. It is in the long-term interest, therefore, of both the most needy segments of our nation and of social workers to strengthen the public and private, not-for-profit sectors of the social welfare system. Participation in for-profit organizations by social workers produces the opposite effect and contributes to the destruction of responsive and sensitive policies and services to the vulnerable populations whose betterment should be our paramount concern.

REFERENCES

Abramovitz, M. (1986). The privatization of the welfare state: A review. *Social Work,* July–August, 257–264.

Abramovitz, M. and Epstein, I. (1983) The politics of privatization: Industrial social work and private enterprise. *Urban and Social Change Review,* 16, 13–19.

Ehrenreich, J. (1985). *The altruistic imagination: A history of social work and social policy in the United States.* Ithaca, New York: Cornell University Press.

Jacobs, S. (1982–1983). Advocates for children v. Blum. *The Advocate,* Winter.

Kettner, P.M., Netting, F.E., and McMurtry, S.L. (1989). Privatization of human services: Who will serve those who cannot pay? Unpublished paper presented at the 1989 Council on Social Work Education Annual Program Meeting, Chicago.

Lewis, H. (1988). "Ethics and the private non-profit human service organization," In M. Reisch and A.C. Hyde (Eds.), *The future of non-profit management and the human services.* San Francisco: San Francisco State University Monograph.

National Association of Social Workers (November 1987). Delegate Assembly, policy resolution.

Reisch, M. and Wenocur, S. (1984). "Professionalization and voluntarism in social welfare: changing roles and functions." In F. Schwartz (Ed.), *A growing partnership: Voluntarism and social work practice.* New York: University Press.

Rosner, B.L. (1980). Psychiatrists, confidentiality and insurance. *The Hastings Center Report,* 10, 5–7.

Shank, B.W. (1985). Considering a career in occupational social work? *EAP Digest,* July/August, 55–62.

Stoesz, D. (1988). Human service corporations and the welfare state. *Society,* 25, 53–58.

Titmuss, R. (1985). *Essays on the Welfare State.* London: Allen & Unwin.

Wenocur, S. and Reisch, M. (1989). *From charity to enterprise: The development of American social work in a market economy.* Urbana, Illinois: University of Illinois Press.

ANNOTATED BIBLIOGRAPHY

Abramovitz, M. (1986). The Privatization of the Welfare State: A Review. *Social Work,* July–August, 257–264.

Provides an excellent summary of the economic and ideologic underpinnings of conservatives' favorite social policy buzz word of the 1980s.

Kettner, P.M., Netting, F.E., and McMurtry, S.L. (1989). Privatization of Human Services: Who Will Serve Those Who Cannot Pay? Unpublished paper presented at the 1989 Council on Social Work Education Annual Program Meeting, Chicago, March 1989.

A concise analysis of the effects on clients of the phenomenon of privatization.

Lewis, H. (1988). Ethics and the Private Non-Profit Human Service Organization. In M. Reisch and A.C. Hyde (Eds.), *The Future of Non-Profit Management and the Human Services*. San Francisco, San Francisco State University Monograph.

In this elegant exposition on ethics in the nonprofit sector, Lewis makes some telling comparisons between the underlying assumptions of for-profit and nonprofit human service providers.

Stoesz, D. (1988). Human Service Corporations and the Welfare State. *Society* 25(5), 53–58.

This article places the development of for-profit human service organizations in the context of the rise and decline of the welfare state in the United States.

Rejoinder to Professor Reisch   DALE A. MASI

There is no doubt that this discussion centers on my opponent's belief that a for-profit enterprise is basically antithetical to social work values. His thesis assumes that capitalism is the evil and disregards our topic, i.e., whether social workers should or should not work for for-profit entities.

He excludes the private practice of social work as an example of a for-profit social service setting but, of course, that is precisely what it is. He claims the for-profit organization does not allow the social worker to work for the client first. Does any social welfare system allow this? Last, he accuses the for-profit of screening out the most needy. In no way is this the issue. Of course the poor and the underprivileged need social workers. However, there are also poor employed persons. As Director of the EAP for the US Department of Health and Human Services, I know we had many women working at Social Security who used the Health Clinic for prenatal care. (EAPs, incidentally, are required by law for all federal employees—would Dr. Reisch only support EAPs in this sector?)

His reaction is singularly one-dimensional, i.e., the United States. He does not discuss the fact that in socialist countries such as France, Italy,

Germany, and Switzerland, profit-making employers are required to have social workers. This author recently met with the Executive Director of the International Federation of Social Workers from Geneva, who talks about how alive and well occupational social work is throughout socialistic Europe in for-profit corporations. In addition, it is taught as a major in schools of social work. Does he then say the Italian social worker should not work in Fiat? That the Swiss social worker not work for Rolex?

As I reread his response, it is clear to me that the issue he raises is political, not professional. At no time does he substantiate his argument that social work values will be compromised professionally. It is always an issue of productivity and for-profit as being a negative influence. I refuse to follow such a definition.

It is time to place occupational social work where it belongs alongside the other professions: occupational medicine, occupational nursing, and occupational law, for example. Certainly these professions have value systems as strong as ours and they, too, have practiced in this arena for decades. My opponent does the profession of social work a disservice as well as all of us who practice in it to assume we would have our values compromised. If anything, we should be applauded for being willing to break new ground for social work, especially in the United States, where this specialty has lagged behind.

Is Social Work Inherently Conservative— Designed to Protect the Vested Interests of Dominant Power Groups?

EDITOR'S NOTE: Historically, the purpose of social work was to improve the quality of life for the disadvantaged of society—the poor, the sick, the disabled, the old, the unemployed. Some would argue that this still remains the primary purpose of social work and have become increasingly concerned that current social services not only do little to alter structural, economic, and social factors that contribute to personal and social problems of concern to social workers, but in addition, contribute to the perpetuation of these conditions. They raise questions such as: do social services provided do anything to change the likelihood of personal and social problems addressed by social workers? Or, are they really a smoke screen, a "pap" to the citizens that the government really cares and is doing something when in reality services are offered in large part to "keep the cap on," that is, to contain conflicts that might occur without these services? Others would argue the opposite position—that social work is not inherently conservative in the sense described above. They would argue that social workers are and have been in the vanguard of efforts to alter inequitable conditions related to many personal and social problems. Is social work inherently conservative?

Rosemary C. Sarri says YES. She is a professor of social work and a faculty associate of the Institute for Social Research of the University of Michigan. In addition to teaching social work at Michigan and several other schools in the U.S. and in several countries overseas, she has done research on the impact of policy change on programs and services, on single mothers and their children, and on juvenile justice and child welfare. With J.

McDonough she is the author of *The Trapped Woman: Catch-22 in Deviance and Control* (1987), Newbury Park, CA: Sage, and also the author of numerous other books and papers. She has served on several federal and state advisory commissions.

Carol H. Meyer, DSW, argues NO. She is Professor at the School of Social Work at Columbia University and past editor of *Social Work*. She is the author of four books and 50 articles and chapters about social work practice and its purposes.

YES

ROSEMARY C. SARRI

Social work, like other professions, is shaped by the society in which it exists, but when compared with other helping professions, it operates with less autonomy and is charged with explicit social control functions vis-a-vis populations variously defined as handicapped or disadvantaged. Because social work is primarily a woman's profession, and was one of the few open to women, its history reflects women's position in Western society—that of low power and subordination. It was expected to address "expressive" and person-oriented tasks of caregiving and nurturing viewed as more appropriate for women than policy development, reform, and action. Some writers went so far as to say that women were more effective in these roles because of their experiences as mothers and housewives.

Although some of the early social workers in the late nineteenth and early twentieth centuries were members of upper middle class society, they performed their roles as volunteers in organizations dominated by powerful male elites who sought to maintain both their class and gender interests. These men were quite willing to allocate what they saw as innocuous caregiving responsibility for the poor, ill, dependent, and handicapped to women. The majority of female social workers responded by various patterns of accommodation, thereby excluding themselves from roles of reform and leadership. Such a response is not surprising; groups that are oppressed often respond in a cautious and conservative manner.

Many social work leaders in the early part of this century had a strong interest in social reform and change, and that pattern is still present in 1990, but the development of this second pattern has been more sporadic and has received less support from the rank and file membership. This second group was led initially by Jane Addams, Edith and Grace Abbott, Florence Kelly, and their colleagues, followed later by Frances Perkins, Harry Hopkins, and Bertha Reynolds, all of whom led efforts toward major societal reform and change. Throughout the history of social work in the United

States there have been members who were outstanding leaders of reform, but often they relied more on groups outside the profession rather than within. Ehrenreich (1985) has characterized the profession as a "house divided," especially since the 1960s and the period of the War on Poverty.

Conservatism also springs from the pattern of development of the profession's body of knowledge. It was informed more by practice experience and wisdom developed within a limited range of agencies than by social theory. Mental health professionals, especially psychiatrists and psychologists, strongly influenced the development of social work practice, because social workers readily accepted their directives and often defined themselves in terms of these professionals. Principles were developed that were appropriate to organizational maintenance and client conformity. Only periodically in times of major societal upheaval (1930s and 1960s), brought on by other forces, did theory guide practice, or when there were strong incentives for the application of theory (e.g., behavioral theory). The influence of Mary Richmond directed the profession toward a "scientific case work," but little, if any, independent research was completed to provide the basis for scientifically-based practice. There were few similar admonishments for community organization or social policy staff. Casework was to work toward the development of the individual in her or his social environment while the community worker, by way of contrast, focused on the development of the community so that it could meet its own needs. Active citizens, it was felt, would then act on their own behalf to effect change. Obviously, even community change would require substantial effort to secure adequate resources from the larger society. Community practice was not theoretically based either, but because of its basic orientation to change, it ended up as more reformist in most instances.

Systematic biases against women in social work theory grew out of the psychiatric orientation that had been adopted. Not only did they effect interpersonal practice, but they also were reflected in the position of women in social agencies. Women were the majority, but ever since World War II their presence in administrative and policy leadership positions has declined. Some reversal may be under way in the late 1980s, but their position certainly does not reflect their majority in the total profession. The present linkage of administrative practice to business administration is a conservatizing influence in terms of reform goals as well as the status of women professionals.

The bureaucratic structure of social services in both the public and private sectors has influenced the profession toward conservatism, as Richan (1987) and Withorn (1984) have cogently argued. Workers were rewarded for conformity and compliance, not for action and reform. The achievement of high levels of professionalization in limited fields (e.g., medical and psychiatric social work) led to disengagement from the poor and from clientele in the public welfare sector, partly because it was not felt that a high level of expertise was required for the latter sector. Street (1979) and others have argued that social workers perpetuate poverty and a sense of injustice because of the manner of treatment of disadvantaged and minority clients in most agencies.

The focus of the national professional organizations and the majority of the membership on services to individuals has been a conservatizing influence because the emphasis was on clients' accommodation or coping in the extant society. Few concentrated their efforts on collective social action at the community, state, or national level. This pattern has become even more pronounced since 1970 with the rapid growth in private or clinical practice. Three of four professionally trained social workers now have their primary employment as providers of direct services to clientele. Preference for clinical practice rather than community organization, policy and planning, or social development seems to have become almost antithetical to social reform and action, as evidenced by the content of papers presented at professional social work meetings and in journals.

The more conservative trend in social work since 1970 reflects greater conservatism in United States society as a whole. However, as major social problems of racism, poverty, AIDS, homelessness, family violence, substance abuse, lack of health care, environmental pollution, and out-of-home placement of children have increased rapidly in the 1980s, social workers have not been in the forefront proposing solutions for these problems (Abramowitz). Instead, the profession's response appears to have been one of "wait and see." When the issue is firmly established on the political agenda and resources are available, the profession has enthusiastically joined the efforts to alleviate and treat the problems. A social reform approach would have required far earlier intervention to prevent and control or alleviate the problem when it emerged. Moreover, the reform approach would have also required a more universal or structural approach, not a residual one confined to special populations or even to the United States only. Obviously the latter is far more difficult when powerful economic and political forces oppose such reform, but a significant challenge to the status quo is likely to achieve some redefinition of the situation.

Social work has been and is still very concerned about professionalization because it is viewed as a necessary prerequisite for enhancement of the professional community (Friedson, 1986). Concern then centers on protection of the community's domain as well as the education and practice of its members. Social work, to some extent, functioned as a social movement in the early 1900s, the 1930s, and in the 1960s. In recent decades, however, it has evidenced many more characteristics of a community, particularly in the behavior of the professional organizations. Schools of social work have contributed to the situation today in which very few persons are trained for change-oriented practice because they have adopted a consumer approach—training persons for extant positions or for what the students prefer rather than for what is needed in the society. Moreover, the reliance on practicum training in agencies with professionally trained social work staff operates to maintain the status quo. New and innovating agencies will not be selected for practicum training in most instances. It is also rationalized that training people for change-agent roles is futile because there are too few open positions. Recent experience of public health professionals in community development is an example to the contrary.

The lack of professional concern about racism and public welfare, criminal justice, and chronic ill health also reflects a lack of priority concern about populations in greatest need where only major social change can successfully alleviate the problems. The profession's unwillingness to fundamentally address the plight of minority groups in this society remains a serious obstacle because social workers are the functionaries who control the operation of public welfare and thereby contribute unwittingly to the maintenance of the status of those populations.

There is a tendency to accept the view that social work is an industry in capitalist society, and as such, these types of problems are beyond its legitimate concern as a profession. However, individual social workers as citizens may be very effective in promoting redistribution of benefits for the at-risk populations. The very favorable response of many social workers to the privatization of social services is further evidence of this acceptance of the capitalist perspective.

A related type of behavior has been that of the professional response to the child welfare problems in the United States. Social workers have responded to massive changes in family structure, to the impoverishment of women and children, to the AIDS and drug epidemics by quickly removing children from an environment that is deemed to be deleterious, or else with intensive application of interpersonal technologies while little or nothing is done about the major economic and social problems confronted by the family. Children are placed in a foster care system where the abuse may be even greater and where the long-term outcomes are dismal. Efforts of individuals close to reform in children's institutionalization and empowerment of poor and troubled families has been met with strong resistance from within the professional social work community, as have some of the efforts at intensive home-based intervention.

One significant influence toward greater emphasis within the profession on reform has come from those interested in feminist practice and the status of women as clients and as workers. They have argued convincingly for redefinition of practice theory, for professional priorities toward the addressing of major social problems of poverty, discrimination, racism and sexism. Although this influence within the profession is that of a minority, it can be expected to grow significantly within the next decade when there are likely to be major forces toward social change in the environing society. We may well be entering a period not unlike that of the 1930s and 1960s as far as social change is concerned. Similarly, the role of minority professionals in the profession has been constrained, but it is also possible that they will emphasize the need for greater attention to reform and social action. Certainly there are major demographic and political forces that have the potential for initiating major social reform, and social work can play a significant role in the early stages to set the agenda for change, if it desires to do so.

REFERENCES

Abramowitz, M. (1988). *Regulating the lives of women.* Philadelphia: Temple University Press.

Addams, J. (1926). How much social work can a community afford: From the ethical point of view? Proceedings of the National Conference of Social Work (pp. 108–126). Chicago.

Ehrenreich, J. (1985). *The altruistic imagination: A history of social work and social policy in the United States.* Ithaca, NY: Cornell University Press.

Friedson, E. (1986). *Professional powers: A study of the institutionalization of formal knowledge.* Chicago: University of Chicago Press.

Richan, W. (1987). *Beyond altruism: Social welfare policy in American society.* Philadelphia: Temple University Press.

Street, D., Martin, G., & Gordon, L.K. (1979). *The welfare industry: Functionaries and recipients in public aid.* Newbury Park, CA: Sage.

Withorn, A. (1984). *Serving the people: Social services and social change.* New York: Columbia University Press.

Rejoinder to Professor Sarri   CAROL H. MEYER

The concept of this book, to provide debate about controversial issues, has proven valuable in exposing the persistent, apparently insoluble conflict about the purposes of professional social work practice. I emphasize "practice" because professions are obligated to do something; in fact, my preferred definition of a professional is from the dictionary: "[one] manifesting fine artistry or workmanship based on sound knowledge and conscientiousness."[1] Another more poetic definition says: "though an amateur in politics, he had been a professional in diplomacy." Thus, one of the questions being debated here is: can one who is a professional (lawyer, doctor, nurse, teacher, engineer, architect, or social worker) participate in the politics of social change in his or her professional role?

A more important question perhaps is: should social work have become professionalized in the first place? Had it taken a different route, we might have claimed Norman Thomas and Martin Luther King as twentieth century social (work) reformers. But once having entered the professional status, (and oh, how social workers have yearned for it!) we have assumed obligations to perform in "artistic and workmanlike ways based on sound knowledge and conscientiousness." Of course social reform is necessary; of course social workers should participate individually and collectively in a range of political activities that would promote the social good; of course social reformers like Jane Addams and Florence Kelley (in the preprofessional Progressive Era) operated in the political environment. They also used their autonomy, charisma, and clout to achieve noble ends. But how does one create a 1990 "artistic and workmanlike" model of political behavior, which is of necessity, messy, impassioned, biased, and righteous? Professor Sarri seems to be calling upon rank and file social workers to assume a "social change" role, and that is where one has to consider the issues raised in the "Con" statement. Is it not possible that professionalism is the antithesis of social activism? Not surprisingly, the "pro" statement takes precisely the positions argued against in the "con" statement. (This is definitely a testament to the authors' wisdom in conceiving of this book.)

Professor Sarri has made it difficult to offer a convincing rebuttal to her statement that social work is inherently conservative, because she begins with an indisputable premise. For the reasons she cites, this has been a "woman's profession," this having shaped its conservative directions. She also cites the conservatising influence of the professional association, an argument with which I am in close agreement. Both Professor Sarri and I recognize conservatism when we see it, and both of us share a sorrow that social workers are not more visible in social reform; both of us wish that we could hear more loudly social workers' expressions of outrage at the presence of poverty, injustice and oppression in today's world. Both of us rale against professional withdrawal from the hardest problems found in public child welfare and corrections; both of us worry about the privatising of social welfare. Both of us worry about the increasingly narrow focus of psychotherapy in clinical social work, promoting the selection of the smallest (and most unrepresentative) sector of society to work with, and leaving the poor, minority, and troubled populations with whom social workers should be working, to untrained "human service" workers. But agreement upon these matters should not obscure a more fundamental difference, that Professor Sarri may view social work as a failed social movement, and I view it as a (possibly) failing profession. It is unlikely that true social reformers ever need social work "practice theory." In fact, I would imagine that its use would dampen the reform process, not because such theory is necessarily conservative, but because it addresses a different purpose. Social reform ought to derive its knowledge and effectiveness from politics perhaps, or at least from theory that is more related to social movements than is professional practice theory.

Will this controversy ever be laid to rest? Should it be? Do social workers have more important tasks to do than to expend their energies on old conflicts of purpose? A serious concern today is that social workers have abdicated an expanded professional role in society, never mind their lack of interest in social reform. For example, Professor Sarri views prevention of problems as part of social reform. Conversely, I view preventive programs and practices as an essential part of professional practice. Professor Sarri is concerned about the loss of social welfare protections and services, and views activist attention as entree to the problem. Conversely, I view social welfare as the primary domain of professional social work, about which, incidentally, social workers have been noticeably disinterested. Let us all hope that whether social movement or profession, social workers will come to a renewed awareness of and commitment to the central problems about which both Professor Sarri and I are in agreement. Without such a renewal, then it is conceivable that society will not much care if social workers are present as professionals or as activists. Then, the next chapter marking our history will be entitled, "Was Social Work Inherently Conservative when it used to be a Profession?"

NOTES

1. *Webster's Third International Dictionary* (unabridged) G. & C. Merriam Co. Springfield, Mass. 1971 p. 1811

NO

CAROL H. MEYER

The question has to be answered in the context of social work's role and status in society. If social work is a social institution, then it shares certain features with the total fabric of society. On the other hand, if social work is a freestanding enterprise, then it can shape itself along whatever dimensions it chooses. All evidence points to the fact that social work is a social institution, as well as a profession, and sometimes a self-defining activity.

Is social work conservative (Cooper and Krantzler, 1968)? To the extent that the society in which it exists is conservative, social work as one of society's institutions reflects the same conservatism (Wagner, 1989).

When the social and political profile of the country turns left or right, social work follows it exactly. This has been so in every era since social work emerged as a social institution after World War I. Often, social workers are nostalgic for the earliest days in the Progressive Era, when the upper middle class ran settlement houses and served as radical social critics and aggressive advocates for the poor. But that was before professional education and its inexorable affiliation with universities; before public funding of research and training grants; before the emergence of public services. These new forces and events inevitably constrained social work in its efforts to change the very institutions that supported it.

In the decade of the high-stepping 1920s, social work turned "inward" to define itself and to become preoccupied with psychological processes in their clients. But in the Depression Era, social workers joined the nation in becoming involved with the plight of the poor, who were then almost everyone. During World War II, social workers joined the war effort, emerging from that period of history as did the country, to the conservative, peaceable, precivil rights days of the 1950s. The "sixties" (going into the 1970s) was a time of social change when social workers participate in the War on Poverty, the Civil Rights movement, and later the movement to liberate women. In the 1980s, when the "Reagan Revolution" took hold, social workers went into private practice in great numbers, withdrew from public service employment, and became preoccupied with credentials such as diplomate status and licensing. To the extent that professional self concern is a reflection of conservatism, then social work would appear to be conservative. Yet, there is overwhelming evidence that social workers as a group support liberal political candidates, decry war and racism, support women's rights, and align themselves against poverty and in favor of progressive social programs. Although in these 75 years or so, the profession of social work, now a social institution in its own right, has seldom been known for its leadership in matters of social, political, or economic import, there have always been individual exceptions who have been social critics. So, to the question of whether or not social work is inherently conservative, one answer to support the contrary position is that the historical evidence suggests that in its public pronouncements it is not, although in its dependence upon the society that supports it, it has no choice but to be conservative.

But what exactly is meant by being "inherently" conservative? If it means that social work is politically conservative, then it is probably not true, because as a profession (the public voice) it passes each progressive litmus test of politics that it addresses. If it means that social work sides with value positions that are conservative, then it is probably not true, because social workers most often announce themselves in behalf of progressive social issues. Social workers historically have been called "bleeding hearts,'' and most of them do not mind that too much. On the other hand if the term "inherently" conservative means that social work leans toward conserving established institutions, of which it is one, then the answer is probably yes. It is a mixed picture.

When it comes to the issue of social work being designed to protect vested interests of dominant power groups, one might ask if there is any profession or socially supported institution that is not so designed? Where funding is the vital ingredient that drives an institution, and that funding comes from established "power groups" like the Congress, the state legislatures, or philanthropic lay boards, it is obvious that social workers might tilt toward protecting these vested interests—in their own interests. On the other hand, it is possible to distinguish between the idea of this necessary adaptation to conservative forces, and the idea of "inherent" conservatism. Social work, maturing as a profession, has developed a large degree of expertise in knowledge and skills in many fields of practice. There is no "inherent" conservatism in knowing about social problems and about how to practice in cases of teenaged parents, addiction, family violence, homelessness, mental and physical illness, and the aged. While it is often said that social workers use "bandaid approaches" to treat and rehabilitate people rather than to radically change their environments, the impact of those environments, which includes poverty and oppression and their consequences in poor health, nutrition, housing, education, employment and quality of life, is devastating to the people who suffer deprivation. Social work practice with clients who hurt is not inherently conservative or progressive, any more than is law or medicine, with people who need those services.

Of course there is always a choice as to where social workers might locate their interventions so as to mitigate the hurt that afflicts people. Should this intervention be directly with the power groups who maintain these oppressive conditions? With the CEOs of multinational corporations? With politicians who respond to well-endowed PACs? With local governments that feed on corruption? With lay boards that protect their personal goals? With groups who promote racism and sexism? These groups and the forces they generate in capitalist societies like the United States have not been known to respond readily to the challenges of established social institutions and professions like social work, particularly in eras like the present one, when there is an absence of social idealism in the nation at large. Often, as with the nostalgia felt for the Progressive Era at the turn of the century, some social workers yearn for the social activism of "The Sixties." Perhaps that is where the idea of "inherent" conservatism derives from; i.e., if social workers do not engage in social protest, if they do not take to the streets, and if they do not organize communities to protest, then social work is supposedly "inherently" conservative. There has been sufficient debate about the long term impact of these activities, but leaving aside that evaluation (Moynahan, 1969), it is perfectly possible to consider other types of challenges to power groups by social workers through direct practice and engagement in social policy debates (Kahn, Kamerman, and McGowan, 1972). If the purpose of social action is ultimately to challenge power groups on behalf of social progress, then it would seem to be the propitious choice to act in accordance with the existing sociocultural imperatives so as to succeed in the challenge. The actions might appear down beat, but the outcomes could be radical; there is nothing "inherently" conservative about social action through one's professional role.

Social work practitioners who work on behalf of their clients in and with social agencies recognize that agencies are often dysfunctional, or may be punitive to clients. In these instances, in the daily work life of the practitioner, one might question whether the operative issue is conservatism vs. change or effectiveness vs. poor practice. For example, if a client is not obtaining entitlements or services that are due him or her by right or status, it would be both "inherently" conservative, but more importantly, poor practice, were the social worker not to challenge the policies of the agency in question. The secure and knowledgeable practitioner who cares, and who may have supports somewhere to help him or her may well be effective in changing programs and policies in the service of clients. Far from being inherently conservative, practice in this model is both "activist" and appropriately professional.

The issue will shift if one asks if social work administrators, policy analysts, program planners, or educators are as constrained as are practitioners to adapt to "what is," the conservative position, as opposed to "what if," the position of possibilities and change. On this level of professional activity, there are greater opportunities, and safer conditions, for social workers to introduce change in policies. There is no inherent conservatism in the fact of being a social worker, although inevitably there is the matter of strategy to be considered as well as that of maintaining job security in the face of the controlling demands of boards, taxpayers and legislators. Some social workers can take these risks, and others choose not to, but there is nothing in the tradition, code of ethics, literature, or curricula that explicitly or implicitly defines social work as inherently conservative. But there is no escaping the fact that social work as an institution in society must always reflect the mainstream culture, or that culture will not support it. If this society were to interest itself in progressive social programs, and institutionally confront those power groups who would do otherwise, then perhaps social work would no longer have to suffer the misunderstanding of its being inherently conservative. It would probably be the same social work, but its social, political and economic context would be more compatible with its "inherent" value system.

REFERENCES

Cooper, S., & Krantzler, B. (1968). A polemic in response to a tribute. Social Work, 13(2), 3–4.

Kahn, A.J., Kamerman, S., & McGowan, B.G. (1972). Child advocacy. Child Advocacy Research Report, Columbia University School of Social Work.

Moynahan, D.P. (1969). Maximum feasible misunderstanding. New York: Free Press.

Wagner, D. (1989). Radical movements in the social services: A theoretical framework. Social Service Review, 63(2), 264–284.

Rejoinder to Carol Meyer   ROSEMARY C. SARRI

The argument of Professor Meyer in her negative response to the question: "Is social work inherently conservative?" is qualified. Throughout most of her essay she seems to argue for the "pro" side, that social work is conservative, although she properly wonders about the meaning of "inherent" in this context. She states that whenever the social and political profile of the country turns left or right the social work profession must and will follow it exactly. She even goes on to conclude that, "social work as an institution in society must always reflect the mainstream culture or that culture will not support it" (p. 7). Many great social work reformers would strongly object to that position.

Although I have maintained that the profession has been and is conservative and protective of the vested interests of dominant power groups, I do not believe that it is inevitable that it operate in that manner. Professions are organizations mandated by society, but it is expected that they will be autonomous with respect to major areas of their responsibility. They are authorized to control the behavior of their members so that the needs and interests of clients are paramount. The major constraints are the adequacy of their knowledge base, their skill in practice and the ethical principles for practice that they accept as a profession. The larger the knowledge base and the greater the skill, the greater the autonomy that the profession exerts relative to societal pressures. Examination of the behavior of other professions such as law and medicine or even nursing and education indicates that they do not view themselves as inevitably buffeted in one direction or another by society.

Meyer acknowledges that there have been periods of liberal or progressive behavior as well as periods of conservative behavior, but she suggests that social workers had little or nothing to do with these shifts. As I documented in my "pro" response, there is ample evidence that social workers have been outstanding leaders of social reform in this country. The evidence also would not support such a position because the development of the profession from a social movement during much of the first quarter century of its existence to that of a community (á la Goode, Greenwood, and Friedson) is more attributable to explicit actions of the profession to enhance its status and restrict access to membership than to any force in the society. Moreover, Friedson (1986) argues that graduate professional schools have played a significant role in the practice areas that they have chosen to emphasize in knowledge development.

One is uncertain by what is meant by the statement, "all the evidence points to the fact that social work is a social institution, as well as a profession, and sometimes a self-defining activity" (p. 1). Certainly, these are not mutually exclusive entities.

Social work has had periods of outstanding political leadership in the early 1900s, in the 1930s, and in the 1960s when it was far from conservative. But, in its rush to professionalize and specialize, social workers removed themselves from public social welfare, thereby rejecting the major opportunity for influencing social policy. Today social welfare policy and programs are dominant factors in the United States at Federal, state and local levels. However, the profession does not view public social services as an area of professional concern, although individual social workers, as citizens, may view it as important. In addition to rejecting public social welfare the profession rejected from membership many minority persons and restricted all but a few women to nonleadership positions. Social work has not just been reactive to external pressures, as Meyer suggests; rather, it has deliberately chosen to maximize its professional status in a capitalist society in a particular fashion that mimics the developments in its sister professions of psychology and psychiatry. Strangely, as a female-dominated profession it has not been as militant as either education or nursing in recent years in advancing the position of women in this society.

Should Social Workers Be Licensed?

EDITOR'S NOTE: Licensing is one of the prime means of claiming special expertise in an area. A license to practice in a profession usually requires a particular kind of education and perhaps clinical internship as well, in addition to successful completion of written and oral examinations. The alleged purpose of licensing is to ensure that services offered to the public will be high quality; that is, it is assumed that the screening process used in the licensing process will winnow out those who are not competent to practice a profession. Although some professions require additional competency performances over one's career, social work is not one of these. Thus, once a social worker is licensed and completes the few minimal hurdles that are required to maintain his or her license (such as attendance at certain required training programs), he or she has it for life unless found guilty of some ethical lapse that results in the removal of the license, a rare event. Does licensing protect the public or does it mislead the public in terms of offering false assurances of competence? What other issues should be considered in discussing this question?

James M. Karls, DSW, LCSW, ACSW, argues that social workers should be licensed. He is a field work consultant at San Francisco State University, Department of Social Work Education, and a consultant and therapist in private practice in Marin County, California. He is coauthor of *Case Management and Human Service Practice* (Jossey-Bass, 1987) with Maria Weil, as well as author of a variety of journal articles on mental health subjects. He has served as president of the California State Chapter of the National Association of Social Workers and is currently a member of the NASW Health/Mental Health Commission and coordinator of the NASW P.I.E. (Person-in-Environment) project.

Thaddeus P. Mathis, Ph.D., argues against the licensing of social workers. He is a Professor in the School of Social Administration at Temple University. He has just completed a manuscript entitled *The Politics of Black Liberation: A Critical Examination of the Role of Black Elected Officials in the U.S.* He was a founding member of the National Association of Black Social Workers and the Philadelphia Theoretical and Ideological Center.

YES

JAMES M. KARLS

In the Ian Fleming novels, secret agent James Bond is "licensed to kill." He is permitted by society to take the lives of other people under certain circumstances, and he is not held liable, as would others doing the same thing. While this is a rather dramatic example of a license, it is what licensure is all about. Licensure is permission to certain persons in our society to do things to other people, things that are not permitted to the general population. The surgeon is permitted to cut the human body; the physician is permitted to probe body orifices; the engineer is permitted to build certain structures or objects; the nurse is permitted to inquire into health matters and to dispense medications; the pharmacist is permitted to make and sell various drugs, and so on. The social worker is permitted to explore aspects of human relationships not usually permitted to others.

Licensure is officially defined "as a process by which an agency of government grants permission to an individual to engage in a given occupation upon finding that the applicant has attained the minimal degree of competency required to ensure that the public health, safety, and welfare will be reasonably well protected." Licensure is also de facto recognition that an occupational group has a special body of knowledge and special skills, mechanisms for transmitting this knowledge, and the means (through professional associations or member organizations) of guaranteeing ethical behavior on the part of its members. Although the term *license* is used here to describe societal sanction to practice, currently the movement toward "licensure" of social work is better described as in evolution from "certification" to "licensure." Certification is the process by which a government grants recognition to an individual who has met certain predetermined qualifications. It constitutes "title control" but does not prohibit uncertified individuals from practicing in their occupations or professions doing the same things that others might do. Most licensing laws are referred to as "practice acts" because they usually contain "scope of practice" statements that define what the licensed practitioner may do. It is illegal for any unlicensed person to engage in any of the activities defined by "scope of practice." A group proposing that it be licensed must usually convince a legislative body that the public is being harmed by the absence of regulation. Licensing is the most restrictive type of occupational regulation because the power to grant or withhold a license can be used to deny individuals the opportunity to earn a livelihood in their chosen occupation. The purpose of certification is to enable the public in general and employers in particular to identify those practitioners who have met a standard that is usually set well above the minimum level required for licensure. For both certification and licensure the bottom line is protection of the consumer.

Because "scope of practice" in social work is still in process of definition, most states with licensing laws for social workers might be more properly referred to as certifying the title. Although it is probably growing clearer that society wants to protect itself from potentially harmful "social workers," it is not yet clear what practices of social work could or should be regulated. Thus, currently in most states, social workers are really certified as having special knowledge and skills rather than licensed to practice. But because the movement seems clearly in the direction of licensing "scope of practice" the term *licensure* will be used in this debate.

The fact that almost all states in the United States now have licensing laws for social work perhaps makes the question whether social workers should be licensed moot.

In asking and attempting to answer the question "should social workers be licensed?" one is really asking how social workers have come to be licensed in this country at this time. The question narrows to (1) whether social workers have special knowledge and skills and the other characteristics of a profession, and (2) whether society's health, safety, and welfare will be protected by licensure.

The answer to the question whether social workers have special knowledge and skills and other characteristics of a profession is still in the process of being answered, but is generally in the affirmative. To many studying the process of professionalization, social work is still a "semiprofession," that is, it does not yet have all the characteristics of a "full profession." Although there does appear to be a basic body of abstract knowledge, a network of professional schools, a national professional association, a code of ethics, societal sanction, and an ideal of service, the profession still lacks a common language (an agreed upon way of describing the problems of its clientele), exclusivity (areas of practice that are exclusively those of social work and not shared with other professions), and a clear acceptance by the consumer public of the social worker's ability to provide remedy for many social interaction problems that it purports to solve (a public image of expertise in dealing with or treating social and other problems in the human condition).

Do social workers need official state government and societal sanction to conduct their business, and does this sanction by licensure really protect the public? There would seem to be little question that there needs to be special permission by "the authorities" or by society to allow a stranger to ask questions about thoughts and behavior, finances, relationships with others, and other matters normally considered "private" and not usually permitted to others to ask about. Given that social workers have been asking personal questions of others, placing children for adoption, recommending incarceration or hospitalization and other changes in social conditions for most of this century, why now do we need to assure clientele and the general public that social workers are competent to do so?

The movement to license the social worker appears to be a byproduct of the growth of the social work profession in this country and the growth, in numbers and complexity, of the population. The growth in both the numbers of those who formally train in and identify themselves as "social workers" and the growth of the range in social work practice areas has increased dramatically in the last thirty to forty years. In the 1950s there were fewer than twenty schools of social work in this country producing "professional social workers"; BSW programs were nonexistent, and only two schools offered doctoral level training. In 1984, 346 BSW programs were training over 20,000 students a year: 88 master's degree programs had over 20,000 enrolled, and 51 DSW programs had over 2000 students. The tremendous increase in numbers has created serious problems of control of quality of training and practice. Whereas voluntary control exists through the professional associations, a large number of practicing social workers do not choose to submit to professional association codes of ethics or peer review procedures (it is estimated that some 40 to 50 percent of social workers do not join a professional association in which they would be subject to codes of ethics and peer review). With this "looseness" has come concern among the leadership of the profession, by government officials and by the general public about social workers, both in terms of knowledge and skill and also in conformity to professional ethics. With over 100,000 social workers currently members of the National Association of Social Workers (suggesting almost 200,000 social workers currently in practice), the task of monitoring practitioners on a voluntary basis has become overwhelming. It becomes clear that the increase in numbers has forced a stage in the evolution of social work (societal sanction) that probably would not have otherwise occurred until much later.

Change in locus of practice of social work, notably the development of private practice and "for profit" agencies is another important factor in the move to licensure. Prior to 1960 the very idea of private practice for profit was seen as alien to basic social work tenets. Today, thousands of social workers are practicing in the privacy of their personal offices and charging and collecting service fees directly from the client or from insurance providers. This movement has placed social work in the same position as other entrepreneurial groups and, without the sanction of the church or tax-supported institution, has put social work in the marketplace where the purchaser must beware (and where the vulnerable client must be protected by government from the unethical or unskilled provider of service).

Whereas these first two factors that seem to press for licensure can be seen as arising from society wanting to protect its members, a third, very strong factor in the movement to licensure derives from pressure within the profession of social work itself. Licensure grants a degree of prestige to occupations that would otherwise have lower status in society—the barber or cosmetologist, the vocational nurse, the psychiatric technician. The social worker is not immune to this very human need for prestige and status and compensation for service. Another force driving the licensure movement within the profession is the need for the practicing social worker to compete in the market place. With the increase in the number of social workers in recent decades have come equivalent increases in other human service professions as well, many of them providing services that had once been the unique turf of the social worker—counseling families, working with the elderly, dealing with substance abusers, as well as working with the poor and the disenfranchised. This area is now shared with psychologists, nurses, psychiatrists, rehabilitation counselors, drug and alcohol counselors, and the ubiquitous marriage, family, and child counselor. To gain a "fair share" of the market (as the profession has adapted to the business management language of this era), social workers must be able to market themselves as having special competence to provide certain services that, hopefully, the client in need will buy.

In summary, the question of whether social workers should be licensed is a rhetorical one being answered in the affirmative by the action of state legislatures. In the United States most professional social workers are already licensed or are at least certified as having a certain level of knowledge and skill to practice their profession. This action seems to be an inevitable and even desirable phase in the evolution of the profession. In the general scheme of things it offers the consumer public some guarantee of protection and it enhances the profession of social work. The movement toward licensure is the result of several factors: (1) the dramatic increase over the past 30 years in the number of social workers in practice in this country, accompanied by public uncertainty about the qualifications of the social worker; (2) the movement away from church and other nonprofit agency-sponsored practice toward private practice; and (3) a movement from within the profession to improve the image of the social worker so as to better compete in the marketplace for the funds of those who would purchase the services of the social worker rather than those of other "human service" providers.

REFERENCES

Etzioni, A. (1972). *In the semi-professions and their organization.* New York: Free Press.

Hopps, J.G., Pinderhughes, E.B. (1987). Profession of social work: Contemporary characteristics. In *Encyclopedia of social work, ed 18.* National Association of Social Workers, 351–364.

United States Department of Health, Education and Welfare, Public Health Services. (1977). *Credentialing health manpower* (DHEW Pub. No. 05–77–50057). Washington, D.C., July.

Rejoinder to Dr. Karls   THADDEUS P. MATHIS

The movement toward social work licensing is a manifestation of changing structural forces within a postindustrial American political economy. More specifically, it reflects a set of overlapping political, professional, and economic tendencies whose overall impact is to exacerbate preexisting racial and class inequalities. This conclusion is substantiated by the analysis provided by Dr. James M. Karls. Though his attempt is to argue in support of licensing, Dr. Karls acknowledges the three basic motivations underlying the social work licensure movement. These are, according to Dr. Karls,

> the dramatic increase . . . in the number of social workers in practice in this country, accompanied by public uncertainty about the qualifications of the social worker; . . . the movement toward private practice and . . . a movement from within the profession to improve the image of the social worker so as to better compete in the marketplace. . . .

Dr. Karls is correct. His conclusion that this movement is inevitable and that it guarantees public protection is unwarranted and unsubstantiated. Dr. Karls' characterization of licensing efforts as inevitable is at best speculation and, at worst, little more than an exercise in mystification. Licensing efforts are the result of human aspirations and activity, not some metaphysical phenomena beyond our control. As such, they are subject to human intervention.

That the licensing movement may reflect the choices and values of a majority of current social work leadership may be conceded. However, by Dr. Karls' own estimates, this encompasses only a majority of those fifty percent of social workers who choose to affiliate with the established leadership. This number is diminished further if one deducts those Afro-Americans and others within the profession who oppose licensing efforts. In other words, the current majority is potentially illusive and certainly an historically specific circumstance. In no way can it be described accurately as an irreversibility. It merely reflects the balance of political forces extant at this particular historical juncture and remains subject to the laws of historical movement. The ultimate outcome can still be shaped by the conscious activity of those social forces committed to the creation of a just and humane future.

Whereas some who favor the licensing of social workers may have innocent and just motives, the licensure movement itself may be viewed as a self-conscious political attack on Afro-American interests and leadership and the interests of poor and oppressed people as a whole. It is a movement advanced in the interests of those who now dominate the profession. By advocating the public licensing of social work, current social work leadership is seeking to consolidate and institutionalize its existing privileges and authority, thereby hoping to forestall any emergent challenges to its domination. Any genuine solution to the current crisis of social work must avoid these antidemocratic tendencies.

Social work has an opportunity to play a leading role in the creation of a just and humane future, but only if it develops a set of democratic practices capable of extricating it from its own internal contradictions regarding race and class inequality. Abandoning the effort to repressively establish the boundaries of the profession and its standards of practice is a first step toward this goal. The just choice can still be made.

NO

THADDEUS P. MATHIS

For various professional, political, ideological, and ethical reasons, social workers should not be licensed by the state at this time. Despite the claims of its proponents, licensing does not upgrade the quality of goods and services delivered by social workers. On the contrary, under current circumstances, licensing serves merely to reinforce social stratification and institutional racism. Specifically, the major case against the licensing of social workers at this time is that it has a deleterious effect on Afro-Americans and other people of color and low social status.

The argument may be summarized as follows: social work licensing narrows the scope and the nature of services delivered to people of color and other disadvantaged communities. Secondly, it restricts job opportunities for people of color. Moreover, by utilizing invalid and biased testing and formal, university-based education as the basic screening mechanisms for entering the profession, it limits the entry of people of color and unorthodox perspectives into the profession. Finally, it reflects an inherent political bias, serving to screen out disproportionately militant, progressive, and other nonmainstream perspectives. To some extent, also, licensing may be viewed as an attempt by the NASW leadership to establish hegemony over professional practice and participation by requiring, ultimately, membership in NASW as the criterion for ''membership in good standing.''

This argument is rooted in the premise that the impetus for the licensing movement within the profession of social work is being generated by contradictions within the broader American political economy and the manifestation of these contradictions within social work. Thus, it is a series of concerns other than quality of care that motivates this effort, and these same concerns are at the basis of the fundamental problems that the profession exists to serve.

With the advent of industrialization and the ever-increasing specialization required by the division of labor into more and more discrete units, the identity and allegiance of individuals has come to be shaped in significant ways by their location within the overall division of labor. Occupational sociologists and other scholars have long documented the centrality of the ''job'' in the formation of social values and commitments.

Individuals who perform similar intellectual and physical tasks and share a similar social location tend to evolve subcultures for the purpose of protecting their particular area of activity. The conflicts generated by the diversity of conflicting interests in professional and other occupational groupings usually manifest themselves in disputes over the intellectual bases for practice, the methods of recruitment, the norms governing the relationship between these professionals and others who are not members of the particular profession, and the professional codes of ethics that motivate and govern the professionals in the pursuit of their art and the ''public good.''

Professional social workers are no different. Since the institutionalization of the profession there have been ongoing tensions among the diverse elements that comprise it. It is this diversity of conflicting interests, inherent in its founding, that constitutes one of the principal contradictions confronting the social work profession. These diverse interests are evident in the political struggle to enact licensing statutes in the various states (Baker, 1986).

Though the diversity of disciplines, approaches, perspectives, and interests has been problematic, from the point of view of the development of a consolidated professional identity and a discrete knowledge base within the profession of social work, it has also been the source of vitality and innovation over the years. The effort to have the government license social workers threatens this vitality by both narrowing the scope of professional activity across disciplinary and race and class lines as well as the pool of eligible recruits from which practitioners may be chosen. The attempts to specify the boundaries of the profession, a requirement of all licensing statutes, results in either preempting the self-help efforts of community activists and grassroots service providers or the abandonment of these functions by professionally-trained social workers. The vital mix of personnel and perspectives currently existing is diminished considerably by the enactment of licensing statutes. This has been clearly evident for quite some time in those professions that have already become fully licensed, such as law, medicine, and psychology.

The implementation of public licensing requires establishing artificial boundaries for the profession at the level of knowledge, skill, and activity. For example, licensing tests and standards force a political and administrative resolution to the inherent contradictions within the profession, rather than allowing a more natural resolution of these contradictions through the dialectic of development and struggle. Also, given the ongoing criticism in the literature regarding the current scope and relevance of social work curricula, the timing of the licensing movement is at least questionable. The long-term impact of licensing on social work curricula will be the selection of content related to the tests. Or, alternatively, licensing tests will be based on local curricula, injecting a geopolitical bias into an already stringent recruitment process. This is already evident in those states that have enacted licensing statutes. For example, Cummins and Arkava (1979) have documented the lack of validity in existing licensing tests. Similarly, Johnson and Huff (1987) found that specific social work knowledge and work experience had little impact on licensing test scores in Idaho. The major predictor for success was the applicant's grade point average, followed by the extent of graduate education and race of the applicant (p. 160). They conclude that

> The written test, used for social work licensing, falls short in measuring knowledge unique to the profession; furthermore, there is not a demonstrated relationship between passing a written exam and practice competence. (p. 160)

In California, the only variable correlated with passing the licensing examination was the candidate's personal therapy experiences (Borenzweig,

1977). Finally, not only are the licensing tests invalid, they are racially biased as well (Johnson and Huff, 1987).

The contradictory location of social work in the larger American political economy and its attendant social assignment is the source of another set of principal conflicts within the profession (Galper, 1975 and 1980). These conflicts are evident in the debates over cause and function throughout the profession's history. Historically, the broad diversity of social forces within social work, including racial, educational, cultural, theoretical, and ideologic differences has promoted a healthy tension within the field. Although social workers have been expected to, and, at the same time, have been criticized for controlling the poor, they have also frequently been at the cutting edges of social change as well. This has been due, in large measure, to the tension emanating from the diversity of views and values within the profession. It is precisely this diversity of interests that is jeopardized by licensing.

Finally, the licensing of social workers functions to reinforce and perpetuate the racism already existent within the profession. This racism is evident at all levels of professional activity within social work, from its theoretical base and its code of ethics to its methods of recruitment and the norms governing the behavior of its members. The struggle against racism within the profession, begun as early as the 1920s with the efforts of E. Franklin Frazier (Platt and Chandler, 1988), erupted in 1968 and resulted in a withdrawal of large numbers of Afro-American social workers from the "parent" body (NASW) of the profession. This struggle has continued unabated over the past two decades, led by Afro-American leadership, under the aegis of the National Association of Black Social Workers and African American and other interest groups within the Council on Social Work Education. Much of social work theory is rooted in conservative, system-supporting assumptions about individuals and their relationship to society. This same knowledge base has served to justify racial inequality and other victim-blaming social policies. Although there has been some improvement in the recruitment of Afro-Americans and other people of color into the top ranks of the profession in recent years, the situation is still deplorable. Licensing would only aggravate this situation further. Social work education has an even more dismal record.

Afro-Americans and other people of color are dismally underrepresented on faculties in schools of social work. Moreover, when they are present, they tend to be concentrated in marginal roles and receive lower rates of compensation. The curricula of these schools are still predominately Eurocentric and clinically oriented. The unique perspectives and needs of people of color are often neglected. Again, these negative outcomes would only be reinforced and perpetuated by public licensing.

The primary impetus for the licensing of social workers at this time is generated by the clinical wing of the profession, those who would benefit from direct access to third-party payments and those who desire to function as private practitioners. This segment of the profession has been liberally estimated to be less than 20 percent of all professionally-trained social workers. Yet all practitioners and educators would be constrained by licensing statutes, without the corresponding benefits.

Another impetus for licensing is the attempt to improve the image and raise the salaries of social workers. Many believe that the low status accorded social workers is more a function of the low social status of its clientele in the eyes of the broader community than it is the absence of licensing. Improvement in this area, under current conditions, is likely to come at the expense of low-income and low-status clients, particularly people of color. Historically, this has taken the form of disengagement of professionally-trained social workers from these types of communities. Similarly, the effort to elevate the salaries of social workers will come at the expense of already disadvantaged communities, particularly communities of color. Biased testing, exclusion from institutions of higher education, and alienating curricula are effective instruments for achieving racial hegemony within social work. The consequent increase in social work salaries is likely only to come from limiting the number of new recruits to the profession. Given current realities, people of color would be disproportionately excluded from the profession. The organized Afro-American social work leadership has been the clearest in its opposition to the effort to license social workers. Others, including public service workers, have expressed varying levels of dissatisfaction as well.

In summary, although efforts to protect occupational and professional privileges and prerogatives are a natural byproduct of industrial and postindustrial political economies, there are a number of reasons why the public licensing of professionally trained social workers ought to be opposed at this time. Chief among these reasons is that the institutionalization of racial and class inequalities would be unnecessarily abetted.

At the current stage of American political economy and social organization, efforts might best be addressed to the development of more democratic processes among the various interests internal to the profession. This approach might enable the profession of social work to develop a more unified view of itself. Thus, clearer standards, more uniform methods and techniques, and a greater sense of agreement on knowledge and values among the disparate interests might evolve in a more organic fashion.

Perhaps efforts can be directed more fruitfully toward the development of uniform standards of practice and more appropriate enforcement methods, including the possibility of public licensing. As it stands now, the movement to license social workers represents a repressive tendency on the part of elements within the leadership of the social work profession to consolidate the institutionalization of its privileges and to diminish the likelihood of any emergent emancipative challenges to its authority.

If a pluralistic profession is desirable, then social work licensing, as currently formulated, should be opposed. We must not succumb to the imposition of standards and practices from forces external to the profession and those whom we serve. Consensus must be allowed to evolve organically from the struggle of forces internal to the profession and its clientele. Only then will the profession of social work be capable of realizing its highest stage of development as an instrument of human betterment.

ANNOTATED BIBLIOGRAPHY

Baker, E. (1986). The quest for professional licensure: A case study of the social work profession in Georgia, 1970–1980 (public protection, statutory regulation). University of Georgia, DPA Dissertation.

This is an excellent description of the political forces involved in the licensing struggle in one state.

Borenzweig, H. (1977). Who passes the California licensing examination? *Social Work*, 22, 173–177.

This was the first published study of the actual examinations administered by state licensure boards. The study group was composed of MSW social workers in California who took the examination to be licensed for clinical social worker.

Cummins, D.E., & Arkava, M.L. (1979). Predicting posteducational job performance of BSW graduates. *Social Work Research and Abstracts*, 15, 34.

This is a brief but excellent overview of the validity of social work licensing examinations.

Galper, J.H. (1975). *The politics of social services*. Englewood Cliffs, NJ: Prentice-Hall, Inc.

This is a first rate analysis of the fundamental contradictions within social work and why a radical perspective is needed.

Galper, J.H. (1980). *Social work practice: A radical perspective*. Englewood Cliffs, NJ: Prentice-Hall, Inc.

This is still probably the most coherent statement of the radical perspective within the social work literature.

Johnson, D.A., & Huff, D. (1987). Licensing exams: How valid are they? *Social Work,* 3–4, 159–161.

Platt, T., & Chandler, S. (1988). Constant struggle: E. Franklin Frazier and black social work in the 1920s. *Social Work,* 33, 293–297.

Rejoinder to Professor Mathis   JAMES M. KARLS

Professor Mathis' argument against licensure seems based on his opinion that "Afro-American" and other social workers "of color" will not be able to pass licensing exams and that "Afro-American and other clients of color" will consequently be less effectively served if licensure of social workers is required.

The argument that social workers of color have lower scores on written tests than other social workers is partly true. Some Hispanics and Afro-American men in particular have a lower rate on tests such as the NASW ACSW examinations. Most of the newly developing state licensing examinations by law have to be color blind, so that pass-fail rates or test scores on social workers of color are not known. Why some people have difficulty with written examinations is not definitely known, although various explanations have been offered. Whether the problem lies in the examination or the examinee, the fact is that all but a small percentage of eligible candidates (including social workers of color) pass these examinations. If we accept Professor Mathis' position, we are put in the untenable position of saying that licensing should not occur because some people who seem qualified cannot pass the licensing tests now in use. If the problem is in the testing, we should devise a better method for certifying competence. If the problem lies with the candidate, we should use some of our social work techniques to help.

It should be noted that other fields in which large numbers of people of color are employed (nursing, vocational nursing, psychiatric technology, to name a few) have similar problems around the written test procedure. This has not prevented access to these fields by people of color, and the passing of licensure examinations has both enhanced these occupations as well as served the public interest. I believe Professor Mathis puts down "social workers of color" by implying that they are not as capable as their colleagues.

Professor Mathis' concern about the hegemony of the NASW is in error. It is true that NASW has actively supported the movement for licensure, but hardly out of self-interest. As licensing of social workers passes to the states, the role of the professional association in certifying competence decreases. It is conceivable that the ACSW, which has served to identify the professional social worker for over 25 years, may be replaced by the licensing titles assigned by the many states that now license social workers.

The argument that people of color will not be adequately served if licensure proceeds is questionable. Certainly for individual and family problems people of color want the best help they can get regardless of the color of the provider. And despite all the arguments to the contrary, "better" usually comes from people who know more about what they are doing. In social work that means knowing about human behavior and society and the methods and techniques for helping individuals and groups. The role of professional social workers in helping the disadvantaged and oppressed gain empowerment has not been very prominent for many decades. Those who have led or helped have come from fields other than social work and have had other credentials or licenses to give them legitimacy (among them Martin Luther King, Jesse Jackson, Cecil Williams, Cesar Chavez, and Saul Alinsky). To suggest that licensure of social workers would prevent efforts to empower the oppressed and disadvantaged is to ignore the strong role played by other professions and community leaders.

We would like to think that it is the prerogative of the social worker to develop "militant, progressive, and other non-mainstream perspectives," but unfortunately for social work, it is not. Most social workers in this country serve to relieve the distress of individuals affected by social conditions; relatively few serve to resolve the underlying social problems in the society. Whether that should be so is, as Professor Mathis notes, one of the inherent contradictions in social work and in the American political economy. Delaying or stopping the movement to license social workers is not likely to affect this issue.

Licensure can bring about better and more effective help for the clients of social workers by assuring the recipient of service that the social worker is trained and knowledgeable. Such an effect can only be good for the client, the social work profession, and society!

Should Social Workers Blow the Whistle on Incompetent Colleagues?

EDITOR'S NOTE: The code of ethics of the National Association of Social Workers emphasize the importance of competent social work practice. Yet there is a well-known reluctance on the part of professionals to "blow the whistle" on incompetent colleagues. Options include talking to the person, reporting the individual to a supervisor or to an agency board of directors (if an agency is involved), reporting the matter to NASW Board of Ethics, and going to the media. There is also general agreement that there are indeed incompetent people in the helping professions. Consider, for example, the nationwide compendium of *6892 Questionable Doctors* published by Public Citizen Health Research Group (1990). Included in this list of disciplined doctors are 327 cases of substandard care or negligence, 105 instances of sexual abuse of a patient or sexual misconduct, 601 instances of overprescribing or misprescribing of drugs, 369 criminal convictions, and 338 instances of alcohol or drug abuse. It is estimated in this report that the 2600 total disciplinary actions taken by medical boards in 1987 are "a pittance compared to the 150,000–300,000 Americans who are injured or killed each year as a result of medical negligence" (p. iii). Moral dilemmas are especially common with borderline cases, those that are not blatant in terms of general agreement on what should be done. The reluctance to go outside of the profession is highlighted by the two replies to the case example discussed in this debate.

Frederick G. Reamer, Ph.D., would go outside of the agency but not to the media. He is Professor in the School of Social Work, Rhode Island College. His research and teaching interests include mental health, public welfare, criminal justice, and professional ethics. Professor Reamer is the author of numerous publications, including *Ethical Dilemmas in Social Service* (Columbia University Press, ed 2, 1990), *Rehabilitating Juvenile Justice* (with Charles Shireman, Columbia University Press, 1986), and *The Teaching of Social Work Ethics* (with Marcia Abramson, the Hastings Center, 1982). He is also the author of the chapter on professional ethics in the *Encyclopedia of Social Work*.

Deborah H. Siegel, Ph.D., would not go outside of the agency. She is Associate Professor in the School of Social Work, Rhode Island College. Her research and teaching interests include clinical practice with children and families and the evaluation of clinical social work practice. Her most recent publications include "Effectively Teaching Empirically Based Practice," *Social Work Research and Abstracts*; "Defining Empirically Based Practice," *Social Work; and "How to Integrate Research and Practice,"* in Richard M. Grinnell, Jr., (Ed.), *Social Work Research and Evaluation*.

YES

FREDERICK G. REAMER

Case Presentation

Sarah Russell, MSW had been employed for six years at Rhody Family Service, a private nonprofit agency. Sarah provided counseling to families who had children placed in the agency's foster care program. Michael Long, MSW, another social worker at the agency, had worked closely with Sarah for the past two years in his capacity as case manager for children placed in the agency's foster care program. Michael and Sarah liked each other and got along well. Michael found Sarah to be gracious and warm, and his family and hers occasionally got together socially.

As the months passed, however, Michael began to feel uncomfortable with Sarah's professional behavior at work. In discussing cases with her, in joint supervision sessions, and in group psychiatric consultation meetings, he was continually struck by her superficial assessments and clinical naïveté. Her knowledge of basic human development and treatment theory was unusually weak. Michael also thought that Sarah was much more defensive than most other colleagues when anyone suggested alternative ways of assessing and intervening in her clients' cases. She often responded with nonsequiturs when Michael or other colleagues tried to explore with her concerns about cases they shared.

Michael realized that every social worker has clients who are dissatisfied with them, but it seemed to him that Sarah had an unusual number of dissatisfied clients. At least once a month, a member of a family that he and she worked with would complain to him about the quality of Sarah's work. The complaints were similar. Clients said that Sarah did not listen well, she talked about her own life rather than about theirs, she criticized them, at times she insisted that they explore deeply personal issues, and, once they had begun to do so, she abruptly shifted to another topic. They told Michael that they felt violated and overexposed when she did this. The complaining clients, although angered, usually acknowledged that Sarah was sweet-natured.

Based on the complaints he had received and his own experience with Sarah, Michael concluded that she was an incompetent social worker whose behavior jeopardized her clients' welfare and the agency's reputation. Yet because he was fond of her, he did not want to threaten her job or career. He felt torn about what to do. Should he inform the agency's director about the complaints he had received from clients and about his own concerns regarding Sarah's work? Should he blow the whistle on his colleague and friend?

Commentary

Michael faces a difficult dilemma that, regrettably, nearly every professional faces at some point in his or her career: a decision about whether to blow the whistle on some form of unprofessional behavior. These are among the most difficult decisions professionals must make.

What makes whistle-blowing decisions so difficult? In some instances, social workers are reluctant to blow the whistle because doing so may get a valued colleague in trouble. Or they may be concerned about the possible consequences for their own careers if they are seen within the organization as a "snitch" or trouble-maker. In other instances, social workers simply may want to avoid getting involved in what may turn out to be a complicated, unpleasant, and awkward inquiry. Despite the noble intentions of many whistle blowers, the process is rarely smooth.

Once we put aside self-interested considerations, however, most social workers will acknowledge that circumstances can arise that lead us to feel compelled to blow the whistle. In the face of extreme cases of professional misconduct, for example, involving sexual abuse of a minor or extorting money from vulnerable clients, social workers generally agree that our obligation to protect takes precedence over whatever concerns we might have about jeopardizing a dangerous colleague's career or about sullying our own reputations. Egregious instances of unethical behavior warrant forceful and direct responses. As the NASW Code of Ethics states: "The social worker should take action through appropriate channels against unethical conduct by any other member of the profession" (Principle V.M.2).

Yet, it may be naïve to conclude that every instance of unprofessional behavior warrants full-scale whistle blowing. Whistle blowing can disrupt agency functions terribly and can lead to irreparable damage to agencies' reputations. Whistle blowing can destroy professional careers, even when the suspicions and claims are never substantiated. A decision to blow the whistle must be made with great prudence. In many cases, intermediate measures may be perfectly effective.

The cases that are most troublesome are those on the margin; that is, cases that are neither trivial nor extreme. These are cases in which social workers often feel paralyzed by divided loyalties, caught among the clashing interests of one's agency, clients, colleagues, and self (Reamer, 1990). As Barry (1986: 239) notes in his comments about whistle blowing in organizations:

> Truthfulness, noninjury, and fairness are the ordinary categories of obligations that employees have to third parties, but we can still ask: How are workers to reconcile obligations to employers or organizations and others? Should the employee ensure the welfare of the organization by reporting the fellow worker using drugs, or should she be loyal to the fellow worker and say nothing? Should the secretary carry out her boss's instructions, or should she tell his wife the truth? Should the accountant say nothing about the building code violations, or should she inform authorities? In each case the employee experiences divided loyalties. Resolving such conflict calls for a careful weighing of the obligations to the employer or firm, on the one hand, and of those to the third party, on the other. The process is never easy.

The dilemma involving Sarah Russell and Michael Long is typical of cases involving divided loyalties. Here we have a trained professional whose skills and judgment are being questioned by a colleague. Given the possible risk to Sarah's clients, the consequences for Sarah's and Michael's respective careers and for the agency's reputation, and the effect on Michael's and Sarah's relationship, should Michael blow the whistle? Eventually he may need to, but let's first consider the process he ought to use to make this decision.

There is considerable consensus among contemporary professionals that anyone who contemplates blowing the whistle ought to proceed with considerable caution, rather than blowing the whistle suddenly and shrilly, Michael Long, or any social worker, for that matter, must ask himself several important questions. First, what are my motives? Am I considering blowing the whistle on my colleague because of a sincere wish to protect clients, or am I interested in making life difficult for my colleague? For whistle blowing to be justifiable, we must satisfy ourselves that our motives are honorable rather than self-interested or retributive.

The second question is: is the evidence of wrongdoing available to me compelling and valid? The evidence must suggest serious wrongdoing or incompetence that violates well-accepted standards in the social work profession. Without solid evidence that is virtually incontrovertible, whistle blowing would be irresponsible. If Michael's "evidence" were only circumstantial or based primarily on hearsay, for example, his position would be weak.

The third question every professional must consider is: have I adequately pursued every reasonable internal mechanism and intermediate option in an effort to resolve the problem? Social workers should not jump the gun. Rather, the responsible course of action should entail doing one's best to mediate disputes and rectify misconduct first by speaking directly to the individuals involved. Premature whistle blowing is provocative and uncalled for.

The final question, and perhaps the most difficult to answer, is: how likely is it that whistle blowing will be effective? A social worker may have unimpeachable motives, ample evidence, and may have exhausted every conceivable intermediate avenue of recourse, but if whistle blowing in a particular case is not likely to be effective, it is difficult to justify.

Given the limited details provided in this case, it is difficult to know how pure Michael Long's motives are, how ample his evidence is, how well he has pursued intermediate options, or the likelihood that his whistle blowing will be effective. Let us assume, however, that Michael's principal motive is his deep-seated concern about protecting the agency's clients. Let us also assume that he has tried for months to address his concerns with Sarah directly and with her supervisors and the agency director, all without success. And, finally, let us assume that Michael is confident that the agency's Board of Directors is likely to be responsive, conscientious, and skillful in its handling of Michael's concerns. If these conditions are met, and this is clearly a tall order, Michael would be justified in bringing his concerns to the Board of Directors. The complaints made about Sarah are serious. Clients who may be in need of competent professional skill may be at risk because of the allegedly inferior quality of care provided by Sarah. Michael may be obligated to pursue whatever steps are necessary to safeguard the agency's clients.

But what if, then, the agency's Board of Directors also is not responsive? Suppose the Board members are unwilling to treat Michael's concerns seriously? Should Michael give up at this point?

No, this would be a mistake, assuming that Michael has good reason to believe that clients being served by Sarah are at risk of significant harm. Under these circumstances, Michael would have an obligation to protect the agency's clients, and now that he has exhausted every reasonable option within Rhody Family Service he must consider bringing the matter to an appropriate audience outside the agency. As the NASW Code of Ethics states, "The social worker should seek arbitration or mediation when conflicts with colleagues require resolution for compelling professional reasons" (Principle III.J.7).

The most appropriate organization for Michael to approach is the local chapter of the NASW, which sponsors a Committee on Inquiry designed to address ethical concerns raised by association members. The Committee on Inquiry is charged with hearing grievances filed against NASW members charged with violation of one or more principles in the NASW Code of Ethics. In this case, Michael might cite the code's principle that states, "The social worker should serve clients with devotion, loyalty, determination, *and the maximum application of professional skill and competence*" (Principle II.F.1, emphasis added).

The Committee would review Michael's formal complaint about agency staff (which might include Sarah and the executive director, if Michael believes that both have violated the code of ethics) and, if it accepts the complaint, would conduct a formal hearing to review its merits. The Committee may try to resolve the matter through mediation or negotiation. Although each NASW Committee on Inquiry typically seeks constructive resolution of complaints rather than punitive action, in extreme cases sanctions are necessary. Possible sanctions include revocation of NASW-issued credentials, expulsion from NASW, notification of the public and local regulatory authorities, and letters of censure (National Association of Social Workers, 1989).

Michael's decision to file a formal complaint with NASW is a serious one, because the process for adjudicating grievances can be quite taxing. Michael needs to consider the possible consequences for his own career if he is this earnest about blowing the whistle. To what extent is it legitimate for him to factor this consideration into the equation? It would be naïve to argue that professionals should always be expected to suspend concern about their own well-being when faced with decisions of conscience. Perhaps we would all like to live in a world in which individuals place duty to others before self-centered concerns. But human nature seems to get in the way of such pristine altruism. Like it or not, professionals are, to varying degrees, going to consider the implications of whistle blowing for their own careers, their ability to provide for their families, their reputations, and so on. Perhaps it is not fair to expect otherwise. What we must expect, however, is that social workers will recognize their fundamental obligation to meet clients' needs and to protect clients from foreseeable harm. Occasionally this responsibility may entail blowing the whistle on unprofessional conduct or irresponsible behavior. Accepting this responsibility is part of what it means to be a professional.

72   Debate 5

REFERENCES

Barry, V. (1986). *Moral Issues in Business,* ed. 3. Belmont, CA: Wadsworth.

National Association of Social Workers. (1989). NASW Procedures for the Adjudication of Grievances, rev. ed. Silver Spring, MD: National Association of Social Workers.

Reamer, F.G. (1990). *Ethical Dilemmas in Social Service,* ed 2. New York: Columbia University Press.

Simmons, N., McCarthy, P., & Wolfe, S. (1990). *6892 Questionable Doctors Disciplined by States or Federal Government.* Public Citizen Health Research Group.

ANNOTATED BIBLIOGRAPHY

Bok, S. (1980). Whistleblowing and Professional Responsibility. In D. Callahan and S. Bok (Eds.), *Ethics Teaching in Higher Education.* New York: Plenum Press, 277–295

This chapter provides a succinct summary of issues involved in whistle blowing. Bok provides a useful overview of questions that potential whistle blowers ought to address before making a firm decision.

Bowman, J.S., Elliston, F.A., & Lockhart. P. (1984). *Professional Dissent: An Annotated Bibliography and Resource Guide.* New York: Garland Publishing

This book provides a valuable list of references on the subject of whistle blowing. Citations cover whistle blowing in the professions and in government and include references from the philosophical literature.

Peters, C., & Branch, T. (1972). *Blowing the Whistle: Dissent in the Public Interest.* New York: Praeger

This is one of the earliest and most comprehensive works on the subject of whistle blowing. It provides a useful introduction to the difficult decisions professionals must sometimes make, particularly in the public policy arena.

Rejoinder to Professor Reamer   Deborah H. Siegel

Clearly, there is agreement that sometimes whistle blowing is ethically required. Disagreement occurs when we try to establish guidelines to help us decide when, how, and to whom we should blow the whistle.

Professor Reamer poses four very helpful questions that we must ask ourselves before we blow the whistle; these questions provide a useful framework to guide decision making in difficult situations. Is it always the case, however, that in order for whistle blowing to be a valid response to a situation, the motives of the whistle blower must be untainted by self-interest or retributive impulses? Conceivably, an offense could be serious enough that the whistle should be blown although the whistle blower has something to gain by that action. If, for example, Michael personally disliked Sarah, should he turn the other cheek simply because he might get personal satisfaction from calling attention to her behavior?

Similarly, it may not be realistic or reasonable to require that every whistle blower in every instance must first assemble a mass of compelling and incontrovertible evidence of malfeasance. There may be instances when the whistle blower has ample valid and reliable information up to a point but does not have access to complete knowledge about a colleague's misbehavior. Does that mean that the whistle should not be blown? Mandatory child abuse laws in many states, for example, require that we report child abuse when we so much as suspect that it might have occurred; it is the state child abuse investigator's job, not the reporter's, to determine whether or not abuse has in fact taken place.

One might also question whether it is always necessary to share one's concerns with the offending colleague before one blows the whistle on her or him. Although I agree that it is highly desirable that one do so, I do not think that it is a necessary prerequisite to further corrective action. There may be compelling reasons, other than my own cowardice, that may make it difficult for me to share my concerns directly with a colleague. If, for example, I feared for my own physical safety, I might bypass the colleague and go directly to supervisory personnel.

Finally, I am not sure that one must be confident that blowing the whistle is likely to be an effective course of action before one does it. There may be instances in which a wrong must be exposed as a matter of principle, regardless of the outcome. Who among us can accurately predict the future? If we insist that our whistle blowing must have a high likelihood of effectiveness before we undertake it, we may have set a criterion so unattainable as to make future whistle blowing virtually impossible.

If we accept Professor Reamer's criteria for the moment, however, the details of the Rhody Family Service case as they are presented here do not justify Michael's involvement of the Board of Directors or the Committee on Inquiry. The case summary does not provide evidence of malfeasance serious enough to merit filing a formal ethics grievance against Sarah outside the agency. Blowing the whistle to the Board and the Committee on Inquiry is an overreaction to the severity of Sarah's misdeeds.

NO

DEBORAH H. SIEGEL

In sports, the referee's job is to observe the action to ensure that all parties play the game according to the rules. The referee, a truly neutral actor, "blows the whistle" when foul play occurs, thus stopping the game and initiating corrective action. In the typical human service agency, there is no formally designated referee. It is commonly assumed that each professional social worker referees her or his own professional behavior and functions ethically and responsibly. Although generally this assumption is accurate, every social worker is aware of instances in which a colleague has violated the NASW Code of Ethics or has used poor judgment in carrying out professional responsibilities. What is the social worker's obligation when she or he becomes aware of an instance of a colleague's irresponsible or unprofessional behavior? And what is the social worker's responsibility when such behavior occurs thematically over time and supervisory personnel appear neither not to know about or not to have responded to it?

There is little question that every social worker has an obligation to blow the whistle when serious malfeasance occurs. In our dealings with other social workers we all occasionally encounter incompetent practice, poor judgment, or unethical behavior. We all have at one time or another decided to keep silent about it for various reasons. Not every mistake is consequential enough to merit immediate corrective action by a potential whistle blower; we know that we have made mistaken professional judgments and so we are reluctant to call others on the carpet for that, we feel that it is not our place to point out someone else's error, we fear serious repercussions on ourselves if we blow the whistle, or something else deters us. The question is, therefore, specifically under what circumstances should we blow the whistle? To whom and for how long should the whistle be blown?

In order to determine under what circumstances one ought to blow the whistle, it is helpful first to ascertain whether or not a behavior violates the NASW Code of Ethics. Clearly, Sarah's behavior has been harmful to clients and has violated principle IB of the code: "The social worker should strive to become and remain proficient in professional practice and the performance of professional functions." One might also argue that in her clumsy interactions with clients, Sarah has also violated principle IC2 of the code: "The social worker should act to prevent practices that are inhumane or discriminatory against any person or group of persons" as well as principle IVO1: "The social worker should base practice upon recognized knowledge relevant to social work." The Code of Ethics does not always point so clearly to ethical violations, but in this case it does. By mishandling already troubled clients, it is reasonable to assume that Sarah has perhaps exacerbated their distress and made it harder for them to seek or accept help from professionals in the future.

The next step is to examine the NASW Code of Ethics in order to ascertain (1) whether or not Michael has an obligation to act, and (2) if so, what form that action should take.

Three statements in the Code clearly indicate that Michael is obliged to take some kind of action in this case:

- The social worker should create and maintain conditions of practice that facilitate ethical and competent professional performance by colleagues (principle IIIJ3)
- The social worker should work to improve the employing agency's policies and procedures and the efficiency and effectiveness of its services (principle IVL1)
- The social worker should act to prevent the unauthorized and unqualified practice of social work (principle VM3)

Having determined that Sarah's behavior has violated the Code of Ethics and that Michael is required by the Code to respond, one must then decide how Michael ought to proceed. Again the code offers some guidance. Principle IIJ4 states that "The social worker should treat with respect, and represent accurately and fairly, the qualifications, views, and findings of colleagues and use appropriate channels to express judgments on these matters." Principle VM2 indicates that Michael must . . . take action through appropriate channels against unethical conduct by any other member of the profession." Thus, Michael must determine what "appropriate channels" means in this case.

Principle IIJ11 indicates that "the social worker who has the responsibility for evaluating the performance of employees, supervisees or students should share evaluations with them." Although Michael has no official supervisory responsibility for Sarah's work, Principle IIJ11 can be interpreted to suggest that he first share his concerns directly with Sarah herself, in the hope that once she knows of his concerns, she will take corrective actions to improve her social work practice. Most of us prefer, as a matter of common courtesy and human decency, to be told face-to-face first, before a negative message about us is delivered behind our back.

In this case, it seems reasonable to assume that Sarah's immediate supervisor and other workers in the agency have also directly observed Sarah's lack of professional knowledge and skill. One has to wonder, then, what, if any, corrective action has already been taken; if some action has occurred, why Sarah continues to function below professional standards; and why, given her incompetent performance, she continues to be employed by the agency. Let us suppose that Michael shares his concerns with the supervisor, and nothing happens. Sarah remains employed at Rhody Family Service and client complaints continue.

Michael might next share his concerns directly with the agency director. But if the agency director fails to take corrective action that results in an improvement in Sarah's performance, her reassignment to other responsibilities in the agency, or her dismissal, Michael may have exhausted all of his reasonable options. He may be tempted to go over the agency director's head and blow the whistle to the Board of Directors, the agency's funding sources, or the media. But these courses of action would be inappropriate and would open the possibility of generating more harm than good. They are drastic measures out of proportion to the severity of Sarah's conduct. These actions could erode trust among colleagues in the agency and could leave Michael scapegoated and ostracized. Furthermore, going to the Board, funding sources, or the media means going outside of "appropriate channels" in this case. A Board of Directors is responsible for hiring and firing the executive director, not line staff. The Board's role is to set agency policy and monitor programs, not oversee an individual staff member's performance. Michael has to weigh the possible benefits of publicly exposing Sarah's incompetence and the agency's failure to deal with it against the costs of threatening agency funding entirely and discrediting the agency in the eyes of the community. Would the community be better off if they did not trust any agency personnel? Would the community be better off without the agency? If we assume for the moment that all of the other social workers at Rhody Family Service function at a high professional level and provide quality service to their clients, then jeopardizing the entire agency's program seems to be a rather far-fetched alternative.

Deciding whether to blow the whistle can be a very painful choice. Most of us are offended and troubled by the injustices we see. Social workers especially are inclined to intervene on behalf of vulnerable people. Nonetheless, we must carefully weigh the costs and benefits of our well-intended actions. An action as potentially disruptive as whistle blowing should not be done impulsively out of pent-up frustration.

ANNOTATED BIBLIOGRAPHY

Compton, B.R., & Galaway, B. (1989). *Social Work Processes,* ed 4. Belmont, CA: Wadsworth Publishing Co.

This comprehensive and widely used introduction to social work practice includes chapters on the knowledge, values, and skills crucial for competent social work practice regardless of agency setting, worker's role, or client system or target system size.

National Association of Social Workers. (1980). *Code of Ethics of the National Association of Social Workers*. Silver Springs, MD: NASW.

> Every social worker, in joining the social work's national organization, agrees to adhere to this code of ethics. The code is intended to serve as a guide to everyday conduct and as a basis for adjudicating ethics grievances against social workers and their employing agencies.

Reamer, F.G. (1990). *Ethical Dilemmas in Social Service,* ed 2. New York: Columbia University Press.

> This book presents a typology to help social workers recognize ethical issues in micro and macro practice and develops guidelines to facilitate ethical decision-making.

Waldfogel, D. & Rosenblatt, A. (1983). *Handbook of Clinical Social Work*. San Francisco: Jossey-Bass Publishers.

> The sections titled "Knowledge Base of Clinical Social Work," "Theories for Producing Change," "Education and Methods for Clinical Practice," and "New Applications of Research in Clinical Practice" provide a concise and comprehensive overview of the areas of theoretical and empirical knowledge necessary for competent clinical social work.

Rejoinder to Professor Siegel   FREDERIC G. REAMER

Professor Siegel is right to dwell on the implications of the NASW Code of Ethics. She has made a number of valuable points about the code's principles concerning professional proficiency, inhumane practices, social workers' knowledge, agency policies, and collegial relations.

One difficulty with this approach, however, is that the broad principles contained in the Code of Ethics allow for considerable selectivity and varying interpretations. In short, it is not too hard to find principles in the code to support either position in this case—whether or not to blow the whistle.

This is an inherent limitation with perhaps all codes of ethics, whether in the field of law, nursing, psychology, journalism, engineering, advertising, law enforcement, social work, or business. Most codes include broad statements of principle and are written at a fairly high level of abstraction. There are exceptions, of course. A number of codes contain very specific prescriptions and proscriptions concerning professional conduct, for example, with regard to fee-splitting, sexual contact with clients, or misrepresentation of credentials. Surrounding these specific statements, however, one usually finds rather general principles concerning professional ideals and obligations. Their function is an important one because they set the tone for a profession's mission. It is often difficult, however, to apply such general principles to complex, concrete circumstances.

Such is the case in the dilemma involving Sarah Russell and Michael Long. In addition to looking at the Code of Ethics for a resolution to this case, which may lead to considerable frustration, it is important to emphasize the process that the social worker involved ought to follow in order to make an informed, principled decision. Difficult ethical choices, of the sort we find here, rarely lend themselves to quick solutions. What they demand is careful analysis of competing claims and interests and a disciplined application of ethical considerations and professional wisdom.

In this case, Michael Long might find it helpful to review the Code of Ethics to ensure that he is raising important questions about professional responsibility. But he must also look beyond the code if he is to thoroughly weigh reasons for and against whistle blowing. He must think through various issues that the code does not broach concerning his own motives, the adequacy of his evidence of incompetence, his efforts to resolve the matter without blowing the whistle, and the likelihood of a successful outcome.

Whistle blowing may be necessary in this case. The Code of Ethics includes language that supports this conclusion, although admittedly one can also find in it language to support an opposing point of view. In the end, one's decision must be defended on grounds that are more substantial and firm than one typically finds in a code of ethics.

Should Social Workers Be Well-Trained in Behavioral Principles?

EDITOR'S NOTE: Behavioral principles describe relationships between behavior and environmental consequences that have been found across a wide range of situations and species. For example, hundreds of studies have explored the effects of different patterns of reinforcement on the rate and durability of behavior. The differential effects of positive and negative control on behavior have been explored in hundreds of experimental and applied reports. These principles describe empirical relationships. There are many different theories that may account for them. One of the hallmarks of social work is an emphasis on the social environment. Thus, a question naturally arises: Should social workers be well trained in behavioral principles? That is, should they understand and be able to apply knowledge concerning the relationships that have been found between behavior and environmental consequences? Would such an understanding accompanied by performance competencies enhance the quality of services offered to clients? Reactions to this question will depend in large part on one's view of how knowledge related to social work practice should (and can) be generated (see discussion in the introduction as well as Debate 8: Should social workers base practice decisions on empirical research?).

Bruce A. Thyer, Ph.D., LCSW, argues YES. He is Professor of Social Work and a Faculty Fellow, University Affiliated Program, at the University of Georgia, and an Associate Clinical Professor of Psychiatry and Health Behavior with the Medical College of Georgia. He is a member of the Editorial Board of the *Journal of Applied Behavior Analysis* and will

serve as Editor of *Research on Social Work Practice*. His publications
include *Treating Anxiety Disorders: A Guide for Human Service Professionals* (Sage, 1987) and *Professional Social Work Credentialing, and Legal
Regulation* (with M.A. Biggerstaff) (C.C. Thomas, 1989). He is the editor
of *Behavioral Family Therapy* (C.C. Thomas, 1989).

Herbert S. Strean, DSW, argues NO. He is Professor Emeritus,
Rutgers University, and director at the New York Center for Psychoanalytic
Training, where he directs the training of social workers, psychologists, and
psychiatrists in psychoanalysis. He is the author of twenty-three books and
100 articles. Recent books include: *Resolving Marital Conflicts: A Psychodynamic Perspective* (Wiley, 1985) and *Resolving Resistance in Psychotherapy* (Wiley, 1985).

YES

BRUCE A. THYER

A number of themes have made themselves evident during the past decade
or so of social work practice and education. Foremost among these themes
is the concept of accountability. Accountability in social work may take a
number of forms. In professional practice this involves attempting to empirically document the outcomes of service at the level of the individual
social worker. Another dimension of accountability is the concept that the
selection of social work methods of intervention should be based upon one's
familiarity with the relevant research literature, and that one should initially
attempt methods of intervention that have been empirically shown to actually be of help to people in need. In the field of social work education,
accountability takes the form of teaching students theories of human behavior that similarly have a sound empirical foundation, and not to devoting
large amounts of valuable classroom time to the exploration of human
behavior theories that either have been shown to be erroneous or to those
that lack an adequate empirical foundation. Additionally, accountability in
social work education implies that the professoriate keep up to date with the
latest developments in practice research and to convey this knowledge to the
classroom environment. Practice classes should be devoted to students
acquiring skills in specific procedures that scientific evidence demonstrates
are helpful to clients, and the agencies that provide field instruction should
be able to reinforce such classroom instruction with appropriate supervision
from experienced social workers who are well-trained in these methods of
empirically-based practice.

Given these propositions, I believe that a strong case can be made in
favor of the contention that social workers should be well-trained in behav-

ioral methods for the following reasons. The experimentally derived principles of human behavior comprising contemporary social learning theory, those of respondent, operant, and observational learning, possess an extremely strong foundation of empirical support. There is a large scientifically credible literature (largely ignored in contemporary social work textbooks) concerning the validity of social learning principles in accounting for many of the phenomena we call human development across the life span. For this reason, a thorough grounding in the basic and intermediate principles of social learning theory should form an important component to human behavior in the social environment courses in the social work curriculum. In many respects, the behavioral approach, with its strong focus upon a person's history of transactions between behavior and their psychosocial environment (which provides reinforcing and punishing consequences), is the approach to practice that is most congruent with the profession's historic person-in-environment perspective.

Social work research courses should include a strong element pertaining to the methods of scientific inquiry labeled the experimental analysis of behavior (EAB). Also known as single system research designs, EAB provides the practitioner with a set of practical research principles with direct applications to the conduct and evaluation of social work intervention at all levels, including work with individuals, therapy with couples, families and small groups, community practice, and policy analysis. The basic tenets of EAB include using reliable and valid means of defining and measuring a client and systems' problems; to periodically take such measures before, if possible, during, and after treatment to ascertain the effectiveness of social work intervention; and to rely more upon the visual analysis of graphically presented data as opposed to the use of obtuse inferential statistics. All these practices are compatible with and perhaps essential to contemporary ethical social work treatment. Teaching students to apply the principles of the EAB in their own practice affords the profession with one means of bridging the often lamented gap between the social work practitioner and the researcher. A recent bibliography on the use of single system research designs in social work found over 250 citations (Thyer & Boynton, 1989), illustrating the vitality of the approach.

It is in the teaching of social work practice classes that it is most apparent that skills in behavior analysis and therapy should be an obligatory part of the intervention armamentarium of contemporary social work professionals. More than 15 years ago a task force assembled by the American Psychiatric Association (1974) concluded that at that time ". . . behavior therapy and behavioral principles employed in the analysis of clinical phenomena have reached a stage of development where they now unquestionably have much to offer informed clinicians in the service of modern clinical and social psychiatry" (p. 137). The task force also found

". . . that a course in psychology with special attention to the experimental analysis of behavior should be recommended . . ." (p. 114).

Today the authoritative *Comprehensive Textbook of Psychiatry* provides an excellent and concise overview of the role behavior analysis and therapy plays in the field on mental health care. Liberman and Bedell (1989) note that extensive and well-controlled bodies of practice research have convincingly demonstrated that among the psychosocial therapies, behavior therapy may be considered to be the initial treatment of choice for a wide variety of disorders, including but not limited to the anxiety disorders, schizophrenia, depression, eating disorders, psychosomatic complaints, sexual dysfunctions, substance abuse, childhood disorders, mental retardation, and other developmental disabilities such as autism. They provide a comprehensive chart illustrating that every year since 1965, the application of behavioral principles has consistently expanded into more difficult and increasingly complex so-called mental disorders. It is widely acknowledged that these behavioral studies are among the best designed and controlled investigations in the social and behavioral sciences.

In the areas of administration, supervision, community and organizational practice, and policy analysis and development, compellingly large bodies of empirical research currently exist (and remain largely ignored by most social work academics), which offer parallel positive developments for our profession's educational curricula and practices (e.g., Greene et al., 1988).

I chose to respond to the question, "Should all social workers be required to be well-trained in behavioral principles?" in the affirmative because I believe that such approaches have much to offer our profession and that the social worker who remains unfamiliar with this burgeoning area of theory and practice will be seriously handicapped in terms of his or her ability to effectively help others. I take this position not to authoritatively dictate to my peers (although the Council on Social Work Education has been doing that for years) but to challenge my colleagues to dispute the validity of the contentions contained herein, to point to another model of human behavior with such a robust degree of empirical support, or to provide an example of another approach to social work services with the scope and applications of behavior analysis and therapy.

The acceptance of behavioral principles and of behavior analysis and therapy is rapidly growing. Approximately 65% of all newly hired faculty in the field of clinical psychology claim that social learning theory is their preferred theoretical orientation. Certain states are adopting behavior analysis as their official treatment modality for the care of persons with developmental disabilities (Johnston & Shook, 1987). In contrast, training in dynamically oriented psychotherapy is no longer a required component of the professional training of psychiatrists in Great Britain, and similar initiatives have been proposed for residency training of psychiatrists in the United States. Although psychodynamically based theories and practices continue to dominate the clinical training of social workers, there has not been a single well-controlled study demonstrating that such therapies are of benefit to social work clients. Currently, behavioral principles afford the best our profession has to offer in terms of practice theory and intervention. Until another, more comprehensive, approach appears on the scene, ethical practice and academic integrity require that behavioral principles be an important component of social work education.

REFERENCES

American Psychiatric Association. (1974). *Behavior therapy in psychiatry*. New York: Jason Aronson.

Greene, B.F., Winett, R.A., VanHouten, R., et al. (1988). *Behavior analysis in the community*. Lawrence, KS: Society for the Experimental Analysis of Behavior.

Johnston, J.M. & Shook, G.L. (1987). Developing behavior analysis at the state level. *The Behavior Analyst*, 10, 199–233.

Liberman, R.P. & Bedell, J.R. (1989). Behavior therapy. In H.I. Kaplan & B.J. Sadock (Eds.), *Comprehensive textbook of psychiatry*, Vol. II, ed 5. Baltimore, MD: Williams & Wilkins, pp. 1462–1482.

Thyer, B.A. & Boynton, K.E. (1989). "Single-subject research designs in social work practice: A bibliography." Unpublished manuscript, School of Social Work, University of Georgia.

ANNOTATED BIBLIOGRAPHY

Cooper, J.O., Heron, T.W., & Heward, W.L. (1987). *Applied behavior analysis*. Columbus, OH: Merrill

A highly recommended introductory textbook to the field of applied behavior analysis. Covers basic and intermediate principles of behavior, the methodology of the experimental analysis of behavior, and extensive applications to direct practice.

Pinkston, E.M., Levitt, J.L., Green, G.R. et al. (1982). *Effective social work practice: Advanced techniques for behavioral intervention with individuals, families, and institutional staff*. San Francisco: Jossey-Bass

An excellent compilation of a large number of cases illustrating the application of behavior analysis to a wide variety of situations encountered by social work workers at all levels of practice.

Thyer, B.A. (1988). Radical behaviorism and clinical social work. In R.A. Dorfman (Ed.), *Paradigms of clinical social work*. New York: Brunner and Mazel, pp. 123–148

A more detailed overview of the philosophy of behaviorism and of behavioral methods as applied to a complex clinical case.

Rejoinder to Professor Thyer HERBERT S. STREAN

One of Professor Thyer's major preoccupations in choosing a theoretical perspective from the social and behavioral sciences that can be utilized in a major way in training social workers "is the concept of accountability." Thyer correctly points out that "accountability in social work may take a number of forms," but his central concern is that social work students should not be subjected "to the exploration of human theories which . . . have been shown to be erroneous."

On the basis of Thyer's prescriptions and caveats, behavioral principles should be ruled out of the social work curriculum. Why? Because behavioral theories do not account for many of the dimensions of the human being that are absolutely necessary for a social worker to master in order to understand and to help therapeutically men, women, and children who are in stressful conflict. Behavioral principles tend to disregard unconscious wishes, ego defenses, superego mandates, and ethical ideals. They have very little to say about what really motivates and governs the behavior of human beings—fantasies, day and night dreams, psychosexual development, character armor, romantic ideals, "the child" inside all adults, and love in all its forms, healthy and immature, to name just a few of the variables that behavior therapists tend to disregard.

In addition to overlooking many crucial dimensions of the human organism, the empirical research of the behaviorist is unscientific. To rely to such an extent on numbers and chi squares, percentages, and decimal points renders much of their research close to irrelevant. How can one really measure the apathy of a neglected baby, the desperation of a single parent on welfare, or the dependency of an abandoned spouse? The very nature of the complex human being, living in a complex society, is such that to measure him and her rather than try to understand and to describe him or her comprehensively, tends to subject our social work students to a very limited and extremely mechanical perspective on human beings and on their interactions and transactions with others.

Just as the principles of behaviorism omit much of what we know as part and parcel of the human organism, its orientation to therapy does likewise. Rarely does the therapy reported by a behaviorist deal with one of its most pertinent variables, the therapist's countertransference. If the therapist's own values, conflicts, history, and anxieties are not considered in studying therapy, a large part of the therapy is just not being studied. One could say the same thing about the behaviorists consistently overlooking the client's transference reactions, which, more than any other feature of therapy, account for the positive or negative outcome of the treatment. Resistance, too, in all its forms, covert and overt, conscious and unconscious, which is a "given" in all therapy, is rarely addressed by the behaviorist. When these crucial variables in any treatment are omitted in the study, evaluation, or research on therapy, the validity and reliability of the study, evaluation, or research must be questioned.

Behavioristic principles tend to move away from central values of social work practice. Self-determination of the client and acceptance of the client are bypassed as the client is rewarded and punished. Often when behavior is being rewarded (reinforced) or punished (aversely deconditioned), the behaviorist, in many ways, is acting out his countertransference biases under the guise of "the scientific method."

Like most ardent champions of behavioral principles, Professor Thyer distorts the efficacy of psychoanalytic treatment, or what he calls "psychodynamic" therapy. Psychoanalytic treatment, despite Thyer's contentions, is the most researched and most successful therapy on the market today. Although behaviorists and others may deny this truism, reports from such researchers as Fisher and Greenberg in *The Scientific Evaluation of Freud's Theories and Therapy,* Sarnoff in *Testing Freudian Concepts,* Firestein in *Termination in Psychoanalysis,* and Colby in *Psychoanalytic Research* clearly demonstrate how psychoanalytic treatment does help different types of individuals in rigorous and sustained ways. This is probably why the noted behaviorist, Dr. Arnold Lazarus, was able to conclude in his paper, "Where Do Behaviorists Take Their Problems?" that behaviorists take their problems where they believe they are going to be helped: to psychoanalytically oriented psychotherapists.

NO

HERBERT S. STREAN

As one who has constantly argued that there is room, in social work for many different theoretical perspectives and room for many different practice modalities, I find myself feeling somewhat uncomfortable in doing a "con job" on what is probably the most popular orientation to practice in social work today. Although I will argue against the proposition that "social workers should be well trained in behavioral principles," I would like nonetheless to point that there are certain notions of behaviorism such as reinforcement, positive and negative, and other learning concepts that many social work practitioners from different "schools" can and do find useful.

There are several reasons why I believe that behavioral principles should not be stressed in social work training. First, the behaviorist omits in his assessment of clients much of what personality theory has contributed to practice. As a matter of fact, the behaviorist tends to eschew all of personality theory. Second, there are many variables in the treatment situation that the behaviorist omits. Third, while the behaviorist champions "a scientific approach" to treatment and research, his omission of the internal dimension, e.g., the client's unconscious, makes the consumer of behavioral research somewhat skeptical. Finally, there are certain values that have been part and parcel of social work that the behaviorist tends to overlook.

In a well-regarded social work text that adheres closely to behavioral principles, the authors contend:

> . . . a youngster who, for whatever reasons, is judged to be a problem because he will not attend school can be thought of as successfully treated when his school attendance becomes reasonably frequent. A child who suffers from enuresis is "cured" when he no longer wets himself. The case of an impotent man can be closed when he experiences erections. An unemployed father is satisfactorily treated when he obtains gainful employment (Briar and Miller, 1971, pp. 167–169).

The above statement tends to demonstrate many of the weaknesses of the behaviorist's approach. Diminution of symptoms (external behavior) tells us little about the human being and his progress in treatment. For example, a youngster may improve his attendance at school and concomitantly become more neurotically compliant, more frightened of authority figures, and more terrified of his aggression. When the client's self image, object relations, ego functions, superego pressures, and defenses are overlooked, we cannot be sure what a shift of symptoms means. It can be for the better, but it could be for the worse. Behaviorists, while touting their "conditioning," often wish to ignore that human beings have wishes, form transferences, fear change, and seek to understand the many dimensions of their intrapsychic and interpersonal lives.

To use the language of the behaviorist, a behavioral approach to social work does not take account of several "intervening variables." One crucial intervening variable is the client's internal environment. When unconscious wishes, superego mandates, introjects, ego ideals, and transference reactions to the therapist are ignored, much of the client is being rejected by the practitioner.

Once we start dealing with intervening variables, as psychologist Reuben Fine points out, the whole fabric of behaviorism becomes radically altered.

> If we must rely on inference again, why should we eliminate introspective data? Introspection after all leads to another series of inferences, which can then be collated with behavioral data. But then the original argument of behaviorism, that we should only deal with observables, obviously collapses. . . . Thus behaviorism, when pushed to its conclusion, . . . leads to an inherent logical contradiction. If we confine ourselves to purely objective data, we cannot explain them. And if we try to explain them, we get away from pure objectivity . . . The behavioristic position rests upon certain essential misconceptions of scientific method. The crucial role of inner psychological data cannot be denied (Fine, 1983, p. 35).

Well-established scientific data tell us that behavior involves some inner experience, conscious or unconscious, and that without a specification of the inner, even the outer becomes merely an empty shell. If it is easier to get at the outer than at the inner experience, this does not make the latter less important (Fine, 1983).

Essentially, the behaviorist approach stresses method, arguing that it alone has the right approach to science, an approach derived from that used in the physical sciences. In principle this claim is mistaken, because method does not make science. Rather, the reverse is true; the scientific attitude creates the method most suitable to the data under investigation.

Preoccupation with method and removal from the scientific attitude is most clear in the behaviorist's stance in the treatment situation. What dynamically-oriented therapists have been able to demonstrate over and over again for decades is that a client's experience of the therapist is going to influence enormously how the client responds to interventions. When the notion of transference is overlooked, much of what transpires in treatment cannot be understood. Psychoanalytic therapy has been able to demonstrate that a client's chronic complaints are really unconscious wishes, and if responded to neutrally by the therapist, they will become recapitulated in the transference. Consequently, a man who says over and over again that his wife is cold and frigid unconsciously wants such a wife. If the therapist does not reward or punish the client for his views, but instead listens empathically to his story in breadth and depth, the client will experience the practitioner the same way he experiences his wife. Slowly the client begins to see how he writes his own marital script (Strean, 1985). This more comprehensive and more scientific approach surpasses, in my opinion, any form of therapy that the behaviorist offers. It embraces crucial intervening variables such as transference, resistance, psychosexual development, and the unconscious, all variables neglected by the behaviorist.

The behaviorist's approach to research tends to mirror its superficiality in diagnosis and treatment. For example, if one human being asks another a question, the answer will be a variable one, depending on the question, the relationship between question and subject, and many other factors. What a subject tells the experimenter (whether in response to written questionnaires or interviews) depends on the transference-countertransference relationship between the two. Unless the motivation of the subject is taken into account in research experiments, the observations will be contaminated. The fact that, unlike certain other types of behavior, motives cannot be enumerated does not mean that research should dispense with this important dimension of the human being. Because so many examinations of behavioristic practice, perhaps examinations of most social work practice, have failed to take into account the client's internal evaluation of the social worker and agency and the relationship between the subject and the investigator, the results of the research have to be questioned (Strean, 1978).

From time to time, some of my social work colleagues and I have wondered about some of the values of the behaviorists. According to Skinner (1971), one of the foremost exponents of behaviorism, the human being is not activated by purposes, is "beyond freedom and dignity," and may not have an unconscious mind. One might ask, "If man has no purposes, hopes, dreams, or ideals, how do we account for an institution like the United Nations?" The behaviorist rarely talks about enhancing the client's capacity to love, diminishing his hatred, helping the client have a role in the family and in the social order, values that most social workers endorse and use in their work.

Basically, the scientific statements of Skinner and the behaviorists are simply incorrect. Freedom and dignity do exist; man is activated by purposes, aims, and goals. On the behaviorist's notion that introspection is not a valid scientific method, Bertrand Russell (1948) commented, "his view seems to me to be so absurd that if it were widely held I should ignore it."

REFERENCES

Briar, S., & Miller, H. (1971). *Problems and Issues in Social Casework.* New York: Columbia University Press.

Fine, R. (1983). *The Logic of Psychology.* Washington, D.C.: University Press of America, Inc.

Russell, B. (1948). *Human Knowledge: Its Scope and Limits*. New York: Simon and Schuster.

Skinner, B.F. (1971). *Beyond Freedom and Dignity*. New York: Alfred A. Knopf.

Strean, H. (1985). *Resolving Marital Conflicts*. New York: John Wiley and Sons.

Strean, H. (1978). *Clinical Social Work*. New York: The Free Press.

Rejoinder to Professor Strean   BRUCE A. THYER

In his response, Dr. Strean sets forth a number of remonstrations regarding the general field of behavior analysis, concerns that are commonly found in the social work and psychodynamic literatures. Dr. Strean's objections are based on an inadequate familiarity of the behavioral perspective, as I will attempt to illustrate here.

Most psychodynamically-oriented practitioners seem to be unaware of the substantial literature in the fields of behavior analysis and therapy devoted to so-called personality theory (PT). The text by Lundin (1986) reviews much of this research. Current survey textbooks on PT usually devote a large number of pages to social learning theory approaches to understanding the human personality (e.g., Mischel, 1986), as do texts on human development in general (e.g., Perry & Bussey, 1984). The behavioral approach to studying human personality is in fact a thriving perspective with substantial empirical support.

From the inception of behavior therapy, its practitioners and theorists have devoted considerable attention to relationship variables and how they affect the course of treatment. Controlled studies have found that behavior therapists' use of empathy, warmth, and genuineness in working with clients rivals or exceeds the use of these core conditions by psychodynamically-oriented therapists (e.g., Fischer et al., 1973). What behavior therapists bring to this field is a much more rigorous approach to the measurement and analysis of relationship variables in treatment (e.g., Milne, 1989) than earlier, less sophisticated, theoretical orientations.

Far from ignoring the client's internal environment, behaviorists have pioneered in the scientific investigation of private events and their relationships to overt behavior (e.g., Hefferline & Bruno, 1971). Among Skinner's early (1953) writings may be found theoretical extrapolations of behavioral positions on the inner life of human beings. The radical behaviorist is highly concerned with developing a natural science of all human phenomena, including verbal behavior, thinking, creativity, delusional and hallucinogenic states, and other private events (e.g., Layng & Andronis, 1984). The original position of John Watson, the founder of an early form of behaviorism, was that the subject matter of psychology was limited to observable behavior. However, a cursory reading of Skinner and other contemporary behaviorists will reveal that this view has not correctly characterized a behavioral perspective for over 50 years. Surely five decades is enough time to lay this particular canard to rest!

Concerning the value base of the behaviorist position, it is worth noting that in 1972 the American Humanist Association presented its Humanist of the Year award to B.F. Skinner. The earnest efforts of behavior therapists have done much to promote greater degrees of freedom and dignity among developmentally disabled, psychotic, severely depressed, and chronically anxious individuals. It is difficult to recouncil Dr. Strean's criticism of behaviorists, who have done so much to improve the human condition, with the psychoanalytic perspective that he advocates. It has been the seminal work of Freud and his followers who gave us the degrading concepts of "penis envy," "oedipal desires," homosexuality as a psychopathological state, and a pejorative view of women. Where lies "freedom and dignity" in these ideas?

Contrary to the assertion of Dr. Strean, behaviorists have a keen interest in understanding the etiology of psychosocial problems and incorporating this understanding into the development of interventive plans (e.g., Bailey & Pyles, 1989). We seek to understand current behavior in terms of a person's history of environmental transactions; however, not in terms of hypothetical mental mechanisms that lack an adequate empirical base. The reader may decide which approach is most congruent with social work's person-in-environment perspective.

Behaviorists do not assert that they have the only valid approach to the study of the human condition. We do state with confidence that we have a very useful approach that has proved its worth in developing a wide variety of effective psychosocial treatments. We do ask that the advocates of alternative theories and research methods provide convincing evidence of the usefulness of their approaches. The dignity and worth of our clients and the importance of their problems demands no less than an empirical approach to practice.

REFERENCES

Bailey, J.S., & Pyles, D. (1989). Behavioral diagnostics. In E. Cipani (Ed.), *The treatment of severe behavior disorders: Behavior analysis approaches.* Washington, DC: American Association on Mental Retardation, pp. 85–107.

Fischer, J., Paveza, G., Kickertz, N., et al. (1975). The relationship between theoretical orientation and therapists' warmth, empathy and genuineness. *Journal of Counseling Psychology*, 22, 399–403.

Hefferline, R.F., & Bruno, L.J. (1971). The psychophysiology of private events. In A. Jacobs & L.B. Sachs (Eds.). *The psychology of private events*. New York: Academic Press.

Layng, T.V., & Andronis, P.T. (1984). Toward a functional analysis of delusional speech and hallucinatory behavior. *The Behavior Analyst*, 7, 139–156.

Lundin, R.W. (1986). *Personality: A behavioral analysis,* ed 2. Malabar, FL: Kreiger.

Milne, D. (1989). A multidimensional evaluation of therapist behavior. *Behavioral Psychotherapy*, 17, 253–266.

Mishel, W. (1986). *Introduction to personality, ed 4*. New York: Holt, Rinehart and Winston.

Perry, D.G., & Bussey, K. (1984). *Social development*. Englewood Cliffs, NJ: Prentice Hall.

Skinner, B.F. (1953). *Science and human behavior*. New York: Macmillan.

Is International Social Work a One-Way Transfer of Ideas and Practice Methods from the United States to Other Countries?

EDITOR'S NOTE: The French philosopher Montesquieu once said, "I don't know why that man dislikes me so. I've never done anything for him!" Most people have experienced the alienation that often arises from exchanges between friendly parties. Most grievous is a relationship characterized by a one-way flow of benefits. The problem of "overwhelming benefactions" exemplifies the point. It refers to the circumstance where 1) donors offer something recipients want and so accept, but 2) the recipients then find that donors refuse a benefit offered in return. The consequence for the recipient is a diminished status and, ultimately, the distress that comes with frustrated repayment obligations. Public welfare has been characterized this way. In the international realm this is also frequently said to be the case between the world's powerful nations (i.e., more capable of large scale giving) and the poorer or less developed ones (i.e., dependent on gifts). The question here is, "is this also true regarding the relationship of social work in the United States to the comparable enterprises in the rest of the world?"

James Midgley, Professor of Social Work and Dean of the School of Social Work at Louisiana State University, says YES. His major books include *Professional Imperialism: Social Work in the Third World* (Heinemann, 1981); *The Social Dimensions of Development* (with Margaret Hardiman) (Wiley, 1982); *Social Security, Inequality and the Third World* (Wiley, 1984); *Community Participation, Social Development and the State* (Methuen, 1986); and *Comparative Social Policy and the Third World* (with Stewart MacPherson) (St. Martins, 1987).

The NO case is made by Manny Toors, which is a pseudonym for a social worker who has extensive knowledge and experience of international affairs. He has traveled and published widely on issues of international social work and social welfare. (The explanation for masking the author's identity is found in the introduction to the volume.)

YES

JAMES MIDGLEY

The term "international social work" is widely used in social work circles today to refer to the exchanges that take place between social workers from different countries (Mohan, 1987). As international travel and communications have become easier, exciting opportunities to enhance intercountry collaboration have been created.

Despite these opportunities, international social work has been characterized by the one-way transfer of ideas and practice methods from the United States to other nations. As the United States has become a world superpower, so American social work approaches have been widely exported. Although the diffusion of American social work has not been a conscious or deliberate attempt to compel social workers in other societies to adopt American approaches, it has involved the subtle, gradual spread of ideas and practice methods that has been facilitated by American influence, the availability of funds for American social workers to travel internationally, the provision of scholarships to students from abroad, and the export of American textbooks and other publications.

The Diffusion of Social Work

Although the word "imperialism" refers to a situation in which one country controls events in other countries, it does not accurately describe global realities today. Whereas many nations were previously ruled by foreign powers, most people today live in sovereign nation states. Nevertheless, the term "imperialism" is still widely used, especially with reference to the military, diplomatic, economic, and social influences exerted by the world's superpowers. Through these "imperialistic" tendencies, institutions emanating from the superpowers have been widely diffused. And, in the climate of opinion created by superpower influence, confidence in local institutions has waned. Consequently, there has been an increased willingness to adopt practices from abroad because they are perceived to be superior or "advanced." It was precisely this attitude that facilitated the export of American social work to other nations.

Modern professional social work is a Western institution that emerged in Europe and North America toward the end of the nineteenth century. The idea that professionally trained personnel should deal directly with individuals, groups, and communities to combat social problems was promoted by the charities and settlement houses that were trying to respond to the high incidence of poverty and deprivation accompanying rapid industrialization and urbanization. Through their efforts, social work gradually became established, and by the 1920s it had diversified into various fields of practice. By this time, professional training schools had also been created, and numerous books and journals that gave the subject a theoretical base had been published. Within a relatively short period of time, social work emerged as a new profession responsible for meeting human needs (Lubove, 1969).

Although the settlements and the Charity Organization Society were British inventions, the emergence of social work as a profession was promoted most effectively in America. Britain was a major world power at the time, and it is not surprising that these institutions were exported to the United States and other countries. But American social workers were more successful than social workers in England in obtaining public recognition, establishing links with the older professions (such as medicine, law, and psychiatry), and in getting social work education established within their country's universities. By the 1950s, as the United States became a world superpower, American approaches to social work attracted international attention and were widely emulated in many parts of the world.

Many examples of the diffusion of American social work to other countries can be given. Approaches to social work education that evolved in the United States have been widely copied in other countries. In Britain, where social work training programs emerged independently of external influences, American curricular approaches were gradually adopted. One of the earliest examples of the replication of American educational ideas occurred in 1929 when the University of London established a program in psychiatric social work that relied extensively on American clinical theories and methods. As Irvine (1978, p. 176) pointed out, American psychoanalytic theory occupied an important place in the program, "and the dominant diagnostic (or mainline Freudian) school of social work in the USA had great influence." In India, American experts played a major role in establishing the country's schools of social work, and they significantly influenced the character of social work education. As one Indian writer noted, "The main currents of inspiration for social work training in India have come from and continues to come from America" (Thomas, 1963, p. 67).

Social work education in many other developing countries has also been modeled extensively on American approaches (Midgley, 1981). A study of schools of social work in twenty-two Third World countries undertaken by Adler and Midgley (1978) found that American textbooks and journals were widely used, that curricula generally gave emphasis to clinical training, and that many faculty had been educated in the West. Local textbooks and other educational materials were underdeveloped and where such resources existed, they were often neglected. In Africa, a text-book by Clifford (1966) that was designed specifically for African students was prescribed only at one of the African schools included in the study.

Practice methods developed in the United States have also been repli-cated in different parts of the world. Social work practice in Britain was for many years highly specialized, but the "generic" approach that emerged in the United States was eventually adopted. As Vickery (1977) pointed out, increasing exchanges between British and American social workers in the 1950s resulted in a preference among British social workers for the way Americans integrated different practice methods. This eventually resulted in a major overhaul of the country's public social work services and in the adoption of the so-called "generic" approach in British social work (Young-husband, 1978). American approaches to community organization have also been exported to many countries. With financial aid from the United States Federal government, many developing countries have adopted com-munity development programs that rely extensively on American theories. In Britain, where community organization was not a well-developed method of social work practice, the American War on Poverty program of the 1960s had a significant effect on British social workers who began to copy the poverty program's community-based practice approaches and apply these ideas in dealing with inner city problems (Higgins, 1978).

Another example of the diffusion of social work ideas is the provision of financial aid to students from other countries. American schools of social work have long enrolled international students on their professional programs although these programs are not designed to educate them for practice in their own countries. When these students return home they often unwittingly facilitate the transfer of American ideas. This process is being exacerbated as more American colleges are establishing satellite programs in other countries (DeLoughry, 1989).

Problems of the One-Way Transfer of Social Work

Although the international diffusion of knowledge can facilitate learning and understanding, the one-way transfer of ideas and practice methods from the United States to other countries has created numerous problems.

One problem is the inappropriateness of American approaches to these societies. Social workers from various nations have pointed out that the unique economic, social, and cultural circumstances of their countries require concepts and methods that are uniquely relevant to local conditions. Writing about social work practice in the Philippines, Almanzor (1967) pointed out that many American social work ideas do not fit the country's cultural realities and cannot be effectively implemented. Khinduka (1971) questioned the usefulness of American approaches in developing countries where, he argued, the problems of economic underdevelopment, mass poverty, and deprivation require techniques that differ significantly from those in use in the industrial nations. In England, the emphasis that is given to clinical skills in the curriculum as a result of the diffusion of American ideas has been questioned because most social workers practice in statutory agencies and not in clinical settings (Brewer and Lait, 1980). Enrolling international students on MSW programs designed for American students has also created problems. Huang (1978), a Chinese social work educator who studied in the United States, described how he and other foreign students often experienced difficulties trying to absorb the cultural ideas that were being communicated through their courses; describing his educational experience as "cultural footbinding," he criticized the practice of enrolling international students on programs designed to train American social workers.

Another problem is that a dependency on foreign ideas and practices stifles local initiative, and the development of new knowledge. If social workers in different countries rely on one country for their concepts and methods, they are unlikely to formulate new approaches that help the subject to evolve in new directions. This has negative implications for social work, which, like other professions based on scientific knowledge, must constantly seek to renew itself and its accepted wisdom.

A related problem is that the dominance of one country's approaches in the international arena inhibits the sharing of knowledge and experiences. Although social workers from many different countries now attend international conferences, American ideas exert considerable influence over the way social workers from different countries approach the subject. Like other professions, social work can benefit by sharing ideas but this is only meaningful if international exchanges are reciprocal and equal.

Finally, the absence of intercountry collaboration has been detrimental to social workers in the United States. Confident of their own theories and practice approaches, American social workers have not sought to learn from their colleagues in other countries. By studying and, where appropriate, adapting ideas from abroad, however, they could enrich American social work. For example, the experiences of Asian and African social workers who work in situations of great cultural diversity can be of value to American social workers. Having recognized the increasingly multicultural character of their society, American social workers are seeking to enhance the profession's sensitivity to cross-cultural realities. Similarly, occupational social work that has emerged as a new field of practice in the United

States has much to learn from India, where this field of practice has been well established since the late 1940s. The rising incidence of poverty in the United States requires a new commitment from social work that can be usefully informed by sharing experiences with Third World social workers who have long been engaged in the delivery of services to the poor.

As suggested earlier, the one-way transfer of American ideas is not a deliberate attempt to impose ideas on other nations but rather the result of a tendency to accept the superiority of institutions that are associated with superpower status. Social workers need to be aware of these subtle "imperialistic" influences and make a conscious attempt to resist them. By challenging the one-way transfer of social work concepts and methods, international social work can foster truly reciprocal exchanges and enrich the profession throughout the world.

REFERENCES

Adler, S., and Midgley, J. (1978). Social work education in developing countries. *Social Work Today,* 9, 15–17.

Almanzor, A. (1967). The profession of social work in the Philippines. In *Council on Social Work Education, An intercultural exploration: Universals and differentials in social work values, functions and practice.* New York: Council on Social Work Education.

Brewer, C., and Lait, J. (1980). *Can social work survive?* London: Temple Smith.

Clifford, W. (1966). *A primer of social casework in Africa.* Nairobi: Oxford University Press.

DeLoughry, T.J. (1989). As the race to internationalize U.S. Colleges heats up, concern rises over programs' quality and standards. *Chronicle of Higher Education,* June 21, A21.

Higgins, J. (1978). *The poverty business: Britain and America.* Oxford: Basil Blackwell.

Huang, K. (1978). Matching needs with services: Shoes for Chinese feet. *International Social Work,* 21, 44–54.

Irvine, E. (1978). Psychiatric social work: Training for psychiatric social work. In E. Younghusband (Ed.), *Social work in Britain: 1950–1975.* London: Allen and Unwin, pp. 176–203.

Khinduka, S. (1971). Social work in the Third World. *Social Service Review,* 45, 62–73.

Lubove, R. (1969). *The professional altruist.* New York: Atheneum.

Midgley, J. (1981). *Professional imperialism: Social work in the Third World.* London: Heinemann Educational Books.

Mohan, B. (1987). International social welfare: Comparative systems. In A. Minnahan, et al. (Eds.), *Encyclopedia of social work.* Silver Springs, MD: National Association of Social Workers, pp. 957–969

Thomas, P.T. (1963). Social work education and training in India. In *India, Planning Commission, Social welfare in a developing economy*. Faridabad: Government of India, pp. 62–75.

Vickery, A. (1977). Social work practice: Divisions and unifications. In Specht, H., & Vickery, A. (Eds.), *Integrating social work methods*. London: Allen and Unwin.

Younghusband, E. (1978). *Social work in Britain: 1950–1975*. London: Allen and Unwin.

ANNOTATED BIBLIOGRAPHY

Midgley, J. (1981). *Professional imperialism: Social work in the Third World*. London: Heinemann Educational Books

This book examines the influence of Western social work ideas on the social work profession in the developing countries. It offers a controversial critique of the replication of Western approaches in these countries and describes some of the consequences of "professional imperialism."

Mohan, B. (1987). International social welfare: Comparative systems. In A. Minnahan, et al. (Eds.), *Encyclopedia of social work*. Silver Springs, MD: National Association of Social Workers, pp. 957–969.

This entry in the *Encyclopedia of Social Work* provides a comprehensive survey of the field of international social welfare and social work.

Munday, B. (Ed.). (1989). *The crisis in welfare: An international perspective on social services and social work*. New York: St. Martin's Press.

This recently published edited collection contains chapters about the problems facing social work and social welfare programs in seven different countries. Although it does not deal specifically with the diffusion of social work, it provides useful information about how the social work services are organized in different societies.

Rejoinder to Professor Midgley   MANNY TOORS

James Midgley believes that international social work is dominated by American ideas and practice approaches. He has produced some empirical evidence in support of his claim, but his argument is really inspired by his overriding concern with "imperialistic influences." The idea of imperialism has been the prevailing theme in his previous writings on international social work, and indeed one of his books on the subject included the word "imperialism" in its title (see Midgley's references: Midgley, 1981).

Midgley's obsession with imperialism is difficult to understand because there is little evidence to show that any one country dominates the globe. The idea that the United States and the Soviet Union control the destiny of humanity is old fashioned and does not fit reality. The economic power of Japan, the assertion of freedom in Eastern Europe, the growth of the newly industrializing economies of East Asia, and the existence of nonaligned powerblocks such as the Organization of Petroleum Exporting Countries (OPEC), demonstrate the obsolescence of this idea.

Another problem is Midgley's incorrect use of the concept of "imperialism." If peasants in Indonesia enjoy American movies, if Bulgarians develop a taste for cola, or if Australians wish to adopt American medical technologies to improve the quality of their health care, can this be described as imperialism? When Americans purchase French cosmetics, go to see Russian ballet, or watch British documentaries on public television, does anybody criticize this as "imperialistic?" Surely the notion of imperialism involves coercion. While it is imperialistic to *force* people in other countries to adopt American (or Soviet or European) culture, Midgley's account of social work "imperialism" provides no evidence of anybody being forced to accept anything. If other societies choose to adopt American social work theories or practice ideas, it can hardly be described as imperialistic. Midgley's definition of imperialism is not only unsatisfactory, but undermines the basis of his argument.

Midgley claims that social work in different parts of the world faces serious problems that he attributes to the dominance of American ideas and practice approaches. This is difficult to accept. Most of the problems facing social work as a profession are indigenous in origin and need to be dealt with by social workers in their own countries. To imply, as Midgley does, that these problems will magically disappear once Americans stop exporting their ideas abroad is naive.

The view that social work in the United States can learn from other countries is commendable. But while much more needs to be done to enhance international exchanges of this kind, it is not true that American social workers have failed to learn from other countries. American social workers travel abroad and have extensive international contacts with social workers in other countries and they obviously learn a great deal from their experiences. The question is how innovations in other countries can be transferred to the United States. Instead of spending his time attacking American social workers for being "imperialistic," Midgley could make a more positive contribution by helping to identify ways of adapting lessons from other countries to solve America's own pressing domestic social problems.

NO

MANNY TOORS

Although the term "international social work" is sometimes used to describe a field of practice in which social workers are employed by international agencies such as the Red Cross or the United Nations (Healy, 1987), most experts use it to refer to the exchanges that take place between social workers in different parts of the world. As this definition suggests, international social work is fundamentally reciprocal: social workers who have international links learn from each other and treat each other as equals.

Historical and factual evidence will be provided to refute the argument that international social work is the one-way transfer of ideas and practice methods from the United States to other countries. It will also be argued that the values that characterize professional exchanges between social workers from different nations are inimical to the imposition of American (or indeed any other nation's) ideas and practice approaches on social workers in other countries. International relationships in social work are based on a foundation of mutual respect, understanding, and cooperation, and not on the premise that one country's theories and practice methods are superior to those of others.

The Reciprocal Nature of International Social Work

International social work is as old as the profession itself. In the latter half of the nineteenth century, when social work first emerged to help needy people in the rapidly growing cities of Europe and North America, social workers in different countries developed links with each other. For example, there were close contacts between the founders of the Charity Organization Society (which played a major role in establishing social work as a profession) in Britain and the United States. The first Charity Organization Society in the United States was founded in Buffalo, New York, in the early 1870s by Rev. Steven Gurteen, who had worked with the Society in London (Leiby, 1978). Jane Addams, the famous founder of Hull House, visited Europe and spent some time at Toynbee Hall in London, which was the first settlement house in the world. In turn, many European social workers visited the United States to learn from their American colleagues. Sidney and Beatrice Webb, who were among the most influential leaders of the profession in England, visited Hull House and were enthusiastic about its activities (Addams, 1910).

As these historical events suggest, social workers in Europe and North America regarded each other as colleagues. British social workers did not believe that their ideas and practice methods were superior to those of their American counterparts. Nor did American social workers see themselves as ignorant inferiors who lacked ideas of their own. Social workers in both countries were capable of developing their own social work theories and practice methods, although they readily exchanged information in an attempt to learn from each other.

Subsequent developments in the field of international social work have reinforced the reciprocal nature of professional exchanges between social workers from different countries. One important factor in promoting these exchanges has been the creation of international professional associations such as the International Council on Social Welfare, the International Federation of Social Workers, and the International Association of Schools of Social Work. Since their inception these organizations have advocated professional contacts based on mutual respect, understanding, and cooperation. Indeed, they were founded primarily to facilitate contacts of this kind, and for this reason, have sponsored international conferences and workshops and published books, reports, and journals that seek to enhance understanding of social work in different countries. In promoting exchanges between social workers around the world, they have certainly not advocated the adoption of American approaches. A cursory glance at any issue of the journal *International Social Work* (which is published by these organizations) will show that its articles deal with social work in many different countries and regions of the world. This includes the United States, which, from the point of view of professional social work, is just one among many partners in the enterprise of international social work. The journal is certainly not dominated by articles from the United States, nor does it advocate the adoption of American ideas in other societies.

This is also true of conferences and workshops arranged by the international organizations. Participants come from all over the world, and the topics presented deal with practice issues and problems in many different nations. The claim that these international forums provide an opportunity for American social workers to impose their ideas on unwilling participants from other countries is absurd. Social workers do not attend international meetings to hear about social work in the United States: they come to obtain information about the professional developments in many different parts of the world, and they would soon be bored (and annoyed) if these meetings were exclusively concerned with American social work.

The evidence shows that international exchanges in social work are reciprocal and supported by values and beliefs that reinforce mutually valued relationships. Social workers from other countries who exchange ideas with their American colleagues expect to be treated as equals. The idea that international social work is the one-way transfer of American ideas and practice methods is insulting to social workers from these countries because it suggests that they are passive and too feeble to resist the imposition of foreign approaches.

The Diversity of Social Work Education and Practice

A review of the historical development and contemporary characteristics of social work in different nations also negates the argument that international social work is the one-way transfer of American ideas and practice methods to other countries. If the argument were true, then social work throughout the world would be using the same theories and practice approaches that have been adopted in the United States. This is not the case.

Social work emerged in different countries under different conditions as a result of very different influences. In Europe, American ideas played a small part in the historical growth of social work. Although there were instances when Europeans copied development in the United States, they were far more influenced by indigenous developments. The argument that American social workers are primarily responsible for shaping social work in the developing countries of the Third World has been popular. Midgley (1981) is one of the leading proponents of the view but, as he himself admits, the evolution of social work in the developing countries was influenced by different factors. In the former British colonial territories, for example, social work depended more on ideas emanating from England than the United States. In these countries also, indigenous ideas have played a significant role in the development of social work.

Many different approaches to social work practice have emerged in different parts of the world, and these contrast sharply with the patterns of professional practice that prevail in the United States. For example, while American social workers are extensively engaged in private practice, this is not the case in other countries. The growth of clinical social work, the emergence of licensing and third party reimbursement, and the popularity of psychotherapy as a practice modality is unparalleled. Indeed, the term *clinical social work* is not widely used in other parts of the world. In most countries, social workers are primarily engaged in public service. In Latin American countries, for example, social workers are frequently employed in national social security organizations, and in Britain and other European nations, they work primarily for local government authorities. In many African and Asian developing countries, they are extensively involved in government sponsored adult education, agriculture, nutrition, and community development programs (Midgley, 1984). These activities bear little resemblance to the professional roles of social workers in the United States.

The diversity of professional social work roles in different parts of the world is accompanied by different approaches to social work education. In the United States, social work education is now highly standardized and is offered either through a 4-year Bachelor's degree or a 2-year Master's degree. This model is not emulated in other countries; indeed, the international surveys of world social work education undertaken by the International Association of Schools of Social Work (Rao and Kendall, 1984) reveal that professional education in other countries has taken many diverse forms. In some countries, such as Britain, there are even significant differences between the social work programs offered at different educational institutions. In others, where a greater measure of standardization has been achieved, professional education bears little resemblance to the American model. Even within Europe, as a recent study demonstrated (Brauns and Kramer, 1986), social work education has adopted various forms. These diverse patterns show that there is no universal model of professional education in social work based on approaches emanating from the United States.

As international communications and exchanges have expanded, it has become possible to know about developments in other countries within a very short period of time. This does not mean, however, that events, fashions, and trends in other countries are eagerly imitated. Today, the world of social work is too diverse to adopt (or wish to adopt) one theoretical orientation or one approach to professional practice. Indeed, with the growth of nationalism as a major ideologic force and the weakening of the United States as a world power, the view that international social work involves the one-way transfer of American ideas is both implausible and erroneous.

REFERENCES

Addams, J. (1910). *Twenty years at Hull House.* New York: Macmillan.
Brauns, H., and Kramer. D. (1986). *Social work education in Europe.* Frankfurt: Eigenverlag des Deutches Vereins für offentliche und private Fursorge.
Healy, L. (1987). International agencies as social work settings: Opportunity, capability and commitment. *Social Work, 32,* 405–409.
Leiby, J. (1978). *A history of social welfare and social work in the United States.* New York: Columbia University Press.
Midgley, J. (1981). *Professional imperialism: Social work in the Third World.* London: Heinemann Educational Books.

Midgley, J. (1984). Social work services in the Third World: The integration of remedial and developmental orientations. *Social Development Issues,* 8, 89–104.

Rao, V., and Kendall, K. (1984). *World guide to social work education.* Vienna: International Association of Schools of Social Work.

ANNOTATED BIBLIOGRAPHY

Thruz, D., and Vigilante, J.L. (1975). *Meeting human needs: An overview of nine countries.* Beverly Hills, CA: Sage; and Kahn, A.J., and Kamerman, S.B. (1980). *Social services in international perspective: The emergence of the sixth system.* New Brunswick, NJ: Transaction.

Both these books present an overview of social work and human services in different countries and demonstrate that patterns of professional practice and service delivery in the human service vary significantly between different countries.

Mohan, B. (1987). International social welfare: Comparative systems. In A. Minnahan, et al. (Eds.), *Encyclopedia of social work.* Silver Springs, MD: National Association of Social Workers, pp. 957–969.

This contribution to the *Encyclopedia of Social Work* discusses different aspects of international social welfare and social work and is a useful introduction to the field.

International Social Work.

This journal which is published by Sage for the major international social welfare organizations contains many articles on the subject. It is published quarterly.

Rejoinder to Mr. Toors JAMES MIDGLEY

Toors has argued emphatically that American ideas and practice approaches do not dominate international social work. He has claimed primarily that international exchanges are essentially reciprocal, and that there is, therefore, no one-way transfer of American ideas and practice approaches to other countries. He has also argued that social work has taken many diverse forms in different countries, and that because of this diversity, no common dependence on American ideas can be found. Although these assertions may appear to be convincing, they need to be examined more closely.

Toors confuses the idea that international exchanges in social work are reciprocal with the idea that they should be reciprocal. Few would disagree with the view that reciprocity in international relations is desirable. In the hard world of international politics, however, some countries are more powerful than others, and they have been able to exert influence over others. Social work has been inadvertently caught up in this situation. Although social workers undoubtedly desire genuine reciprocity in international relationships, the global power game impedes the realization of this ideal. Instead of naïvely believing that power differentials do not exist, social workers need to acknowledge these realities and strive consciously to combat them. Mutuality in international relationships does not come automatically, but needs to be accomplished through purposeful action.

Toors ignores the empirical and historical evidence that shows that American social work has excessively influenced social work in other countries. If the argument concerning the one-way transfer of American ideas is to be refuted, this evidence must be discredited. Toors has conspicuously failed to deal with this evidence or to rebut its incontrovertible conclusions.

Toors does make an important observation at the end of his statement, however: he notes that the growth of nationalism and the weakening of American (and Soviet) hegemony has affected contemporary global realities. There is indeed evidence to show that people around the world are resisting imperialistic forces and asserting their freedom. This has happened in both the Western and Soviet spheres of influence. Social workers in many countries have also sought to assert their independence from external influences, and they have made considerable gains. The fact that international conferences are not dominated by American theories and practice approaches, and that the content of international journals is now more encompassing, is because of the efforts of social workers such as Hans Nagpaul (1972) in India and Angelina Almanzor in the Philippines (1967), who campaigned for a more broadly based approach. Today, social workers from other countries do not eagerly emulate American developments and they can, with justification, demand to be treated as equals

The diversity of social work in different parts of the world is also a consequence of the efforts of these and other social workers. But this was not always the case. In the 1970s, American social work textbooks were being prescribed in countries of very different social, cultural, and economic circumstances. Even indigenous literature reflected American influences: in countries as diverse as the Philippines and Kenya, where textbooks had been written to cater to the needs of local social work students, their dependence on American ideas and practice approaches was unmistakable

(Clifford, 1966; Hebbert, et al., 1972). As more social workers in these and other countries assert their autonomy and experiment with indigenous approaches (Walton and Abe el Nasr, 1988) the diversity, reciprocity, and multicultural character of international social work will be further enhanced to the benefit of the profession as a whole.

REFERENCES

Almanzor, A. (1967). The profession of social work in the Philippines. In Council on Social Work Education: *An intercultural exploration: Universals and differentials in social work values, functions and practice.* New York: Council on Social Work Education.

Clifford, W. (1966). *A primer of social casework in Africa.* Nairobi: Oxford University Press.

Hebbert, V., et al. (1972). *Social work practice: A Philippine casebook.* Quezon City: New Day Publishers.

Walton, R., & Abo el Nasr, M. (1988). Indigenization and authentization of social work in Egypt. *International Social Work,* 31, 135–144.

Should Social Workers Base Practice Decisions on Empirical Research?

EDITOR'S NOTE: This question addresses the key issue in debates about criteria for selecting knowledge in social work. There is little agreement among social workers about whether selection of assessment, intervention, and evaluation methods should be based on available empirical research. Differences of opinion assume increased significance in terms of effects on practice as related data from empirical research accumulates. One reason for this debate is lack of understanding of and agreement about "the scientific method." Misunderstandings are the norm rather than the exception (see Singer, B. and Bernassi, V.A. (1987). Occult beliefs. *American Scientist* 69:49–55.) For example, it is often assumed (incorrectly) that use of the scientific method requires a reliance on linear accounts of behavior. Different views of the utility of empirical research are discussed in the statements that follow.

Edward J. Mullen, DSW, argues YES. He is Professor and Associate Dean at the Columbia University School of Social Work. He has taught in the areas of direct practice and research methods in both the masters and doctoral programs at several universities. His publications include contributions to the empirical foundations of direct practice, methods for using information in practice decision-making, and evaluation research.

Howard Goldstein, DSW, argues NO. He is Professor at the Mandel School of Social Work, Case Western Reserve University, where he teaches direct practice and qualitative research in Masters and Doctoral Programs. He is the author of many articles and three books on social work practice:

Social Work Practice: A Unitary Approach, Social Learning and Change, and *Creative Change.*

YES

EDWARD J. MULLEN

It has generally been thought that social work knowledge should be built from scientific methods of investigation and that intervention skills should be developed through the systematic application of that knowledge. Currently, however, much of social work's practice knowledge has not been developed in this way. Instead, social workers frequently rely on knowledge that has been formed from impressions gained in practice experience sifted through what might be called *common sense*. Whereas such a common sense method is of obvious value in everyday life, an approach to knowledge that enhances the strengths of common sense while minimizing the weakness is desirable. The scientific approach has been developed for these purposes. This chapter proposes that social work practice knowledge should be developed through the application of scientific methods whenever possible. Central to this position is the idea that scientific work is essentially a disciplined spirit of inquiry involving the use of a wide range of procedures, and that the primary goal is to develop knowledge of the empirical world. Scientific work cannot be equated with particular procedures because scientists are continually improving their procedures as the technology of investigation matures. Therefore, this chapter does not discuss particular procedures of scientific inquiry, but rather focuses on the characteristics of the scientific spirit that distinguish scientific work from other forms of investigation.

There is little disagreement with the idea that social work knowledge should be based on an understanding of people and their institutions. The issues have more to do with how that understanding is reached. At a general level it is not difficult to observe how people most frequently develop an understanding of the world. Events are experienced, thought over, compared with prior beliefs, and conclusions are reached. The problem with this rather common method is that it depends greatly on each person's rather haphazard experiences, the peculiarities of an individual's thought processes, and the nature of the individual's prior beliefs. Although this approach can provide a kind of personal understanding, it does not provide professional knowledge, that is, an understanding shared by the professional community, because each individual will be prone to arrive at quite different conclusions. What makes sense to one person often does not make much sense to another person. It is abundantly clear that honest, well-intentioned, reasonable people frequently disagree. Even when a particular group of people come to agree in this way, thereby establishing a belief system, theory, or tradition, the resulting shared understanding rests on a problematic foundation, difficult to modify and correct because it typically becomes so firmly held. These beliefs tend to be elevated to the level of knowledge and disseminated by people who are considered by their belief communities to be authorities. Generally, people outside this belief community do not consider these beliefs to be valid nor the authorities legitimate.

Professional knowledge must have some of the characteristics previously described. That is, it must be shared by the professional community and it must be promulgated by professional authorities such as teachers. Those people outside the profession must also consider professional knowledge to be valid, however, and authorities who promulgate that knowledge to be legitimate. Professional knowledge, therefore, must find its validity outside the community of believers. Criteria that are respected by both the professional community and the larger community are necessary. Because in a diverse society there will always be diverse beliefs about the nature of people and their institutions, knowledge should be developed by means of an approach that is capable of testing one belief against another so as to build more confidence in one position and less confidence in another position. Also, because in a diversified community individual experiences will be highly varied and sifted through a great range of individual perspectives, the approach should be capable of finding a way through these differences. Furthermore, because people and their institutions change and because erroneous conclusions are always possible, the approach should be both capable of adapting to these changes and capable of correcting errors. These are the requirements that the scientific method addresses that make it a suitable source for social work practice knowledge.

The scientific approach is fundamentally a set of values that is shared by a group of people called scientists. This set of values motivates social scientists to pursue an understanding of people and their institutions. This understanding is sought through the systematic testing of alternative beliefs, using methods that attempt to reduce various sources of bias. Also, all conclusions are held suspect until empirical verification has been demonstrated to the community.

Because social workers are practical professionals whose interventions are intended to affect people and their institutions, practice knowledge should not only provide understanding, but it should provide support for interventions in specific situations. This applied knowledge should be sufficiently precise so as to provide guidance in specific practice situations. Although broad generalizations can be useful to social workers, practice knowledge must incorporate an understanding of specific types of situations. This is an unusual challenge because it is difficult to develop knowledge that applies to broad categories of events and also is sufficiently precise so as to take into account the specifics of individual practice situations. Yet, applied scientists share this value, and their work is characterized by attempts to develop increasingly better procedures that can provide knowledge for use in specific situations.

Whereas most would agree that professionals should use knowledge developed through scientific methods, there is disagreement about which procedures are most relevant for the study of social work concerns. Currently, some social workers favor objective methods, whereas others favor subjective, qualitative procedures. Some social workers prefer to emphasize the development of rather general explanations about broad categories of events, whereas others seek fairly specific contextual explanations. Perhaps reflecting the vigor of contemporary scientific work, there is a burgeoning of interesting procedures available to social workers. This richness makes the use of scientific methods especially compelling. Whereas methodologists may debate the usefulness and relevance of these various procedures, for the professional social worker the question addressed in this chapter is more fundamental. The question is, should social work professionals base their interventions on knowledge developed through work inspired by scientific principles? That is, should social workers critically examine their practice knowledge to determine the extent to which it has been developed and verified through methods that 1) reduce the possibility of bias; 2) involve the careful examination of alternative explanations; and 3) have systematically referenced empirical observation so as to provide a general level of understanding about some aspect of a social work concern. This chapter has argued that there can be only one reasonable response for an effective and accountable professional social worker.

The use of scientific criteria in social work practice could be illustrated by reference to several examples. Consider several of the more significant social problems of the day, such as AIDS, homelessness, substance abuse, domestic violence and neglect, and mental anguish. What would social work practice knowledge be in each of these areas if scientific criteria were to be rejected. When AIDS was first discovered in the United States, it was unusually prevalent among gay men. Some people thought that there was something about being gay that caused AIDS, and others were not in danger of becoming infected. Whereas some believed that biological factors unique to gay men were causative, others believed that moral factors were causative, explaining AIDS by invoking moral judgment. Some believed, for example, and still believe, that AIDS is caused by immoral behavior, resting their belief on authoritative opinion of some religious groups. This example illustrates an historical trend, that is, the use of moral norms to fix beliefs about social problems. This use of moral norms frequently results in a pattern of blaming the victim by characterizing people who have problems as undeserving, because the morality of their behavior is presumed to be the cause of their problems. What is the source of this type of knowledge? Usually the source is intuition, authority, or tradition. Fortunately, scientific method can examine social problems such as AIDS without invoking moral judgment. As an example, scientific method has found that AIDS is caused by a virus transmitted through certain types of human contact, not requiring a judgment regarding the morality of that behavior to explain the illness. Aside from the moral explanation, scientific method has been able to address the empirical question regarding the biologic factors, demonstrating that people other than those who are gay can just as easily become infected. This understanding has been established through the use of systematic, controlled, empirical study, that is, through the use of scientific methods. The importance of these findings is obvious.

Going beyond cause to intervention, the world looks to scientific research to develop effective interventions that will prevent and cure AIDS. What would we think of a professional who would argue against the use of scientific methods for the development and evaluation of cures for AIDS? Also, from the perspective of the social work planner and policy analyst, who would argue against the use of scientific methods to determine the demography of AIDS and trends in the development of the illness? Or who would not support the scientific study of the service systems required to provide care and treatment for people with AIDS? Perhaps critics of scientific method would focus on clinical practice and the counseling relationship. What is different at the clinical level? It is at the clinical level that the issues are most sensitive. For example, in clinical work the social worker may be called upon to help a person with AIDS live with impending depression. Does scientific method have a place here? Scientific method would require that the practitioner determine what has already been found out through prior study to be effective ways for helping people deal with impending depression and what is known about the use of these methods with people having AIDS. Scientific criteria also would require that social workers systematically evaluate their own attempts to help people with AIDS cope with impending depression. Scientific criteria would also require that the social worker's interventions be modified based on the results of the evaluation. Critics of scientific method would say that reliance on such scientific criteria would impersonalize the clinical relationship and that it would be better to interact in a less constrained manner. This argument can be misleading. A developed professional is one who has integrated whatever criteria are used into his or her professional repertoire. It does not follow that paying attention to feedback from evaluation of effectiveness would depersonalize the clinical relationship. Rather, it is likely that mature professionals would have integrated an ability to evaluate their own practice so that it would enhance the relationship. Failure to systematically attend to the effectiveness of clinical intervention with people having AIDS would be unethical and unprofessional.

The example with AIDS could easily be extended to the other social problems identified earlier. Homelessness is a problem of growing proportions requiring serious attention from social workers at all levels, from policy formulation to clinical practice. Social work intervention should be built on a clear understanding of the characteristics of homeless people, the services and policies guiding current service systems, and direct interventions with the homeless. Systematic evaluations of interventions with the homeless are required to improve services as well as to fit the requirements of accountable professional practice.

This chapter has presented the position that social work practice knowledge should be constructed through scientific methods and that social workers should select knowledge that can be assessed using scientific criteria. The alternative is to base practice knowledge on methods already demonstrated to be flawed. Scientific methods have contributed immeasurably to the advancement of knowledge in many areas, including social work practice. The profession's credibility and effectiveness will certainly be enhanced by the increased use of scientifically developed knowledge. This knowledge, when combined with professional goals, function, and values will enhance skillful social work intervention.

ANNOTATED BIBLIOGRAPHY

Fiske, Donald W., & Richard A. Shweder (Eds.), *Meta-theory in Social Science*. Chicago, IL: University of Chicago Press, 1986.

This book examines the current state of knowledge in the social sciences and sets forth proposals for acquiring valid and useful social and behavioral knowledge.

Mullen, Edward J. Using Research and Theory in Social Work Practice. In R.M. Grinnell, Jr. (Ed.), *Social Work Research and Evaluation*, ed 3. Itasca, IL: F.E. Peacock Publishers, 1988.

This chapter describes a method social work practitioners can use for selecting information from research and theory for use in practice. The method assumes that each social worker needs to develop his or her own approach to practice, and that to a large extent this requires the critical use of research findings as well as theoretical formulations. This chapter describes a way this can be done.

Mullen, Edward J. Methodological Dilemmas in Social Work Research. *Social Work Research and Abstracts* 21:4 (Winter, 1985): 12–20

This article discusses methodological issues currently debated within the profession. Methodological dilemmas are discussed, including issues associated with objectivity, quantification, scientific explanation, and empiricism. Alternatives are critically evaluated.

Rejoinder to Professor Mullen   HOWARD GOLDSTEIN

In his thoughtful chapter, Professor Mullen confirms my observation that the findings of empirical research that are limited to sociologic problems (e.g., homelessness) and biologic factors (e.g., AIDS) might be instructive and informative for social work practice. Although these "facts" have much to say about the disease or condition, they have little to tell the social worker about what it means to be stricken with a fatal illness, to be out on the streets, to lose one's family, or to suffer in other ways. Meaning, in these instances, is shot through with vivid personal images, moral questions, and needs that would be rendered banal and arid by quantification and measurement.

If social work is to make any progress in developing practice-based research, then it must confront a fundamental question. Is the world (and particularly the social world that is our concern) ultimately recognizable in scientific terms, that is, objectively observable, predictable, measurable, and subject to quantification? Or is the social world (as we, ourselves, experience and shape it) known to us by our shared and individualized interpretations and constructions? As one example, "homelessness" provides an answer. To be sure, it is important to know something about its incidence and spread. But more than just a statistical fact, it is a social construct. As a term invented by society, it is fraught with moral, economic, and political value, and, not the least, unique and deeply personal meanings for society and for the victims. If we were a nomadic, hunting and gathering society, it would not even be a statistical fact.

Professor Mullen perpetuates the seductive myth of the scientific method and its promises of professional status and respectability. It defines social work as a technology that can discover the causes of human suffering and despair, devise precise interventions, and predict outcomes. Our heritage and practice prove that social work is not a technology, but rather a humanistic endeavor in which artistry, creativity, intuitiveness, and interpersonal talents are hallmarks of our professional competencies.

A humanistic approach does not excuse professionals from accountability and the ability to evaluate the nature and worth of their efforts. Neither does it impair the advancement of knowledge or deny that the scientific method has certain selective functions. It does shift attention, however, to the interpretive and subjective rather than the statistical and objective methods of inquiry—phenomenologic, ethnographic, hermeneutic, for example—methods that more accurately and helpfully capture the content, process, and outcomes of practice. It is not the static measurements of frequencies and abstract variables that concern the practitioner who is confronted with complex problems of living. Rather, to be helpful and effective, it is the need to comprehend the more profound meanings that our clients give to their definitions of quality of life and well being, to their culture, values, and morals, and to the critical implications of change. The interpretive and reflexive methods of inquiry are more appropriate to this endeavor. They are different but no less systematic and disciplined than are those methods that Mullen recommends, scientific methods borrowed from the natural sciences that are more relevant to the study of inert and nonhuman phenomena.

NO

HOWARD GOLDSTEIN

Should Social Workers Base Practice Decisions on Empirical Research?

Not long ago, readers of social work journals were treated to an uncommon event: a grand debate about social work research and the relevance of its empirical foundations and methods.[1] Professional debates are sometimes beneficial; by polarizing a particular issue, fresh ideas might then be generated. This question, however, seems to have remained polarized as each camp constructs even more robust intellectual barricades to defend its particular position. This outcome, it seems to me, was inevitable, because the debate held to rather heady levels of abstraction and ideology.

As posed in the title, the question now is far more basic and down-to-earth. It is less concerned with the theoretical merits of empirical research and more so with question about the utility of its findings for informing practitioners' decisions and judgments in practice. The question is answered here in "yes, but . . ." terms. Yes, it is useful to the extent that it highlights certain narrow avenues of knowledge. But, no, these findings have little significance for the humanistic qualities of practice.

Empirical findings are useful insofar as they have something to say about specific realms of the human state, the sociological and the biological. In the first instance, empirical-statistical studies of mass behavior, the attitudes and actions of selected populations, often yield informative results. These studies and surveys may, for example, alert us to the general reasons for premature termination by certain client populations, the frequency of use of alcohol or drugs by high school students, or, coincidental with the question we are examining, the rate of success in teaching empirical research in graduate social work education and the extent to which social workers use research findings in their practice.[2] Biological studies, on the other hand, are restricted to inquiries about specific physical and material conditions; for example, memory loss among the elderly, types of organically based depression, and the implications of certain diseases such as Alzheimer's. But the significance of these data must be treated with caution as they might or might not apply to practice. Sociological findings provide a map of sorts, but there is no certainty that any one client actually is part of the terrain that the map purports to represent. Conversely, biological data may serve as indicators or pointers that highlight an isolated aspect of one's physical state at a particular point in time. In itself, however, it has nothing to say about where or how this condition fits in with the client's larger cultural, interpersonal, and adaptive world. The persuasiveness of either of these types of findings can be misleading. The social worker, ever eager for concrete facts in the face of the complexity and ambiguity of the client's circumstances, may be beguiled by an enchantment with numbers.

It would be tempting to take the negative position by using the "proof is in the pudding" argument and leaving it at that. If the findings of empirical research indeed are serviceable for practice decisions, we would expect that social workers would eagerly exploit them. But that is not the case. The products of well-funded and earnest research are not high on the list of resources for practicing social workers.

For this reason alone, it is important to consider if, in down-to-earth terms, empirical research can tell us anything that matters about the human situations encountered in every day practice. To do this, we must examine, as space will allow, just a few of the more apparent characteristics of the human state to see if they lend themselves to empirical investigation.

Unlike the objects that science seeks to explore and explain, the human situation is far more ambiguous and elusive. Our dualistic and Cartesian heritage forces us to think about the two aspects or images of the person, mind and body or brain, and mind or matter and essence (omitting, for the sake of brevity, the more confounding question about how they interact). One image or aspect of the person is the material, organic or constitutional—the brain and its neuronal structures and other structures and systems that make up the purely biologic organism. The other aspect or image is far more fugitive and incomprehensible; this is what is variously called the mind, ego, self, consciousness, self-awareness, or soul or psyche. The organism can be measured, surveyed, and subjected to experimental protocols: our biologic characteristics are more or less static and verifiable. In sharp contrast, our nonmaterial qualities, the essence of who and what we are or are judged to be, do not fit the scientific criterion for investigation, they are not directly accessible to our senses or research instruments. Moreover, unlike the substantial nature of our material selves, what we call mind or consciousness or self is not a thing but a process or activity, we are typically in the act of being conscious or aware as we make our way through our experiences; our selves are usually in the process of transformation in our social relations. We are never exactly what we just were.

The critical differences between the two images have either been grossly overlooked or converted into artificial but utilitarian metaphors by the empirical researcher. As if they were distinct biological items, "motives," "values," "self-concepts," "attitudes," and other synthetic constructs are pared down and molded into unites that will conform to some scale or measurement device. Analogously, mind and brain are blithely equated with the software and hardware of the computer. This, however, is a deceptive comparison. Computers have "memories" but they cannot spontaneously remember anything; they are on line but are not self-conscious; they can generate information but do not know what it means; and they cannot imagine.

The way the mind works suggests a more cogent analogy, that of story, text, or narrative. By way of memory, symbols, language, imagery, and other mental agencies, the person is frequently in the process of creating or redefining a personal or shared version of reality, a story. This occurs in the form of a dialogue in which, in a manner of speaking, one is openly or tacitly in conversation with one's self or with others. Even as I write this sentence a conversation is going on—with myself as I reach inward for words and ideas to convey this message and with you, the reader, as I try to convert these images and ideas in what I hope is a comprehensible form. No doubt this is also the essence of the social work interview as the social worker and the client shift in and out of their respective selves, constantly editing and revising the shared story in the attempt to make sense and create meaning of their own and the other's messages. Empirically factoring out such "variables" as specific interventions or client and worker characteristics or other observable behaviors can only diminish or negate the essentially narrative nature of the relationship, and thus its meaning and significance. Let us consider why this is so.

First consider the importance of history and context for our understanding of our client's words and story. Empirical methods are generally indifferent to the idea that a human situation unfolds within a perceived sense of time and space (unless one or the other is isolated as an independent variable that only serves to freeze that which is experienced as fluid). For more than just a formal social history, we must turn to the client's narrative that will tell us what the current circumstances are all about in auto-biographic terms; in effect, "This is how things turned out because of the way things were in my life." Moreover, this autobiography will be shaded by the felt influence of its social, cultural, and physical setting. Putting this more simply and idiomatically, this is what we are asking in the question, "Where are you coming from?" Difficult as this understanding is to achieve, it is no wonder that we are persuaded by simple cause and effect proposi-tions or formulas, e.g., people who were abused as children tend to abuse their own children.

Such cause and effect findings reflect the identification of empirical social work research with the assumptions and methods of the natural sciences. In the latter, it is presumed that the objects of inquiry are uniform and subject to rational explanation and prediction.[3] Human thought, inten-tion, and behavior are scarcely rational or predictable; more so than not, to be human is to be unpredictable, paradoxical, ambiguous, and sometimes absurd. We have no hesitation about using irrational means to prove that we are indeed rational. The family or marital counselor is familiar with the competing and incongruous justifications clients will insist on to prove who is right and who is righteous. At its best, the capricious or irrational nature of the human mind makes for the remarkable wizardry of adaptation, including the ability to invent extraordinarily novel and creative ways for coping with formerly unimagined dilemma. Can this creativity be measured?

Sol Garfield (1978), an eminent researcher in the field of psycho-therapy, suggests a possible answer. Concluding that many clinical settings are relatively unaffected by research findings, he notes that "[p]art of this problem is undoubtedly related to the fact that many research studies are seen as being unrelated to the 'real world' of clinical realities" (p. 225).

Clearly, the "real world" of social work practice is not shaped by statistical "facts," frequencies, distributions, and correlations. Rather, this world is a rich and complex mosaic inlaid with a fugitive assortment of recollected values, moral questions, myths, and faiths. Although the hard-nosed researcher may discount these beliefs and principles (and their com-panion emotions) as "soft stuff" because they cannot be measured and concretized, overlooking them in practice would transform the social worker into a kind of machinist.

It is the value we attribute to an experience and not the fact of the experience itself that makes the difference and creates meaning. In a single case study, for example, the fact that a married couple has decreased the frequency of their arguments or the fact that a parent increased the rate of attention given to her child's schoolwork over certain time periods is, in and of itself, merely a numerical estimate of specific behaviors. The numbers may be interesting if they are taken as an index of our effectiveness (our own meaning), but what the "change" means to the client is likely to be something else. The parent might interpret her new approach to her child as a means of gaining favor from her counselor, as evidence of her new found strength, as a task she had to endure, and so on.

Meaning is not a static entity, it is what we "discover," "give" or "find." Thus, it cannot be captured by an impersonal instrument (Polkinghorne, 1988). As our perceptions change, so do the meanings we give to our world. And so our account and story of ourselves and our experiences undergo small or great alterations. From this view, it would not be unthinkable to consider the practitioner as an editor of sorts who helps clients revise their unrewarding renditions of reality into stories that will work better and lead to more wholesome ways of coping.

The way practice has been portrayed thus far shows that empirical findings can, at best, play on a peripheral role. The decisions and judgments that are made in practice are responsive to the tentative assumptions that arise out of our moment-to-moment interpretations of what is taking place. This is what Schön (1983) calls "reflection in action," another form of research in its own right. In order to make sense of the unique and puzzling human event, the practitioner (if he or she is not guided by cookbook techniques) creates a progression of low-level theories not only about the client's circumstances but also about his or her actions by questioning, "How do I understand?" "What will happen if . . . ?" and so on. Prior experiences and gained knowledge (including research findings) do have a role in this reflective process, largely for purposes of comparison, e.g., "How does what I already know relate to what I am learning about *this* case?"

Quite simply, the helping experience is an interpretive event. That this is so is appreciated by many researchers in the human sciences who have already abandoned their former romance with ideals of scientific purity and prediction. Rabinow and Sullivan (1987, p. 7) speak of this move as the "interpretive turn." Because human life is an open system it is subject to an infinite range of unpredictable forces and therefore cannot be studied in a vacuum or scientifically controlled environment. As a result, the exactitude that is available to the natural sciences cannot be expected in the human sciences. As they put it:

> Our capacity to understand is rooted in our own definitions, hence in what we are. We are fundamentally self-interpreting and self-defining, living always in a cultural environment, inside a web of signification that we ourselves have spun . . . when we try to understand the cultural world, we are dealing with interpretations and interpretations of interpretations.

Research on social work practice is sorely needed; despite many decades of inquiry, what we really know about what makes the difference in the helping process is something that is too often disparaged because it lacks the aura of scientific verity. That something is called "practice wisdom," the accretion over time of the humanistic knowledge, skills, and values that shape the art of social work. For the extent to which social workers are reflective, are concerned with the interpretation of meanings and values, and deal with metaphors and other symbolic and imaginative representations of thought, feeling, and behavior, so are they expressing creativity and artistry.

What requires investigation are the naturalistic qualities of practice itself, the interpretive wisdom and art of the ordinary helping event, the integrity and wholeness of the event, and not merely its isolated "practitioner" or "client" or "intervention" or other isolated variables. The research question is both simple and profound: "What is going on and what makes the difference?"

If we are satisfied (as we are in ordinary human circumstances) with knowledge that is not absolute, conclusive, or subject to tests of significance, the interpretive and ethnographic research methods of cultural anthropology will prove to be illuminating and instructive. The use of case studies, life histories, participant observation, and interviewing are examples of the ethnographic method (and, as well, examples of social workers' basic skills), which allow the meaning and nature of practice to come forward in their naturalistic and metaphoric forms. There is a certain irony in this complicated argument and its recommendations because they merely restate a basic social work principle: "Start where the client is."

NOTES

1. M. Heineman, The Obsolete Scientific Imperative in Social Work Research. *Social Service Review* 3 (September 1981) pp. 371–395; W.W. Hudson, Scientific Imperatives in Social Work Research and Practice, *Social Service Review* 2 (June, 1982) pp. 246–258; Debate with Authors, *Social Service Review* 2 (June 1982) pp. 311–312; T. Holland, Comments on 'Scientific Imperative in Social Work Research and Practice' and reply by W.W. Hudson, *Social Service Review* 2 (June, 1983) pp. 337–341; M.H. Pieper, The Future of Social Work Research, *Social Work Research and Abstracts,* 5 (Winter, 1985) pp. 3–11; E.J. Mullen, Methodological Dilemmas in Social Work Research, *Social Work Research and Abstracts* 5 (Winter, 1985), pp. 12–20.

2. See, for example D.H. Siegel, Can Research and Practice be Integrated in Social Work Education? *Journal of Education for Social Work,* 3,

1983, pp. 12–20; R.M. Carew, The Place of Knowledge in Social Work Activity. *British Journal of Social Work*, 3, 1978, pp. 349–364; L.E. Beutler, M. Cargo, & T.G. Arizmendi, Therapist Variables in Psychotherapy Process and Outcome. In S.L. Garfield and A.E. Bergin (Eds.), *Handbook of Psychotherapy and Behavior Change*, ed 3. New York: John Wiley & Sons, 1986, pp. 259–301.

3. Even in the natural sciences, the comfortable notions of uniformity, predictability, and order have come into question, (see, for example, J. Gleick, *Chaos: Making a New Science*. New York: Viking, 1987).

REFERENCES

Garfield, S. (1978). Research on Client Variables in Psychotherapy. In S.L. Garfield & A.E. Bergin (Eds.), *Handbook of Psychotherapy and Behavior Change*, ed 2. New York: John Wiley & Sons.

Gergen, K.J. (1982). *Toward Transformation in Social Knowledge*. New York: Springer-Verlag.

Polkinghorne, D.E. (1989). *Narrative Knowing and the Human Sciences*. Albany: State University of New York Press.

Rabinow, P. & Sullivan, W.M. (1987). *The Interpretive Turn: A Second Look*. In P. Rabinow & F.E. Williams (Eds.), *Interpretive Social Sciences: A Second Look*. Berkeley: The University of California Press.

Schön, D. (1984). *The Reflective Practitioner: How Professionals Think in Action*. New York: Basic Books.

Rejoinder to Professor Goldstein   EDWARD J. MULLEN

Social work is a complex profession. Social workers engage in many forms of practice, including policy analysis, social administration, social research, and direct practice. Social workers intervene at various levels, affecting issues at the international, national, regional, urban, and local levels. They are concerned with a wide range of problems and populations cutting across many fields of practice. Social workers are concerned with the destructive effects of discrimination, inequity, racism, poverty, violence, and prejudice at all levels and in all forms. This is the nature of social work practice. It is in this context that my chapter examined whether social workers should base their interventions on knowledge developed through work inspired by scientific principles. In this chapter I suggested that social workers should critically examine their knowledge to determine the extent to which it has been developed and verified through methods that reduce the possibility of bias, involve the careful examination of alternative explanations and systematically reference empirical observation. These are essential qualities characterizing scientific research.

I find it quite remarkable that anyone who recognizes the breadth of the profession's mission could conclude that scientifically derived knowledge and scientific methods have little relevance to anything that matters about the human situations encountered in everyday practice and, at best, play only a "peripheral" role. I find it troubling to hear that social workers are essentially "editors" who help clients revise their autobiographies, especially when I consider the complex range of interventions needed to deal with the broad issues and problems that must be addressed if the profession is to be responsive to its historical mission, I am concerned also for the profession when I read that only a single approach to research is found to be illuminating and instructive (e.g., interpretive or ethnographic methods).

Qualitative methods are important forms of empirical research, and these methods have contributed to the profession's knowledge base, especially enhancing understanding about meanings that people attribute to their experiences, as well as expanding understanding about a wide range of cultural variables. Social workers have additional concerns requiring information and research methods that go beyond these perspectives, however. Social workers require knowledge that will allow them to facilitate social movements, influence public policy development, manage organizations and programs, strengthen neighborhoods, communities, and families, and provide a wide range of vital services. All of this occurs in the context of a society that has benefitted immeasurably from scientific and technologic developments. Why would the profession exclude itself from the reality and richness of our own cultural context?

Elsewhere I have written that each social worker is professionally and ethically accountable for basing practice on the best information available. I have suggested that the accountable professional is also responsible for the development of a personal practice model, including a self-evaluation capability (Mullen, 1988). Such personal practice models can be enriched by information derived from many sources, including personal and professional experience, conceptual-theoretical analyses, and empirical research findings and methods. These forms of information when bound together by a clear sense of values, ethnics, and mission make possible accountable and effective practice. The profession can not settle for less!

The current debate within the profession regarding the importance of scientific methods has been, as Professor Goldstein writes, rather abstract and ideological. Those participating in this debate have at times presented strong arguments for one or another research method, rejecting methods favored by their antagonists. Professor Goldstein joins in this debate supporting those who favor qualitative, interpretive methods and expressing skepticism regarding objective, quantitative, nomothetic approaches. The epistemological issues here are as old as philosophy itself. Nevertheless, they must be once again addressed in the contemporary context. We are currently being urged to reject scientific methods that value objectivity and to embrace methods that are fundamentally subjective[1] Objective methods are seen as reductionistic, that is, reducing people and their creations to no more than material objects. Alternative methods such as "story-telling," which seek to elicit an individual's experience of his or her subjective world, are seen as more appropriate. The epistemological issues raised in the contemporary debate are important, and they will not be easily settled. However, scientific work is not driven by such philosophic discussion. Rather, scientists, including social work researchers, proceed in their investigations using whatever methods hold promise for contributing to the advancement of knowledge. The value of the methods will be determined not by *a priori* criteria, but rather by the extent to which they contribute to the advancement of relevant knowledge, and for social work, to the advancement of the human condition. This fostering of a spirit of open inquiry is the current challenge. Extreme attacks on scientific methods and empirical analysis too often serve to reify intuitive methods that when used alone, have previously been found to be inadequate for the development of specialized expert knowledge.[2] A return to such methods would be regressive and run counter to experience. Social workers can best serve society as well as individual clients by using specialized knowledge that is firmly based on systematic, controlled, empirical study.

NOTES

1. The issue is not whether scientists are objective. By definition scientists as people are subjective. Rather the issue is whether research methods should be used that are designed to control for some of that subjectivity so as to reduce some biasing influences. There is no suggestion that such methods result in purely "objective" investigation, only that some bias is, it is hoped, controlled.

2. Intuitive methods can contribute to what might be referred to as "common sense." Common sense is essential for human survival, providing each person with a general knowledge base as well as an approach to everyday living. The profession has even developed an extensive body of specialized knowledge using what might be considered common sense methods. This is often called "practice wisdom." However, as discussed earlier, expert-specialized knowledge is also needed for social work to be

considered a profession with practitioners capable of providing something in addition to interventions based on common sense.

REFERENCE

Mullen, E.J. (1988). Using Research and Theory in Social Work Practice. In R.M. Grinnell (Ed.), *Social Work Research and Evaluation,* ed 3. Itasca, IL: F.E. Peacock.

Should Social Workers Accept a Disease Model of Substance Abuse?

EDITOR'S NOTE: Most helping professionals embrace a disease model of substance abuse, the view that problematic use of alcohol or drugs will inevitably continue (and usually get worse) without treatment, that one drink leads to other drinks. This view of substance abuse is the heart of most professional as well as nonprofessional programs designed to decrease substance abuse, such as Alcoholics Anonymous. Evidence that some problem drinkers can become controlled drinkers has resulted in heated reactions because these data would seem to contradict the disease model of substance abuse. (This finding is sometimes misinterpreted as implying that all problem drinkers can become controlled drinkers—the substitution of all for some.) Those who accept a disease model of substance abuse argue that the individuals included in these studies were not really alcoholics.

Peter Manoleas, MSW, argues YES. He is a lecturer and field work consultant at the University of California at Berkeley. He has 21 years experience as a therapist, administrator, and consultant in the fields of mental health and substance abuse and has written in the areas of addictions, mental health and architecture, and vocational services for the mentally ill.

Roger A. Roffman, DSW, argues NO. He is Associate Professor of Social Work at the University of Washington, where he chairs the research minor and the chemical dependency specialization. His current research interests include the treatment of marijuana dependence and AIDS prevention.

YES

PETER MANOLEAS

The popularity of the disease model of addictions was given its greatest boost in 1960 with the publication of E.M. Jellinek's *The Disease Model of Alcoholism*. Since that time millions of alcoholics and drug abusers have entered the recovery process free from the stigma previously associated with the dominant view that the abusive intake of chemical substances was due to a lack of strength or to a moral weakness. Recently, however, the disease model has come under attack by investigators questioning its validity and even its utility as a construct. This chapter shall not attempt to shed light on the "truth" of the disease model, but rather its usefulness to social workers and other treating persons in helping addicted clients alter their faulty belief systems and sustain their recoveries. The chapter treats alcohol as a drug, and consequently uses the terms alcoholic and addict (as in other drugs) interchangeably.

A Disease of Lifestyle

Medical researchers in the past 25 years have been giving increasing attention to maladies such as heart disease, diabetes, respiratory disease, certain types of cancers, and others that are chronic disorders, but that are caused or exacerbated by the lifestyle of the patient. Trends in behavioral medicine, prevention, and heath promotion not only recognize the cost effectiveness of exercise, proper diet, stress management, and other habit alteration, but in some cases its curative necessity. It is most useful to conceive of alcoholism and the addiction to other psychoactive substances as this type of disease (Flores, 1988). They have their etiologies in lifestyles or habits, but once one has the disease, one definitely has it. The disease of addiction is chronic, progressive, and degenerative, it is not curable, only arrestible, and one is always prone to relapse. Paradoxically, in order to remain "in remission" from the disease, the addict must alter his or her behavior, i.e., abstain from the substance. The need to introduce the intermediate construct of a disease to accomplish this behavioral change will be explored later.

The disease model is particularly important for social workers and other psychotherapists, most of whom have been trained in another disease model, namely, that of psychopathology. Many such people may tend to view substance abuse as a "symptom" of underlying conflict or other pathology. It is important for such people to see addiction as a primary disease that must be addressed before working on "deeper" problems. Psychotherapy is a waste of everyone's time while the client's brain is still toxic, and his or her feelings are still anesthetized or otherwise chemically altered.

Diagnosis

The use of psychoactive substances is not a problem for most people who take them. Millions of people drink alcohol and caffeine beverages on occasion without ever encountering problems. There are others who experiment with illicit drugs and do not have difficulty. On the continuum of frequency of usage and consequences of use, however, a substance abuse (or dependence) diagnosis is generally given to persons who meet two broad conditions. The first is the compulsive usage of the drug(s) for their effect, and the second is the continued use in the face of adverse consequences that are known to the user. Most chemical dependence professionals made a further diagnostic distinction between "psychologic" and "physical" addiction, or, in the nomenclature of DSM-III-R, substance dependence versus substance abuse. Much of the debate about the "inexact nature" of the criteria for these diagnoses stems, in my opinion, from the fact that diagnosable substance abusers by definition cannot control their intake of the drug and must abstain in order to recover. Increased tolerance has been demonstrated during their years of usage, and controlled usage is not possible. Perhaps no other syndrome has caused as much introspection among practitioners and researchers. It is difficult to ponder these issues without asking, "Is that me?" Alcoholics Anonymous, as usual, provides a way out of the entanglement of convoluted arguments and defenses by keeping it simple with the statement, "Anything that causes a problem is one." The model fits particularly well for the person-in-environment focus of social workers. We are forced to view our clients holistically as biopsychosocial beings. We assess the various spheres of functioning—physical, social, psychological, sexual, occupational, spiritual, legal, and creative—and examine the effects of substance use on each of these areas. Armed with the disease concepts of progression and tolerance, we then decided whether or not the use of alcohol or drugs (licit or illicit) played a role in the diminution of functioning in one or more of these spheres. If it did, the usage is problematic, and a diagnosis can probably be made.

The Role of Denial and Belief

Given that diagnosed substance abusers cannot use alcohol or drugs at all if they wish to sustain their recovery, one of the cardinal symptoms of most people suffering from the disease is the denial of that reality. Because of the fact that their mental processes are often dominated by preoccupations of securing, using, or the recalled (or imagined) positive effects of the drug, most addicts and alcoholics deny the negative effects of usage and cling to the belief that they are in control of their usage, or could be if they only chose to be. This is based on the faulty belief that it is ever possible for an alcoholic or addict to return to "normal" or controlled usage. Herein lies the clinical and ethical danger caused by the studies on controlled drinking. As Flores (1988) points out and my experience corroborates, "If you tell a group of ten alcoholics that research has shown that one out of ten alcoholics can successfully return to normal drinking, each of them will surely believe s/he is that one." From the point of view of the recovering person, such research is not only frivolous, but tampers with their sobriety and perhaps their lives. As any chemical dependence practitioner will acknowledge, abstinence is crucial, and whatever works, works. Consequently, the truth of whether or not controlled chemical intake is possible for addicts is not important. What is important is that they accept as reality the fact that they will never be able to drink or use again. The admission of having the disease and the need for a stable and enduring belief system are absolutely essential. On their way to "hitting bottom," addicts and alcoholics usually receive some external pressure from a variety of sources to quit or "cut down." Many are temporarily able to succumb to covert or overt threats like, "If you come home drunk again, I'm leaving you," or "If your urine test comes up dirty again, you're fired." The ability to temporarily do this represents repeated attempts at control and is not the same as the total admission of having the disease and all that implies. Brown (1986) calls the former compliance and defines it as the conscious acceptance of an external reality (I cannot drink or use). What is necessary is surrender, which she defines as the unconscious acceptance of that external reality.

The Paradox of Control

There are many twelve-step programs designed to help people with various addictions. Alcoholics Anonymous, Narcotic Anonymous, Cocaine Anonymous, and others all have similarities in their approaches. The first step in each, for example, is, "We admitted we were powerless over _____." Each person who gets to the point of this admission has tried, in myriad ways to convince him or herself over a period of years that he or she was in control, usually with disastrous consequences. The disease model allows the person a constructive way out of the intricate web of denial, guilt, externalized locus of control, anger, and despondence. He or she may then take the first steps toward accepting responsibility for current behavior without blame. It is not, for example, the individual's fault that he or she has the disease, but there is treatment, a way out, and it is his or her responsibility to follow through with it. This paradoxic admission of loss of control in order to get back in control of one's behavior or life is not unique to the world of addictive behaviors. Much of human functioning, and many therapeutic techniques, wittingly or otherwise, work this way. Consider the absurdity of "therapeutic" injunctions such as, "Try to relax," or "Be more spontaneous." Obviously, one can only relax when one quits trying and "lets go." Neither can one plan to be spontaneous. Most of us learned the definition of the autonomic nervous system in introductory psychology as that system over which we can have no conscious control. The field of biofeedback, deep relaxation, and other areas of behavioral medicine have proven that this is not the case. Autonomic functioning can be consciously controlled through a process of "visceral learning," which involves "letting go" of traditional attempts to control. Similarly, power struggles in psychotherapy or in families are often paradoxically resolved by focusing away from the symptom.

The admission of being an alcoholic or addict is somewhat reductionistic but necessary. It asks the person to conflate a complex identity into a one-dimensional self. This is crucial to acceptance of the disease and for early stage recovery. There is plenty of time later for the person to "reconstruct" a healthy, complex, self image that may include gender, work roles, familial roles, and much more. There is time to work on historical feelings, unresolved emotional conflicts, and so on, but for the period of primary recovery, abstinence is the most important issue, and the constant and public admission of being an alcoholic or addict is essential.

Twelve Steps versus Therapy

Professional psychotherapists have long been uncomfortable with the nonprofessional basis for Alcoholics Anonymous and other twelve-step programs. Part of this discomfort stems from lack of understanding about how such programs work. Other professional therapists, as they learn about the methods and efficacy of these programs, may confront the question of what their role is in the treatment process or how they can help people to recover. Without a doubt, there has been more dialogue of late about how the two approaches can complement each other. Many alcoholics and addicts who have gotten and remain clean and sober through twelve-step programs have gotten past their anger about experiences with "codependent" therapists who saw them for extended periods of time without directly confronting potentially life-threatening substance abuse. There are still vast differences in perception about which approach constitutes the "therapy," and which the "adjunct," but each group seems to be acknowledging some value in the other approach.

Careful consideration of the twelve steps will reveal that they provide a structure and personal recovery plan within the context of the self-help group. As mentioned, the first step is the admission of loss of control. The subsequent steps ask the client in lay language to do many of the things one actually does in the process of therapy. "Making amends" to those one has hurt with drug use, "correcting character defects," and taking a personal "moral inventory" are lay terms for personal and group processes that are not at all unlike what occurs in many forms of psychotherapy. The approach is also famous for the abundant use of slogans like "keep it simple," and "one day at a time," all of which are designed to correct faulty beliefs and cognitions ("stinking thinking") and eventually provide security and calming with their simplicity, almost like mantras or chants. The holistic approach taken by these self-help groups focuses on all of the "spheres of functioning" mentioned earlier. Positive changes in the physical, emotional, social, spiritual, and other areas of life accompany working the twelve steps. The warning not to let yourself get too tired, too hungry, too angry, or too lonely are good guidelines to healthy functioning and embody common sense. Addicts recognize these as four "red flags" to impending relapse.

Conclusion

There are many theories that claim to isolate causes for addictive disorders or behavior. Most people who work in the field of chemical dependence realize that the causes are many, varied, and complex. Moreover, they are concerned about using whatever tools they can to help people to get and remain clean and sober. The disease model has been explored in this connection. Wallace (1975) cites three ways that the alcoholic's or addict's belief in the disease model can be helpful:

1. It helps explain the past in a way that gives hope for the future;
2. It allows the alcoholic or addict to cope with guilt, anxiety, remorse, and confusion, and;
3. It provides them with specific behaviors (remaining abstinent, attending meetings, working steps, and so on) that will change their life in the desired direction.

REFERENCES

Brown, S. (1985). *Treating the Alcoholic: A Developmental Model of Recovery.* New York: Wiley.
Flores, P. (1988). *Group Psychotherapy with Addicted Populations.* New York: The Haworth Press, pp. 8–19.

Jellinek, E.M. (1960). *The Disease Concept of Alcoholism*. New Haven: Hillhouse Press.

Wallace, J. (1975). *Tactical and Strategic Use of the Preferred Defense Structure of the Recovering Alcoholic*. National Council on Alcoholism.

ANNOTATED BIBLIOGRAPHY

Brown, S. (1985). *Treating the Alcoholic: A Developmental Model of Recovery*. New York: Wiley

> The author, a clinical psychologist in recovery herself, provides us with a conceptual model that goes a long way in bridging the gap between self-help recovery groups and professional therapists. She views the recovery process as occurring in developmental stages, and "translates" twelve-step terms into professional jargon and vice-versa.

Flores, P. (1988). *Group Psychotherapy With Addicted Populations*. New York: The Haworth Press

> The book examines the utility of the disease model in non–twelve-step group therapy with alcoholics and addicts. The author adapts Yalom's principles of group psychotherapy for usage with this special population.

Rejoinder to Peter Manoleas
ROGER A. ROFFMAN

Peter Manoleas builds his advocacy for the disease conceptualization on its usefulness rather than its validity. Two of his statements convey his reliance on this criterion:

> This chapter shall not attempt to shed light on the "truth" of the disease model, but rather its usefulness to social workers and other treating persons in helping addicted clients alter their faulty belief systems, and sustain their recoveries.
>
> Consequently, the truth of whether or not controlled chemical intake is possible for addicts is not important. What is important, is that they accept as reality the fact that they will never be able to drink or use again.

I agree that the disease concept is useful. At any one time in this country, hundreds of thousands of people are using the disease model's precepts in finding their way out of addiction.

But can we so easily rely on usefulness and dismiss accuracy or validity as we choose to accept or not accept a set of beliefs concerning the nature of a phenomenon? Is it ethical to do so? I think not.

In the face of evidence that most people who become addicted are never treated, must we not be open to the possibility that the premises upon which we have built our treatment programs are faulty? Perhaps we are preventing people from seeking help because the only help we are offering is unacceptable.

In the face of fairly poor treatment outcomes for addiction, must we not at least challenge our conventional approaches? Perhaps the treatment model that greatly helps some people actually greatly hinders others.

Some decades ago, Freud's theories had a profound impact on our beliefs about human behavior and development. Therapies built upon those concepts were and are useful to many people. Yet, those theories and therapies deserved to be challenged as evidence emerged that refuted their essential precepts. Today, we see psychoanalytic therapies as coexisting with many other interventive approaches, and we seek ways of better matching individual needs with the best options available. I believe that we can do no less in the field of addictions.

Yes, I believe that the disease model is helpful. But I also believe that its concepts and the interventions based on its premises are insufficient to effectively meet the diverse needs held by the addicted population.

As a social worker, I seek to help clients learn about the array of options they might consider as they grapple with addiction. One such option is a disease model program or fellowship. Yet, many others must be explored. Otherwise, the client loses.

So, shall social workers accept a disease model of substance abuse? If the choice is to accept the disease model and nothing else, my answer must unequivocally be no.

NO

ROGER A. ROFFMAN

Life would be a lot easier for helping professionals but not for a great many chemically dependent people or those headed in that direction if the disease explanation for substance abuse were universally accepted. The often acrimonious debates among workers in the field would be avoided, and those who have valuable contributions but disagree with the disease concept would no longer find themselves discounted by their colleagues.

Irreparable harm would result, however, with universal acceptance of this conceptualization, and for that reason a more accurate model of explanation is warranted. The disease model is obstructing a comprehensive social response to addictive behaviors and their consequences. Fewer people are being helped in this country than otherwise might be the case. We are doing far less than we might in preventing substance abuse.

In the United States today, there are some mighty wide gulfs in the field of addiction. For example, in many, if not most, chemical dependency treatment programs, the services offered represent a far cry from empirically tested interventions. Strongly held beliefs about what good treatment entails are prevailing, despite many of these beliefs simply being unsupported or contradicted by the findings of science. The failure to translate empirically derived knowledge into operational programming in this field is a remarkable manifestation of the hefty power held by ideology in our times. The staff's attitude seems to be: "What worked for me should work for everyone else." No matter that treatment outcomes are modest at best. No matter that many people who are overwhelmed with abusive drinking or drug use refuse to enter currently existing programs because of the labels which they require clients to adopt.

Another gulf is represented by the arguments about the disease concept. The use or nonuse of the term identifies the "us" and the "them" among chemical dependencies specialists, particularly in rehabilitative settings. The word "disease" today seems to be a symbol, unfortunately for many the only symbol, for a certain set of attitudes and beliefs: not blaming the victim, having compassion for his or her struggles, considering genetic transmission as a possible causative factor, and supporting twelve-step fellowships such as Alcoholics Anonymous.

The vocabulary of those who do not accept a disease conceptualization marks them as outsiders, and dangerous outsiders at that. Where's the danger? In a nutshell, it pertains to shame and money. Let me begin with the matter of shame. As seen by many, the only alternative to thinking of alcoholics and drug addicts as diseased is to think of them as bad, unworthy, or morally weak.

That is not how I think. Each of us is largely a product of the environmental influences (e.g., in the home, peer group, community, schools, and employment settings) that shape our attitudes, beliefs, choices, and capacities. Given one set of environmental circumstances, a future humanitarian emerges; given another, a thief or rapist. Sure, we all have choices. But they are heavily shaped by our individual environments. Some physical and psychologic environments literally propel people along a trajectory toward alcoholism or other drug dependency.

We do not have to rely on a disease conceptualization in order to have compassion, be nonjudgmental, consider biologic predisposition, and support twelve-step programs. We can and should have such a perspective based on recognizing that how one learns to think and behave is largely influenced by one's environments and that many environmental circumstances are damaging and negative. None of us can claim to be completely independent from such forces.

Shame needs to be eliminated, in part because it is not deserved and in part because it inhibits taking the necessary steps to reverse a self-destructive behavioral pattern. Many of us respond to shame by hiding and denying. It is painful and adds to the reasons why just one more drink or hit is so very necessary just to get through today. But we do not require a disease formulation to let go of pejorative judgments.

The second "dangerous" consequence of refuting a disease concept is economic. The health care industry is legitimized, via the disease model, as carrying the responsibility for chemical dependency "treatment." With that responsibility also comes profit. Conceptualizing the nature of chemical dependency as learned behavior implies that educational institutions, not clinics and hospitals, ought to be the primary locus for prevention and intervention. A lot of money, counted in the billions, is at stake! Among those who would stand to lose are the many thousands of treatment program personnel who earn their living directly based on a disease concept of chemical dependency. If only their track record warranted their claim to exclusive legitimacy in helping chemically dependent people!

Before we take a look at some of the ways in which the disease concept obstructs vitally important public responses to chemical dependency, we ought to identify just what this concept includes. While not everyone will endorse every part of this definition, these components are commonly listed as comprising the disease model: (1) Chemical dependency is a specific disease, with some people being particularly vulnerable. Genetic factors play a major role in determining vulnerability. (2) With the onset of alcohol or drug use, those people with this specific vulnerability go through a progression of stages of use (e.g., seemingly normal use leads to excessive use, being secretive about use, increased tolerance and withdrawal, blackouts, and ultimately, loss of control). Unless treated or facilitated to understand and cope with the disease via a twelve-step fellowship, death is highly likely. (3) The disease cannot be cured but can be arrested. Abstinence is mandatory.

Much of the above is captured in the phrase: "Chemical dependency is a primary, progressive, and chronic disease." In thinking about this notion, one can quickly think of alcoholics or drug addicts for whom each of the definitional components would readily fit. Their family histories were replete with evidence of intergenerational transmission, they moved steadily through each of the anticipated stages, and they eventually appeared to be out of control. Any use seemed to inevitably lead to profound intoxication. When they attempted to reduce or moderate their use, it was only a matter of time before relapse occurred to highly abusive patterns. Eventually, perhaps after a few false starts, they became active in a twelve-step program. We now see them living healthy and productive lives.

Without doubt, this model fits many people. Moreover, it appears to reduce the barrier of shame erected in the path of overcoming dependence. Why, then, do we not adopt it? The answer is simple. This model is built on numerous erroneous conclusions. In reality, it fits only a fraction of the addicted population. Furthermore, it prevents us from what might be the most effective public responses to addictive behaviors.

Is it primary? Yes, indeed, for some people it appears that abusive alcohol or drug use was not preceded by other dysfunctional disorders that might have led to chemical dependency. Yet for others, there is considerable evidence that the alcohol or drug abuse was symptomatic of an underlying preceding disorder.

Is it genetically transmitted? Perhaps for some. The research findings concerning genetically determined metabolic differences, alterations in brain waves, variations in endorphins, neurological susceptibilities, and the like simply are not sufficiently strong to warrant generalization to more than a small percentage of chemically dependent people. Some other explanations are needed for most people.

Is there a specific progression through stages? Again, for some people a common pathway is manifested. Abundant research concerning drinking behaviors among Americans points to the existence of variations of use patterns, however. For that matter, for many people there appear to be periods of abusive use followed by periods of moderation or abstinence without exposure to rehabilitative programs. No one set of stages accounts for more than a fraction of people who become dependent. Many people experience an evolution of patterns that simply do not fit with the unitary disease conceptualization.

Is loss of control inevitable? If we listen to many of our clients, it sure looks that way. Moreover, the notion of loss of control provides a rational way of explaining how a person could have continued to engage in such destructive behaviors again and again. But if we take a look at the research on loss of control, we are again confronted with evidence to refute this central criterion for the disease notion. Researchers have demonstrated that even debilitated alcoholics, under certain circumstances, can and do exert considerable control over the initiation and continuation of alcohol consumption. Loss of control appears to be a choice.

Is abstinence the only option? Understandably, most chemical dependency specialists, particularly those who themselves dealt with their own dependence, are adamant on this issue. Their belief is based on having tried controlled use and failed. One ought not to argue with what they determined was essential for them. Studies of drinking behavior in the general population clearly indicate that some people who drink abusively for a period in their lives later become moderate drinkers. Moreover, studies of outcomes for those treated in either abstinence or moderation programs demonstrate that durable moderation is attained by some program graduates. When compared with the fairly modest percentage of people who attain durable abstinence as a consequence of treatment, the moderation outcome is highly relevant.

Thus far, I have put forward reasons to question various components of the disease concept. Let me now turn to the most important reason: the disease model inhibits us from developing a comprehensive social response to the prevention of chemical dependence.

The disease concept has led us in the United States to build a treatment system that systematically discourages a great many potential clients from seeking help. Not too many years ago, a Congressional study estimated that only fifteen percent to twenty percent of alcoholics were being served. Why so few? Is rampant denial keeping people from acknowledging their need for help? Are there not enough rehabilitative programs for all who would otherwise accept help? Both are undoubtedly true. Yet another quite plausible explanation is that hundreds of thousands of alcoholics who perceive themselves as being unable to get a handle on a destructive drinking pattern refuse to join a program that requires accepting complete abstinence as the only legitimate goal. Unlike the diverse array of rehabilitative goals and options available in other countries, most notably England, all alcoholics in the United States are essentially treated alike. Distinguishing between problem drinking and alcoholism, with differential rehabilitative methods and objectives, is largely unacceptable in our country. Operationally, problem drinking is seen as early stage alcoholism, and abstinence is the only answer for alcoholism.

There is empirical evidence for the successful attainment of moderation in some alcoholics. What if our rehabilitative system offered that as one legitimate objective, along with careful medical and psychosocial screening? I suspect that we would witness massive increases in the numbers of voluntary applications for help.

The disease concept also clouds our thinking about primary prevention. If alcoholism is a unitary phenomenon that largely affects individuals who are genetically predisposed to this disease, we need only find a way to identify those who are vulnerable and advise them to not drink. This idea is not too different from genetic counseling for couples contemplating having children.

In contrast, if we think of alcoholism as learned behavior that might affect the entire population, with a variety of manifestations and causes, we would design our educational programs and social policies quite differently than we do today. Assuming that we could muster the necessary political clout, we would use our licensing, taxation, and criminal laws and regulations far more in shaping alcohol consumption. Perhaps we would even consider teaching moderation skills to young people who choose to drink.

Some experts have mused that the alcoholism industry has a great deal to gain by supporting the disease concept. It is not all of us who consume alcohol who must be considered by policymakers, it is only the relatively few who are biologically vulnerable. No need to cut too deeply into the industry's profits!

Despite all of the previously mentioned reasons, there is no question but that the disease concept is profoundly helpful to many people. The tragedy is that it greatly obstructs us from being far more effective with a much larger part of our society.

ANNOTATED BIBLIOGRAPHY

Fingarette, H. (1988). *Heavy Drinking: The Myth of Alcoholism As A Disease.* Berkeley: University of California Press

Fingarette offers a well-structured and supported argument for abandoning the disease model of alcoholism. He also provides a thoughtful historical perspective on the evolution of this concept as well as a clear alternative way of understanding the cause of chemical dependency.

Galizio, M., & Maisto, S. (1985). *Determinants of Substance Abuse: Biological, Psychological, and Environmental Factors.* New York: Plenum Press

This volume is a useful recently published reference concerning empirical studies that have addressed the major determinants of substance abuse.

Gerstein, D. (1984). *Toward the Prevention of Alcohol Problems.* Washington, D.C.: National Academy Press

Gerstein assesses the many different ways in which alcoholism prevention might be conceptualized, as well as programs that would naturally follow these diverse ways of thinking about prevention.

Heather, N., Robertson, I., & Davies, P. (Eds.), (1985). *The Misuse of Alcohol.* New York: New York University Press

Heather and his colleagues are strong advocates for a learning perspective. Included in this edited volume are useful chapters pertaining to treatment effectiveness.

Marlatt, G.A. (1983). The controlled drinking controversy. *American Psychologist, 38,* 1097–1110

Marlatt's article offers a history of the controlled drinking debate as well as a reasoned analysis of the perspectives held by debate opponents.

Rejoinder to Professor Roffman

PETER MANOLEAS

The disease model of addictions, like any other conceptualization of human functioning, should not be so uniformly and inflexibly applied that it approaches the status of an ideology. To do so forces potential recipients of service to conform to our notions of them in order to gain access to help. Roffman, however, does not make a convincing case for the assertion that "the disease model is obstructing a comprehensive social response to addictive behaviors and their consequences." Although there is evidence that some alcoholics can control their drinking some of the time (Peele, 1985), these studies are of limited usage for those of us concerned with serving public sector clients because they deal primarily with white male subjects, but moreover, they concern themselves almost exclusively with alcohol abuse. It is clear that some problem drinkers, with the appropriate help, can gain control over their alcohol intake. Those who can should be afforded every opportunity to do so. The disease model is most useful for those who, despite repeated attempts, with whatever type of "professional help," continually fail to gain such control. For these people, the belief that they can control their use of the substance is faulty and we owe them more than continued technical consultation on how to keep trying. They often die trying. The operational definition of addiction encompasses the symptoms of loss of control and repeated attempts to quit.

The disease model should not be confused with a medical model. The former is a construct that embraces symptoms, a progressive and degenerative course, and a possible fatal outcome. Although the etiology of the disease is poorly understood, this is the case for many diseases. It is not necessary to totally understand the cause to know what the indicated treatment is. This treatment can be peer-oriented and inexpensive or free. This model is not the same as the medical model, which has given us 28-day hospital-based programs costing from 9000 to 12,000 dollars per stay. These are often unnecessarily staffed by medical professionals and a variety of 24-hour shift personnel. The recovery process often does not begin in earnest until after this initial 28 days of abstinence. Obviously, these programs are accessible to only a small percentage of those in need of help.

It is precisely the two-tiered system of care that makes the disease model useful in working with public sector substance abusers. In most urban areas in this country, those getting (or not getting) such public services are overwhelmingly ethnic minorities and usually polydrug abusers. Alcohol-based controlled drinking studies yield little useful information about working with such populations. Indeed, the logical positivist tradition, with its emphasis on understanding has not been particularly kind to people of non-European backgrounds. While relevant empirically based approaches need to be developed for Afro-American, Latino, Asian American, and Native American substance abusers, there is no doubt that spirituality will prove to be instrumental in each case. The twelve steps and twelve traditions of Alcoholics Anonymous, Narcotics Anonymous, and Cocaine Anonymous are compatible with this spirituality. They allow and encourage the development or restoration of faith and culturally healthy belief systems. They are flexible enough to be compatible with innovative programs like the acupuncture detox program operated by Lincoln Hospital in the South Bronx area of New York City. The predominantly Afro-American, Puerto Rican, and Dominican clientele of this program find the disease model a convenient way of accepting the new and strange treatments. The program claims about fifty percent negative toxicology screens after three months of treatment (for all drugs). It is clear that the disease model has the flexibility to adapt to such current and future innovative approaches.

REFERENCE

Peele, S. (1985). *The meaning of addiction: Compulsive experience and its interpretation.* Lexington, MA: Lexington Books.

Should Social Workers Use the DSM-III-R?

EDITOR'S NOTE: The purpose of the Diagnostic and Statistical Manual of mental disorders, which is published by the American Psychiatric Association, "is to provide clear descriptions of diagnostic categories in order to enable clinicians and investigators to diagnose, communicate about, study, and treat various mental disorders" (DSM-III, 1980, p. 12). More recent versions have been written as described in the statements that follow. The introduction to DSM-III-R (1987) states that "each of the mental disorders is conceptualized as a clinically significant behavioral or psychological syndrome or pattern that occurs in a person and that is associated with present distress (a painful symptom) or disability (impairment in one or more important areas of functioning) or with a significantly increased risk of suffering death, pain, disability, or an important loss of freedom. . . . Whatever its original cause, it must currently be considered a manifestation of a behavioral, psychological, or biological dysfunction in the person" (p. xxi). This manual is used as key guide to diagnosis in many social work training programs. Does this classification system offer a useful guide for social workers? Does it improve the quality of services provided to clients?

Elizabeth Anello answers YES. She is in the doctoral program in social welfare at the University of California at Berkeley. She is Co-director of social work for Health Care for the Homeless/Tom Waddell Clinic, a public health clinic and outreach program in San Francisco.

Stuart A. Kirk, DSW, and Herb Kutchins, DSW, answer NO. Stuart Kirk is Professor, Columbia University School of Social Work, where he teaches in the areas of management, research, and mental health, and is regularly amused or perplexed by the academy.

Herb Kutchins, DSW, is Professor, Division of Social Work, California State University, Sacramento, where he teaches in the areas of law and social welfare, criminal justice, and mental health, and periodically tutors his coauthor in the special customs of the do-it-yourself university.

YES

ELIZABETH ANELLO

The Diagnostic and Statistical Manual of Mental Disorders (herewith referred to as DSM) describes and organizes the behavioral manifestations of mental and emotional deterioration. Each year the American Psychiatric Association continues to revise and refine the DSM, incorporating new research and clinical findings. DSM's first version appeared in 1952. The current edition is the DSM-III-R. Work on DSM IV is in progress (Millon & Klerman, 1986). Psychiatrists, clinical psychologists, social workers, counselors, psychiatric technicians, nurses, and health workers refer to the DSM in clinical work. The manual classifies the observable behaviors and signs of mental and emotional disorder and organizes these symptoms into syndromes that are characteristically seen in clinical practice. It also provides some statistical data to place behavioral syndromes into perspective within the landscape of mental and emotional life. The system permits the clinician to form various working hypotheses for the client's distress. These diagnoses are often provisional. They serve as models to explain behavior and are often altered during the treatment process as observations of client behavior confirm or refute initial impressions. The diagnostic guidelines are conservative. They require considerable behavioral evidence to support a particular clinical judgment.

Should social workers use the DSM-III to guide their practice? Why should social workers use a document prepared by psychiatrists? Although social work contributions have helped shape the manual in significant ways, the DSM remains psychiatry's property.

DSM: A Useful Practice Tool

The DSM is a useful tool and an accepted handbook for social workers. It is assumed that social workers are and should be working with chronic and acute mental illness as equal partners with other health professionals and that the DSM is the most updated and comprehensive guide for mental and emotional problems. Its companion casebook also has practical reference value. It should be used as a reference for psychiatric assessment along with other technical manuals or analytic tools (and intervention planning). Social workers in nonclinical settings should also be familiar with DSM, because often advocacy requires challenges to problem diagnosis. It is best used by those who have some experience with severe psychopathology. The DSM-III (1980), or alternately the DSM-III-R (1987) is widely used by clinical social workers. Kutchins and Kirk (1988) found that about twenty-five percent of clinical social workers use the DSM almost daily (p. 217).

The context of the debate over the DSM in social work is the larger issue of social work's purpose and the relative emphasis given to helping individuals (a clinical focus) versus helping communities (social change). What are some of the common abuses in assessment and diagnosis and how does use of DSM relate to practice abuses? What is the role of diagnosis in social work and how does DSM affect this role? How well is DSM used by social workers? Is it used in the best interest of the client?

Social Work's Role in Mental Health

Social work is an accepted partner in the mental health field. The DSM may not be the only guide for reference, nor even the most important one for social work; however, it is a standard manual used by mental health practitioners. Social workers should use the means available to them to communicate via a shared technical language with other mental health practitioners. To disavow its psychiatric connection, which social work would do by abandoning use of DSM, would be to place itself outside the arena of contemporary mental health services. Lacking familiarity with DSM, social workers would effectively sever their partnership with other mental health professionals. They would become out of step with the vast health and human services enterprise, which, for better or worse, is thriving today. Instead, social workers should master use of DSM and other psychiatric references.

Social work should provide expertise in the use of DSM. It is vitally important that social work not relinquish its leadership role in mental health and human services because social work has so much to offer these still-emerging fields. Social work brings a special perspective to psychiatric issues, and that perspective must continue to be represented in the development of mental health services. In direct practice in both public and private sectors, social workers supervising other counselors, health workers, and paraprofessionals need expertise in problem assessment and diagnosis and must be able to guide and train others in the appropriate use of classification systems. As advocates, social workers should be able to critique and challenge inaccurate evaluations where sufficient evidence is lacking for diagnostic conclusions offered.

Social workers are often placed in an adversarial position in traditional public social work practice in child welfare and in mental health. Often evaluations are contested. Where social workers are expert in the tools of diagnosis, they can guide the process of evaluation with respect to client strengths and with awareness of the limitations of decision making based on diagnosis. Social workers can then be effective advocates for comprehensive evaluation, of which diagnosis of psychopathology is merely a part.

In accepting a large role in the health and human services and a clinically astute role in the social services, social work can continue to pull the professional perspective away from its emphasis on pathology and toward a holistic or ecologic approach, which is consistent with social work's view of human behavior. Whether from a psychopathological or an ecological perspective, however, or whether from a psychodynamic or behavioral orientation, social workers cannot avoid the task of problem identification or diagnosis in their work with individuals any more than they can in work with communities. Other efforts to develop problem classification systems for social workers are in progress (Karls & Wandrei, 1988). However, changes in language and a focus on roles rather than personality, will not alter the fact that some social work aims to help the individual, and, inevitably, must assess his weaknesses, or, as an esteemed colleague refers to them, his challenges, as well as his strengths. What social work has struggled to do, consistently and historically, is to maintain a rightful balance between the two. This has generally meant highlighting strengths when prevailing sentiment has always preferred to focus on faults (Lewis, 1982; Tolson, 1988).

Social workers are best prepared to offer leadership in health, mental health, and human services when they are fluent in both the analysis of psychosocial pathology and the assessment of personal assets and competencies. Clearly, the DSM can assist with these tasks. For environmental impact assessment, social work should accept the challenge to create a needed model. Dwelling on diagnosis of pathology or etiology or personality characteristics is not social work's preference. Working together with a client, helping him or her develop strategies for problem resolution or practice new ways of coping with difficult conditions and situations is social work's typical emphasis. Current empowerment approaches modernize this traditional conception (Cohen, 1989; Heger & Hunzeker, 1988).

Problems of Misuse and Error with DSM

Misuse of the DSM and errors in diagnosis have been identified as problems and are, in part, what make use of the DSM controversial (Kirk & Kutchins, 1988). Labeling a client by diagnosis can be damaging to the client's self esteem and potentially harmful to his or her reputation. Basing decisions on insufficiently supported evaluations should be considered irresponsible practice. Misuse of diagnostic information is a practice error that can be corrected with clinical supervision in agency-based social work. Responsible assessment should protect the client from unnecessary intervention, inappropriate treatment, or disruptive family or individual dispositions. The DSM demands substantial evidence for diagnosis and includes only those observable indicators that have some reliability (Klerman, et al., 1984). This conservative approach to diagnosis should protect the client against overdiagnosis.

Error in diagnosis can lead to serious treatment errors and harm to the client. Often quick diagnostic impressions lead to routine or standard treatment recommendations. The use of medications for various emotional problems is one area of great potential harm to clients, yet it is often not challenged by social workers. It is not unusual to find antidepressants, for example, prescribed to clients without adequate assessment of psychosocial issues. By demanding full assessment of all contributing variables in the life of the client before medication is offered, social workers can prevent the proliferation of radical pharmacotherapy. Cohen (1988) has challenged the mental health field on its overreliance on medications for the chronic mentally ill. For all presenting problems, the DSM tends to support psychosocial treatment approaches and is an asset to social work clinicians in this regard.

Recognizing the inherent problems of diagnosis and the weaknesses of any classification system, social workers must be willing and able to debate and challenge diagnostic inferences of others when working in interdisciplinary practice or involved in an adversarial process. That is, social workers must foster accountability for responsible assessment among colleagues as well as with adversaries. DSM is clear and manageable for this purpose. It is likely that clinicians will find classifications in DSM that do not hold up as valid. This is not a weakness of the effort to classify. In effect, this psychiatric guide is continuously open to test and revision, and that openness bodes more favorably for the client than a less empirical, more dogmatic nomenclature system would.

The DSM can help nonmedical clinicians avoid the errors of psychologizing conditions that have a physical or organic element. Social work is well-suited to the task of comprehensive assessment of individual distress because it has never been narrowly invested in either organic or intrapsychic causality. Social work's more comprehensive, holistic approach has traditionally recognized the importance of physical and environmental health on personal well-being as well as the psychologic motivations and adaptive value of deviant behavior. Personal distress, in the social work view, is a consequence not only of personal variables but also of external social and economic contingencies.

Social workers in health and mental health can work together with their clients, using DSM, to demystify psychiatric diagnosis and psychiatric treatment. Behavioral indicators can be confirmed by the client, evaluations can be reviewed and revised with client participation, reporting of diagnoses can become matters of consent and dispute. Where illness is experienced by the client, explanation should not in itself be threatening when the overall approach is to refuse to define the clients by their illnesses. Thus, responsible use of diagnostic tools includes the participation of the client and should not be limited to mere consent.

In summary, DSM can aid social work practice inasmuch as it 1) refines classification of clinically observed behavioral syndromes and provides a shared language among helping disciplines; 2) provides a more rational system of problem-identification than clinician impressions, which are subject to numerous kinds of biases; and 3) requires substantial behavioral evidence for any diagnostic conclusion, and supports a comprehensive psychosocial and medical assessment process that can help to thwart the application of quick fixes. DSM is organized in such a way that psychiatric diagnosis can be made accessible to the client as well as to nonmedical clinicians.

Finally, the normative quality of the question addressed here requires the proposal of a principle for practice. The principle should assist decision making in the use of analytic tools and other technologic resources in practice plans and interventions. Kutchins and Kirk (1988) rightly advance the ethical concern that the tool or technology not harm the client. Social work without use of technology can harm clients, however. The best practice is for the expert and the client to use the tools of the trade together. A negotiated interpretation of distress can be most helpful in the long run. Our clients expect and deserve expertise, but ultimately they are their own agents of change.

REFERENCES

American Psychiatric Association. (1987). *Diagnostic and Statistical Manual of Mental Disorders*, ed 3. (Rev.) Washington, D.C.:

Cohen, M.B. (1989). Social work practice with homeless mentally ill people: Engaging the client. *Social Work*, 34, 505–509.

Cohen, D. (1988). Social work and psychotropic drug treatments. *Social Service Review*, 62(4), 576–599.

Hegar, R.L., & Hunzeker, J.M. (1988). Moving toward empowerment-based practice in public child welfare. *Social Work*, 33(6), 499–502.

Karls, J.M., & Wandrei, K.E. (1988). "Person-in-environment: A system for describing, classifying, and coding problems of social functioning." Unpublished manuscript.

Kirk, S.A., & Kutchins, H. (1988). Deliberate misdiagnosis in mental health practice. *Social Service Review*, 62(2), 225–237.

Klerman, G.L., Vaillant, G.E., Spitzer, R.L., Michels, R. (1984). A debate on DSM-III. *American Journal of Psychiatry*, 141(4), 539–553.

Kutchins, H., & Kirk, S.A. (1988). The business of diagnosis: DSM-III and clinical social work. *Social Work,* 33(3), 215–220.

Lewis, H. (1982). *The intellectual base of social work practice.* New York: Haworth Press.

Millon, T., & Klerman, G. (Eds.). (1986). *Contemporary directions in psychopathology: Toward the DSM-IV.* New York: Guilford.

Tolson, E.R. (1988). *The metamodel and clinical social work.* New York: Columbia University Press.

Rejoinder to Anello

STUART A. KIRK AND
HERB KUTCHINS

Anello has the difficult task of defending the use of DSM by social workers. It is so difficult, in fact, that she distorts the nature and actual uses of DSM in order to make her case. Anello's argument is an example that illustrates how common it is for social workers and others to misinterpret DSM in order to transform it into something they would like it to be. For example, she falls quickly into making invalid assertions about the manual. In the first paragraph alone she makes the following incorrect statements: that DSM describes "mental and emotional deterioration;" is revised each year; provides "some statistical data to place behavioral syndromes into perspective within the landscape of mental and emotional life" (whatever that means); and permits the clinician to form hypotheses to explain behavior. Inaccurate observations such as these occur throughout her statement, but space prohibits us from pointing out all of them.

Because our statement addressed some of her arguments, we do not need to comment further on them. She makes other assertions about the potential misuses of DSM with which we are in agreement. However, her statement raises four issues that deserve brief comment.

First, she confuses diagnosis with both social work assessment and with problem identification. Diagnosis, according to DSM, is the placement of a "mental disorder" that exists "within the person" into one of 200 disease categories. This is not the same as social work assessment, although some practitioners argue that it sometimes is a small, technical part of it. Similarly, psychiatric diagnosis is not the same as problem identification, because the latter almost always entails the assessment of interpersonal and contextual resources—factors excluded from the purview of DSM.

Second, she weakens her case by arguing that DSM should be used because it is an established reference manual. Her belief that it should be approved because of its widespread acceptance is a dangerous position.

Many activities and technologies are available that should be resisted. In 1486, an important text of the Inquisition, the *Malleus Malleficarum*, was published. It contained the symptoms and methods for identifying and persecuting witches. The *Malleus* was a universally accepted reference manual that was considered to be infallible: in those early days of printing, it was a bestseller. If we keep the example of the *Malleus* in mind, judgements about the value of a diagnostic manual for clients should be distinct from its availability and its widespread acceptance.

Third, Annello argues that problem identification and treatment should involve the active participation of clients. We agree that this is a worthy objective in social work practice. We see no evidence, however, that DSM facilitates this collaboration. In fact, data from our earlier study indicate that few clinicians use DSM for this purpose. Moreover, the very structure of psychiatric diagnosis presents formidable barriers to mutual collaboration. Imagine, for a moment, a client who believes that he or she is the messiah, among other beliefs and behaviors. How does a mental health worker collaborate with him about a DSM diagnosis? Do they sit together thumbing through the big manual scanning the diagnostic criteria to find the set on which they both agree? Do they decide whether his delusions are symptoms of schizophrenia, paranoid type, or delusional disorder, grandiose type? Do client and worker negotiate the official disorder?

Finally, one of Anello's best arguments for learning about DSM—one that we failed to recognize in our statement—is to advocate on behalf of clients who are victims of misdiagnoses. We are unable to counter this argument. Accurate knowledge about DSM allows social workers to identify when a DSM diagnosis is insufficient for social work purposes, how clients can be harmed, and why it is an inappropriate tool for our profession. Solely for these reasons, DSM deserves to be used by social workers.

NO

STUART A. KIRK AND HERB KUTCHINS

Five Arguments for Using DSM-III-R and Why They Are Wrong

Psychiatry has entered social work like an invading army, bringing with it as its major weapon the DSM-III-R with its enforced official language, strict customs, and world view. Social work as a profession has responded to the intrusion in two ways: one has been to ignore the invasion and treat it as a transitory event with no long-term implications for the profession; the other has been to accept the incursion as a benefit that somehow strengthens the profession and improves practice. We view DSM-III-R from neither of these perspectives. We argue that the infiltration is neither minor nor the the consequences salutary.

What Is DSM-III-R?

The Diagnostic and Statistical Manual, Third Edition, Revised, or DSM-III-R for short, is a 500-page book published by the American Psychiatric Association (APA, 1987). The first edition, DSM-I, was published in 1952; the second, DSM-II, appeared in 1968; and the third, DSM-III, was produced with great publicity in 1980. A revision of the third edition, DSM-III-R, was distributed in 1987. The fourth edition, DSM-IV, is due in the early 1990s. With each new version there has been a substantial increase in the number of diagnoses, from 60 in 1952 to more than 200 in 1987, and more categories are under consideration for the next edition. Like the latest model car, the manual may be purchased with a vast array of accessories: casebooks, tape cassettes, mini-manuals, workshops, interview protocols, and computer programs. The third and later versions have been runaway best sellers among mental health professionals, adding considerably to the influence and coffers of the American Psychiatric Association.

The title of DSM is a misnomer; there is nothing statistical about the manual. The book is a compendium of more than 200 officially approved diagnoses of mental disorders, including well-known entries such as schizophrenia, obsessive-compulsive disorder, and posttraumatic stress disorder, as well as rather unusual ones, such as frotteurism and trichotillomania, and some very controversial ones such as self-defeating personality disorder, postluteal phase dysphoric disorder (commonly referred to as PMS), and oppositional-defiant disorder. Every entry is accompanied by a list of criteria that describes features thought to be associated with each diagnosis. These criteria are to be used in reaching a diagnostic decision. Every category is assigned a five digit code number (e.g., 295.70 for schizoaffective disorder) that has very little substantive or numerical significance, although it conveys an unwarranted image of precision and "statistics." The numbers are merely used to refer to mental illnesses listed in a medical handbook, the *International Classification of Diseases*. The same impression about statistical precision might be conveyed if you were gullible enough to believe that your social security number captured something terribly precise and unique about your personality because it contained nine digits.

How Is Social Work Involved?

Why should social workers be concerned about an ever-expanding list of categories that are called "mental disorders"? There are three reasons why the DSM obsession with codes and categories should not be ignored.

The first is because DSM embodies a particular viewpoint emanating from one professional organization, the American Psychiatric Association, that is being mandated by insurance companies, mental health agencies, and other organizations for use by all mental health workers and clients. The field of mental health is broadly interdisciplinary, involving the activities of many social workers, clinical psychologists, psychiatric nurses, rehabilitation counselors, marriage and family counselors, and others. Although a few social workers, psychologists, nurses, and other mental health professionals participated in advisory committees, only psychiatrists associated with the American Psychiatric Association had decision-making authority in the adoption of DSM. Social work has a viewpoint that is different than psychiatry's regarding mental health problems, a perspective that is much more focused on interpersonal relationships and social conditions (Kirk, Siporin & Kutchins, 1989). Despite claims to the contrary, the social work approach has not been incorporated into DSM-III-R.

The second reason to be concerned stems directly from the first. The viewpoint expressed is that a wide array of human problems should be conceptualized as mental disorders, a subset of medical illnesses. Those who developed DSM were explicit about this controversial point. How is it, you might ask, that being a transvestite (302.30 Transvestic fetishism) or a child's difficulty with arithmetic (315.50 Developmental arithmetic disorder) are illnesses, not simply unusual or devalued behaviors? These are very complex issues about which there are many different viewpoints within psychiatry and among the mental health professions (Wakefield, 1989a; Wakefield, 1989b). Many people have raised significant questions about the medicalization of human problems. DSM obscures that controversy and those complexities by presenting an impression of consensus where it does not exist.

Third, the imperialistic tendencies represented by DSM should concern us because psychiatry has not been known historically to be especially benevolent, particularly to racial minorities, women, and others whom society devalues. Psychiatric diagnoses here and abroad have been used to justify slavery, demean women, strip people of their civil rights, imprison political dissidents, force sterilization, promote punitive electroshock treatment, rationalize brutal brain surgery, and abet genocide. The repeated use of psychiatric diagnoses for nontherapeutic, oppressive purposes forces us to consider carefully and critically psychiatry's attempt to create new diagnostic categories and claim an ever-expanding jurisdiction over community life and personal troubles.

More social workers are employed in the mental health field than any other professional group. Furthermore, mental health is the single most common field of practice among social workers. What happens in the mental health field, consequently, is profoundly important to social work. The use of DSM-III-R is required by almost all service providers and funding sources in the field. Its use is frequently required not only for psychiatrists, but also for all the other mental health professions, including social work. Thus, whether they want to or not, whether they find it useful or not, whether they accept its premises or not, whether they wish to label people or not, social workers find themselves involved with DSM,

The Flawed Arguments for Using DSM

Five arguments can be offered as reasons why social workers should embrace DSM. All are unconvincing.

DSM Is a Product of Scientific Research

The developers of DSM convey the impression that the classification system was based on the best available research, but many of the categories and much of the diagnostic system are far from scientifically grounded. There are many explanations for this failure. A major reason is that our knowledge of mental problems is very incomplete. An effective classification system would be based on known causes or on effective differential treatment. DSM is based on neither because there is a paucity of information about the causes of many mental problems or about their effective treatment. Even in the manual, this deficiency is acknowledged, "for most DSM-III-R disorders . . . the etiology is unknown" (APA, 1987:xxiii).

Although the developers of the manual deny it, DSM is a classification system that assumes operationally that people either have or do not have a disorder. This is a very crude approach to understanding people, and by its very nature it ignores the complexity of human behavior and cognition that can best be described and studied along continua. People vary in the extent to which they feel depressed, anxious, or unsocial. Referring to some as suffering from anxiety disorder or as having an antisocial personality disorder ignores the range of human emotions and behavior. This categorical approach to labeling people is one of the reasons that the validity of many of DSM's 200 plus disorders is questionable. Moreover, the ability of clinicians to use the classification consistently, i.e., reliably, has been seriously questioned. There is almost no scientifically adequate evidence that most of the specific diagnoses can be used accurately. In fact, when DSM-III was published in 1980, no evidence about reliability was offered for 80 percent of the specific diagnoses included in the manual, and the reliability for most of the major classes of disorders was not very good (Kutchins & Kirk, 1986).

The limited scientific grounding of the classification system has made decision-making about diagnostic categories vulnerable to political influence. Prior to the 1980 and 1987 editions, considerable political intrigue surrounded the decisions about the inclusion of homosexuality, tobacco dependence, neuroses, self-defeating personality disorder, and many other issues.

Currently, political battles are occurring over proposals for new diagnoses to be included in the next edition, such as victimization disorder, postabortion depression, and others. The argument that DSM is a product of science, not politics, is a claim most effectively made to the already convinced.

DSM Provides a Common Language among Mental Health Professionals

The essence of this argument is that somehow mental health professionals are having difficulty talking to each other and that DSM remedies this problem. In fact, mental health professionals are having little difficulty communicating; mental health journals are full of articles, national conferences are well attended and active, innumerable case conferences and staffings throughout the country are loaded with psychiatric talk. But what observation of all this communication will quickly reveal is that there is no common viewpoint about what are disorders, what causes them, or how they should be treated. Proponents of DSM attempt to short circuit these debates by suggesting that it is just a matter of everybody using the same diagnostic categories and language. This argument obscures the fact that categories and language are themselves the subject of some of the most intense and acrimonious debates. Witness, for example, the widely publicized debates about the inclusion of masochistic or self-defeating personality disorders.

Proponents say, however, that scientists and researchers need a common category system so that they can advance knowledge by making certain that investigators in different geographical areas are studying the same problems. This is a legitimate concern in all scientific endeavors and goes to the heart of the scientific reliability of DSM. There is evidence that practitioners may not be using DSM reliably, and that, even among skilled researchers trying to apply DSM consistently, its ambiguities can undermine its reliability (Winokur, Zimmerman & Cadoret, 1989). Many researchers, particularly in psychology, believe that the categorical system itself, as opposed to a dimensional one, is an enormous hindrance to communication and understanding of human behavior (Eysenck, 1986).

DSM Represents a Comprehensive Approach to Psychosocial Assessment

This claim usually refers to the fact that DSM is "multi-axial" (Williams, 1982). It has five axes: 1) a list of "clinical conditions" (a concept that is not defined or explained anywhere in the manual); 2) a list of developmental and personality disorders; 3) physical disorders; 4) a one-digit numerical rating of social stressors; and 5) another numerical score that represents a global assessment of functioning. Only the first three axes are part of the "official" system. Surveys of practitioners have found that most do not use axis four or five, the only two axes that might give the DSM some dimensionality, because the first three axes are merely lists of disorders.

But even if clinicians faithfully used axes four and five, they have serious shortcomings. For instance, single numerical ratings of stressors or single numerical ratings of social or psychological functioning hardly qualify as a comprehensive psychosocial assessment. There is no place in the DSM for an assessment of coping capacities, of social networks, of family strengths, of intergenerational ties, of community resources, and so forth. Proponents of DSM quickly and correctly point out that DSM was never intended to include those factors. This is precisely why DSM is inadequate for use by social workers! It does not concern itself with those domains of human functioning that are the sine qua non of social work.

Using DSM Will Lead to More Effective Social Work Treatment

In many respects, this argument is the most important claim that proponents could make—that using DSM helps clients. To our knowledge, no one has attempted to make this argument, and for good reason—there is no evidence that it is true. There is, however, some indirect evidence that it is false. In a recent survey of social work practitioners who use DSM, many indicated that using DSM was not helpful in treatment planning or in accurately reflecting clients' problems (Kutchins & Kirk, 1988). Most social workers see DSM-III-R as an administrative hurdle that must be jumped before they can work with clients.

Social Workers Need to Use DSM Because It Is the Basis for Reimbursement for Services

Failing to persuade social workers that DSM helps clients, some proponents argue that at least DSM helps clinicians to get paid. This argument has two intriguing implications. The first is that financial reimbursement systems that are themselves the result of political battles among insurance companies, government bureaucrats, political ideologists, and professional lobbyists should determine how we label people and their problems. This contradicts the first argument by appearing to elevate political deal making or financial self-interest above judgments about the validity of mental or behavioral problems. By doing so, it appears to imply that the other rationalizations for using DSM are just that—rationalizations, offered to dress up money grubbing and parade it around as scientific practice. Unfortunately, there is considerable evidence that this occurs and on a broad scale. Practitioners routinely report that they use DSM for reimbursement and for not much more (Kutchins & Kirk, 1988). More troubling is the evidence that they deliberately use inaccurate diagnostic labels for clients to gain reimbursements (Kirk & Kutchins, 1988). There are many other ways to finance social services that do not depend on claims about specific mental disorders. For example, people can receive the services they need as an entitlement of citizenship, or practitioners can be paid for services rendered to clients. Labeling people as mentally disordered is not necessary for helping clients or financing care. Thus, DSM seriously distorts professional practice, jeopardizes clients, and leads to practices that are at best unethical, and at times, illegal.

Conclusion

The popularity of DSM-III-R is part of its danger. More effort has been made to develop this edition of the manual than its predecessors. Its prominence and institutionalization, however, have created a situation where there is little tolerance for deviation and almost no room for the development of alternative approaches that would be inconsistent with DSM-III-R. Its control over the definition of mental disorder is complete. Like a country where an army of occupation has been in place for over a decade, the people forget that life could be different. It is this effective and narrow control of the mental health field that in the long run will prove detrimental to social work and its historic concerns about clients.

How did social work allow DSM to infiltrate its professional domain without the social work profession critically examining its implications? Professional leaders may have been busy, attending to other problems, or simply uncritically accepting of the arguments of the proponents. Most likely, social work leaders simply did not know what to make of the DSM blitzkrieg or whether the compendium of codes and categories might not be good for social work because it, like psychiatry, is a profession hungry for a scientific base or at least the appearance of one. It has been 10 years, however, since the appearance of DSM-III, and there has been an outpouring of articles, books, and research in the fields of psychiatry and psychology that indicates many of its limitations. Inattention is no longer an adequate excuse for ignoring the flaws in the arguments for adoption of DSM by the social work profession. Our argument is that there is not evidence that it is good for clients and that the appropriate response for the social work profession is not to use it.

REFERENCES

American Psychiatric Association. (1987). *The Diagnostic and Statistical Manual of Mental Disorders,* ed. 3. Revised. Washington, D.C.: American Psychiatric Association.
Eysenck, H.J. (1986). A Critique of Contemporary Classification and Diagnosis. In Millon, T., & Klerman, G. (Eds.). *Contemporary Directions in Psychopathology.* New York: Guilford, pp. 73–98.
Kirk, S., & H. Kutchins (1988). *Deliberate Misdiagnosis in Mental Health Practice.* Social Service Review, 62 (2), pp. 225–237.
Kirk, S., Siporin, M., & Kutchins, H. (1989). The Prognosis for Social Work Diagnosis. *Social Casework,* 70 (5), 295–304.

Kutchins, H., & S. Kirk (1986). The Reliability of DSM-III: A Critical Review. *Social Work Research & Abstracts,* 22 (4), 3–12.

Kutchins, H., & S. Kirk (1988). The Business of Diagnosis: DSM-III and Clinical Social Work. *Social Work,* 33 (3), 215–220.

Wakefield, J. (1989a). "Disorder as Dysfunction: A Conceptual Critique of DSM-III-R's Definition of Mental Disorder." Forthcoming.

Wakefield, J. (1989b). "Diagnosing Psychodiagnosis: Social Control and the Concept of Mental Disorder." Forthcoming.

Williams, J. (1982). DSM-III: A Comprehensive Approach to Diagnosis. *Social Work,* 26, 101–106.

Winokur, G., Zimmerman, M., & Cadoret, R. (1989). 'Cause the Bible Tells Me So. *Archives of General Psychiatry,* 45, 683–684.

ANNOTATED BIBLIOGRAPHY

Faust, D., & Miner, R.A. (1986). The Empiricist and His New Clothes: DSM-III in Perspective. *American Journal of Psychiatry,* 143, 962–967

A theoretic and philosophic examination of whether the King is properly attired.

Kohn, A. (1989). Suffer the Restless Children. *The Atlantic Monthly,* November, 90–100

Nearly a million children are regularly given drugs to treat "hyperactivity," one of a number of DSM categories that masks our ignorance about the definition, causes, or treatment of something that may not even be a "disorder."

Millon, T., & Klerman, G. (Eds.). (1986). *Contemporary Directions in Psychopathology: Toward the DSM-IV.* New York: Guilford

This book, edited by two DSM insiders, contains many thoughtful articles pointing out the serious shortcomings of DSM-III as we march happily toward DSM-IV.

Mirowsky, J., & Ross, C.A. (1989). Psychiatric Diagnosis as Reified Measurement. *Journal of Health and Social Behavior,* 30, 11–25

Although DSM-III has been heralded as a breakthrough, these sociologists call for the abandonment of diagnosis for research on the nature, causes, and consequences of problematic behaviors.

Zimmerman, M. (1988). Why Are We Rushing to Publish DSM-IV? *Archives of General Psychiatry,* 45, 1135–1138

An insider who argues that rapidly revising the diagnostic manual every few years, although it may boost sales, does not allow enough time for researchers to develop the sound empirical base that could inform the revision process.

Rejoinder to Professors Kirk and Kutchins

ELIZABETH ANELLO

Professors Kirk and Kutchins argue that DSM is detrimental to social work. Their argument has three serious problems. First, they address some key issues for social work, but only indirectly, by griping about the diagnostic code. Second, they use their own survey data to support a single perspective, and this raises concerns about the use of research in practice. Third, their recommendation to abandon DSM would take social workers out of mental health practice.

Non-DSM Issues

There are four good issues raised by Kirk and Kutchins and they are only slightly related to the DSM manual. It may not be fair to place the weight of these issues on DSM. First, there is the issue of the economics of mental health care. The authors complain that psychiatry is invading social work turf. The fact is that social work is taking over some of psychiatry's work, in part because psychiatric care has become too costly. Psychiatrists would like to control diagnosis and limit social work's role (GAP, 1987), but social work is hardly a victim, as implied by the authors' invading army imagery. Inclusion in Medicare (NASW, 1990) and competitiveness with psychiatry (Fairbank, 1989; Haber and McCall, 1989) make clinical social work an important and economical provider of mental health care.

The authors refer to the medicalization of human problems without enlightening us. Some conditions benefit by a medical approach. With alcoholism and addiction, medicalization defuses the moral element of the problem and provides an acceptable explanation for the recovering person. Treatment of severe mental illness often relies on sedation and coercion rather than diagnosis and individualized planning. A medical approach stressing managing the disability rather than altering the personality can benefit many persons with mental disabilities. On the other hand, medicalization of the problems of children and adolescents overlooks environmental and developmental factors and should be strongly challenged by social work. These controversies are not obscured by DSM; on the contrary, the existence of a diagnostic code permits debate and reform.

The implication of an "official" classification system in mental health is that regulation of the practice becomes possible. Kirk and Kutchins deplore "enforced official language" explicit criteria, defined categories, and mandates in the provision of care. How then, are mental health consumers to protect themselves? Enforceable language is the stuff of civil rights and patients' rights and should not be shunned by social workers. Maltreated mental health consumers have clear definitions governing their diagnosis with DSM; the informed client will not permit misdiagnosis.

Related to the regulation of practice is the issue of clinician accountability to the client and to the community. Mechanisms of accountability are necessary to balance the practice of experts and the rights of citizens. The authors criticize labeling and shared guidelines, however, without explicit definitions and guidelines experts risk being a professional aristocracy. Social workers should support an accessible system of diagnosis and professional accountability to the client and the community of consumers and providers. Questions of professional oppression are directly related to accountability, but psychiatrists should not necessarily be singled out as the only offenders. All professionals are subject to the same highhandedness of the privileged and should welcome the means for accountability.

Research in Practice: Surveys, Tests, and Validity

Survey data, like psychological test data, have appropriate and limited uses in the practice of helping. Both can be interpreted in a variety of ways. The authors use their data from a mailed survey of clinical social workers (Kutchins and Kirk, 1988) to support an anti-DSM position. However, only 25 percent of their sample reported that they used DSM "almost daily" (p. 217) and most of the respondents' complaints centered on the inapplicability of DSM to marital and family problems. Social work is such a broad field that a single diagnostic tool is not expected to address all areas of practice. The value of DSM might be better explored with a larger sample of social workers who use DSM regularly.

There is support for DSM as a useful diagnostic tool in Kutchins and Kirk's study. Most social workers reported some importance of the DSM for case review (75%) and treatment planning (78%). Responses suggest that DSM is not the only assessment tool used, and that is wise. However, one third of the social workers sampled found the DSM important for treatment purposes, and that seems to be reasonable support. The authors make much of the reimbursement issue, but their conclusion that social workers use DSM for "not much more" is just not supported by their data. Also, reimbursement uses speak more to issues of accountability, which should be considered apart from treatment uses. The complaint that reimbursement is political is gratuitous; what is not political in the American human services? Given the looseness with which researchers sometimes interpret their data and draw conclusions, it may be preferable for social work research to present hard information and reasoned alternatives and to leave the moral debate to practitioners who are close to the action and its impacts. Confounding accountability with money grubbing is an example of questionable interpretations.

Kirk and Kutchins complain that DSM is not scientific. However social workers have always recognized the value of qualitative knowledge, clinical analysis, and case study. DSM is not statistical because of its code numbers. The statistical information in DSM is contained in references to prevalence rates of particular problems. DSM categories have some reliability because they represent observable behaviors and this descriptive approach may be more useful and protective of the client than the theoretical approach preferred by some of the helping disciplines. Validity of the diagnoses admittedly remains an open issue (Klerman, et al., 1984).

Book-Burning Is Not the Right Response

Professors Kirk and Kutchins offer a book burning response to DSM. It is difficult to understand what they are trying to say. Are social workers to abandon working with the mentally ill? Should they not do clinical work? Not diagnose? Abandon private practice? Not be accountable? The DSM is, after all, a book. Ultimately, no one is compelled to live by it or conform to it. As in all that is written, some of it is irrelevant and even silly. The point is to use what is helpful. If clinicians use it to rule out unsupportable hypotheses and rein in personal biases, it will benefit clients. Even better, if social workers use it together with clients, they may prevent some of the excesses of professional mental heath intervention.

REFERENCES

Fairbank, A. (1989). Expanding insurance coverage to alternative types of psychotherapies: Demand and substitution effects of direct reimbursement to social workers. *Inquiry*, 26(2), 170–181.
Group for the Advancement of Psychiatry (GAP). (1987). *Psychiatry and the mental health professions: New roles for changing times*. New York: Brunner/Mazel.
Haber, S., & McCall, N. (1989). Use of nonphysician providers in the Medicare program: Assessment of the direct reimbursement of clinical social workers demonstration project. *Inquiry*, 26(2), 158–169.
Kutchins, H., & Kirk, S. (1988). The business of diagnosis: DSM-III and clinical social work. *Social Work*, 33(3), 215–220.
Klerman, G.L., Vaillant, G.E., Spitzer, R.L., et al. A debate on DSM-III. *American Journal of Psychiatry*, 141(4), 539–553.
NASW News. (1990). *Push for Medicare payments, Title XX hike ends in victory*. Silver Spring, MD: National Association of Social Workers.

Should Social Workers Participate in Treatment Only if the Client Consents to Such Treatment Freely and without Coercion?

EDITOR'S NOTE: Early in their training, social work students are introduced to the fundamental values of their chosen field. Among the first and most celebrated of these is client self-determination. A logical corollary of this is the right of clients to refuse treatment. Many also say that client self-determination has a technological justification: a true helping relationship cannot develop when the client's participation occurs under duress. The fact is, however, that social workers often are asked or expected to work with clients under more or less coercive circumstances. Should they cooperate? That is the subject of this debate. It is introduced by two brief vignettes that both debaters use to illustrate their arguments.

Lynn Atkinson, Ph.D., answers the debate question YES. She is an Assistant Professor in the Sociology department of Oklahoma State University where she teaches social work and clinical sociology courses. Dr. Atkinson has spent several years working in the child welfare system. In addition to several articles and a book chapter dealing with human service policy, she is the author of *Power and Empowerment: The Power Principle* (Las Vegas: Falcon Press, 1988).

O. Dale Kunkel, DSM, argues the NO position. He is an Associate Professor at the Northeastern State University School of Social Work where he teaches social work and coordinates the field placement program. Dr. Kunkel has been a social worker in mental institutions, prisons, and drug and alcohol treatment for oil companies. His published works are concerned with behavioral therapy, sexuality, and child welfare.

Coercion and Chemical Dependency

Ken Willis is a 32-year-old skilled laborer in an oil refinery. His job involves responsibility for a number of routine but complex procedures involving toxic and highly explosive chemical compounds. He works on rotating shifts, and from week to week his work hours will be different. He has recently been experiencing severe marital problems, which have prompted him to request time off to deal with financial and legal problems occurring in the marriage.

On a Monday morning after a Friday on which Ken had asked to take a day off to deal with his bank on loan refinancing, Ken was involved in a minor spill of toxic chemicals. There were no injuries or significant damage to property resulting from this spill. However, the company has a policy that requires that those involved in all accidents due to human error submit to a drug test.

Three days later, Ken's drug test results are returned. He has been determined to be positive for marijuana. The company requires him to enter a 30-day drug rehabilitation program, to spend 1 year in aftercare, and to report monthly to the employee assistance office for monitoring for 1 year. He is further required to submit to drug testing on demand by the company as a condition of continued employment.

Ken maintains that he does not have a drug problem, that he rarely uses marijuana, and that current use is because of strain in the marriage and drug treatment is an unnecessary waste of time.

Coercion and Child Welfare

Ellen Washington is a 21-year-old single woman with two children. Ellen has a 4-year-old girl named Angela and a 2-year-old son named Derron. The two children have different fathers. Ellen was never married to either man, neither of them currently has any contact with the children, and neither of them provides any financial assistance to the children.

Ellen currently receives AFDC support for herself and her children. She has no other source of income and very little family support. Ellen was removed from her family of origin at age 15 because of parental abuse, and lived with three different foster families until she became pregnant the first time at age 16. She then lived briefly with Angela's father, who left 2 months after the child was born.

Ellen is currently working part time to complete her high school education. She has been dating a 26-year-old man, Everett, who spends two or three nights a week sleeping at Ellen's apartment.

A Head Start worker who works with Angela reported to the child welfare authorities that Angela reported that she sleeps with her mother and the boyfriend whenever he stays at the apartment. The child welfare worker interviewed Angela, Ellen, and Everett in response to the notification.

The investigation revealed that there had been no specific sexual contact between Angela and the adults. Ellen and Everett did sleep together naked, but Angela wore a nightgown when sleeping with them. Ellen and Everett did have sexual contact when Angela slept with them, but could not recall whether they had actually had intercourse while she was present. Angela was aware that sexual activity was going on, but indicated that she would rather sleep with the adults than in the room with her brother, who cries and is fitful at night.

The court determined on the basis of the investigation that Angela was at risk and removed her from the home to a foster care family. Ellen was required to attend sex education and parenting education classes as preconditions for having Angela returned to the home. She was also required to attend group therapy sessions for survivors of childhood incest, although she could not recall that she had been directly victimized sexually as a child.

YES

LYNN ATKINSON

The United States has long been hailed by its citizens as "the land of the free," the place where all individuals are entitled to their own beliefs, their own values, and their own lifestyles. Our right of freedom to control our own destinies without fear of governmental interference provides autonomy and security for ourselves and our families, promotes cultural variation and diversity in our society, and is what separates this country from the totalitarian regimes that rule a large portion of this world.

Social work as a profession recognizes and respects the freedom of the individual and the right of the individual to self-determination. The Code of Ethics of the National Association of Social Workers states, "The social worker should make every effort to foster maximum self-determination on the part of clients." In working with people, social workers must respect the right of individuals to choose their own life paths. Although a social worker may disagree with the choices or the values of a particular person, the social worker must respect that individual's right to believe and do as he or she wishes and honor that right by not forcing the person to do something that is against that person's will.

Freedom of choice for every individual should include a client's freedom to choose whether or not to engage in treatment. Coerced treatment is an infringement of the client's right to self-determination. It denies an individual control of his or her destiny and forces the individual to conform to a social worker's or a bureaucracy's idea of right and wrong. When we begin to "treat" or change individuals' views or ways of living without their consent, we move toward the horror of brainwashing or programming depicted in novels such as George Orwell's *1984*.

The tendency for coerced treatment to infringe on individual freedom is not the only problem associated with its use. Unfortunately, the grounds on which coerced treatment is ordered are very shaky and the results of the "treatment" are often ambiguous, if not detrimental, for the individual or family. Social workers often engage in coerced treatment for the wrong reasons. Rather than being the helpers they were meant to be, these social workers turn instead into psychoterrorists who are dreaded by the clients with whom they work.

The rest of this argument examines problems inherent in situations where coerced treatment occurs, using the opening case vignettes for illustrative purposes. The focus is on two areas of practice where coerced treatment is frequently an issue. These areas are child protective services and drug and alcohol treatment.

Grounds for Ordering Coerced Treatment Are Often Shaky

The mandate for coerced treatment often results from an investigation into the beliefs, values, and lifestyles of the individuals or families in question, as can be seen from both example vignettes. The point of this investigation is to uncover the facts regarding an individual's lifestyle and determine if this lifestyle meets the investigating agency's ideas of what constitutes appropriate behavior.

The results of these investigations are often based on fiction and unsupported assumptions in addition to facts. Rumor and innuendo, information from unreliable resources, and circumstantial evidence are used to build case investigations in coerced treatment situations (Szasz, 1963; Pride, 1986).

In addition, investigators often insert their own moralistic ideas as reasons for ordering coercive treatment. Persuasive arguments have been made (Pride, 1986) that coerced treatment is based on middle-class moralistic assumptions that do not allow for cultural diversity and that treatment models are based on a masculine ideology that does not lead to healthy psychological change for female clients.

Problems inherent in the child welfare system are a source of public concern. Mary Pride (1986) documents incompetency in the child welfare system and provides illustrations of children who are removed from their homes because the homes do not meet professional "experts' " ideas of how children should be raised. Anonymous phone calls are often accepted as basis for a child abuse or neglect case. Child protective service workers would rather err on "the side of the child" than leave a child in a possibly harmful situation.

The vignette on Ellen Washington and her daughter, Angela, is a case in point. In this situation, the results of the investigation are ambiguous. There is no evidence of incest or child molestation, yet in order to err on the side of the child, Angela is whisked away to a foster home until her mother can fulfill agency requirements, which may or may not change the conditions that resulted in Angela's removal. Angela crawled in bed with the adults in order to be able to sleep. Will she be more secure in a foster home with strangers whom she may or may not be able to trust? How will Angela interpret the fact that she was removed from her home because she crawled into bed with her mother?

Drug and alcohol treatment is also mandated based on ambiguous evidence and moralistic assumptions. In the case vignette, Ken Willis is ordered to participate in a 30-day treatment program and 1 year of aftercare in order to keep his job. From the investigation, it is not clear that the minor toxic chemical spill resulted from use of marijuana. It could just as easily have resulted from the emotional strain associated with his failing marriage.

Only a single drug test was used to determine that Ken had an addiction problem. The reliability of specific drug tests varies greatly based on the test used. The whole idea of drug testing still remains controversial. In addition, marijuana is not a physically addictive drug. It is possible for Ken to have used it without developing an addiction. Yet, a single drug test is used to prove that Ken is a liar when he states that he does not have a drug problem and to justify 1 year of coercive treatment to cure this problem.

Results of Treatment Are Often Ambiguous or Detrimental

Not only are the reasons for coercing treatment shaky, the treatment that is ordered to deal with inappropriate values or behavior is oftentimes ineffective, inappropriate for the problem at hand, or damaging to the individual and his or her family. Those providing treatment in coerced treatment situations are often not trained for their jobs and may only possess a high school or college degree. They may not know what proper treatment is or be able to provide it. One of the most important predictors of change while in treatment is the person's desire for change. Those coerced into treatment may not wish to change their behavior, and chances are the treatment will be ineffective. In addition, coerced treatment may often be harmful. "Solomon's Choice" documents the harm many families suffer when they came under the domain of the child welfare system. Drug users and alcoholics have made their connections for continued drug use through treatment centers designed to stop the drug use.

In the case vignette regarding Ellen, she is ordered to attend group therapy sessions for survivors of childhood incest although she could not recall being victimized as a child. Not only does this appear to be an inappropriate referral for Ellen, it subjects other members of the group to a sort of voyeurism as Ellen listens to their problems and situations. Angela's removal to a foster home is drastic in light of the circumstances. Is this the best situation the worker could arrive at? The worker could have asked the family to alter their disturbing sleeping arrangements. If faced with a choice of altering the sleeping arrangement or having Angela placed in foster care, Ellen may have chosen to change the sleeping arrangements, thus ending the disturbing behavior. Angela's removal from the home is certainly harmful to the family, shattering the beliefs that both Ellen and Angela may have held about their control over their destinies and alleviating their faith in a system meant to protect them.

In the situation with Ken Willis, the coerced treatment may also be inappropriate and ineffective. If the problems are indeed a result of the marital strain, marital counseling might be more effective than drug treatment. Again, marijuana is not physically addictive. Time in a treatment center may very well be wasted time. Furthermore, 30-day in-patient treatment is unlikely to reduce the strain in Ken's marriage, and may in fact increase it.

Other Problems with Coerced Treatment

In addition to the infringement on individual rights and the problems associated with both investigations and treatment in a situation of coerced treatment, there are other ethical concerns a social worker should consider before engaging in coerced treatment. One of the problems with treating the individual is that this ignores the social conditions that work to create a social problem in the first place. Both child neglect and abuse and drug and alcohol problems correlate with poverty, unemployment, environmental stress, and other social conditions. Focusing on the individual does not eradicate the conditions that bring about these social problems. Perhaps a worker's attention would be better focused on changing the societal conditions that bring about the problem rather than the individual behavior that is the result.

Coerced treatment services, including child protective services and drug and alcohol services, continue to grow drastically both in number of cases and in cost of services. If these services are effective, then why do the problems continue to grow? Bureaucracies do not wish to work themselves out of existence; they therefore create new cases to treat. In addition, profits for bureaucrats engaging in coerced treatment continue to grow. These factors may be as important as the needs of a client when treatment becomes coerced. Bureaucracies are not likely to say that a client does not need their services.

There are many problems and ethical dilemmas faced by the social worker when dealing with issues of coerced treatment. Because of these problems a social worker should not engage a client in treatment without his or her consent.

Annotated Bibliography

Fabumni, C., Frederick, L., & Jarvis, M. (1985). The codependency trap. Unpublished forum first presented at the National Association For Rights Protection, University of Minnesota

Challenges the concept of codependency and the male models that are used in treatment of alcoholism and drug addiction.

Maeder, T. (1989). Wounded healers. *Atlantic Monthly, 263*, 37–47

Discusses the fact that a large proportion of those in the helping professions are emotionally unstable. They may, in fact, have as many problems as those clients they are trying to treat.

Pride, M. (1986). *The child abuse industry*. Westchester, IL: Crossways Book

Argues the case that the child welfare system does not protect those children who are in danger of abuse but instead enforces a moralistic upper-middle class code of parenting on all of society.

Szasz, T. (1963). *Law, liberty, and psychiatry*. New York: Collier Books

Argues that psychiatry is a form of social engineering.

Zegart, D., & Pedrick, L. (1989). Solomon's choice. *Ms.*, 78–83

Documents some mistakes made by child welfare workers investigating abuse and the devastating effect this has on the families involved.

Rejoinder to Professor Atkinson   O. DALE KUNKEL

The arguments presented against social work involvement in coercive treatment are essentially a manifesto for libertarianism. This argument denies the existence of rights for the society in general. In so doing, the author guarantees the destruction of the liberty and security she professes to advocate. Without an orderly society, the security of all individuals is forfeited.

The argument is made that social workers must respect the client's right to choose his or her own path. Yes, within limits. The right to endanger others through the use of an illegal drug? Society and common sense say no. The right to perpetuate a pattern of failed family functioning, and in the process risk exposure of a child to abuse, incest, and neglect? We passed that point in social responsibility decades ago! Common sense and common decency suggest that Ellen's child deserves the chance to escape a cycle of poverty and neglect that have engulfed the mother.

Is there, as Dr. Atkinson says, a social idea of right and wrong at work here? Indeed there is. She advocates the unbridled exercise of personal freedom as "right." I would suggest that such a notion is doomed, and terrifying should it exist. If the "male, middle class" morality she decries is opposed to use of illegal drugs by persons in safety-sensitive positions and opposed to reckless exposure of preschool children to abuse and minimal standards of care, I guess I can live with that. Dr. Atkinson might be well advised to consider the difference between freedom and license in human behavior.

Another point worth considering is the myth of self referral as a criterion for therapeutic success. Current reports from a number of drug treatment programs indicate that "coerced" patients directed to treatment by courts or employers do as well or better in recovery than those who waited and suffered through the traditional "bottoming out" process. The argument that marijuana is nonaddictive is fatuous, if familiar. Most drug counselors recognize it as a common part of the pathologic denial process.

Dr. Atkinson errs in another regard. Anonymous calls may prompt an investigation by child welfare, but rumors alone do not form a basis for action such as removal of a child from the home. Again, this is the sort of response one gets often from clients who seem more animated in assailing a child protective worker than they are in caring for the child.

Now for psychoterrorism. In my dictionary, terrorism is defined as acts of violence perpetuated for purposes of intimidation. The point of treatment is not terror. It is rehabilitation of behavior deemed dysfunctional. Yes, society has a voice in making that determination. Yes, social work has a role in providing services aimed at rehabilitation. Yes, it is a value laden process.

I give an emphatic No, however, to the notion that we can simply abdicate our role if we are not embraced and appreciated by the client. We will encounter resistance, hostility, even hatred from clients at times. But when the client's functioning is manifestly impaired or when it overtly presents a threat to others in the society, there is a social responsibility to intervene. By continuing to function as if there is no social ethic guiding our professional intervention, we refuse to act responsibly in developing a code of ethics that grapples honestly with practice realities. By refusing to codify those principles, we leave the clients more, not less, at the mercy of the individual worker's values and agency policies. The path forward is the recognition of the fact that anomie represents as much a threat to freedom as does regulation. We might all consider more deeply those sections of the code of ethics ignored by Dr. Atkinson and examine our role in light of our responsibility to society as well as the individual.

NO

O. DALE KUNKEL

The question of whether social workers should be involved in the treatment of involuntary clients is an academic issue at best. In reality, social workers are daily in the business of treating clients in circumstances that can only be described as coercive. If we did not do so, the social work profession would be a greatly diminished enterprise, if it would exist at all. Moreover, if all such interventions ceased, society would be deprived of a powerful and humane resource for promoting the general welfare.

Whenever clients are coerced into treatment, it is invariably because they have come into conflict with some social agency that finds their behavior threatening. This social perception is certainly not always right, but it is most definitely a proper function of society and its agents to attempt to regulate social behavior in the collective interest. Social work and the social welfare institution are among those agents of society that share in this regulatory and rehabilitative mandate. This is a role that every social worker accepts when he or she takes a job in child welfare, a juvenile office, a corrections program, an employee assistance program, and any of a host of other settings. Perhaps only the private practice segment of the profession escapes this charge, and even here a significant number of clients come to treatment on court-ordered diversion programs or in hopes of mitigating criminal or civil matters pending in court.

Perry London made the point 25 years ago that all of psychotherapy is at base a moral proposition. Many therapists, however, either do not recognize or will not acknowledge the moral foundations of the clinical relationship. We make judgments about what behavior is good or bad, except that currently we call those behaviors "functional," "appropriate" or healthy." The effect is the same. The approval of the therapist is given or withheld contingent upon the meeting of some standard. In this way, the therapist is the agent of society. The therapist serves to convey a sense of those behaviors that society regards as good or bad and helps the client modify those behaviors that have served to bring him or her into conflict with some segment of the larger society.

In order to frame this discussion, let us consider the moralistic, pragmatic, and technical issues involved in coercive treatment. Let us begin with three propositions:

1. Society has the right and the duty to defend itself against deviant acts that threaten the social order. Without such power, the result is anarchy.
2. Because society will and must address deviance if social workers will not be a part of that process, something worse may take its place.
3. The techniques of behavior change are increasingly effective and can serve to improve the lives of even those clients who at the time of treatment do not consent to treatment.

Let us now look at each of these points in detail.

The Morality of Coercion

Social workers, indeed all the therapeutic professions, speak to the tensions between the individual and society. Individuals do not exist in a vacuum. The mandate for social work practice is not a mandate for unlicensed individualism. Extreme examples make the point. Murder, rape, assault, robbery, and the like will provoke a societal response. Once upon a time, just as surely, homosexuality, promiscuity, drunkenness, and blasphemy would do the same. Times have changed. The question is not whether society should respond, but when. When is a behavior so outrageous to the common sensibility that society may justly determine it to be a threat? Second, how should society seek to address the deviant?

I would argue that society has a moral right to sanction deviance. In fact, it would be immoral not to address the deviant act. That is part of the social contract. This is not a Rousseauvian perspective, however. Just as an effective parent does not allow a developing child unbridled freedom, so the social contract must define the mutual limits on society and the individual. The definitions of social tolerance will be in constant flux, but those definitions are the living membrane that both joins and separates the individual and society.

Social workers are agents of society as surely as they are agents for their clients. We might briefly consider the NASW Code of Ethics on this point. Section II-F of the code states that, "The social worker's primary responsibility is to the clients." Section II-G goes on to say that "The social worker should make every effort to foster self-determination for the clients." It is interesting to note that every subsection of the code in this area goes on to discuss the legal processes that may abridge the client's right to self-determination.

Section VI-P of the code concludes with the general proposition that "the social worker should promote the general welfare of society." What happens when the interests of the general society conflict with the self-determination of the client? The code would seem to suggest that the client has precedence, but the subsections quickly hedge by characterizing the legal conditions under which client self-determination is not primary. By leaving this determination to the legal system, we allow ourselves the hypocrisy that we function only in the clients interest. More about that later.

In the early days of the social work profession, there were two distinct wings to the profession. One group was frankly moralistic and sought to bring deviants and fallen souls back into the social mainstream. The other wing was populated by social reformers, who saw and sought to change the social injustices that created human misery. Nowadays we decry moralism while practicing it in subtle forms. At the same time, we have retreated from social reform. Our current refusal to stand for or against society may have something to do with the stagnation in the profession. In so doing we deceive only ourselves. Perhaps a look at our own moral foundations as a profession would be instructive.

Pragmatic Considerations

As a practical matter, if social workers do not deal with individuals who are coerced into treatment, what will happen? Quite obviously, some other agent of society will address the behavior of the client. The most likely candidate is the criminal justice system. The technology of the criminal justice and corrections system relies heavily on punishment, which may not be either effective or necessary for many forms of social deviance.

The likely result of not trying to treat some forms of deviance is that it will become criminalized by society. As marginal behaviors become criminal, the society becomes more oppressive. Thus, a frequent fear that social workers could become "mental health police" is wrongheaded. Societies that tend to become oppressive do not in the main offer therapeutic rehabilitation as an intermediate step between conformity and criminality. The obvious exception is the Soviet abuse of the psychiatric system. This occurred in a society whose collectivist sentiments are as pronounced as are the American individualist sentiments. Although we cannot ignore the dangers embodied in the Soviet abuses, they are unlikely to be replicated here. The fascist process has been one of criminalizing marginal deviance and punishing it, not seeking to rehabilitate the deviant.

It is noteworthy that all the while that social work has espoused individual ethical values, it has continued to place most of its members in settings where some or all clients come to treatment under some form of coercion. By saying one thing and doing another, we create a dangerous deceit. By not acknowledging the coercive nature of many social work contexts, we are prevented from developing an ethic that takes deliberate account of the coercive contexts and provides clear and unhypocritical guidelines for practice in such settings. Hysterical protestations about unlimited individual freedoms do not advance this important need in the profession.

A word is in order here about cultural pluralism. It is easy to see our society as an Anglo-Saxon monolith bent on the eradication of legitimate minority cultures. By addressing the realities of a plural society, one of which is a common core of shared values, we can better define the tolerable range of cultural diversity. The elasticity of a culture has limits. A minority culture that practiced human sacrifice, incest, or the like would clearly not be tolerated. A culture that tolerated wife beating or withholding medical assistance to children may challenge many people's personal limits, even if all parties subscribe to the mores. We do not serve society or ourselves, however, by acting as if there are no limits to individual expression. Once again, the issue is not whether we should treat involuntary clients, but how and by whom they should be treated.

Technical Considerations

The preceding discussion is moot if we do not have the technical ability for changing behavior in involuntary clients. Modern psychotherapy has an increasing inventory of techniques upon which we draw for changing client behavior. This fact alone has induced some people to consider therapeutic intervention where before none would be attempted. It has also induced courts to seek treatment alternatives to punishment in an increasing number of circumstances.

As a purely technical matter, the involuntary client presents obstacles to treatment. As we have said earlier, however, in reality social workers have a large body of ongoing experience with coerced clientele, and some of that experience has produced positive changes and refined methods. A couple of examples might be illustrative.

Progress in the treatment of addictions has caused many professionals to recognize that the old saw about alcoholics and addicts needing to "bottom out" and be ready for change may have been in error. Recent evaluations have shown that patients sent to drug and alcohol rehabilitation under the coercive threat of loss of a job or as a result of court orders for criminal offenses such as drunk driving do as well or better in recovery than do those who are voluntarily self referred. This leaves us with the disquieting realization that many who have recovered from addiction and are glad to be free of it might have been spared years of suffering by a more aggressive treatment posture by professionals such as social workers.

The treatment of the chronically mentally ill with more aggressive methods such as behavior modification, neuroleptic drugs (addressed elsewhere in detail in this volume) have allowed many patients to leave custodial hospitals and live lives of greater freedom and latitude. Few of those patients would consent initially to the aggressive treatment regimens that may have ultimately spared them and their families years of suffering.

The proposition is simple. Sometimes, by reason of disease, addiction, or distorting life experiences, our clients are unable to make choices that are in their own best interest. Effective treatment, aggressively and competently provided, is a humane alternative to continued suffering or resorts to criminalization of the behavior. As social workers, we have an obligation to consider the cruelty involved in allowing our fellow human beings to, as they say, "die with their rights on."

Up to this point, for the sake of argument, I have dealt with extreme examples. The crucial question, if we allow the fact that society has a right to intervene at some point in response to deviance, is "Where do we draw the line." When is it possible to determine that individuality has become deviant? The case examples were chosen to try to challenged that margin. Do these cases merit the imposition of a social will on the individuals? Let us look at the two examples.

The case of Ken Willis would sound familiar to many substance abuse counselors. Denial is a key feature of the substance abuse syndrome. It is not uncommon that marijuana is the drug identified in "for cause" occupational tests. It is generally used in concert with other drugs, most commonly alcohol. Are the marital problems related to drug use? Is the accident a product of stress rather than substance abuse? Each of these questions requires clarification.

In Ken's case, the worst that can happen is that he be made aware of the dynamics of drug abuse, the family implications, and the resources available to aid his recovery if he chooses. The company requires that he abstain from the use of an illegal drug, one which is known to impair judgment, coordination, and sense of time, which is a relatively sensible precaution in view of the dangerous potential on the job. Ken protests that treatment is a waste of time. This protest is made by many at the onset of treatment, and many of those have subsequently come to appreciate the insights and changes produced by treatment. In years past the alternative often would have been termination of employment and possibly being reported to legal authorities. Treatment in this case seems a constructive alternative to any of the alternatives, including ignoring the accident, the drug usage, and the family strain.

In the case of Ellen Washington, we find a young woman without financial resources, with a history suggestive of family dysfunction as a child, and the statistical likelihood that this pattern will replicate itself. Those familiar with child abuse scenarios shudder when confronted with a young woman who has been abused herself, who has a pattern of unstable relationships, and who places a minor child in a situation charged with sexual abuse potential.

Does Ellen have the unlimited right to live as she chooses, relying on society for financial support, while placing her own children at risk? Maybe. Is it permissible for society to seek to correct some of her developmental deficits by offering courses in parenting and sex education to a woman who manifestly can benefit from both, but probably has no idea they exist? How could she choose these for herself, because she literally does not know what she does not know?

Certainly foster case is not without its problems, but the experience of far too many children like Angela is that they are exposed to abuse, neglect, or simply poor parental models, and a cycle of marginal existence and economic dependency is perpetuated. The option of foster care and therapeutic intervention seems benign, even perhaps timid, in this example.

In both cases, it is possible to argue that the individual is violated by intrusive social agencies. The experiences to which they are directed, however, serve simply to educate them about the issues that brought them into conflict with social institutions. They raise the possibility of increased awareness and latitude of choice for both clients. These are hardly things for which society need apologize.

ANNOTATED BIBLIOGRAPHY

London, P. (1964). *Modes and morals of psychotherapy*. New York: Holt, Rinehart and Winston

> This is a thoughtful, readable examination of the role that morality, examined and unexamined, plays in therapy. Anyone concerned with client coercion will be fascinated by his reasoning.

Because this argument involves some consideration of the "social contract," a notion philosophically out of fashion for some time (perhaps because it is refractory to solution), it might be instructive to look at two classics, or discussions that compare them. Jean Jacques Rousseau proposed the basic goodness of the individual and the evil of society in *The Social Contract*. Thomas Hobbes, in *The Leviathan*, makes his famous proposition that life is "nasty, brutish, and short," in nature, and that society is created as an absolute sovereign over the bestial impulses of humans. Much food for thought between these two classic extremes.

More conventionally, Frank Loewenberg and Ralph Dolgoff present many ethical issues and dilemmas faced by social workers in practice in *Ethical Decisions for Social Work Practice*, (Itasca, IL: Peacock Press, 1982) with extended discussions of some of the matters outlined here.

Rejoinder to Professor Kunkel   LYNN ATKINSON

Dr. Kunkel frames his argument for coercive treatment in such a manner as to depict coerced treatment as both a benign and benevolent method society has discovered to protect itself from rampant individualism. Dr. Kunkel seems to imply that without the coercive treatment, social chaos would result. Individuals would then rebel against society, closet deviants would crawl out of every corner, and there would be anarchy all over the streets.

Dr. Kunkel's argument rationalizing the use of coercive treatment by social workers as a protective measure for society is persuasive. It is, however, flawed in four major ways. Let us examine each of these flaws in turn.

First, it is ridiculous to assume that by forcing a significant portion of the population to undergo treatment for social deviance, we keep society from anarchy. If Dr. Kunkel's argument were accurate, and it was a fact that coercive treatment must be used to keep anarchy from occurring, one must wonder why we have so many social deviants. If most of our current population consists of social deviants being held in tow only by society's coercive forces, then what portion of the population do these coercive structures really represent? Surely the majority of society is not represented, for the majority exists of closet social deviants who would come out and create a reign of terror and anarchy should the coercive forces ever stop. And if the majority is not represented, how can the force behind the coercive structures be said to represent the general welfare?

Second, Dr. Kunkel's belief that coerced treatment is a benign and benevolent force that is better than other alternatives is just plain inaccurate. For many, many reasons stated in my argument, coercive treatment is very often harmful and not always helpful to both the individuals and the families who are involved in treatment. Even in cases where help occurs because of the coerced treatment, harm also occurs and leaves the memory of the successful treatment a bittersweet memory in the client's mind.

Third, Dr. Kunkel argues that the use of coercive treatment methods is a right of society. Although societies have always had penal systems and methods of punishing unacceptable social behavior, Dr. Kunkel implies that society has the right not only to punish unacceptable behavior, but to reframe the will of any person who chooses not to conform to society's rather ambiguous standards. It is my opinion that giving society control over people's thoughts as well as their behavior is a dangerous precedent. In addition, treatment is not the same as punishment. Therefore, treatment does not end during a certain time frame as punishment does, but can go on forever, haunting the victim for the rest of his or her days.

Finally, Dr. Kunkel's argument assumes the proliferation of coercive treatment bureaucracies is a result of society's concern with the general welfare of its citizens. He does not allow for alternative explanations of this growth, which in my mind are just as feasible. Power and money are strong motivators for both individuals and bureaucracies. I do not believe their influence can be ignored here.

Dr. Kunkel is right when he says that most social workers are employed in situations where treatment could be coerced. It could be, but it does not have to be. If social workers were more aware of the problems they bring upon themselves and their clients when treatment is coerced, they would refuse to participate in this treatment unless they had their client's consent.

Should Volunteers Be Used as Direct Service Givers?

EDITOR'S NOTE: Before there was social work or social welfare, there were spontaneous, voluntary acts of helping between human beings. There always will be such expressions of mutual concern. Today there are both the profession of social work and the institution of social welfare, entities that came into and will remain in existence to rationalize and regulate much of the helping that occurs in a modern society. Everyone agrees that volunteers have a valuable part to play in this arrangement. The question is, what part? The controversy is strongest with reference to the use of volunteers in ways that overlap with the domain many professional social workers believe is best left to them, the realm of direct service giving. The debate presented below is introduced by a background statement prepared by both debaters.

Rosalie N. Ambrosino, Ph.D., argues the YES position. She is Associate Professor and Undergraduate Program Director in the School of Social Work at the University of Texas at Austin. Her current scholarly activities reflect interests related to child welfare and family services, domestic violence, and school social work. Dr. Ambrosino is a coauthor of *Social Work and Social Welfare—An Introduction.*

Stephen C. Anderson, Ph.D., who presents the NO case, is Associate Professor and Practicum Coordinator in the School of Social Work at the University of Oklahoma. He teaches practice courses in both the undergraduate and graduate programs. His current scholarly activities reflect interests related to mental health issues, child welfare, and the delivery of social services to American Indians.

Background of the Debate

STEPHEN C. ANDERSON AND ROSALIE N. AMBROSINO

The role of volunteers in meeting human needs has varied greatly over time. Prior to the development of social work "professionalism" and social work education in the early part of this century, most of the human services directed towards children and families were delivered by volunteers. Mutual aid and charity and philanthropy were two of the earliest means of meeting human needs. In particular, the Charity Organization Societies and the settlement house movement that grew out of the charity and philanthropy efforts in the nineteenth century were primarily staffed by volunteers. These volunteers were often referred to as "friendly visitors." Levin (1969) reports that when paid staff were hired, their duties were clerical or administrative, while the volunteers maintained their positions as decision makers and service providers. Porter R. Lee (Bruno, 1957), in his presidential address to the National Conference of Social Work in 1929, described the way in which professional methods grew out of the initial lay attempts to meet social problems. Specifically Lee stated that:

> Social work begins by someone seeing an unmet need, and setting about to provide for it. For example, if it is a neglected child that arouses his sympathy, he makes arrangements for its care. In this phase, the worker is a missionary, a propagandist, rousing others to see the need, and to join with him to meet it. (pp. 278–279)

As the scope of this country's social needs expanded with a resulting demand for greater governmental resources and the development of professional social work education and a cadre of social work professionals, however, the role of the volunteer became less certain. The shift from the provision of direct services by volunteers to professional social workers in the early 1900s allowed for the development of another challenging role for volunteers. With their intimate knowledge of social problems gained in their volunteer direct service experiences, they began working to seek social and legislative reforms. Levin (1969) asserts that their success in improving community conditions, garnering resources, and advocating for the passage of humanistic legislation produced the "Golden Era of Social Legislation" (p. 87).

With the ending of this reform period at the close of the 1920s and the growing development of a professional identity among social workers, there seemed to be little need for widespread citizen participation in the human services. During the Depression Era and World War II, however, social workers were forced to reconsider using volunteers because of increased social needs and severe personnel shortages. Thus, volunteers again became involved in providing direct services (Suarez & Ricketson, 1974).

During the early 1950s, volunteer roles reflected a partnership with professional social workers. This "partnership" defined the role of the volunteer to be one of policy maker (i.e., board member) and provider of nonspecialized service activities. Thus, the "traditional roles" for volunteers centered around functions that included driving, fund raising, education and public awareness, office assistance, and other auxiliary roles (Levin, 1969). Beginning in the mid to late 1960s, this trend changed as volunteers began to break out of these traditional roles and to move again into providing direct services. This return to the provision of direct services has continued to the present time. Today, there are many examples of programs utilizing volunteers as probation officers, lay therapists in child abuse and neglect programs, counselors on telephone crisis or help lines, advocates in domestic violence programs, and in the burgeoning number of self help or mutual aid groups.

The primary question for the ensuing debate is whether or not volunteers have overstepped their boundaries in providing direct services to client populations who might be better served by professionals. This debate reflects a long-existing tension between professionals and volunteers who have not been able to arrive at a definition of roles satisfactory to both.

REFERENCES

Bruno, F.J. (1957). *Trends in social work 1874–1956*. New York: Columbia University Press.

Levin, H. (1969). Volunteers in social welfare: The challenge of their future. *Social Work,* 14, 85–94.

Suarez, M.L., & Ricketson, M.A. (1974). Facilitating casework with protective service clients through use of volunteers. *Child Welfare,* 5, 313–322.

YES

ROSALIE N. AMBROSINO

Increasingly, volunteers are filling direct service roles that in the past might have been filled by paid social workers. Social problems such as poverty, unemployment, homelessness, school dropouts, teenage pregnancy, substance abuse, child maltreatment, spouse abuse, and the needs of the elderly are placing a greater demand on human service programs. Funding cuts in these programs have resulted in large numbers of individuals with unmet needs and minimal efforts directed toward prevention. The Reagan and Bush calls for assistance from the private sector and individual citizens, contrasted with overburdened social workers' struggle for recognition and pleas for adequate funding of social programs, have also resulted in increased tension between volunteers and employed social workers. Most social workers are aware that human services agencies cannot survive without volunteers; however, concern exists that the glamour placed on the volunteer role denies the importance of social work's valuable contributions to meeting human needs. Because of this conflict and resulting misunderstandings regarding the potential uses of volunteers, many social workers have not learned the skills needed to use volunteers effectively (Haueser & Schwartz, 1980).

Although many social workers embrace volunteers and use them to their fullest potential, others continue the debate about their usefulness or keep them at arm's length. Even the terminology used in this debate is often demeaning: "professionals" versus "volunteers," "paraprofessionals," or "subprofessionals." For purposes of this debate, a volunteer will be defined as a person who performs direct service roles with clients without receiving monetary remuneration. Another issue often debated is what constitutes "direct services" provided by volunteers. Most definitions of direct services include services provided directly to clients, either face to face or by telephone, such as counseling and therapy, tutoring, transportation, and child care. Indirect social services are often characterized as those that have an indirect impact on clients such as establishing resources, advocating, or promoting public awareness. For this debate, "direct services" will refer to those services that involve direct relationships with clients for purposes of behavior change.

One final caveat must also be included: in order for volunteers to be effective in the provision of direct services, careful screening, orientation and training, and supervision and monitoring must take place. A successful volunteer program requires skilled social workers and other paid professional staff who understand the potential uses of volunteers, as well as their needs, and who value volunteers as important as the clients they serve.

A Qualitative Means for Agencies to Extend the Services of Paid Staff

Most observers and participants in the human services field agree that human services workers do not have the time necessary to meet all the needs of individual members of families experiencing crisis. The dilemma is whether to hire more paid staff or to seek alternative methods of service delivery. Proponents of volunteerism argue that unless alternate methods are used, fewer clients are able to be served effectively, or large numbers of clients are served ineffectively. Paid human services professionals "must be trained in ways to multiply their effectiveness by working through other less

extensively and expensively trained people" (Hobbs, 1969, p. 21). Margaret
Rioch, well known for her National Institute of Mental Health-sponsored
program that trained middle-aged housewives to provide psychotherapy
under supervision, suggests:

> The challenge to the mental health professional should be, after
> establishing his/her own basic clinical competence, to work out ways
> in which he/she can multiply his/her effectiveness by a factor of say
> six, by discovering ways of working through other people. (Hobbs,
> p. 21)

Volunteers can provide direct services to many individuals and families. For example, parents experiencing the development of their first teen-
ager who suddenly is resistant to following family rules can be assisted by a
trained volunteer, particularly a person who has already experienced parenthood with teenagers. Persons within multiproblem families who have
never developed a trusting relationship with a worker or agency may require
6 to 10 hours of time each week with a helping person just to develop a
beginning supportive relationship and more time once the relationship is
developed to meet their many needs.

Increasingly, volunteers are both men and women of all ages who are
representative of all cultural and economic groups. Members of a specific
cultural or ethnic group, or inhabitants of a specific geographic area or
neighborhood, often can establish relationships with clients who share
similar ethnic and neighborhood experiences and thus bring a wealth of
information to paid staff not otherwise possible. Because there is less social
distance between such volunteers and clients, they are able to circumvent
class and ethnic differences and the alienation clients might feel toward paid
service providers (Riessman, 1969).

A Potent Resource for Bringing about Behavioral Change in Clients

With appropriate training, volunteers can serve as an excellent resource for
bringing about behavioral change in clients. Sobey (1970) found that in
comparison to professionals, nonprofessionals in many mental health programs were more likely to be engaged in activity group therapy, socializa-
tion groups, and milieu therapy, while they were almost as likely to be
equally engaged in providing individual and group counseling. In a residential treatment program for emotionally disturbed children, social workers
observed parents, teachers, and other persons who already had significant
relationships with residents. The lay person was able to build on the already

existing positive relationship with the child using the techniques learned in the program when the child left and returned home.

Carkhuff and Bergenson, evaluating laypersons who had received limited, but specific training, found that

". . . lay trainees function at levels essentially as high or higher . . . and engage clients in counseling process movement at levels as high or higher than professional trainees." (1969, p. 5)

Rioch's (1963) homemakers trained to provide psychotherapy were found to be satisfactorily providing services to even difficult cases. Successful use of lay persons in providing marriage counseling, therapeutic crisis services, and treatment to hospitalized and outpatient schizophrenics has also been observed. Volunteers often can form relationships with hostile clients or those parents requiring extensive nurturing before they can relate to their children:

The client can readily accept that the volunteer is involved because he or she cares and can identify the volunteer as an ally. The volunteer does not have the apparent authority of control over the client's life inherent in the caseworker's role and therefore is less likely to be perceived in a threatening light. (National Center on Child Abuse and Neglect, 1977, p. 13)

Berkeley Planning Associates (1978) found that those child abuse and neglect programs where clients were in treatment for at least 6 months and where volunteer lay therapists or self-help programs were used (Parents Anonymous) were more likely to show improved functioning of clients than in other programs studied.

Individuals who have experienced child abuse, substance abuse, emotional problems, parenting children with special needs, or problems with elderly parents themselves often can lend support more readily than paid professionals who have not. As the social work profession continues to emphasize prevention, increased numbers of self-help groups, hot lines, and mentoring programs will be needed, coupled with a more extensive cadre of well-trained and supervised volunteers to work with these programs (Haueser & Schwartz, 1980).

Building a Constituency Group

The more volunteers become involved in the provision of direct services to clients, the more sensitized they become to legislative, policy, and funding issues that have an impact on their clients. Volunteers who wait with clients to receive care, complete an eligibility interview, or attempt to locate treatment services where none are available can provide first-hand information about client needs. As volunteers, they also have much more freedom to advocate for social service needs and are often more likely to be listened to than paid professionals. Many traditional human services programs now recognize the significance of volunteers as their strongest program supporters:

> The volunteer often becomes an advocate for the agency, for the client, and for broad-scale social changes in the community. The dedicated and informed volunteer is a citizen advocate whose lack of self-interest permits and gives credibility to public support for programs where professionals would be accused of vested interest. (Haueser & Schwartz, 1980, p. 599)

A Way for People to Engage in Meaningful Human Relationships

Direct service opportunities for volunteers are more likely to sustain volunteer interest because they offer a chance to promote individual growth and self-awareness and to develop new skills. Experience from self-help programs demonstrates that individuals who give help to others grow themselves. As volunteers work with others directly and develop meaningful relationships with clients, their own self-esteem increases, leadership skills begin to emerge, and other personal growth takes place (Riessman, 1969).

Erikson (1963) and Gilligan (1977) suggest the importance of meeting developmental needs through interpersonal relationships. This need can be seen particularly in Erikson's life stage of middle adulthood, when acquiring a sense of generativity is pitted against avoiding stagnation or self absorption. The key to achieving generativity is a person's need to be needed and the need to care, experienced particularly through giving of self. Growing individuals need to experience a continuity in their lives by investing energy and ideas into something new, both in their children and in their communities (Withey, et al, 1980, p. 643). For women in particular, serving as a volunteer can provide an important means of meeting relationship needs when children leave home. The National Association of Social Workers (NASW) policy statement on volunteerism (Haueser & Schwartz, 1980), for example, points out that "volunteer opportunities for self-realization may be particularly important for women in a time of role transition" (p. 596).

Direct service relationships for older adult volunteers have also been found to meet personal needs. Hunter and Linn (1981) found significant differences in both emotional and physical well-being when comparing elderly volunteers and nonvolunteers. Volunteers had fewer hospitalizations, were taking less medication, had less anxiety and depression and fewer somatic symptoms, and were more likely to report a strong will to live and a higher level of life satisfaction than nonvolunteers.

A Means to Exploring Career Interests and Gaining Employment

Use of volunteers in direct service roles also offers opportunities for individuals to explore career interests and to obtain employment in human service programs. Many individuals begin volunteering because they are interested in careers in human services and want to explore these interests prior to seeking education or employment. Others decide on a career in a helping profession as a result of volunteering. Most social work students have had at least one volunteer experience prior to entering a social work program. The more varied the experiences, the more likely the student is to have a realistic viewpoint of the social work profession.

Many volunteers are hired as paid staff as a result of their volunteer experiences. Social workers in corporate personnel programs, health care settings and nursing homes, child care programs, and schools often create jobs for themselves after providing direct social services to clients as volunteers. Adolescents, young adults, homemakers reentering the labor force when children are older, persons seeking a second career, and social workers seeking entry into a new area or additional challenges all benefit extensively by volunteering.

In summary, volunteers have not overstepped their boundaries in providing direct services to client populations. A strong partnership between paid social work professionals and volunteers is vital in order to meet the many needs of today's individuals. The 1977 NASW Delegate Assembly's policy statement on the use of volunteers in human services, while establishing clear boundaries differentiating the functions of volunteers from those of paid staff, provides a clear mandate to the profession that volunteers are critical allies. The statement calls for the strengthening of social work education in the area of screening, training, and effectively using volunteers, including emphasis at the graduate level placed on a career as a volunteer administrator (Haueser & Schwartz, 1980). Training volunteers to provide direct services to clients to supplement the roles of paid social worker professionals will result in a delivery system that is more responsive to meeting human needs.

REFERENCES

Anderson, S., & Lauderdale, M. (1986). *Developing and managing volunteer programs.* Springfield, IL: Charles C. Thomas.

Carkhuff, R.R., & Bergenson, B.G. (1967). *Beyond counseling and therapy.* New York: Holt, Rinehart and Winston.

Erickson, E. (1963). *Childhood and society,* ed 2. New York: W.W. Norton.

Evaluation of child abuse and neglect demonstration projects, 1974–1977, Vols. 1 and 2. Washington, DC: Conducted by Berkeley Planning Associates for the U.S. Department of Health, Education, and Welfare.

Gilligan, C. (1977). In a different voice: Women's conceptions of self and morality. *Harvard Educational Review,* 47(4), 481–517.

Hobbs, N. (1969). Mental health's third revolution. In Bernard Guerney (Ed.), *Psychotherapeutic agents: New roles for nonprofessionals, parents and teachers,* pp. 14–27. New York: Holt, Rinehart and Winston.

Hunter, K., & Linn, M. (1981). Psychosocial differences between elderly volunteers and non-volunteers. *International Journal of Aging and Human Development,* 12(3), 205–213.

Promising practices: Reaching out to families (1981). Washington, DC: National Center on Child Abuse and Neglect, U.S. Department of Health and Human Services.

Rioch, M., et al. (1969). National Institute of Mental Health pilot study in training mental health counselors. In Guerney, B. (Ed.), *Psychotherapeutic agents: New roles for nonprofessionals, parents and teachers,* pp. 545–557. New York: Holt, Rinehart and Winston.

Riessman, F. (1969). The "helper" therapy principle. In Guerney, B. (Ed.), *Psychotherapeutic agents: New roles for nonprofessionals, parents and teachers,* pp. 87–95. New York: Holt, Rinehart and Winston.

Sobey, F. (1970). *The nonprofessional revolution in mental health.* New York: Columbia University Press.

Withey, V., Anderson, R., & Lauderdale, M. (1980). Volunteers as mentors for abusing parents: A natural helping relationship. *Child Welfare,* LIX(10), 637–644.

ANNOTATED BIBLIOGRAPHY

Anderson, S., & Lauderdale, M. (1986). *Developing and managing volunteer programs.* Springfield, IL: Charles C. Thomas

This is an excellent step-by-step manual that addresses all of the major components necessary to develop and manage successful direct services volunteer programs.

Haueser, A., and Schwartz, F. (1980). Developing social work skills for work with volunteers. *Social Casework 61*, 595–601

Haueser and Schwartz make a strong case for the use of volunteers in many social service roles and pay particular attention to the need for social work educators and professionals to develop ways to teach social workers appropriate skills in using volunteers effectively.

Rejoinder to Dr. Ambrosino   STEPHEN C. ANDERSON

In the context of this argument, two terms are most critical: "volunteer" and "direct services." In her opening statements, Dr. Ambrosino accurately reflects the confusion that surrounds the use of the term "volunteer." Ambrosino argues that a "volunteer" is a person who does not receive monetary remuneration for the services that they provide as contrasted with a "paid professional" who does. I agree with this distinction, but I also feel that it falls short of providing enough clarity for the purposes of our debate.

In the context of using volunteers for direct service roles, a "volunteer" is a person recruited from the community without a professional social services experiential or educational base. Thus, a paid professional social worker who donates his or her time for community service is not the type of situation to which I am opposed. Many professionals volunteer their professional services without monetary benefit. However, these individuals are performing their work based upon their professional education, experience, and commitment to the delivery of services in adherence to professional values and ethics. This activity is far different from that to which I pose my objections.

Ambrosino in her section of "A Means to Exploring Career Interests and Gaining Employment" fails to address the issue at hand in a direct manner. The issue is not one of undergraduate or graduate social work students engaging in volunteer activities or of professionals voluntarily demonstrating the worth of their professional contributions in a nontraditional social work setting. What I am against is the use of individuals as volunteers to perform tasks they have neither the educational or experiential background to perform.

I concur with Dr. Ambrosino that the term "direct services" means those services that involve direct relationships with clients for the purposes of behavior change. The essential part of this definition that I want to underscore is "for the purposes of behavior change." It is for this purpose that I am most opposed to using volunteers as direct services providers. Thus, I am not against the use of volunteers in self-help groups; for example, I am not against the use of high school students as volunteers in activities such as hospital Candy Striper programs. Much of Ambrosino's argument blurs this distinction.

There are many appropriate roles for volunteers to fulfill. These roles can include office support, client transportation, fund raising, acting as board member, babysitting, and program advocacy to name a few. All of these roles can ably assist those volunteering to meet their life needs and to engage in preentry to the work force experiences. In many communities, agencies such as the Boy Scouts, Girl Scouts, Big Brothers/Big Sisters, YWCA, and the YMCA all rely heavily on volunteer support for their programming. However, most of the volunteer roles in these settings do not involve "engaging in behavior change."

One of the most critical points that Ambrosino raises is that volunteers provide a means to extend agency services in a time of fiscal restraint. Social workers in areas such as child welfare and mental health are so overloaded that their effectiveness is greatly reduced. I concur with Ambrosino's observation that it is unlikely that sufficient funding will become available to reduce this strain.

I disagree with Ambrosino, however, that one answer is to focus on and expand the use of volunteers to provide direct services in human services programs. If anything, the arguments that she makes are but additional evidence of the need for fundamental welfare reform in this country today. To suggest that social workers need to find innovative ways to do more with less is a conservative response to our current crisis. If social work as a profession wishes to be proactive to this crisis, I suggest that a more radical advocacy stand be taken in promoting such concepts as nationalization of health care, full employment and livable wage policies, and comprehensive income redistribution.

Volunteerism has been and always will be a part of how we respond to social need. How we use volunteers in light of the ethical, legal, and professional issues that I have raised needs to be carefully considered. There are many appropriate roles for volunteers to fill, but providing direct client services is not one of them.

NO

STEPHEN C. ANDERSON

Volunteer Role Ambiguity

Volunteers engaged in indirect service roles in an agency are involved with a set of clearly defined behavioral expectations. Volunteer roles such as board member, driver, children's group attendant, clothes closet helper, or office assistant are all roles that can be defined and articulated in a written job description. These roles represent typical needs of many agencies, and volunteers can be recruited on the basis of their bringing to the agency the requisite skills to adequately perform their assigned role. The recruitment of volunteers to perform direct service roles with agency clients presents a distinct dilemma because direct service roles are assumedly based upon the possession of professional skills. It is questionable that nonprofessional volunteers either can or should be even partially responsible for the provision of direct services to clients.

Professional relationships are inherently distinct from a personal or social relationship. Pincus and Minahan (1973) identify three basic characteristics that mark a professional relationship. These characteristics are:

1. First, social workers form relationships for a professional purpose.
2. Second, in professional relationships the worker devotes himself to the interests of his clients and the needs and aspirations of other people rather than his own interests.
3. Third, the worker forms relationships based on objectivity and self awareness that allow him to step outside of his own personal troubles and emotional needs and to be sensitive to the needs of others. (Pincus & Minahan, 1978, pp. 69–70)

Volunteers simply cannot meet the above criteria in developing a direct relationship with a client. Volunteers may be altruistically and other-oriented in their motivation, but they are also motivated by what they can gain from their experience for themselves. It is more likely that a volunteer will form a relationship with a client that is closer to that of being a friend rather than that of a professional. As a result, there will be a tendency for volunteers to become more personally invested in the client relationship as a way to meet both their own needs and the needs of the client. The type of relationship that is formed makes it difficult for the volunteer to engage with the client on the basis of objectivity and self-awareness.

Direct services to clients are either professional or they are not. If the services rendered are professional ones, they are services that are based on a directed course of formal education and are embedded in an identifiable body of knowledge, a unique set of values, and specific skills. Volunteers engaged in the provision of direct services are ultimately placed in an ambiguous role situation. It is a situation in which they have neither the appropriate orientation nor the knowledge, values, and skills to do the job adequately.

Lack of Knowledge and Skills to Meet Client Needs

The use of volunteers and paraprofessionals in direct service roles largely had its beginning in the idealism and social activism of the 1960s. There was a belief that life experience was as or more valuable than professional knowledge and skill. Beginning in the late 1970s, the shortcomings of programs emphasizing indigenous leadership became apparent. Increasingly, emphasis was placed on the view that the delivery of direct client social services was best provided by professionals. Over the past decade, most states enacted licensure or certification legislation for social workers, and accreditation organizations and health insurers have increasingly required that services be provided by licensed professionals. These developments have taken place out of a concern that the services clients receive are qualitative and meet the minimum standards of good care.

Providing services to clients in need is a complex task that requires a diverse array of knowledge and skills that depend on far more than "life experiences" and the ability to be warm, empathetic and genuine. The provision of services is a dynamic and ongoing process. Working with clients continually requires the processing of new information and the making of "executive," and at times immediate, decisions. There is no way to predict the needs or demands of a client in the future. Thus, a client who is assessed today as primarily needing social support and a positive role model may become depressed and suicidal tomorrow.

Social work professionals are educated to know that often the immediate "presenting problem" is only what exists on the surface. Being an active listener and then knowing what to do with the information obtained are professional rather than lay functions. Volunteers may well be able to be trained as active listeners, but short of enrolling in a professional degree program they cannot be trained in knowing what they are listening to, how to process that information, and to then take appropriate action. Volunteers through their orientation and training sessions may learn pieces of the process of working with clients, but they can never realistically learn the whole process.

The lack of knowledge and skills possessed by the volunteer poses risks for the client, agency, and possibly others. In situations where a volunteer does not pick up on subtle suicidal or homicidal ideations of a client, the risk is possible loss of human life. The risk of death or severe injury may also be present in those cases involving abusive behavior toward either children or spouses.

Failure to pick up on these warning indicators also poses a risk to the agency. Increasingly, case law is emerging that focuses on the "duty to warn and protect" (Corey, Corey, & Callanan, 1988). Agencies have been held liable for damage awards because of their failure to warn potential victims of threatened harm, commit a dangerous individual, or to protect suicidal clients through notification of family or significant other. Although agencies may attempt to screen out and not assign such cases to volunteers, there is no guarantee that this kind of screening can be successfully done. Essentially, the ability to adequately assess risk behaviors and the ability to take decisive action requires the knowledge and skills of a professional.

Can an Agency Afford Volunteers?

The recruitment, training, recognition, and supervision of volunteers take both money and the time of professional agency staff. A common misconception is that volunteers are cost savers. Volunteer programs are not a "panacea" for the problems associated with large caseloads, money shortages, staff burnout, and lowered staffing levels. A mistake that many programs make is to not adequately plan for all of the costs associated with the development and implementation of a volunteer program. One of the most critical aspects of running a volunteer program is to provide for the adequate supervision of volunteers.

Supervision of volunteers includes tasks related to the selection of appropriate cases to assign to volunteers, being available for telephone contact with the volunteers, and having weekly supervisory meetings with volunteers. These tasks not only include the actual time spent with the volunteers, but also the time it takes for preparation and planning. The failure to provide for the adequate supervision of volunteers can lead to a number of negative consequences for an agency. Liability issues can pose one of the more severe dangers to an agency. The lack of adequate supervision, particularly of volunteer staff, can potentially lead to the filing of malpractice suits. Inadequate supervision can also lead to volunteer dissatisfaction, dropout,and a resulting negative community reputation. Even worse is when volunteers decide upon their own direction and begin to reshape the direction of the agency and its services to meet what they believe needs to be done. For an agency already strapped for adequate resources, any of the above situations will only serve to make a bad situation worse.

The above costs are in addition to the time necessary for the recruitment and training of volunteers. Volunteer recruitment, training, and supervision are all costs to the agency. The failure to anticipate these costs can result in any number of negative consequences for both the agency and its clients. If there is a breakdown in time spent on the recruitment and screening of volunteers, programs run the risk of volunteers who may be so engrossed in their own needs that those of the clients are overlooked and not met. The lack of adequate training and supervision can result in the lack of control over volunteer activities and risk harm to clients.

Before using volunteers to direct service roles with clients, an agency must carefully weigh the assets and liabilities of such a program. The potential liabilities of such a program are immense and the risks not worth whatever potential value the program may have to clients. Programs and their clients may well be better served by recruiting volunteers instead to lighten support tasks, thus freeing professional staff to better focus their unique knowledge and skills on clients.

Ethical Dilemmas

The last argument against using volunteers in direct service roles deals with a number of ethical dilemmas. A growing body of literature is emerging, which brings emphasis and focus to the issue of professional ethics (Lowenberg & Dolgoff, 1988; Wells & Masch, 1986; Corey, Corey, & Callanan, 1988). The NASW Code of Ethics (1979) serves as a guide for social work professionals in carrying out their professional responsibilities. While professionals may be held accountable for their professional behavior, the same does not apply for volunteers. While the various "do's and don'ts" of working with clients may be covered in volunteer training sessions, there is little way of holding volunteers accountable for their actions. In the end, the unethical behavior of a volunteer will become the unethical conduct of either the professional social worker or their agency for allowing such a volunteer to have contact with clients.

The first ethical concern is that of confidentiality. There is a tendency on the part of volunteers to either loosely or rigidly adhere to client confidentiality and privacy. The loose adherence to this principle may result in the sharing of client information in any number of innocent ways. Out of their enthusiasm to share with others what they are doing or to talk about the "shocking" lifestyles or problems of their clients, a volunteer may unwittingly be the source of damaging social gossip. Likewise, a rigid adherence to client confidentiality can also result in harm. Confidentiality is a complex issue and one that has any number of limitations. Knowing the limitations and who to consult with requires a great amount of professional judgment. The failure to report potential harm to self or others, suspected abuse or neglect, and subtle symptoms of mental illness can all have serious consequences for both the client and their family members.

The NASW Code of Ethics under the section pertaining to the ethical responsibility to clients states: "The social worker should serve clients with devotion, loyalty, determination, and the maximum application of professional skill and competence" (Section II.F.1.). The question to be asked is whether the use of volunteers represents this "maximum application of professional skill and competence." While ideally a client should be receiving a range of services, often the volunteer is used because there is a scarcity of other resources. In this situation, it is questionable whether the clients of an agency are getting their needs met to the fullest extent possible.

Other ethical issues such as the imposition of values and the creation of a dependency relationship that violates the client's right to self determination are also problematic in the use of volunteers. Engaged in an ambiguous role, the volunteer in their "quasi" friendship relationship will often resort to becoming the moralizing "advice giver." Rather than listen and see life from a different perspective, emphasis is given to the "should" or "what I did" messages as a way to help and save the client.

Conclusion

Volunteers have and will continue to make vital contributions to the social service delivery system and all of its participants. In making these contributions, there is a wide variety of meaningful roles for them to fill. However, these roles need to be ones that are supportive to the agency itself and not roles that place responsibility on volunteers for the delivery of direct social work services. Volunteer and professional roles cannot be combined. Volunteers simply do not possess the knowledge, values, and skills that undergird a profession in how it provides services to people. To place volunteers in such direct service roles is to place professionals, their agency, and most of all their clients at risk. As delineated in this article, the risks are too great to take.

REFERENCES

Corey, G., Corey, M., & Callanan, P. (1988). *Issues and ethics in the helping professions.* Pacific Grove, CA.: Brooks/Cole Publishing Co.
Lowenberg, F., and Dolgoff, R. (1988). *Ethical decisions for social work practice.* Itasca, IL: F.E. Peacock Publishers, Inc.
National Association of Social Workers (NASW) (1979). *Code of ethics.*
Pincus, A., & Minahan, A. (1973). *Social work practice: Model and method.* Itasca, IL: F.E. Peacock Publishers, Inc.
Wells, C., & Masch, M.K. (1986). *Social work ethics day to day.* New York: Longman, Inc.

ANNOTATED BIBLIOGRAPHY

Anderson, S.C., & Lauderdale, M. (1986). *Developing and managing volunteer programs: A guide for social service agencies.* Springfield, IL: Charles C. Thomas

This is a process-oriented book that provides the reader with practical guidelines for developing a successful volunteer program in ten steps. The steps are presented in an order that challenges the readers to develop their own program philosophy and to then engage in a program development sequence designed to assist the readers in avoiding damaging pitfalls.

Volunteer—The National Center. *Volunteer readership.* Arlington, Virginia: Volunteer—The National Center; 1111 N. 19th St.; Suite 500; Arlington, VA 22209

This resource is published by the major volunteer program and leadership association in the United States. This publications is a yearly presentation of major texts and pamphlets published on topics related to volunteerism. The association also publishes a quarterly journal, *Voluntary Action Leadership.*

Rejoinder to Professor Anderson
ROSALIE N. AMBROSINO

Dr. Anderson raises many important issues regarding the use of volunteers in direct practice roles. Programs that use volunteers in such roles have been able to address those issues successfully through effective recruitment, screening, training, and supervisory and monitoring efforts.

The issues Anderson raises are no different from those faced by programs using paid helping professionals. Role ambiguity, maintaining appropriate professional boundaries with clients, and ensuring high ethical standards are issues all human services administrators encounter, regardless of the type of client served and the level of staff used.

Just as clearly defined job descriptions can be designed for volunteers in direct service roles, they can be designed for volunteers in direct service roles. Maintaining clearly defined volunteer roles also requires strong support from professional social work staff. Role boundary violations by volunteers are much more likely to occur when they receive inadequate support.

Well-trained volunteers are also able to form professional relationships with clients and to keep roles separate and focused. Proponents of using volunteers in direct service roles argue that clients are often more receptive to change if they are involved in relationships with volunteers whom they view as truly interested in their needs, as opposed to paid professionals who may be viewed as working with clients because they have to if they want to keep their jobs.

Although it is impossible to transmit to volunteers the knowledge, skills, and values upon which the social work profession is based in the same ways that social work professionals are educated, a good volunteer program should create an organizational context as well as extensive training that teaches necessary content and reinforces it on an ongoing basis. The issue is whether information learned by volunteers can be applied consistently without a professional knowledge base. Proponents of volunteer programs would argue that with sound social work supervision it can, especially when the volunteering occurs with in the context of a social work organization that reinforces the essence of the profession. Effective volunteer programs are neither cost free nor time free. A partnership with social work paid professionals and volunteers is necessary for volunteers to be effective practitioners.

Anderson also points out the ethical implications of not providing competent professional staff to work with clients when volunteers are used. Ethical concerns can also be raised when potential resources are not developed to serve clients with unmet needs. Haueser and Schwartz (1988) argue that the real ethical issue is the failure of the social work profession to use volunteers more extensively and of social work educators to prepare social work professionals to use volunteers in direct service roles. Volunteers can be used effectively to enhance the social work profession in serving clients. To not use them jeopardizes those individuals to whom our profession is supposedly most dedicated.

REFERENCES

Haueser, A., & Schwartz, F. (1980). Developing social work skills for work with volunteers. *Social Casework* 61, 595–601.

Should Social Workers Evaluate Their Practice Based on Clearly Defined Objectives?

EDITOR'S NOTE: The diversity of social work practice theories reflects sharp differences among social workers about the goals that should be pursued and how clearly they can (or should) be described. Some social workers believe that clearly defining service goals often (if not inevitably) requires the trivialization of goals, that the goals involved in helping clients are complex, and that they defy clear description in a meaningful way. Those who argue the other side of this argument believe that accountable social work practice requires clear description of service goals and that this clarity requirement does not mean that the goals pursued will be trivial or irrelevant to client concerns. Indeed, they would go further and argue that only if goals are clearly described can intervention options be wisely selected and progress clearly indicated. Thus, lying behind the common vagueness of goals pursued by social workers are not only issues of competence (can social workers clearly describe relevant goals that are related to outcomes desired by clients) but should they do so.

Martin Bloom, Ph.D., argues YES. He is Professor of Social Work at Virginia Commonwealth University and is the author of numerous articles and chapters concerning social work practice and evaluation. He is coauthor of *Evaluating Practice: Guidelines for the Accountable Professional* (with Joel Fischer, Prentice-Hall), author of *Lifespan Development: Bases for Prevention and Interventive Helping* (1984, Macmillan) and *Introduction to the Drama of Social Work* (1990, Peacock).

Sophie Freud, ACSW, Ph.D., argues NO. She is Professor at the Simmons College of Social Work. She came to academic life after 20 years of social work practice. She has written many articles and chapters dealing with the theory, teaching, and practice of psychotherapy as well as with feminist issues. In addition, she has written over 50 book reviews and is the author of *My Three Mothers and Other Passions*. She was happy to contribute to this controversy, which she considers an important feminist and political issue having to do with one's general world view.

YES

Martin Bloom

Of course social workers should evaluate their practice based on clearly defined objectives, if the alternative is to evaluate their practice based on unclear objectives and vague and diffuse goals. The issue at question is much more profound than that, however. It revolves around the fundamental point of whether social workers should evaluate their practice objectively as an integral part of the process of practice itself. It is clearly possible to practice the arts of social work without objective evaluation—most of the history of social work has been so practiced. The question arises as to whether objective evaluation adds anything significant to the social work process, while not detracting anything significant from that process.

Because most of the history of social work involved practice without objective evaluation, we should inquire as to what sort of evaluation was used. There can be no doubt that any social work practitioner eagerly sought evidence about how well the client's problems (presented, underlying, or otherwise defined) were being resolved during the course of service, and afterward when services were terminated. The evidence they obtained was largely subjective, based on impressions and reports from others about the client situation. These kinds of evidence were essentially from the same sources of information on which the practice itself was based, and thus were biased and limited, but had the feeling of verisimilitude because of the closeness to the source of the problems.

It was no surprise that social workers were outraged at the discouragingly long series of studies of social work practice using experimental control group designs that yielded negative results—from the Cambridge-Sommerville Project, to the Girls at Vocational High, the Cleveland Protective Services Project, the Chemung County Study, and others. The tendency was to blame the messengers bearing the bad news, rather than look at the situation in a constructively critical light. I point out that the messenger in these cases was research, that is, formal, experimental designs involving outside researchers looking at complex services to large numbers of persons with the hope of contributing new information to the scientific knowledge base. Contrast this with evaluation, which often involves the practitioner analyzing the process and outcome of his or her own services with a given client (individual or group) for the purpose of obtaining rapid feedback so as to correct the course of the intervention. I submit that the current debate about the CSWE Accreditation requirement that all students (BSWs and MSWs) must know how to evaluate their own practice has confused classical research with recent innovations in evaluation. And if this distinction were properly understood, there would be little question from any sector of social work but that we should insist on objective evaluation for the sake of our clients, our profession, and the society we serve.

Social work, as Zimbalist (1977) has pointed out, has had a long love/hate relationship with research, for very good reasons. Research has at times produced as many problems as answers, sometimes promising the sun and delivering merely sunburn. But now we have entered an age where a methodology exists that permits relatively simple, approximate, but useful evaluation of practice. So the question "Should social workers evaluate their practice based on clearly defined objectives?" takes on an entirely new complexion. Let us focus this discussion on the potential utility and hazards of using single-system designs to provide the objective basis for practitioners evaluating their own practice. Evaluating practice based on clearly defined objectives is one aspect of this new mode of evaluation. Let us consider some of the potential benefits of social workers using single-system designs to evaluate their practice.

First assumption: The more clearly that a client's problems are identified and explicated, the more readily will the practitioner be able to retrieve relevant information from the profession's knowledge base and plan relevant strategies for dealing with the client's concerns.

In order to identify the target objectives clearly, the social worker must interact with the client to obtain a clear understanding of the total problem. The worker cannot hope to resolve what he or she cannot grasp clearly. Vaguely or globally defined problems are the bane of the social work profession and a chief cause of ineffectiveness. Even a best-loved theory is no friend if it permits or encourages practitioners to be imprecise about what they are targeting with their interventions. Once a clear fix has been made on a given problem, anchoring that understanding with clear operational definitions enables worker and client to continue working on it over time.

The values that the client seeks to attain are embodied in the targeted objectives. Clarifying the particular objectives means that the client also discovers more clearly what his or her values are. These values are incorporated into the evaluation process by indicating preferred states of affairs, and then measuring objectively how closely current performance approximates these goals.

All client situations are unique, messy, and complex. It is part of the art of helping that the practitioner can observe some general patterns of behavior from the specific instances the client presents. By attaching conceptual labels to these patterns, practitioners are enabled to locate relevant information and use theories or empirical evidence to guide their actions in making appropriate changes in these patterns of behavior so that the client will attain his or her goals. Every theory of behavior change (therapy) of which I am knowledgeable seeks to identify client problems as the basis for practitioner actions. The single-system evaluation method is theory free in the sense that any conceptual framework may use its methods for ascertaining whether or not significant change has occurred in an identified target.

"Clearly defined objectives" has several possible meanings. First, the client may identify the problems and their converse, the objectives or conditions that would prevail if the problems were no longer present. It is important to keep close to the client's sense of problems and objectives in the mutual interchanges that is at the heart of competent social work practice.

A second meaning of "clearly defined objectives" involves the practitioner's assessment of the situation and the specific targets that are identified to reflect this perspective. The set of targets on which the client and practitioner agree to work represents the major dimensions of the whole problem. No one can work on every aspect of a client's life situation; we must identify some major representative patterns and help the client to help him- or herself in dealing with these patterns. Thus, the worker's "clearly defined objectives" for the client represents the underlying themes in the client's problems. Resolutions of these themes should empower and teach the client to deal with other ordinary problems in life. It is critical that the practitioner make sure that the targets of intervention are in fact the ones for which the client seeks help and are the basic problems in the case. We can know this only if the objectives are clearly defined and are made public so that client and worker agree on what it is they are doing together.

Admittedly, some client problems are difficult to define objectively, such as internal states or existential conditions. However, even the most subjective or existential condition is known by means of some observable indicator of that problem. Just ask the client how he or she experiences the supposedly ineffable, and you have a rough but sufficient indicator of the problem. If the problem exists at all, then it can be measured by some objective indicator (Hudson, 1978). If you cannot tell whether or not whatever you do affects the problem, then you have not completed the first step of problem solving, which is identifying the problem. That would be one instance of incompetent social work practice.

Second assumption: The more that focused interventions are applied to clearly defined target problems, the more likely are these objectives to be resolved. Clearly specifying the target of intervention means that the worker can also assess how consistently or reliably he or she is "reading" the client over time. If the worker cannot get a clear fix on the target, then it is likely that he or she will be unable to work consistently toward its resolution. More importantly, if the worker cannot get a clear fix on the target, then he or she cannot be certain what the problem is or when the problem is resolved. A subjectively defined problem (or one on which there is no objective agreement) is an invitation to irresponsible practice.

Once the objectives are clearly defined in terms that are public and behaviorally clear, then the practitioner can work on connecting a specific set of interventions with the specific targets to achieve specific kinds of outcomes. Interventions must contain the ingredients that affect the targets in appropriate ways. Models of therapy tell us what theoretical linkages may exist between the client and worker interactions and possible changes in the targets. Objective observation and measurement tell us whether the hypothesized relationships appear in this specific concrete instance. Only if we have clearly defined our target objectives are we able to measure whether the changes that were theorized to happen did in fact happen in this specific case.

We can monitor the changes that are occurring in clearly defined target objectives so as to know when our intervention strategy is on the right path toward attaining some valued goal. This is a critical part of teaching and maintaining competent social work practice. At each step along the way (such as at each interview session, or through various direct and indirect record keeping methods), we can know objectively where the client is in regard to specifically-defined targets.

When the ongoing monitoring of clearly defined target objectives shows that the client seems to be making reasonable progress toward the objective, then the social worker is supported in maintaining his or her intervention. If the client is not showing reasonable progress, then the social worker has the information immediately and should inquire about what is happening that prevents the client from attaining objectives. Obviously, many possibilities present themselves, from poorly defined targets, weak interventions, unclear instructions, poor client training to perform the needed actions, and so forth. But whatever the problems, the social worker will be able to identify that a concern exists that needs correction so as to be able to get back on the path toward problem resolution. Without knowing what the target objective is through clear definitions, the practitioner would not be able to benefit from this feedback during the helping process.

Third assumption: The more successful a practitioner is in resolving clients' problems, the more likely he or she is to accumulate efficacious methods that can be applied in new situations.

Students learn from clear experiences connecting theory, evidence from research, practice methods, and the ongoing evaluation of the mix of these in field practice. However, there is also life after social work school, and practitioners are fully capable of benefiting from their self-instruction on successful outcomes, so as to build a repertoire of efficacious methods. To know what worked, as well as that something did work, is vitally important. The more clearly the target objectives are specified, the more readily the worker can connect a given intervention with a given outcome, thus building the fund of objective practice wisdom. A worker who knows that some method is not working will be more likely than not to seek consultation; if the worker knows that very little he or she is doing is working, then the worker may seek further training or other career options. Evaluating one's own practice with clearly defined objectives and the other aspects of single-system analysis is thus a form of continuing education, a dignified self-corrective to ineffective practice that the individual can engage in before others take the unpleasant step of removing the incompetent worker.

Knowing that something worked demonstrably well with clients should also build the worker's sense of professional self-esteem, which also contributes to the development of professional competence. With a stronger sense of self-confidence, a practitioner will be more open to continuing corrective feedback on his or her performance.

In the larger sense, social work as a profession has to demonstrate its effectiveness and humaneness as part of societal accountability. The profession is probably as strong as its weakest link—the less-than-optimally-competent social worker. Thus, I advocate building into everyday practice (and everyday student education) ways to evaluate objectively one's own practice. This begins with all practitioners clearly defining targeted client problems so that ongoing practice may be monitored and corrected as part of objective evaluation.

ANNOTATED BIBLIOGRAPHY

Barlow, D.H., Hayes, S.C., & Nelson, R.O. (1984). *The scientist practitioner: Research and accountability in clinical and educational settings*. New York: Pergamon Press

This book is a brilliant exposition of clinical research methods for practitioners in applied settings, emphasizing single case designs and methods of analysis.

Barlow, D.H., & Hersen, M. (1984). *Single case experimental design: Strategies for studying behavior change, ed 2.* New York: Pergamon Press

This is a brilliant exposition of clinical research methods for practitioners in research and applied settings, emphasizing single case designs and methods of analysis.

Bloom, M., & Fischer, J. (1982). *Evaluating practice: Guidelines for the accountable profession.* Englewood Cliffs, NJ: Prentice-Hall

Modesty prevents me from describing this book as a brilliant exposition of clinical research methods for practitioners in applied settings, emphasizing single system designs and methods of analysis.

Hudson, W.W. (1976). First axioms of treatment. *Social Work, 23,* 65–66

One of Hudson's many brilliant contributions to clinical thinking and research. You will either love or hate this brief statement; there is no intermediate position.

Zimbalist, S.E. (1977). *Historic themes and landmarks in social welfare research.* New York: Harper and Row

A delightful and provocative history of six major themes in social work research, including studies of poverty, evaluative research, and the multiproblem family. Excerpts from classic studies are included.

Rejoinder to Professor Bloom   SOPHIE FREUD

The dialogue between two thinkers, Dr. Bloom and I, who have different premises about the nature of human existence and therefore have adopted different languages, is a difficult one.

The array of subtle human experiences are reduced, in Dr. Bloom's phenomenologic world, to clear quantifiable "target" problems that, like a clogged up sink, can be fixed. I mean clearly fixed. I counted a dozen "clearlys," "clear fixes," and "clears" (apart from clearly defined objectives) in Dr. Bloom's text before I gave up counting. Where Dr. Bloom perceives clarity and rationality I perceive ambiguity, complexity, and unpredictability.

Clients come to us with pain and unhappiness that they attribute to a set of internal and external causes. The social work encounter then becomes a common construction of the client's problem. This process of creating an identifiable issue, far from being a first diagnostic step, strikes me as the essence of the helping process. Dr. Bloom thinks of it as a rational process that is guided by logical reasoning, while I view it as an intuitive exchange, undergirded by images, metaphors, and analogies.

Frequently, it is not the problem but only its meaning that can be changed, and intervention might be geared to such a change of meaning, or at least new perspectives on meaning.

Dr. Bloom writes about "attaching conceptual labels" to unfortunate patterns of behavior, whereas I would think it more useful to avoid conceptual labels that may become rigid self-fulfilling prophecies.

Instead of having one particular problem that can be mastered, the client may become embedded in a conceptual label, may indeed become the label itself. Moreover, once a problem is defined, it may prematurely close the field of inquiry. While the social worker sets about fixing a clearly defined problem, the client's interest has shifted. Problems do not stay still; they change from day to day and from hour to hour.

Dr. Bloom talks about social workers "making appropriate changes" in clients' behavior. I think we can at best encourage or support, perhaps guide or even try to persuade clients to change their lives, but the idea that we can "make changes" in our clients' behavior seems quite presumptuous.

Clearly defined objectives are used by industry defining the number of cars to be produced by a certain deadline. They are used by the space program, albeit not always successfully so, because their effort to meet their clearly defined deadline recently led to catastrophe. So have other attempted conquests of nature by technology. Dr. Bloom himself refers to "the art of helping" and artistic endeavors that are destroyed by clearly defined objectives. I would hope that our new appreciation of the fragile interdependent nature of our natural and human ecology has led us to be more cautious about tenacity of purpose in any enterprise. We know from experience that trying too hard can be counterproductive and result ultimately in "more of the same." Often it is the art of letting go, rather than focusing more intensely on some issue, that effects change.

Dr. Bloom highlights the need for social workers' belief in themselves and their competence. We happily agree on this point. We warn parents not to enter their children's life with a fixed agenda, but to enter their children's subjective world and expand its boundaries. Nevertheless, we hope to give parents clear guidelines on their own optimal behavior. It is such clearly defined guidelines about their professional comportment that will enhance social workers' self-assurance and confidence in their helping mission.

NO

SOPHIE FREUD

The struggle for recognition, justification, respect, and respectability with ensuing allocation of fair and sufficient financial and human resources for social work as an institution, as well for its practitioners and clients, has been central to the field since its beginning. The ongoing debate regarding the effectiveness of social work practice is one manifestation of this effort. This debate has taken different forms, depending on the sociopolitical forces of a particular historical period. Currently the call for accountability is embedded in a technocratic climate in which people and activities are measured by their technical expertise in the production of visible goods. Indeed, the powerful watchdog of the field, the Council on Social Work Education, expects that students be taught "a scientific analytic approach to knowledge building and practice" (1988, p. 127). The council includes in such a scientific approach, learning "designs for the systematic evaluation for the students' own practice" (1988, p. 96). Single-subject design research attempts (also called single-system designs or single-case research) have thus been the latest answer to this call for accountability. I shall argue that the related expectation that social workers evaluate their own practice based on clearly defined objectives cannot be met. Indeed I consider both the concept of "clearly defined objectives" and the possibility of knowing whether one has reached them and whether they have been helpful, illusory, and presumptuous.[1]

Background Assumptions

The wording of the proposition entails a number of assumptions. The language implies that social work practitioners are people who have clear goals that they will or will not reach. Social workers are thus viewed as people who do things to other people. Indeed, the language reflects the image of a practitioner who is outside his or her practice, conscientiously using a scientific analytic approach, a technique, a suitable intervention, to bring about a predetermined goal. It places the social worker apart from the client and in control of what will happen. It is surprising that the field of social work, which has been in the forefront of embracing an ecological context related practice, should become mired in its accountability efforts in a language, imagery, and thinking that reflect an outdated nineteenth century paradigm of energy, unilateral control, and objectivity. Our current second order cybernetic thinking (Keeney, 1983) suggests that the observer is inevitably part of the observed; the encounter between two people is thought to develop in unpredictable steps and sequences that neither one nor the other participant can control. Indeed, it is suggested that the very attempt and illusion of control can become toxic.

A second outdated assumption in the above proposition is that of linear, deterministic causality. We set up objectives, pursue them, one objective at a time or several at once, week by week, or perhaps twice or three times a week with urgent matters until our goal is reached. It is as simple as walking from A to B. Or is it? In the middle of that short walk the client becomes dependent on the social worker and calls her at inconvenient moments at night, and the objective now becomes the effort to stop this behavior; the client changes his mind as to the objective because something else that is more urgent has happened; the agency runs out of funds and the client has to be transferred elsewhere; the client's or perhaps the social worker's children get arrested for drug charges; the social worker is writing a paper on single subject design and needs the client's data. Enough said; I must be writing about absurd unusual contingencies, and shall instead fall back on the growing literature that questions linear, deterministic causality, substituting accidental and unpredictable occurrences as equally likely outcomes of human events (Zimmerman, 1989).

The statement regarding clearly defined objectives also implies a philosophy of positivistic scientific objectivity which has been rejected by many social work scholars as an unsuitable philosophic basis for our field (Imre, 1984).

Whose Clearly Defined Objectives?

Clear objectives, we are told, will combat social workers' hidden agendas and arbitrary personal goals. Presumably they are negotiated by a consensus between worker and client.

Is this indeed the case most of the time? If we speak about organizationally based practice we have to deal with the objectives and normative standards of the community that funds the agency, private or public, with the agency that may have its own, for example, sectarian rules, and probably with other members of the client's family. There are, as well, the values of the social work profession that the social worker has absorbed at her school. It would be a rare situation indeed, that did not pose a whole set of contradictory objectives that need to be sorted out.

A social worker investigates a complaint of child neglect. Her first objective is to assess the facts—they are ambiguous. Her second objective is to help the mother with parenting skills and attitudes. Because the mother has not asked for help, this is a protective objective of the community on behalf of the child. The mother will have to be persuaded of the value of this objective, which leads us back to the social worker's own agenda for which clearly defined objectives were to be a remedy. If the mother remains uncooperative, a new clearly defined objective of removing the child from this protesting family needs to be established and eventually evaluated for its short-term and long-term benefit to the child, the mother, and the community. Nothing should be easier to evaluate, as long as we start with clearly defined objectives.

The adult children of an old man ask for social work help with placing him in a nursing home because he has become confused and it is unsafe for him to live alone. The man wishes to stay in his familiar surroundings. The clearly-defined objective is to find a solution to this dilemma. The man is placed in a nursing home and dies soon after the move. The objective was a nursing home placement that was achieved and so the case must be evaluated as a success. The man might have died in any case.

Assuming, however, that we have a cooperative voluntary client, should social workers accept the client's objective for change, following our proud principle of self-determination? Or could it be a primary treatment goal to question a client's objectives, introducing new options and perspectives? What about a gay man who wants help with becoming heterosexual because he had learned that it is wrong to be gay? The very process of defining new objectives for this client, by an enlightened social worker— perhaps self-acceptance and contact with the gay community—might be the essence of their engagement, confounding "intervention" with the process of setting up objectives.

Clear objectives are easiest to set in behavioral therapies, although the attempt at single-study designs has invaded more traditionally psychodynamically-based casework practice as well (Dean & Reinherz, 1986). Regardless of theoretical frame, it is concrete, observable behavior that is most easily measured and modified. Another cooperative student client contracts for help with coming to her classes on time. Indeed, as the weeks go by, the student's increasingly frequent punctuality (as confirmed by her teachers), can be beautifully upwardly graphed. Yet, at bottom, the student's lateness may be an expression of a lack of interest in a program that might be wrong for her. In work with a parent, the goal of praising the child more often is cooperatively set. Here again, our graph shows excellent progress. Yet, her son reminds this mother of her abusive former husband and the essence of the relationship continues unchanged. These are some of the many plausible situations in which the contract for specific narrow goals obscures higher, more important ones.

A judicious setting of objectives may, of course, assure successful outcome. Dean and Reinherz report how students have to learn to give up "unrealistic expectations" (1986, p. 92). In other words, clearly defined objectives may well be influenced by much less clearly-defined theoretical assumptions that dictate realistic and unrealistic goals.

Evaluations Based on Clearly Defined Objectives

Long-Term and Short-Term Effects

The difficulty, or I would say the impossibility of objective evaluations, has already been touched upon when I discussed a child placement or the transfer of an old person to a nursing home. Because each situation is unique, we cannot know whether an alternate intervention or none at all would have had better or worse consequences, either for the client, a member of his or her family, or the community. Although short-term effects of our interventions may look promising, long-term effects are usually impossible to assess. It is, of course, an axiom of traditional psychotherapy that it causes short-term anguish and discomfort while having long-term beneficial effects. A woman once told me that her "effective family therapy" had persuaded her to stay with her husband long enough to raise his children, leaving him when they were of age. She later thought with bitterness of all "the lost years" spent raising another woman's children. The children were glad and grateful that she had stayed with them, and we cannot know whether her own life would actually have been better or worse if she had left them earlier. All of us constantly make decisions that have unpredictable outcomes and we cannot know the alternate life that different decisions might have led to.

Cause and Effect Links

Even convinced empirical scientists would hesitate to make direct cause and effect links. Life is complex and multiply determined, and there is no guarantee that a particular intervention has led to a specific outcome, especially when considering individual cases. People's lives continue and their experiences may be much more powerful than the best intervention. Whereas even the link between intervention and change cannot be established with certainty, what particular aspect of the intervention might have been effective remains an unanswered question. An informal survey I once made on this subject revealed such astonishing answers as "The most significant therapy event was when the therapist picked me up at the train station to save me taxi fare" or "The one thing I shall never forget is that the therapist, breaking her therapeutic rules, gave me a cup of hot tea when I got wet on a rainy day."

It is well known that unintended learnings are an ubiquitous phenomenon. It is even possible that receiving good professional advice might inhibit someone from relying on their own opinions in the future, or that inept advice that is rejected allows the client to feel more self confident.

There are many writers in the field who believe that regardless of specific technique, it is above all the social worker and client relationship that accounts for outcome. It is a pity that complex relationships and subtle interpersonal processes have proven recalcitrant to quantitative measures.

Difficult Measurements

The whole process of measurement is infused with dubious assumptions. In single-subject design there is an attempt at a baseline measure that may even take several sessions until "treatment" starts. If the problem disappears too fast, the baseline measure is spoiled because of "reactivity" (Nelson, 1988, p. 12) and the worker must wait for the symptom to reappear until a new baseline can be taken. The fact that the very decision to seek help may change a client's problem is thus discounted; discounted as well is the possibility that a skillful social worker could find a new frame in which the problem disappears. Indeed the artificial distinction between assessment and treatment seems like a quaint relic of outdated thinking.

Changes are often measured by means of client self reports or by administering objective "reliable" scales. Self reports rely heavily on the client's cooperation, hopefully uncontaminated by a human tendency to self-deceit, or a wish to please or frustrate the social worker. The use and misuse of objective scales rests on the uncertain assumption that attitudes exist within the client and outside a context. In Keeney's (1983) words, "A perfect score on a so-called objective test is indicative of perfect trivialization" (p. 79).

Conclusion

Given that it is difficult, impossible, or undesirable to define one's objectives clearly at the beginning of a social work encounter, and that it is quite impossible to ascertain the long-range effects of a human interaction, should we conclude that social workers need not be accountable to their clients and society? Not at all. My quarrel is not with the need for accountability but with its assessment.

The field has always known that it would be unfair, impractical, and unrealistic to assess students by the outcome of their cases. Our students are evaluated by process criteria such as their ability to form relationships, to be empathic and attentive, to carry out a plan of action, to understand how their own feelings and values enter a situation, and to respect professional boundaries. Although the evaluation of mature workers might differ from that of students, it seems appropriate to focus in both cases on the person engaged in practice, rather than on disembodied objectives. We must reject the image of the social worker as a technocrat who engages in instrumental relationships for a well-defined purpose. Indeed, the relentless pursuit of deliberate purpose with technical expertise but without respect for the ecological system in which a client is embedded may breed pathology. Keeney (1983) warns us against purposeful rationality that does not include an esthetic orientation. Wahn (1986) and Imre (1984) reject the image of social workers as social engineers and the social work process as a scientific experiment. Instead, they view the worker and client interaction as a moral engagement between two persons, an existential encounter that is sustained by the social worker's humanistic values and professional integrity. I suggest that it is the nature of such professional integrity rather than objectives that needs to be more clearly defined and to which all social workers must indeed be held accountable.

NOTE

1. I would like to thank my colleague Ann Fleck Henderson for sharing her many ideas and her valuable references to the relevant literature.

ANNOTATED BIBLIOGRAPHY

Dean, R.G., & Reinherz, H. (1986). Psychodynamic practice and single system design: The odd couple. *Journal of Social Work Education,* 22(2), 85–95

This article offers a clear illustration of the application of single system designs to psychodynamic practice. It stresses the value of student learning through such an exercise, while admitting to some limitations of the model.

Imre, R.W. (1984). The nature of knowledge in social work. *Social Work,* 29(1), 41–45

The author vigorously rejects locial positivism as an appropriate basis for social work practice. She suggests that relationship principles are more important than techniques.

Handbook of accreditation standards and procedures. (1988). Curriculum Policy Statement. Washington DC: Council on Social Work Education

Keeney, B.P. (1983). *Aesthetics of change.* New York: The Guilford Press

This book offers the clearest and most compelling introduction to cybernetic theory that I have found in the literature.

Nelson, J. (1988). Single-case research and traditional practice: Issues, possibilities, solutions. Paper delivered at the Simmons College School of Social Work, April 27

Whan, M. (1986). On the nature of practice. *British Journal of Social Work,* 16, 243–250

Mr. Whan offers a convincing argument that social work is a moral rather than a technical or scientific enterprise.

Zimmerman, J.H. (1989). Determinism, science and social work. *Social Service Review,* 63, 53–62

The writer attacks deterministic thinking as coming from an outdated scientific paradigm. He stresses the negative impact that belief in determinism has had on social work research.

Rejoinder to Professor Freud

Martin Bloom

Goodness! So the concept of "clearly defined objectives," as well as the possibility of knowing whether one has reached them, is a "presumptuous" and "absurd illusion," and the very attempt to achieve control over these "disembodied objectives" is "toxic" and may "breed pathology." That does put the modest enterprise of trying to figure out how matters are going in our attempts to help clients in a bad way. But because CSWE has mandated that all BSW and MSW students should know how to evaluate their own practice, which implies objective measurement of client targets, I will try to reply to Dr. Freud's splendiferous discussion.

First, Dr. Freud appears to be operating on incorrect assumptions on the nature of scientific practice. Evaluation is an integral part of practice, not a foreign imposition on it. That means that whenever possible client and worker mutually define goals and objectives, and work together in both attaining them and monitoring progress toward that end.

Second, the death of the philosophy of scientific objectivity is greatly exaggerated, to paraphrase Mark Twain, because some practicing social workers and researchers still think in such quaint linear terms. For example, Dr. Freud herself approvingly describes a case in pure linear terms as if these "unsuitable" ideas might just convey something of use to the practitioner. In describing the case of the tardy student, Dr. Freud concludes that ". . . at bottom, the student's lateness may be an expression of a lack of interest in the program that might be wrong for her." Dr. Freud's interpretation sounds like (lateness) is caused by (lack of interest). By the way, the practitioner might evaluate his or her effectiveness with this case by measuring 1) punctuality and 2) degree of interest in the program, and then try to increase interest in the given program, or in some alternative program. With Dr. Freud's help in supplying the linear theory in this case, and with clearly defined objectives (punctuality; expressed interest in a program of study), we can provide the practitioner with a simple evaluation tool to know how well his or her interventions are succeeding. With this kind of approximate information, the practitioner can know whether to continue or to change the intervention, according to this useful feedback. I fail to see why this evaluation enterprise deserves to be called toxic.

Dr. Freud suggests that the "field has always known that it would be unfair, impractical, and unrealistic to assess students by the outcomes of their cases." I must not be in that field because I can think of nothing more important to students than to know what it is they did that helped or did not help a client to some demonstrable degree. Such knowledge may include objective information on whether or not they were "empathic, attentive." It may include information on how well they delivered their interventive strategy. But it certainly must include whether the client's problem is resolved or not, if we want to stay in business as a helping profession and teachers of helping professionals.

I am in full agreement with Dr. Freud that scientific practice should include "respect for the ecological system in which the client is embedded." Indeed, I have spent the last decade trying both to develop this ecological or configural perspective along with the evaluation processes illustrated by single-system designs. However, I wish that Dr. Freud had developed with equal clarity her point about the fundamental nature of the helping encounter, that existential moment that is "sustained by the social worker's humanistic values and professional integrity." I strongly suggest that we manifest such professional integrity when and only when we solve client problems. A warm, humanistic relationship is not an end; it is merely the beginning of effective and humane practice.

Should Social Workers Use Written Contracts?

EDITOR'S NOTE: One of the many differences of opinion about how social work practice should be conducted concerns the use of written service agreements between social workers and their clients. These are case management tools not legal documents. That is why some writers prefer to call them service agreements rather than service contracts. Those who argue in favor of their use believe that clear written service agreements can enhance the quality of services offered and increase the likelihood that some of the ethical and legal requirements of high quality practice are insured such as informed consent. Those who argue against their use believe that written agreements offer false assurances and are not actually ethical when parties of unequal power are involved.

Theodore J. Stein, DSW, argues YES. He is Professor of Social Welfare at the School of Social Welfare, State University of New York at Albany. Professor Stein was director of the Alameda Project, an experimental effort to counter foster care drift, and of the Illinois-West Virginia Project in which procedures for decision making at child welfare intake were developed and tested. His publications include *Children in Foster Homes: Achieving Continuity in Care* (with Eileen D. Gambrill and Kermit T. Wiltse, 1978), *Decision Making at Child Welfare Intake: A Handbook For Practitioners* (with Tina L. Rzepnicki, 1983), and *Child Welfare and the Law* (1990).

Stewart Collins, MA, and Chris Rojeck, MA, argue NO. Stewart Collins is Senior Lecturer in Social Work, University of Wales, Bangor, where he teaches social work theory and practice. He is the author of numerous articles as well as coauthor of *Social Work and Received Ideas* (with C. Rojek and G. Peacock). He is currently contributing to and editing *Alcohol, Social Work and Helping* (Forthcoming, 1990).

Chris Rojek is Senior Editor in Sociology with Routledge Publishers. He is the author of numerous articles and author, coauthor, and coeditor of four books. His current research interests include leisure, travel, and post-modernism. Forthcoming books include *Ways of Escape: Transformations of Leisure and Travel in Modernity and Post Modernity;* a coedited book (with E. Dunning) *Sport and Leisure in the Civilising Process,* and a coedited book (with B. Turner), *Forget Baudrillard?*

YES

THEODORE J. STEIN

Contracts, service agreements, and case plans refer to written agreements between social workers and clients. This article begins with a brief review of the use of written contracts in social work and other helping professions. Arguments for their use, based on professional ethics and accountability, are presented.

Background

In the mid-1970s, Stein, Gambrill, and Wiltse argued that written contracts between caseworkers and the parents of children in foster care should be routinely used. They presented data showing that 70 percent of children whose parents signed contracts were reunited with their families of origin, compared to 16 percent of those whose parents did not sign contracts.[1]

A spate of articles followed in which scholars debated the merits of using written contracts. But the social work literature on the use of written service agreements is not extensive. A computer search of social work and psychological and sociological abstracts shows that only ten of fifty-one articles (20%) published between 1976 and 1988, in which the use of written service agreements between clients and service providers are discussed, were in journals directed specifically to a social work audience (e.g., *Social Work, Social Casework*). The remaining articles were published in journals directed toward professionals in psychology, vocational rehabilitation, and medicine.

Regardless of the disciplinary focus of journals reviewed, most discuss the use of written contracts as a therapeutic tool or refer to their use with specific populations, such as those in methadone treatment programs, in inpatient facilities, with borderline patients, and with clients who are suicidal.[2]

Written case plans for children in foster care are required by federal law.[3] Federal and state courts have ruled that written case plans are an entitlement that cannot be withheld without due process of law[4] and that child welfare workers must develop behaviorally specific case plans that meet the basic requirements outlined in the next section.

The literature on the use of written service agreements suggests that they have become a normative aspect of social work practice, although some people question whether contracts must be in writing and whether they are appropriate for all populations.[5] Rojek and Collins (1987) argue against the use of written contracts on both abstract and concrete grounds. They suggest that the different meanings people assign to "words, expressions, and propositions" (p. 206) undermine the notion that contracts can effectively communicate shared agreements.[6] On the practical level they state that a contract between a social worker and client cannot be an "agreement between equals," (p. 203) because social workers have more power than their clients.

Ethical Issues

Ethical concerns arise when the actions of one person have an effect on others. Helping relationships are particularly susceptible to ethical concerns. Involuntary clients may think that they have no choice but to comply with service providers to regain custody of their children, for example, or to obtain their release from programs to which they have been remanded by the courts. Voluntary clients may feel unable to participate fully in making the choices that affect their lives because of the mystique that surrounds many therapeutic endeavors; a mystique that is reinforced by professionals through their use of esoteric jargon that limits the lay person's access to full participation.

The potential for abuse in helping relationships is explicitly recognized in the code of ethics of the National Association of Social Workers. It admonishes professionals to: 1) provide clients with accurate and complete information regarding the extent and nature of the services available to them; 2) apprise clients of their risks, rights, opportunities, and obligations associated with social services provided to them; and 3) make every effort to foster maximum self determination on the part of clients.

These precepts offer a general sense of the professional's responsibilities but are useful only to the extent to which they can be operationalized. Service agreements that are written in descriptive language that is accessible to lay persons provide a framework for operationalizing these guidelines. Written agreements should state the 1) client's long-term objective in working with a service provider; 2) goals that refer to the outcomes that will be observed when the problems that must be resolved to reach the client's objective are remediated; 3) tasks that are to be undertaken by clients, social workers, and community providers in helping clients achieve their objectives and goals; and 4) timeframes for achieving the overall objective, for accomplishing intermediate goals, and for undertaking specified tasks. The consequences for clients for adhering or failing to adhere to agreements should also be specified. The amount of information that must be communicated to clients argues against verbal contracts. Even when made with the best of intentions, verbal agreements may lead to misunderstandings and disagreements regarding responsibilities and expectations.

Accountability

Accountability takes on different meanings in relation to the question: "Accountable to whom?" Social workers are accountable to the public that funds service programs, to the agencies that administer them, to the profession, to clients, and often to the courts. Written service agreements provide a framework for accountability to all.

In child welfare, for example, federal and state law requires written service agreements for which minimum content is specified. Review of case plans every 6 months is mandated by law. If developed in accordance with the standards set forth in the law, case plans satisfy minimum criteria for accountability.

Written service agreements provide protections for clients who have a document showing the conditions that were established for them to obtain their objectives. Such documentation provides a measure of safety from arbitrary and capricious decision making by service providers. Service providers also have a document that shows their effort to inform clients of their rights and responsibilities.

Written service agreements provide a framework for ongoing monitoring of the effects of service provision. For example, if one of the goals in a case plan states that "the client will acquire and demonstrate skills at using noncorporal methods of discipline," and the responsibilities of clients and social workers in approximating this goal are spelled out with timetables for task accomplishment, workers can monitor compliance with each task and, if needed, intervene if tasks are not being accomplished according to agreements in the service plan.

Discussion

Written service agreements provide an ethical framework for practice and for establishing accountability. For the latter reason some may shy away from their use, develop written agreements in ways that undermine their potential (by using vague language, for example), or use verbal rather than written agreements.

The arguments made against the use of written agreements are not persuasive. The suggestion that inequality in the relationship between clients and social workers prevents mutuality and mitigates against the use of written agreements seems to argue more persuasively for than against their use. The possibility that a therapeutic relationship is unequal places a significant burden on the practitioner to show that every effort was made to fully inform clients of their rights and responsibilities and of what they can expect from working with social workers and other service providers.

That clients differ in their literacy skills argues for developing written agreements using language that is accessible to clients and for using different methods for communicating essential information. For example, tape recordings are helpful for those who are not able to read, as is the use of interpreters to assist in wording agreements in the client's primary language.

The use of written service agreements is not a guarantee that clients fully understand their rights and responsibilities, nor can one ensure that a client's signature on a service agreement was freely given. Written service agreements are not a perfect tool, but they do provide a systematic means for communicating necessary information to clients.

NOTES

1. Stein, T.J., Gambrill, E.D., & Wiltse, K.T. (1974). Foster care: The use of contracts. *Public Welfare,* 32(4), 20–25; Stein, T.J., Gambrill, E.D., & Wiltse, K.T. (1978). *Children in foster homes: Achieving continuity of care.* New York: Praeger Publishers, p. 91.

2. Barker, R.L. (1987). Spelling out the rules: The written worker-client contract. *Journal of Independent Social Work,* 1(2), 67–77; Pearson, J., Thoennes, N., Mayer, B., et al. (1986). Mediation of child welfare cases. *Family Law Quarterly,* XX(2), 303–322; Magura, S., Casriel, C., Goldsmith, D.S., et al. (1987). Contracting with clients in methadone treatment. *Social Casework,* 68(8), 485–493; Levendusky, P.G., Berglas, S., Dudley, C.P., et al. (1983). Therapeutic contract program: Preliminary report on a behavioral alternative to the token economy. *Behaviour Research and Therapy,* 21(2), 137–142; Rudestam-Kjell, E. (1985–1986), Suicide and the selfless patient. *Psychotherapy Patient,* 2(2), 83–95; McEnany, G.W., & Tescher, B.E. (1985). Contracting for care: One nursing approach to the hospitalized borderline patient. *Journal of Psychosocial Nursing and Mental Health Services,* 23(4), 11–18.

3. The Adoption Assistance and Child Welfare Act, 42 U.S.C. Section 670, *et seq.*

4. *Joseph and Josephine A. v. The New Mexico Department of Human Services,* 575 F. Supp. 346 (1983); *Lynch v. King,* 550 F. Supp. 325

(1982), upheld *sub nom Lynch v. Dukakis* 719 F.2d 504 (1983); *L.J. v. Massinga,* Civil No. JH–84–4409, "Memorandum an Order" (MD. July 27, 1987), 838 F.2d 118 (4th Cir. 1988), *cert denied* 109 S. Ct. 816 (1989); *G.L. v. Zumwalt,* 564 F. Supp. 1030 (1983); *Del A. v. Edwin Edwards,* Class Action: No. 86–0801 (February 1986).

5. Seabury, B.A. (1985). "The beginning phase: Engagement, initial assessment, and contracting." In Laird, J. & Hartman, A. (Eds.), *A handbook of child welfare: Context, knowledge, and practice.* New York: Free Press, pp. 352–359.

6. Rojek, C., & Collins, S. (1987). Contract or con trick? *British Journal of Social Work,* 17, 199–211.

ANNOTATED BIBLIOGRAPHY

Court, J.H. (1987). Addressing undressing. *Australian Psychologist,* 22(1), 17–28

This article discusses the use of written contracts from the standpoint of ethical issues that arise in working with clients.

Seabury, B.A. (1985). The beginning phase: Engagement, initial assessment, and contracting. In Laird, J., & Hartman, A. (Eds.), *A handbook of child welfare: Context, knowledge, and practice.* New York: Free Press, pp. 352–359

This article contains a general discussion of the use of written contracts in social work and describes the different ways in which written contracts may be used.

Stein, T.J., Gambrill, E.D., & Wiltse, K.T. (1978). *Children in foster homes: Achieving continuity of care.* New York: Praeger Publishers

The use of written contracts with the biological parents of children in foster care is discussed and data describing the relationship between a parent's willingness to sign a contract and the likelihood of their working to regain custody of their children are presented. Examples of written contracts are contained in this report.

Rejoinder to Professor Stein
STEWART COLLINS AND CHRIS ROJEK

Dr. Stein presents evidence from small scale empirical research with "specific populations" of foster parents, methadone users, "borderline" patients, and suicidal clients. In fact there are limits imposed on empirical research in contract work that support our earlier arguments. Empiricists equate reality with what can be perceived in interactions between individuals and are uncomfortable with abstractions such as class, race, and gender. They are in danger of forgetting that "Empirical social research cannot get around the fact that all the data it investigates, the subjective no less than the objective, are mediated by society" (Adorno, 1976, p. 255). Therefore, subjective motivations (wills, hopes, wants) can be exaggerated at the expense of objective social influences (class, race, gender). Writers advocating written contract work are thus constantly in danger of ignoring forces beyond the individual's control, and support "the existing state of affairs by refusing to engage seriously with structural questions" (Rojek & Collins, 1988, p. 619).

Dr. Stein goes on to present arguments in favor of written contracts that emphasize the significance of ethical practice and accountability. He talks about social work's accountability to the law, the profession, to clients and the public, arguing that contracts provide barriers to arbitrary and capricious decision making. Unfortunately, Dr. Stein neglects the power of social work discourse to overwhelm the client. Laudable though his intentions may be, written contracts are informed by social work discourse. For example, accountability has one meaning to social workers because it links in with certain social work concepts and exists as part of the language of social work and the social work world, while it may have a very different meaning to a client or user, as it links in with their concepts, their language, and their world. To repeat, the client's language and world is usually characterized by much less power than that encompassed by the social workers sphere of operations. At one point Dr. Stein talks about "the consequences for clients for adhering or failing to adhere to agreements" without mentioning any similar consequences for social workers who fail to meet agreed requirements (Stein, 1990). This reinforces our argument that social workers have more power than the client and it is likely to be the client who suffers the consequences of any failure in implementing written agreements, not the worker.

Nor can we see that Dr. Stein's emphasis on the code of ethical practice for social work and expectations of ethical behavior by social workers as being likely to lead to more equitable contract work, to overcome the wider enmeshment of the worker in structural matters. Issues of class, race, and gender will still dominate and are bound to effect written contracts made by social workers. Codes of ethical practice, while providing valuable guidelines, cannot compete with the structural giants that dominate our social world, including the use of written contracts in social work.

REFERENCES

Adorno, T.W. (1976). Sociology and empirical research. In Connerton, P. (Ed.), *Critical sociology*. Hammondsworth: Penguin.

Rojek, C., & Collins, S. (1988). Contract or contrick revisited? *British Journal of Social Work* 18, 611–622.

NO

STEWART COLLINS AND CHRIS ROJEK

The first point we would wish to make is that we are not suggesting that social workers should not use contracts. We are in favor of attempts to create genuine partnerships between social workers and clients. Some of the most common arguments given in favor of contract use are that contracts recognize the limited and reciprocal nature of rights, conditions, and obligations; they cut down suspicion and opportunities for mistrust, misunderstanding, and avoidance of key issues. Secondly, it is claimed that contract making leads to more ethical forms of practice, with greater scope for openness, honesty, and power sharing. Thirdly, contracts are advocated as an aid in managing complex and difficult workloads. And finally, they are seen as versatile; they can be used in a wide variety of settings including work with individuals, couples, family groups, and in residential settings.

Contract work is thus part of a growing movement that recognizes the role of the client, consumer, or user as an active, empowered participant in relationships with social workers. We actively support such trends and have written about them elsewhere (Rojek, Peacock, & Collins, 1989). However, we have reservations about some of the claims that have been made about contract work. We develop our argument by using critical material from the field of social work and link contract making into a wider framework of social and economic relations in society. We contend that contract work also reflects contradiction around issues, such as power, inequality and ambiguity in social work. We believe social workers should be alerted to these issues.

Opponents in the field have expressed reservations about the openness, honesty and reciprocity of contract approaches. Is an "equal" relationship possible between social workers and clients? Social workers accumulate expertise, knowledge, and skills through training and work experience. Clearly most clients have not had the same work experience; they cannot, by definition, draw upon similar knowledge and skills. In both a positional and real sense, social workers have much more power than their clients.

A second reservation should be noted. Contract work is largely helpful in the short term to increase clients' confidence and provide a small sense of achievement, satisfaction, and success. Yet its success in achieving change in the long term is problematic. Contracts are usually quite specific and narrow in their focus. Long-term problems may not be amenable to change, and problems in work, emotional life, or wider social relations may well continue. A contract cannot usually provide long-term genuinely supportive solutions—only short term palliatives.

Furthermore, social workers do not operate as isolated individuals. They are part of the wider agency that employs them. Agency resources, guidelines, and policy may well be incompatible with what the social worker views as being "right" for a particular client. It follows that contract work cannot be concerned simply with what is "right" for the client, because the worker is involved in a complex system of obligations to the agency, accountability to middle and senior managers, and sometimes to legislation that restricts possible courses of action. In addition, the required agency resources may simply not be available. It follows that contract work cannot be said to be free, open, and flexible because it is preempted by the legal and economic framework in which social work is located.

The question of measuring what is achieved by contracts also suggests problems. While it is not difficult to quantify contract work in terms of frequency and length of sessions, it is quite another thing to measure the quality of such encounters. When social workers and clients formulate and follow through contract work, is the social workers contribution nonauthoritarian and nonjudgmental? Does the social worker's behavior maximize opportunities for mutuality and participation? Contract work is about making judgments, and the process of negotiation is not open ended because it has a purpose—to improve the client's capacities and social orientation. The worker "cannot avoid expressing a practical morality and an ideology in addressing situations . . . every possible response is value laden" (Clark with Asquith, 1985, p. 35). Is it possible, therefore, for workers to avoid imposing their values and their morality in subtle and unknown ways? Even the worker's shake of the head, smile, grimace, and raising of eyebrows will all influence contract negotiation as values intrude despite the worker's best intentions.

We would now like to move on to look at some wider themes linked to sociology and philosophy that raise further questions about contracts. These can be split into three sections: surrounding freedom and contracts, meaning and signifying systems, and control and discipline. First, freedom and contracts. Most social work clients are working class and poor. Usually, their experiences of education, work, housing, health, and social security have been at the rough end of contract relations:

> "They are the real experts in the metaphysics of contractual inequality. It is an expertise founded on years of experience of state assistance, low pay, struggling to make ends meet and living in continual fear of debt and dispossession. Compared with this, the attempt to build open, equal and fair contracts in social work is certainly very worthy.

It is indeed likely to give clients a fleeting sense of freedom and possibility. But it is a caricature of the contract relation which clients experience outside the social work setting. The economic inequality and bureaucratic organisation of capitalist society prevents the individual from developing fully and freely" (Rojek & Collins, 1988, p. 205).

Therefore, we suggest that when social workers enter into contract relationships, their intentions to provide clients with a genuine or consistent experience of freedom are seriously flawed, however well intended, because the contract approach operates with a concept of freedom that has little application in wider society. Most contract relations in "everyday life" are rarely open to mutual evaluation and joint reconstruction. We suggest that when social workers engage in contract work with clients it generates false, artificial assumptions, precepts, and demands about life under capitalism. For example, from a Marxist viewpoint, in relation to employment, work contracts may be said to be unfair because the division of power between the worker and capitalist is uneven. We endorse the Marxist conclusion that the creation of genuine partnership and openness in society requires political and economic changes of a very basic kind. At the same time we also believe that profound cultural changes are required, relating especially to race and gender, and Marxism does not adequately provide for these. Yet we would be more critical of contract approaches in social work because its capacity for providing such cultural and attitude change around race and gender issues is even more severely limited. The approach consistently underplays the structural dimensions of personal problems and can act only as a palliative in relation to these wider issues.

We now wish to move on to examine our second section: meaning and signifying systems related to contracts. We state unequivocally that the viability of contract making depends on the common meaning that workers and clients read into written agreements. Contract work is clearly a linguistically grounded enterprise. Words can easily acquire new and unanticipated meanings, and different people interpret the same words in different ways. Thus, in the mind of the social worker, the connotative means of key concepts in contracts such as "mutuality," "participation," "explicitness," and "accountability" are different from those in the mind of the client. Each person locates or places these terms in different signifying systems; the social worker in the language of social work, the client in the language of the layperson. Thus the social worker is equipped with a technical and theoretical language that the lay person does not possess.

If we put this point in the terminology of discourse theory, social workers have a notion of what contract signifies (means) because we are aware of how it differs from other signs (social work concepts) in the signifying system (language of social work) (Barthes, 1957). As Pêcheux puts it "Words, expressions, propositions . . . change their meanings according to the position held by those who use them" (Pêcheux, 1975, p. 111).

The writings of Derrida and Foucault have considered the role of power in those institutions in society that intend to be facilitative and progressive, such as hospitals, educational institutions, psychiatric units, and, of course, social work. The social worker approaches contract encounters with normative expectations about negotiating agreements, selecting tasks, goals, and criteria of monitoring that the client does not possess Thus, the worker's experience of contracts makes him or her a theorist, whereas the client is a nontheorist. Hence it is hard to see how the social worker can be anything other than at an advantage in managing contract work. The poststructuralist approach reveals how power and ideology are mediated through the language of contract work, even where relationships are intended to go beyond relations of power and ideology.

There are important social and institutional dimensions in generating meaning in contract work, but at the same time discourse theory argues that communication generally is highly problematic because meanings are never concrete, fixed, definite, and unambiguous. This has significant implications for the viability of contract work, because the poststructuralists claim that precision and explicitness as personified by contracts are impossible objectives. Meaning continues to be fluid and flexible as relationships between a social worker and client develop, because communication necessarily involves misunderstanding and "undecidability" (Lacan, 1977; Eagleton, 1982). Such thinking encourages social workers to have a critical attitude to the supposed sharpness, precision, certainty, and clear language said to be involved in contract work.

Our final section is concerned with control and discipline and some other negative features of contract work. Contracts fragment the social work relationship into a number of narrow goals and tasks; the contract primarily supplies well-defined criteria to evaluate the quality of a client's efforts. Evaluations may be jointly conducted, but it is largely the social worker's recording of evaluation that determines how line management and other workers will perceive and may eventually relate to the client, despite recent movements that allow clients greater access to records. A record that labels the client as either uncooperative or negative could have serious implications for his or her future: for example, such material could be included in a court report. Thus, "failures" in contract work can have unintended negative consequences and "spin offs" for the client despite intentions to be open and mutually evaluative; the client can be still "blamed," with long-term implications for his or her future contacts with the agency.

Furthermore, contract encounters could be used by line managers to monitor the productivity of social work staff. Written contracts provide a careful record of the clients' problems and the content and results of the contract relationship. The written form is also compatible with standardization; the growth of proforma contracts would greatly strengthen the position of line managers, perhaps enabling them to dictate centrally the contract encounter and standardize the results. The total effect would be to produce a strong argument for rationalizing the use of labor in social work. This brings us to a further alternative point. If contracts clearly lay down specific rights and obligations between worker and client, then equally this could be interpreted as a bid to limit liability between the parties. Contracts are joint agreements that the client enters into freely. In real terms they require the client to cooperate with the social worker to establish the means and ends of the relationship. The contract is therefore tantamount to the client, partially indemnifying the social worker against the collapse of the relationship.

If something goes wrong with the relationship then the contract can be used as proof that the social worker is not solely to blame. In this way the contract limits the liability of the social worker to the client; this should prove attractive to line managers wary of the moral panics and accusations sometimes linked with state social work.

In conclusion, we argue that contract work has been used to "bring the client in" but "keep society out." Contract work involves a narrow view of social work that treats the personal problems of individuals and isolates them from a wider societal context, characterized by class inequality, patriarchy, and racism. The real inequality between social worker and client in organizational power and theoretical knowledge cannot be set to one side. Clients' general, past experiences of contracts in low-trust relations are neglected and the language of contract work is not neutral. Confused perceptions, misunderstandings, and ambiguous messages are hard to avoid. In particular, the language of contract approaches is not merely technical. It is underpinned by moral, social, and political values that must be confronted.

REFERENCES

Barthes, R. (1957). *Mythologies*. St. Albans: Paladin.
Clark, C., with Asquith, S. (1985). *Social work and social philosophy: A guide for practice*. London: Routledge.
Eagleton, T. (1982). Wittgenstein's friends. *New Left Review,* 135.
Lacan, J. (1977). *Ecrits*. London: Tavistock.
Pecheux, M. (1975). *Language, semantics and ideology*. London: Macmillan.

Rojek, C., & Collins, S. (1988). Contract or contrick? *British Journal of Social Work,* 17, 199–211.

Rojek, C., Peacock, G., & Collins, S. (1989). *The haunt of misery.* London: Routledge.

ANNOTATED BIBLIOGRAPHY

Rojek, C., & Collins, S. (1988). Contract or contrick? *British Journal of Social Work,* 17, 199–211

This paper offers a critical examination of the contract approach in social work. It argues that the claims made on behalf of contract work are extravagant and untenable. Critical material is used from social work practice, sociology, and philosophy.

Rojek, C., & Collins, S. (1988). Contract or contrick revisited? *British Journal of Social Work,* 18, 611–622

This paper is again concerned with the limitations of contract approaches. Significant contributions are drawn from discourse analysis and the limitations of empiricism. It highlights the importance of structural analyses in contract work—related to class, race, and gender. Also the value of open dialogue in social work is emphasized, based on a wide variety of theories.

Rojek, C., Peacock, G., & Collins, S. (1988). *Social work and received ideas.* London: Routledge

One of the first books to examine the language of both traditional Marxist and feminist social work as forms of power. The will to help and care for people in distress can unintentionally result in new types of dependency, control, and domination. The book draws on major theoretics of social power such as Foucault and shows how these ideas apply to questions of welfare, need, and care.

Rojek, C., Peacock, G., & Collins, S. (1989). *The haunt of misery.* London: Routledge

Many social workers feel angry, confused, and stranded. In Great Britain, The New Right's triumphant march has been matched by the apparent exhaustion of collectivism. This is a series of critical essays for critical times. Written by academics and professionals, the essays cover social work and unemployment, the crisis of AIDS and HIV infection, drug use, client collectives, the elderly, ethnic minorities, mental health, and social worker and client self-management.

Rejoinder to Stewart Collins and
Chris Rojek
THEODORE J. STEIN

Rojeck and Collins take issue with the use of written contracts between social workers and their clients. The potential power differential between parties is at the heart of their critique. They express this concern in various ways, asking whether an equal relationship between social workers and clients is possible, pointing out that the context within which many social workers practice precludes an exclusive focus on what is "right" for a client, and arguing that the limits of language and shared meaning constrain a client from full participation in the contract process. I have taken the position that the potential for inequality in helping relationships argues for, rather than against, the use of written agreements.

Inequality may be an inherent feature of helping relationships because of the expertise of the helper and the likelihood that a person, when seeking help, may be more vulnerable to persuasion than at other times. The involuntary status of many clients may exacerbate problems of inequality. However, beyond offering a critique of written contracts, Rojek and Collins do not suggest ways out of the dilemma they identify. One might infer, especially from their sociological and philosophical critique, that relationships between social workers and their clients are so vulnerable to abuse as to render the entire helping enterprise bankrupt, thus leading to the conclusion that we must restructure totally the profession's approach to working with clients. In the introduction to their article, however, these authors endorse efforts to "create genuine partnerships between social workers and clients," but they give no hint as to how this would be accomplished.

One final point is that Rojeck and Collins make the use of written contracts synonymous with the helping relationship. After noting that "contract work is largely helpful in the short term," they state that ". . . *its* success in achieving change in the long term is problematic" (emphasis added). Use of the pronoun its implies that contracts, in and of themselves, are expected to create the kinds of changes that social workers and their clients seek, rather than recognizing that contracts are but one tool in an armamentarium of interventions. The process of developing a contract with a client may have therapeutic benefits and the contract itself may be viewed as a form of intervention. However, to assume that the contract can by itself create change seems a narrow view and one that invests in contracts a power that they cannot have.

Is Private Practice a Proper Form of Social Work?

EDITOR'S NOTE: The increased interest in counseling among those able and willing to pay for such services was not lost on social workers who engage in private practice in increasing numbers. There has been a continuing debate in the field of social work about whether private practice is a proper kind of work for social workers to pursue. Does private practice not drain resources away from populations of traditional concern to social work? Do the skills required in agency based and private practice complement each other or are there harmful carry over effects? On the other hand, what is the harm of social workers engaging in private practice, especially when this is on a part-time basis, perhaps supplementing income gained from agency-based employment? Perhaps private practice enables social workers to persevere in often excessively challenging public agency jobs.

Jerome C. Wakefield, DSW, answers YES. He is Assistant Professor in the Columbia University School of Social Work, where he teaches courses in clinical practice and personality theory. He has practiced clinical social work in both public and private settings. Current projects include a critique of DSM-III-R's concept of mental disorder, an article on the conceptual foundations of personality theory, an article (with Robert Spitzer) on the diagnosis of adjustment disorders, and a book on the relationship of Freud's theory to contemporary cognitive approaches.

Cheryl A. Richey, DSW, and Gail A. Stevens, MS, answer NO. Cheryl Richey is Associate Professor, School of Social Work, University of Washington, where she teaches graduate courses in clinical practice and research. Her publications include *Building Assertive Skills* (with J.C. Morton and M. Kellett) and *Taking Charge of Your Social Life* (with E. Gambrill). Professor Richey's current research and writing interests include social network characteristics of and social support facilitation with diverse populations.

Gail A. Stevens, MS, is a Ph.D. candidate at the School of Social Work, University of Washington, where she is completing her dissertation on the future practice interests of graduate social work students, with special attention to factors associated with plans to pursue careers in the public sector with less "appealing" client groups. Her research interests include the social, cultural, and biological correlates of interpersonal violence.

YES

JEROME WAKEFIELD

The question of whether social workers should engage in private practice is really a question about the professional mission of social work and about the compatibility of private practice with that mission. Private practice is a noncontroversial option for teachers, doctors, and lawyers simply because private practice is perceived by those professions as merely one more way to pursue their essential missions of education, health, and legal representation, respectively. Social work's unique concern about private practice is due to the fact that some social work educators believe that private practice is antithetical to the achievement of the profession's mission. I will try to show that objections to private practice are all variations on this argument regarding the mission of social work, but that the objections are based on an inadequate appreciation of the multifaceted nature of that mission.

There can be no doubt that private practice has become an accepted part of social work; many states legally recognize such practice through licensing laws, most clinical practitioners consider private practice to be a legitimate social work activity (Alexander, 1987), and private practice is a common goal of students entering clinical social work training. There is even a journal, *Journal of Independent Social Work,* devoted exclusively to issues of concern to the private practitioner. Despite this, many social work educators continue to dispute the appropriateness of private practice, and their objections must be taken seriously because they can have a substantial impact. Such objections can influence course offerings, admission criteria, and other educational resource allocation decisions; they can deepen the rift between private and agency practitioners, weakening the profession; and they can cause students to experience painful conflicts about the acceptability of their professional goals and the appropriateness of social work as a career choice. Any disparity between student aspirations and institutional ideology about private practice could also encourage a corrosive dishonesty and hypocrisy in admission procedures and student-faculty relationships. Consequently, it is important to establish whether the objections to private practice are valid.

On the face of it, an ethical and skillful professional should be able to practice in any setting he or she prefers. Thus, the burden of proof in the private practice debate is on the objector, who must show that there are special reasons for thinking that private practice is not a proper practice setting for social workers. I will examine the four most plausible objections to private practice and argue that they are all misguided. In doing so, I will address only the question of whether there is something intrinsically objectionable about social workers engaging in private practice. Critics of private practice often point to a broad range of practical problems, like the need to ensure that practitioners have sufficient training before entering private practice and the problem of adequately staffing public agencies that must compete with the allure of private practice. Critics also emphasize negative aspects of private practice such as lack of interaction with colleagues and income insecurity. These problems exist in many professions, however, and can be addressed in various ways; they certainly do not justify a wholesale rejection of private practice as a legitimate service delivery system. Proponents of private practice often emphasize the rewards and advantages of private practice, such as independence, enhanced income, flexible hours, and the opportunity to develop clinical skills. However, the fact that private practice provides such benefits in no way proves that it is a proper form of social work. I will ignore all these practical pros and cons in order to focus my analysis on "in principle" objections that aim to show that, even if all the practical problems could be resolved and even if all the touted benefits and rewards exist, there is still something inherently wrong with a social worker being in private practice.

The "Fee" Argument against Private Practice

The first objection is that clients must pay for private practice services rather than getting the services free or at token cost. This objection ignores the fact that private practice fees are often paid by insurers. However, because universal insurance is not imminent, the objection remains. To understand the objection, we have to understand what is supposed to be wrong with a client paying for private social work services.

The "fee" objection seems to be based on the presupposition that social work provides services that people are owed as a right and for which they therefore should not have to pay. The notion that social work services are a matter of right is based in turn, I think, on a correct intuition about the nature of social work: social work services are concerned with "distributive justice," that is, with the just and fair distribution of basic resources needed for social functioning (Wakefield, 1988a, 1988b). Certainly everyone should have access to such justice-related services, regardless of ability to pay.

Nonetheless, the "fee" objection is mistaken. Even when a service is owed to everyone as a right, people may still be required to pay for the service if they can afford to do so. For example, a person accused of a crime has a constitutional right to legal counsel, but only indigent defendants are provided with a court-appointed attorney. Otherwise, the right to counsel is exercised by arranging for private services. Similarly, in city hospitals where there is a de facto right to medical care, patients who can afford treatment must pay, while indigent patients do not pay. Moreover, even where there is free service available to all, as in the case of education, people have the option of choosing available private alternatives, such as private schools or tutors. Social work services are indeed a matter of justice and a person's right and should be available to everyone regardless of ability to pay, but it does not follow that such services should be available free of charge to those who have the ability to pay, or that providing private alternatives is inappropriate.

The "Middle Class Clientele" Objection

Clients who enter private practice, whether they pay for their own treatment or they possess adequate insurance to cover the fee, are likely to be in the middle socioeconomic class or higher. The second objection is that, by treating middle class clients, private practice turns its back on the profession's true constituency, the economically deprived. This argument would not apply if there were some sort of voucher system enabling clients to choose private practitioners over agencies, but such a system is certainly not imminent. To understand this objection, we have to understand what is supposed to be wrong with social workers serving a middle class clientele.

The belief that social work should limit its clientele to the economically deprived again seems to be based on an implicit and, I believe, correct understanding of the mission of social work as distributive justice. That is, social work seeks to ensure that each individual has at least a fair minimal share of the resources provided by society that enable the individual to function socially. Liberal theories of justice from which the social work profession's values are derived imply that it is unfair for any person to be deprived of a minimally decent level of basic resources, which in the case of economic resources is known as the "poverty line." Given that social work's task is to alleviate distributive injustice, and given the additional and common assumption that economic resources are the only kind of resources that are unjustly distributed, it would follow that social workers should treat only economically deprived clients.

It is a mistake to think that economic resources are the only ones that are subject to distributive injustice, however; in fact, there is unjust deprivation of social and psychological resources, as well. Recent work in the theory of justice (e.g., Rawls, 1971) has made it clear that the concept of distributive justice applies to any sphere where resources necessary for basic functioning are produced through social cooperation and interaction and are distributed in accordance with social structures and processes. An element of social fairness always enters into the distribution of such resources. Resources like opportunities, liberties, social supports, and family environments, as well as many important psychological traits, are to one degree or another "distributed" in accordance with social structures, processes, and rules, and are therefore subject to considerations of distributive justice. For example, the field of child welfare is largely concerned with the redistribution of childhood family environments in those cases where the basic distributive system, under which each child is raised by its natural parent(s), deprives the child of a minimally decent environment for growth.

Psychological resources such as self-respect, self-esteem, impulse control, social skills, and many others are certainly as important to people's well-being and ability to function effectively as are economic resources. There are specific social processes and opportunities through which such psychological traits develop. Thus, someone who has been deprived of the appropriate experiences and consequently is extremely low in these traits is suffering from a form of psychological deprivation that is just as much a matter of distributive injustice as is economic poverty. Moreover, the very same moral reasons that justify intervention to help the economically deprived also apply to the psychologically deprived. In both cases, society has not provided an individual with the basic resources necessary for the individual to function at even a minimally sufficient level. Thus, intervention with clients who are psychologically deprived is squarely within the traditional mission of social work, whatever the psychologically deprived client's economic status. This is not to downplay the critical importance of economic deprivation on social work's agenda or the critical importance of agency and public practice. It is rather to emphasize that other forms of deprivation, including psychological deprivation, should also be of concern, and that such forms of deprivation often occur independently of economic deprivation and therefore can appropriately be treated in private practice.

The "Psychotherapy" Objection

The third objection to private practice is that private practitioners do not perform true social work services because they generally rely on psychotherapeutic models of treatment, particularly psychodynamic or behavioral models, that focus on the individual and do not fit the social work profession's essential person-environment focus. I accept the premise that at the heart of social work there lies a concern for person-environment interaction. This idea is wholly compatible with the notion that social work is concerned with distributive justice. Justice, after all, consists of a relationship between the social environment and the person, namely, a relationship in which social, psychological, and economic resources are distributed by society in such a way that the individual is not unfairly deprived.

Although it is true that social work focuses on person-environment interaction, this fact implies very little about the proper focus of intervention. As systems theorists have pointed out, the most effective point of intervention does not necessarily correspond to the locus of the problem; problems in a person-environment interaction may be best dealt with in many instances through intervention with an individual just as, conversely, problems in the individual, such as medical problems, can sometimes most effectively be dealt with through public health or environmental measures. Many social work practitioners have come to the conclusion that the most effective and practical treatment of many cases of deprivation involves changing the individual's psychological capacities and motivations so that they can interact with the social system more effectively, rather than trying to directly change social opportunities. Certainly in the case of psychological deprivation, which often results from early social interactions that left maladaptive psychic structures in their wake, social intervention is sometimes neither appropriate nor possible. So, in a wide range of cases, the constraints of the private practice setting do not affect the appropriateness or effectiveness of social work treatment.

The common notion that psychodynamic or behavioral intervention is intrinsically incompatible with a person-environment perspective is also incorrect. It is true that in such interventions the social worker may address the client's problem through interaction with the client rather than through direct intervention in the client's environment. However, as noted, the problem being treated can still be one of deprivation because of person-environment mismatch. Indeed, both psychodynamic theory and behavioral theory have built-in mechanisms for addressing person-environment interaction through the intervention with the client. Psychodynamic theory considers the meanings that determine the individual's actions, and environments generally affect a person's psychologic functioning through the person's attribution of meaning to the environment. Thus, by exploring meaning, psychodynamicists explore the environment's impact on the client and attempt to change the pattern of interaction through a reconsideration of those meanings. Similarly, behaviorists consider a person's actions to be strongly influenced by the person's interaction with the environment, and particularly by the reinforcement of behavior experienced in the environment. Behavioral treatment can intervene in the person-environment interaction by helping the person to change the pattern of reinforcers. So, even if private practitioners do tend to intervene with the individual and use psychodynamic or behavioral models, this is not an "in principle" objection to private practice. An individual intervention can be used to treat what is or originally was a person-environment problem, and both psychodynamic and behavioral approaches are equipped to do precisely that.

The "Mental Health" Objection

I have used the notions of "psychological resources," "psychological deprivation," and "psychological justice" to explain why psychotherapeutic intervention is part of social work's traditional mission of helping those who are unjustly deprived of basic resources necessary for social functioning. However, not all psychological problems are caused by the maldistribution of psychologically supportive interactions and early family environments. For example, some psychological problems, such as some forms of psychosis, are primarily biological in nature. Moreover, not all psychological problems that are distressful to the individual are serious enough to constitute deprivation analogous to poverty in the economic realm; for example, an airplane phobia may be a serious inconvenience, but it does not deprive a person of a basic minimal level of psychological resources. Thus, not all mental health problems are problems of unjust psychological deprivation in the sense I have defined it. This provides a way of distinguishing the task of the clinical social worker from the goal of the psychiatrist or clinical psychologist; the other psychotherapeutic professions are concerned with the mission of alleviating mental disorder as such, whereas clinical social work is concerned with the alleviation of mental disorder only to the extent that it serves the purpose of alleviating psychological deprivation. The values of psychological justice and mental health overlap but are not identical, and psychological justice alone is the central value of clinical social work.

The above observations lead to a fourth objection to private practice, namely, that private practitioners often provide general mental health services, and thus abandon the aim of alleviating deprivation and injustice— even psychological deprivation and injustice—as their specific professional goal. This makes them professionally indistinguishable from other mental health professionals. In this case, the objectors are correct that private practitioners who serve a general mental health population are not doing social work as it is traditionally conceived. The problem of social workers becoming straightforward mental health practitioners with no regard for traditional social work values is not limited to private practice, however, but is endemic in public and private agencies as well, especially community mental health agencies. Thus, the "mental health" objection is not really a specific objection to private practice. Rather, it suggests that there are problems with social work education and practice in general, and that a clearer conceptualization of the distinctive nature of the profession, and one that can be persuasively communicated to students, is desperately needed.

There is a complexity to the "mental health" objection that is worth briefly exploring. It was suggested earlier that the tasks appropriate to a profession are those that promote the profession's essential mission. However, there are some legitimate exceptions. There are other "derived" tasks that are not part of the essential mission of the profession, but that are taken on by a profession as a result of an implicit agreement with society, usually because that profession is the most appropriate to handle the task on the basis of skills and manpower. Such derived tasks are just as much a part of the profession's responsibilities as are the essential tasks directly related to its mission. Think, for example, of physicians performing cosmetic surgery. Such interventions do not directly serve the mission of the medical profession, which is health, yet doctors are socially sanctioned and even mandated to perform such interventions because they have the appropriate skills. I believe that the social work profession has a similar implicit contract with society under which the profession gets resources and opportunities, as well as legal recognition and protection, beyond what we would otherwise receive, in return for providing society with much needed skilled mental health professionals. Certainly the profession has received much of its governmental training support from grants that focus on the treatment of mental health problems. In fact, social work is the largest provider of mental health care in this country.

If mental health service is indeed a derived task of the social work profession, then private mental health practice is an appropriate and socially mandated task for those with clinical social work degrees who want to engage in this task, although such a role is not entirely consistent with the traditional "justice" mission of social work. However, such mental health personnel are social workers in professional degree and professional affiliation only; in mission, they really belong to the profession of psychotherapy. Most importantly, this derived legitimacy of social work private practice is not relevant to the question that is the focus of this article, namely, whether private practice is legitimate as an activity for social workers within the framework of the traditional goals of the profession. That question has been answered above in the affirmative, quite independently of the mental health responsibilities of the profession.

If mental health practice is a derived task of the social work profession, this situation is changeable. It could certainly be argued that the profession has erred in making its "psychotherapy" contract with society, and that we as a profession are losing our identity in pursuit of the rewards that involvement in the mental health industry can bring. A renewed and more exclusive devotion to the traditional mission of social work, with the practice trade-offs that that would entail, is an option for the profession and for schools of social work. Or we might decide to enjoy the fruits of our mental health responsibilities but to simultaneously renew our efforts at clarifying and supporting traditional goals as well. However, these decisions would not impact on the issue of whether private practice is a proper form of social work. No matter what the future relationship between social work and mental health services, private practice and psychotherapeutic intervention have a proper role in pursuing social work's essential task of justice, because the amelioration of psychological deprivation is a central task of a justice-oriented profession.

This completes my response to the arguments that private practice is not a proper form of social work practice. I have argued that private practice is not antithetical to the essential social work mission of distributive justice and the relief of deprivation. Psychotherapeutic intervention of the sort often provided in private practice can serve the essential and traditional social work aim of justice by alleviating psychological deprivation. The degree to which private practitioners focus on these traditional goals no doubt depends in part on the quality of training they receive and the conceptual and theoretical clarity with which what is distinctive and valuable about social work is presented to them during their education. I have also argued that social work is currently committed to going beyond its traditional mission in the area of mental health if it is to keep its implicit contract with society, but that this can be changed. I hope that recognition of these points will help to put the private practice issue to rest. Professional energies can then be directed at improving education and services, public and private, rather than debating which services are legitimate or which social workers are the real social workers.

REFERENCES

Alexander, M.P. (1987). Why social workers enter private practice: A study of attitudes and motivations. *Journal of Independent Social Work,* 1(3), 7–18.

Rawls, J. (1971). *A theory of justice.* Cambridge, MA: Harvard University Press.

Wakefield, J.C. (1988a). Psychotherapy, distributive justice, and social work, Part 1: Distributive justice as a conceptual framework for social work. *Social Service Review, 62*, 187–210.

Wakefield, J.C. (1988b). Psychotherapy, distributive justice, and social work, Part 2: Psychotherapy and the pursuit of justice. *Social Service Review, 62*, 353–382.

Rejoinder to Professor Wakefield

CHERYL RICHEY AND GAIL STEVENS

Professor Wakefield's support of the private practice option for social workers reflects several core assumptions including that private practice is a legitimate activity and that it functions to ameliorate psychological deprivation. We are not in disagreement with the first assumption. Our position is that, although "proper," the private practice option remains an exclusory career pathway because it can restrict service and professional opportunities.

We do take issue with Wakefield's premise that psychological deprivation is independent from socioeconomic status or economic deprivation. His carefully conceived argument that the concept of distributive justice applies to psychological resources—apart from economic factors—is not empirically supported. Many comprehensive, multivariate studies document the significant connection between economic status and child abuse and neglect, family violence, depression among single mothers, drug and alcohol problems, and debilitation among the elderly. Although psychological deprivation clearly cuts across socioeconomic strata, research suggests that psychological deprivation is inextricably linked to and exacerbated by economic deprivation.

Although the philosophical position that individuals deserve a fair minimal share of all society's resources is appealing, even elegant, it is problematic in application. Political realities teach us that establishing minimal standards for meeting human needs, the proverbial safety net, can be arbitrary and punitive. Fairness does not necessarily take precedence over political expediency and cost containment. Therefore, the real issue is not whether social work should limit its clientele to the least empowered segments of society, but whether ability to pay ensures greater access to "basic" and elective services and thus to a disproportionate share of all possible resources. In a pluralistic society, social work must not become complacent about either the quality or quantity of services available to deprived groups by rationalizing that minimal levels of resources are technically available.

Wakefield charges academics with the responsibility for instructing social workers in the "essential task of distributive justice." This mandate is premature because the organizing principles of distributive justice are not currently integrated into social work practice theory nor is there any assurance that educators, students, and practitioners agree on their interpretation and application. The distinction between psychological justice and mental health is particularly elusive and requires special vigilance by social workers who want to adhere to traditional service ideals. Referring to the airplane phobia example, if continued employment hinged on frequent flying, would treatment undertaken to preserve economic resources qualify as a professionally mandated task? How are employment options balanced against self-esteem?

Finally, we believe schools of social work, especially those at state-supported universities, have a clear mandate to train professionals for competent practice in the public sector. Predicted job market increases for social workers by the year 2000 will occur in services for high-risk children, the elderly, the chronically mentally ill, and in case management jobs with agencies and hospitals. In the mental health field, an area identified by Wakefield as especially suitable for independent social workers, effective practice in the future will require both micro and macro skills, including the ability to function effectively in interdisciplinary teams and as advocates and community support brokers, not just as psychotherapists.

NO

CHERYL A. RICHEY AND GAIL A. STEVENS

Despite the ever-widening domain and scope of the profession, social work practice has historically focused on: 1) improving or restoring social functioning of individuals, groups, and communities; 2) creating favorable socioenvironmental conditions that promote mutually beneficial interactions between individuals and society; and 3) matching resources with human needs. Concurrent with these general aims is an abiding emphasis on the profession's service mandate with disadvantaged, oppressed, and underserved populations. Finally, the arena for service provision continues to be bureaucratic organizations.

Against this backdrop is the private social worker who practices professionally outside the aegis of governmental or voluntary agencies and takes responsibility for negotiating conditions of service with clients. For purposes of this discussion, the key aspects of private practice are 1) work autonomy or independence, and 2) a fee-for-service received directly from or in behalf of the client (Barker, 1984). Although private practitioners include social group workers, community organizers, planners, consultants, and researchers, by far the majority offer direct clinical services to individuals, couples, and families (Neale, 1983). Thus, while clinical or therapeutic methods are not the only form of independent practice, they have become almost synonymous with the term. Our discussion will reflect this emphasis, but many of the points raised here could be applied to social workers who contract independently with groups or organizations for nonclinical services.

Ostensibly, this essay makes a case for why social workers should not engage in private practice activities. The debate surrounding the nature and status of private practice vis-a-vis the profession as a whole has waged for 60 years. We will not attempt to summarize the arguments of private practice opponents. These arguments, for the most part, have attacked the private practice option but have provided little support for its alternatives. Our strategy will be to explicate the benefits of public sector or agency-based practice, or what positive professional and personal outcomes might be lost if private practice is pursued in favor of careers in public service. For purposes of this discussion, "public" practice arenas include a range of governmental as well as voluntary or private not-for-profit agencies that are sanctioned by and accountable to the community or some community group.

The section that follows elaborates on four benefits of public practice, including: 1) personal satisfaction derived from altruistic pursuits and a sense of mission; 2) opportunities for professional development; 3) client and service diversity; and 4) freedom from the business demands of practice. To provide a more balanced commentary, the discussion of benefits will be followed by a section on the challenges of public agency practice, including perceptions of restricted professional autonomy, reduced flexibility of and control over the work environment, and lower incomes. Our commentary draws upon the literature and a recently completed survey of practice interests among incoming, continuing, and graduating MSW students at the University of Washington.

Benefits of Public Practice

Altruism

Reducing the magnitude and severity of social inequities is a unifying concept within social work and one that is pivotal in decisions to pursue careers in public service. Our student survey indicates that altruism is a primary motivation for many reporting a preference for public sector careers. Students stated their desire to "serve the public good," "serve the underserved," and "reach those in greatest need."

Ensuring access to services regardless of clients' ability to pay was also a recurring theme. Students challenged fee-for-service practice models because of their implied "elitism." A recent study of randomly selected NASW members confirms students' perceptions of the exclusionary reality of private practice. This study reported that fifty-four and four-tenths percent of 164 private practitioners surveyed charge an hourly rate of $51 to $75 (Jayaratne, et al, 1988). As these researchers point out, this fee structure directly affects who can and cannot obtain fee-based services. Whereas private practitioners may be reimbursed by a third party for some services, the fact that almost 20 percent of US citizens are uninsured suggests that a good many individuals and families cannot afford private services. Even proponents concede that "the majority of private practitioners are not readily accessible geographically, socially, or financially to a significant portion of the economically disadvantaged" (Barker, 1984, p. 10).

In addition to desires to promote the interests of traditional social work clients, students underscored their commitment to social and institutional reform. As one student wrote, "[The public sector] offers the opportunity to shape public policy, influence a broad range of services, and affect change at the macro-level." Of necessity, the development of social policies and professional practice models consistent with social work values requires collective action. Compared to private practitioners, social workers preferring public practice feel that they are more strategically situated to mobilize forces for improving services and delivery systems for the truly needy.

Professional Development

Transformation from student to professional extends beyond formal study. Analogous to medical internship or residency programs, public sector employment can serve as an extension of supervised field instruction or a training ground where social workers perfect their craft and learn in depth from more experienced professionals or mentors about political process, social policy functions, and how caregiving systems work. Within this experiential framework, professional competencies are fostered and confidence grows. Survey respondents cited "experiencing different treatment modalities," "expanding a professional repertoire," "learning the system," and "discovering how to make use of social service resources" as possible continuing education benefits of public practice. Agencies further support professional development by providing staff with released time or educational leave. In contrast, private social workers must underwrite their own costs, which include course fees and lost client income.

Agency-based practice also offers the social worker the option of sampling numerous professional roles with different clients or with the same client over time. These roles include "diagnostician," "therapist," "advocate," "expeditor," and "case manager" (Weissman, et al, 1983). A wider exposure to diverse intervention roles enables both beginning and experienced practitioners 1) to identify and pursue over the span of a career professional talents not otherwise utilized, 2) to strengthen functions and skills found to be inadequately developed, and 3) to continue to challenge and "stretch" themselves personally and professionally.

Opportunities for consultation and peer review abound in public agencies. Formal and informal interaction, idea sharing, and support and stimulation from colleagues can promote practice proficiency by:

1. facilitating identification and correction of clinical judgment errors based on such ubiquitous factors as worker preconceptions and stereotypes, and failure to search for disconfirming evidence;
2. increasing exposure to new or uniquely combined assessment and intervention technologies;
3. supporting consistent and unflinching consideration of values, ethics, quality control, and legal issues;
4. enhancing intrapersonal and interpersonal problem solving about individual cases or broader constituencies and issues by helping to reframe the nature or definition of the problem and encouraging the creation of diverse solutions or alternatives; and
5. facilitating a sense of professional interconnectedness, collaboration, or "team spirit" that can mitigate feelings of isolation and occupational stress.

Client and Service Diversity

Public practice offers expanded opportunities for the novice and the experienced practitioner to work with diverse clients. For example, a study of 134 social workers reported that agency, as compared to private, practitioners worked with more people of lower incomes, minority members of color, children, and individuals with more severe psychiatric disorders (Borenzweig, 1981). Work with clients who represent variant backgrounds, resources, world views, and life experiences allows the practitioner to continue to 1) discover and challenge personal vestiges of ethnocentrism; 2) expand capacities for openness and empathy; 3) attend consciously or mindfully to each client's frame of reference; and 4) experiment with and refine service modes in the context of multicultural, developmental, and intergenerational realities. Private practitioners are unlikely to experience this heterogeneity and the resultant benefits.

Along with greater client and problem variety, agency practitioners also have expanded opportunities for service diversity, including providing interventions which are more innovative or experimental (Borenzweig, 1981). In organizational settings, which have wider funding bases, individual staff may elect or be encouraged to offer or pilot test new and perhaps more "expensive" procedures, secure in the knowledge that these offerings can be balanced financially by routine agency activities. Agencies may regularly challenge staff to develop innovations as they strive to meet the ever changing needs and demands of their constituencies or funders.

In contrast, private practitioners must always be concerned with developing and marketing services that are profitable. Independent social workers may not have the resource stability to venture far from routine client problems or business-as-usual practice.

Freedom from the Business Side of Practice

Job security, income stability, and benefit packages were frequently mentioned by student respondents as assets accruing to agency-based employment. Practicing within an organizational context emancipates the individual social worker from the hassles and headaches of running a small business, including locating and equipping an office, securing adequate malpractice and business liability insurance, planning for retirement, satisfying tax requirements, maintaining records and referral systems, marketing and advertising, and fee scheduling, monitoring, and collection (Barker, 1984; Margenau, 1989). The time, energy, and resources that must be devoted to these start up and maintenance activities understandably siphon attention away from matters more directly focused on practice delivery. Furthermore, social workers unbound by an entrepreneurial mandate are at greater liberty to pursue service pathways, case by case, that are not profit making. For example, the salaried, agency-based practitioner will likely feel less conflict than the fee-per-hour practitioner about 1) referring clients to other professionals; 2) engaging in advocacy, resource provision, and other nontherapeutic interventions on behalf of clients; 3) extending the duration and parameters of service beyond the 50-minute hour, like scheduling intensive home-based family visits; and 4) terminating service when treatment goals have been achieved. Thus, the exemption of the agency-based social worker from the responsibilities of business management may have additional positive effects on services by removing the subtle but ever present edicts of a market system mentality.

Challenges of Public Sector Practice

Most social workers begin and build careers in public settings. In a recent survey of 1985 NASW members, 62 percent of the respondents reported current and exclusive employment in an agency (Jayaratne, et al, 1988). The remaining one third reported engaging in some form of private practice—12 percent full time and 22 percent part time. The authors suggest that these data, when compared with results from previous studies, reflect an increasing trend toward fee-for-service practice. Whereas others predict that demand for private services has peaked and is declining (Barker, 1984), the charge to agency-based practice continues to be how to attract and retain professionally trained and committed practitioners in public employment arenas. The potential liabilities within these arenas—restrictions in professional autonomy, in control over the work environment, and in financial rewards—are frequently mentioned by social work students and practitioners as reasons for pursuing private practice. The challenge is acknowledging and correcting these potential sources of job dissatisfaction rather than dismissing them as groundless or chiding practitioners who avoid or flee agency work for their lack of professional identification and commitment.

Given that there appear to be higher concentrations of women in private (67%) versus agency (58%) practice (Jayaratne, et al, 1988), gender factors may operate to make organizational life more confining for and less supportive of professional women. The reality in many service agencies continues to be a hierarchical system dominated by men in higher levels of administration (Kravetz & Austin, 1984). Overt and covert sexism in organizational structure and processes—sex stereotyping, wage and job discrimination, sexual harassment—may well contribute to female employees feeling constrained, powerless, and undervalued (Weil, 1987). The negative effects of these and other restrictive agency environmental elements may include reduced opportunities for 1) professional growth and challenge; 2) impacting service design and delivery; 3) advancement to positions that pay more; and 4) combining the multiple role demands of worker, mother, and caregiver of older parents. Given these regrettable outcomes, it is understandable why some professional women, propelled by the quest for more personal and professional freedom and control, opt out of the organizational service arena altogether.

Because a modest percentage of students and practitioners select private practice as their initial or single career pathway (Getzel, 1983), most are employed for some period in an agency before shifting to independent practice. Consequently, agencies have considerable opportunities to engage, support, and challenge "fresh" professional talent. Because most of these professionals are women, attention and vigilance should focus on 1) equity in pay and promotion opportunities, 2) strategies for combating sexual harassment, 3) supporting the coordination of life phase or role demands with career development needs and priorities, and 4) organizational structuring that provides greater staff participation in decision making.

Schools of social work can contribute significantly to the retention of professional service providers in public settings by training future practitioners in how to finesse, cope with, confront, and change the bureaucratic arrangements of agency practice. With such preparation, professionally trained social workers will be better equipped to "stay in the game"—to enjoy the benefits of public practice while remaining resilient to the stressors. Ultimately, when the practitioner is better prepared for organizational membership and the agency environment is more affirming, the promise of agency-based practice will be realized.

REFERENCES

Barker, R.L. (1984). *Social work in private practice.* Silver Spring, MD: National Association of Social Workers.

Borenzweig, H. (1981). Agency vs. private practice: Similarities and differences. *Social Work,* 26(3), 239–244.

Getzel, G.S. (1983). Speculations on the crisis in social work recruitment: Some modest proposals. *Social Work,* 28(3), 235–237.

Jayaratne, S., Siefert, K., & Chess, W.A. (1988). Private and agency practitioners: Some data and observations. *Social Service Review,* 62(2), 324–336.

Kravetz, D., & Austin, C.D. (1984). Women's issues in social service administration: The views and experiences of women administrators. *Administration in Social Work,* 84(4), 25–38.

Margenau, E. (Ed.) (1989). *The encyclopedia handbook of private practice.* New York: Gardner.

Neale, N.K. (1983). Private practice. In Rosenblatt, A., & Waldfogel, D. (Eds.), *Handbook of clinical social work.* San Francisco: Jossey-Bass, pp. 1037–1055.

Weil, M. (1987). Women in administration: Curriculum and strategies. In Burden, D.S., & Gottlieb, N., (Eds.), *The woman client: Providing human services in a changing world.* New York: Tavistock, pp. 92–100.

Weissman, H., Epstein, I., & Savage, A. (1983). *Agency-based social work: Neglected aspects of clinical practice.* Philadelphia: Temple University Press.

ANNOTATED BIBLIOGRAPHY

Barker, R.L. (1984). *Social work in private practice.* Silver Spring, MD: National Association of Social Workers

This handbook offers a practical and balanced discussion of issues facing the private social worker, including continued professional ambivalence toward practice as a business, and the occupational hazards of and outlook for private practice.

Jayaratne, S., Siefert, K., & Chess, W.A. (1988). Private and agency practitioners: Some data and observations. *Social Service Review,* 62(2), 324–336

This study of randomly selected NASW members compares private and agency practitioners on demographics, education and training, and perceptions of job performance and satisfaction.

Weil, M. (1987). Women in administration: Curriculum and strategies. In Burden, D.S., & Gottlieb, N. (Eds.), *The woman client: Providing human services in a changing world.* New York: Tavistock, pp. 92–110

This book chapter examines the extent and effects of and reasons and remedies for overt and covert sexism in social agency organization.

Weissman, H., Epstein, I., & Savage, A. (1983). *Agency-based social work: Neglected aspects of clinical practice.* Philadelphia: Temple University Press

This book explores the numerous roles assumed by clinical social workers in agency-based practice settings. Chapters examine the knowledge, tasks, and skills required to carry out such roles as advocate, expeditor, casemanager, counselor, and colleague.

Rejoinder to Professors Richey and Stevens
JEROME WAKEFIELD

I agree with Cheryl Richey and Gail Stevens that the continued vitality of public agency practice is of critical importance to social work's mission. I also share their hope that the conditions of agency practice will improve and that agency practice will flourish in the future. Their article is useful for sensitizing us to the benefits of public sector work, even if at times they present an idealized and one-sided picture. As an argument against the legitimacy of private practice as an option for social workers, however, Richey and Stevens's article fails to make its point for several reasons.

Richey and Stevens's basic argument is that public sector practice provides many personal and professional benefits and that these benefits would be lost if private practice is pursued in favor of public service. However, proponents of private practice do not argue that public practice and its benefits should be abandoned or even deemphasized; they only argue that, for some social workers and some clients, private practice is a legitimate alternative that has its own benefits. Unfortunately, opponents of private practice tend to take a more exclusionary "either/or" approach that ignores the diversity of practitioner needs and roles.

Richey and Stevens list the benefits of public practice, but they do not attempt to balance the benefits against the serious problems that, they note, are causing social workers to "flee" public practice. Moreover, they do not systematically compare the benefits and costs of private and public practice. Without such comparisons, their list says little about the relative merits of the two forms of practice. In any event, costs and benefits vary with person, situation, and agency. Even a thorough cost and benefit analysis of the two types of practice would not address the issue of whether private practice is a preferable option for some workers some of the time. Rather than making summary judgments about which form of practice is better, it would seem preferable to trust each individual social worker's judgment of where his or her energies will yield the greatest personal and professional benefits.

The deeper issue is not about benefits and costs, but about whether private practice effectively contributes to the mission of social work. Richey and Stevens emphasize that social work is concerned with the "disadvantaged, oppressed, and underserved," a point with which I heartily agree. However, like most critics of private practice, they tend to equate all such forms of deprivation with economic deprivation. This is neither practically nor theoretically the case. Practically, many social work services are not related to socioeconomic status; for example, family violence, child abuse, delinquency, and drug abuse represent disadvantages that are as much social work concerns when they occur in middle class families as when they occur in poor families. Middle class people experience breakdowns in social functioning that are just as painful, urgent, and debilitating as those of poor people.

On the theoretical side, I argued in my article that what a society provides to its members as a matter of right goes beyond sheer economic resources and includes the psychological resources a person requires to function socially. These psychological resources are to some degree (though not completely) independent of economic resources; that is, one can be deprived of the proper psychological resources even if one is financially well off, and one can possess the relevant psychological resources even if one is quite poor. John Rawls, the most prominent contemporary theoretician of justice, has argued that psychological resources, especially such properties as self-respect, self-esteem, and self-confidence, are the most critical goods that a society can distribute to its members, beyond the minimal goods needed for survival. Without some degree of these psychological properties, a person will be unable to effectively utilize or enjoy other resources. Certainly the social work profession is keenly aware of the frequency with which human suffering is due to more than sheer lack of economic resources. Thus, without in any way downplaying the importance of economic deprivation, it can be said that the social work profession is committed to work on psychosocial deprivation in all forms and in all socioeconomic classes, and that private intervention with psychosocially deprived middle class clients is entirely within the profession's essential mission. However, the profession's responsibility to economically deprived clients does suggest that participation in a system of voluntary treatment of the economically deprived and of others who would not otherwise have access to private practice should be part of the private social worker's ethical commitment.

Lastly, I found myself disturbed by Richey and Stevens's response to their observation that there appears to be a higher concentration of women than men in private practice. Rather than defending women's right to this option, Richey and Stevens argue that public practice should change in the future to accommodate women's needs. This does not help women who are faced with life decisions now under current conditions. Moreover, it is questionable whether agency practice can ever provide the special advantages, such as control over the scheduling of work, the ability to increase or decrease work commitment at will, and the higher income per hour, that many women (and men) have found to be critical in satisfactorily balancing their family and professional commitments. It seems odd to present oneself as defending women's interests at the same time that one attacks an option that many women find to be invaluable in making their lives manageable.

A profession's mission is defined not by its form of service delivery, but by its goals. I have argued here and in my article that private practice is an effective means to achieve some of the essential goals of the social work profession, and that it is complementary to public practice. If I am correct, then an exclusive commitment to public over private service delivery constitutes a violation of our professional mandate. Rather than divisively construing public and private practice as being in opposition, we should be cultivating and building on the deeper unity of purpose that motivates all social workers.

Should Social Service Administrators Have Master of Social Work Degrees?

EDITOR'S NOTE: George Schulz left one of the world's leading engineering firms to become Secretary of State. Robert McNamara went from being an automobile company executive to lead the Department of Defense, and from there he went on to head the World Bank. John Scully gave up his high administrative position with the huge company that makes Pepsi-Cola soft drinks to become the chief executive officer of the huge company that makes Apple computers. The story is heard over and over again: persons possessing general administrative and leadership skills move from one industry to another, from one kind of organization to another. The question is, is this appropriate for social services? Or do those who administer social welfare agencies have to have specialized graduate training in social work to get the job done well?

Nancy Johnstone, MSW, answers the latter question YES: those who administer social service agencies should have MSW degrees. She is Executive Director of Youth Guidance, a Chicago agency dealing with troubled teenagers. She is also involved in the broader area of developing programs and policies to improve the delivery of human services and has served with such organizations as the United Way of Chicago, the Citizen's Committee on the Juvenile Court and the University of Chicago School of Social Service Administration.

Edward Rimer, DPA, argues NO. He is Assistant Professor at the University of Illinois, Chicago, and chair of the American Society for Public Administration Section on Human Services and Health. Before taking up his academic career, he served for 15 years in public social service agencies as a social worker and administrator. His research interests include administrative decision making in human service organizations and the education and training of administrators for social service and other not-for-profit organizations.

YES

NANCY JOHNSTONE

I believe that administration encompasses both management and leadership functions and that the most effective administrators are those who are closely related to the work of their organizations by virtue of their training and experience. In social work, where the end product is service to clients achieved through a process of interpersonal relationships, an MSW, along with basic management skills and a good dose of direct service experience, constitute essential credentials for the top administrator. To support this argument I will first identify some contributions of social work training to good administration, and I will then describe why these are critical to the organizational leadership function.

Contributions of Social Work to Administration

The important attributes that social workers bring to administration fall into three categories: framework, values, and skills.

The framework within which social workers understand people and their problems is a "big picture" world view, seeing the broad context in which people live their lives and the systems impacting on them. Culture, socioeconomic class, and the immediate environment are critical to the social worker's assessment of a given situation. For example, a high school student who is unable to sit still or concentrate may have a learning disability such as an attention deficit disorder. However, if he or she attends a tough inner-city school, he or she may be unable to pay attention because he or she is being harassed by gangs whose members are armed and move freely inside and outside of the school. A contextual, or systems perspective, broadens one's understanding and alters traditional definitions of "normal" and "pathological" behavior.

A corollary to this contextual approach is seeing individuals as "whole" people with a range of emotional, physical, social, and concrete needs. Failure to recognize this renders any single intervention ineffective.

Holistic agencies are an outgrowth of this approach, frequently offering an array of services such as counseling, health clinics, legal assistance, education and job training. Doctors have learned that the root causes of physical symptoms often relate to psychological stress.

A second attribute that social workers bring to administration is in the realm of values. The decision to pursue social work is usually driven by a set of values that is reinforced in the formal training program. It is a philosophy that puts people first, a belief in the worth and dignity of human beings, the importance of process and relationships in making decisions and solving problems, the uniqueness of each individual, self-determination, and freedom to grow and reach ones potential.

In addition to framework and values, social workers bring to administration a set of specific skills learned through clinical training and experience. There are a number of management functions that can be delegated to experts, such as fiscal operations, data and contract management, fund raising, marketing and public relations, and the technical side of personnel management. It is these responsibilities that are most effectively carried out by people who have specialized training and who see the organization through a different set of eyes. A classic example of these different viewpoints is the tension between direct service staff who are paid for being client and program focused, and the business and data managers who are organization-focused as they carry out their fiscal and statistical accountability functions.

Other key management functions require the direct participation of the administrator—organizational structure; program development; staff development and supervision; planning; board relations; networking and other external activities. These management functions are significantly enhanced by the presence of clinical skills. The most important of these are listening; understanding and diagnosing people and situations, including self insight; interpersonal skills; group process; problem solving and conflict resolution. For example, working effectively with a board of directors demands far more than progress reports and the presentation of financial data. It also requires an understanding of the members' explicit and implicit agendas, the framework out of which they are operating, individual and group dynamics, and insight into one's own interactional patterns and one's responses to challenge and criticism.

I have described three general areas where social work training enhances administration: framework, values, and skills. This is not to suggest that social workers have cornered the market on contextual frameworks, human-oriented values and process skills, but these are at the heart of good social work practice for those providing direct services as well as for administrators.

Social Work Skills and Leadership

Although core content will differ across various fields, my thesis is that in order to be a leader (in addition to managing), having a background in the content area of the organization will substantially increase administrative effectiveness. Therefore, in social work, it is in the arena of leadership where social work education and experience are most important.

A leader is responsible for organizational cohesiveness, a consistency between philosophy and program. Philip Selnick articulates this point when he states, "Organizations become institutions as they are infused with values . . . The infusion produces a distinct identity. Where institutionalization is well advanced, distinctive outlooks, habits and other commitments are unified, coloring all aspects of organizational life and lending it a social integration that goes well beyond formal coordination and command" (Peters & Waterman, 1982, p. 99). In social work, the way in which an administrator thinks, structures the organization, and functions on the job will have a profound effect on every aspect of the organization, and it is ultimately, and most importantly, reflected in how services are delivered on the front line. For example, clients will play a more active role in determining treatment goals, and client strengths rather than deficits will be emphasized in an agency where the administration appreciates the uniqueness of staff members, responds to their needs for self determination, and seeks their input in decision making. Related to this point is the delicate, intrinsic reward system that motivates social workers to "hang in there" with difficult people and frequently negative work environments. Feeling supported in their values and understanding of human behavior and having the freedom to pursue their work with clients based on these are essential to maintaining a motivated and productive workforce.

Warren Bennis and Burt Nanus (1985) describe key leadership functions as directing organizational change, creating visions for the future, and empowering employees to create new ways of doing things. They describe managers as problem solvers, leaders as problem finders—a creative process of discovery and identification of new directions for the organization.

Equally important to internal organizational cohesiveness and vision is the role of the social work administrator as the link between the agency and the wider community. The social service administrator is the chief spokesperson and "image projector" for the agency, to its board and all of its publics. Kanter (1989) points out that the primary role of the leader is not to manage but to communicate the philosophy and focus of the organization. The viability of an agency over time—its ability to survive and prosper—is inextricably linked to the administrator's effectiveness in interpreting the agency's mission and work to its constituencies and in understanding the impact of broad environmental trends on the present and future work of the agency. The era when we could get by because we were "good people doing good things" has long since passed. If we are to be successful in an increasingly competitive environment, one that is often hostile to our cause, we must knowledgeably and persuasively make the case for our agencies and those we serve. This will require a passionate commitment to social work approaches and values, an in-depth knowledge of the agency's work, and specific skills in relating and communicating with a wide variety of people, all of this backed up by a strong, relevant, productive organization. It is unlikely that an individual without social work training and experience could be successful in delivering this product!

REFERENCES

Bennis, W., and Nanus, B. (1985). *Leaders: The strategies for taking charge.* New York: Harper & Row.

Kanter, R.M. (1989). *When giants learn to dance.* New York: Simon and Schuster.

Peters, T.J., and Waterman, R.H. (1982). *In search of excellence.* New York: Warner Books.

ANNOTATED BIBLIOGRAPHY

Peters, T.J., & Waterman, R.H., Jr. (1982). *In search of excellence.* New York: Warner Books.

The authors studied forty-three successful American companies and distilled their findings into eight basic success-generating management principles. The major message is product quality, small work units, and "turned on" people who are treated decently and expected to "shine." Of special interest is the authors' review of social and economic theory related to business.

Bennis, W., & Nanus, B. (1985). *Leaders: The strategies for taking charge.* New York: Harper & Row.

This book addresses a "chronic crisis of governance" and focuses on effective leadership (differentiated from management) as the critical force behind viable organizations. The authors conducted an in-depth analysis of ninety top leaders and discovered through this process that leadership does not just happen, it is a learned competence. The key concept is "transformational leadership" that focuses on people, motivating them to take action and to become leaders and agents of change.

Kanter, R.M. (1989). *When giants learn to dance*. New York: Simon and Schuster.

Rosabeth Kanter uses case histories as the basis for business and career strategies to meet today's business challenges fueled by "global olympics" and corporate takeovers. Neither traditional hierarchical nor purely entrepreneurial companies will be successful in this new environment. A major strategy in Dr. Kanter's "postentrepreneurial agenda" is one that establishes performance and contribution to the company, not job title and status, as the basis for compensation, within the framework of "cooperative efforts of the whole corporate team."

Rejoinder to Ms. Johnstone
EDWARD RIMER

Nancy Johnstone, a practicing social service administrator, argues that specialized management training (MSW) is necessary because of the unique characteristics needed to manage human service organizations. The premise of the argument is that the nature of social work is so different from other enterprises that one needs a "good dose of direct service experience" in order to be an administrator. She identifies three basic areas: framework, values, and skills. To some extent these characteristics described by Johnstone are simply another feature of the argument for specialized training based on the theoretical distinction between social service organizations and other types of organizations, a distinction that is critiqued in detail in my full statement that immediately follows this rebuttal.

How different are the framework, values, and skills that social workers bring to the job? Not very different. A world view that purports to understand the "broad context" is essentially an acceptance of the fact that the environment plays an important part in determining an organization's activities, an elementary assumption for any business, private or public, profit or not-for-profit. System theory is also a well established and a popular modus operandi for understanding complex society.

The social work profession does not have an exclusive monopoly on the values enumerated by Johnstone. It is safe to say that the health care professions, as exhibited in their zealous pursuit to save and extend lives, also believe in the "worth and dignity" of each individual, that all should have the opportunity to "grow and reach one's potential."

I agree with Johnstone's identification of the key management functions; however, empirically based studies indicate that social work administrators with clinical training frequently lack the skills to perform effectively as administrators. Other professional administration education programs (MPA, MBA, MPH) also emphasize the development of these very same skills. This is recognized by certain segments of the social work education community who have established joint and dual degree programs between the MSW and those aforementioned programs. For example, the University of Pennsylvania, The University of Michigan, Washington University, and Boston College all have joint MSW accredited and MBA programs.

Of the ninety-three schools accredited by the Council on Social Work Education in 1987, twenty-one established thirty-nine distinct joint or dual degree programs. Of the thirty-nine, fifteen are predominantly in the area of administration. Limiting social service administration positions to those with an MSW ignores the fact that other professional disciplines are training individuals with similar frameworks, values, and skills. This unnecessary restriction often means that social service organizations do not get the best person for the job, and this has negative consequences for the delivery of social services.

NO

EDWARD RIMER

The belief that one needs an MSW to be an administrator of a social service organization is based on the premise that social service organizations are different from other organizations, and therefore, successful social service administrators need to possess a distinct set of skills, knowledge, and values that can only be disseminated through schools of social work.

The sanctity of the MSW is preserved and operationalized by requiring that administrators first serve as clinicians in the organization. Prospective administrators thus have to be trained in both clinical and administrative skills. While many argue that there is considerable similarity between these two areas, it is obvious that the overlap is not total. Social work students are therefore put at a disadvantage compared to students of other administrative degree programs because they are forced to take at least some courses that lack any administrative content.

Additionally, administration is considered a "field of practice," taught from the perspective that social service organizations are different from other organizations. This emphasis detracts from the opportunity to identify and develop those skills necessary to administer a complex organization.

The notion, however, that social service organizations are unique is fallacious and requires an extensive rebuttal that will form the basis for my position that one does not need an MSW to administer a social service organization.

Differences between social welfare and other organizations are at best illusive, frequently based on antiquated notions of what administration is and how organizations really function. To be sure, there are some differences, but these are inconsequential to the practice of sound administration.

We will start by examining some of the "myth-conceptions" of the uniqueness of social welfare organizations and then identify those functions of administration that are generic to all organizations and serve as the basis for sound practice.

Social Welfare Organization Myths: Social Service Organizations Are Not Profit-Making Enterprises

The objective of social welfare organizations, we are often told, is to bring about some desired change in people, whether in their behavior, functioning, or living conditions rather than to make a profit. The implication of this statement is that these two facets (helping people and economic gain) are not merely mutually exclusive, but also somehow contradictory. Unfortunately, such a belief ignores the recent enormous growth of for-profit corporations in the nursing home, child care, and health care fields (Stoez, 1984). Accepting the distinction between not-for-profit and for-profit implies that significantly different administrative skills are necessary if one is managing a not-for-profit as opposed to a for-profit organization. This illusion will be addressed later.

In Social Service Organizations People Are the Raw Material

Some argue that while the ultimate objective may be different, the nature of social service organizations sets them apart from other organizations:

> Human services, as a class of organizations, share a unique set of characteristics because they all work with and on people. First, the fact that the "raw material" consists of people vested with moral values affects most of their activities. The service technologies must be morally justified because every activity related to clients has significant moral consequences. . . . The organization and its staff are limited by what they can do *to* [emphasis in original] their clients and how they carry out their work with them. (Hasenfeld, 1983, p. 9)

The activities of all individuals in the work place must be morally justified. We certainly do not condone individuals who knowingly put unsafe merchandise on the market or pollute the environment. We question the ethical integrity of all individuals involved in allowing the massive oil spill in Alaska to take place. In fact, the social work profession, from its beginnings with the Settlement House movement, has devoted considerable effort through social action to instill in others, through legal reform, certain standards of ethical behavior.

Armies work on people as the "raw material," yet we would not suggest that the values of social service administrators ought to resemble those of our military leaders or that social service organizations be administered like the military.

All organizations face certain constraints in terms of what they produce and the means of production. Government regulations and labor laws are far reaching. The constraints faced by social service organizations may be different, but that in and of itself hardly seems to be sufficient cause to require a distinct administrative discipline.

The actions of social workers are directly felt by their clients. It is ingenuous to suggest, however, that the activities of workers in other types of organizations do not impact their customers or that managers of these organizations are unaware and unconcerned about the relationship between worker behavior and client satisfaction with the product. Most for-profit organizations perform product safety and testing (often called quality control) and marketing before an item is made available for public consumption. They also have a customer relations department. The performance or real objective of such organizational activities can be questioned, but no more so than peer case reviews, case consultations, or fair hearing requests. They are essentially the same activities that originate from a need to continually assess the behavior of the organizational members because their behavior has not just financial but moral consequences as well. And I might add, in many organizations including social service organizations, the two are related.

Social Service Organizations Have Vague Goals

The lament that social service organizations do not have specific, measurable goals has been used not merely to justify a distinct administrative framework but also to serve as a rationale for the lack of program effectiveness. The significance of this false assertion is that there are many other types of organizations that can make the same claim.

The goal of a police department is to prevent crime, of the military to provide for the national defense, of a fire department to prevent and put out fires. All of these are as "vague, ambiguous, and problematic" as those commonly ascribed to social service organizations. The assertion of imprecise goals has meant a lack of serious attention to program evaluation (what is to be measured) and is an indication that social service administrators lack an understanding of one of their primary tasks, the evaluation of organizational performance.

Social Service Organizations Operate in a Turbulent Environment

All organizations are affected by the social, economic, and political conditions within which they exist. Most public organizations are impacted by a variety of governmental jurisdictions, just as private, for-profit organizations must conform to city and state building, fire, safety, and labor codes.

Automobile manufacturers have had to respond to changing consumer demands as well as government regulations regarding safety and emission standards. It is only recently that social service organizations have had to contend with competitors, a fact of life for organizations operating in the for-profit sector. To some extent even government agencies have to face the threat of competitors because there are always discussions about the appropriate level of government to provide specific services.

A case has not been made that environment faced by social service organizations is qualitatively any different than that faced by other types of organizations. It would appear that consumer choices are much more fickle than the values and beliefs regarding human problems. Indeed, the belief that poverty is caused by some individual defect has been with us for hundreds of years.

Again, what is critical here is that the assertion about the turbulent environment justifies the "management of crisis" style so endemic to social service organizations and thus negates the value of planning and evaluation.

Generic Administrative Functions

Administrators of all organizations must have skills in managing money, people, and information. The emphasis on the uniqueness of social service organizations ignores, or at best, trivializes these similarities between social service organizations and other organizations. It also tends to minimize the importance of these activities as part of an administrator's job.

Managing money involves being able to develop, revise, and analyze a budget. The functions of a budget are to plan, manage, and control an agency's activities. Analysis means determining what aspects of the organization are most efficient (producing the greatest benefit for the least cost), whereas planning is deciding where to allocate resources based upon the prior analysis. This is necessary in any organization, whether the objective is to make a profit or remove children from unsafe situations. Administrators trained as social workers who have in fact worked as social workers tend to view the budget as a control mechanism limiting their actions on behalf of clients. The budget as a planning or evaluation tool is thus neglected.

Administration is the art of getting things done, and in organizations that means directing others to accomplish specific tasks. Managing people involves personnel recruitment, motivation of staff, development of career ladders, and evaluation. Although the specific aspects of these functions may be different for social service administrators (how and who to recruit), the underlying objectives are the same (hiring the right person for the job). Too frequently, the emphasis in social service organization is on people as the raw material leading to a focus on clinical supervision as the primary personnel function, rather than one of providing a supportive work environment (physical plant, emotional and administrative assistance) for staff to perform the job to the best of their ability.

In order to manage information the administrator must know what information is needed and be able to collect, interpret, and act upon his or her analysis. It is through this process that the administrator fulfills a major aspect of his or her responsibility making decisions. As was inferred earlier, social service administrators are not the only ones confronted with dilemmas about data reliability and validity. The emphasis on the ambiguity of goals in social service organizations leads to a lack of interest and, hence, skill in evaluation. The managerial function of data collection, when it does take place, focuses on output rather than outcome measures. This, in turn, serves to reinforce the notion that social service organizations are not well-managed.

Conclusion

Schools of social work have only recently recognized the validity of specialized training for administration. Some 25 years ago administration was conveniently ignored or tolerated, an area for old social workers to retire to after growing weary of seeing clients, or a reward for good clinical practice. We should not be surprised, therefore, that the initial conceptualizations of social service organizations and administration suffers from the errors of youth.

At times it appears that the policy of limiting administrative positions to those with an MSW is based more on economic pragmatism (preserving higher paying jobs for those within the profession) than on any intellectual basis. There is nothing wrong with this economic rationale. Unfortunately, the elaboration of the uniqueness of social service organizations does more than camouflage our intentions.

Requiring only an MSW degree for administrative positions (rather than accepting other degrees as well) limits our ability to provide the best training, because the theoretical foundation is faulty. Social service organizations are not significantly different from other organizations. Efforts to substantiate these differences detract from attention that should be given to core administrative functions, functions that are essential to administration and that are at the heart of other administrative degree programs. By continuing to advance the position that social service administrators must have an MSW we impose a constraint on our ability to train future administrators. As a result, social service organizations will continue to be perceived as being poorly managed and promote the belief that social workers do not make good administrators.

REFERENCES

Hasenfeld, Y. (1983). *Human service organizations.* Englewood Cliffs, NJ: Prentice-Hall.

Stoesz, D. (1984). *Corporate welfare: The third stage.* Washington, DC: Policy America.

ANNOTATED BIBLIOGRAPHY

Scurfield, R.M. (1980). Educational preparation for social work administrators: A survey. *Journal of Education for Social Work,* 16(1), 49–56

The author surveyed 285 practicing social work administrators who reported significant gaps in their educational training to be administrators. These gaps existed whether the student had clinical or macro training, indicating that the theory, structure, and content of MSW programs need to be reevaluated in order to provide adequate preparation for social work administrators. This empirical study clearly demonstrates that the present policy of requiring an MSW for administration positions is a contributing factor to the less-than-satisfactory state of social service administration.

Stoesz, D. (1984). *Corporate welfare: The third stage.* Washington, DC: Policy America

The author documents the growth of for-profit health and welfare corporations. The continued expansion of proprietary agencies in the area of child care, nursing home, and home care means that revenues for the corporate sector will overtake the voluntary sector by 1990, thus further obscuring the distinction between social service agencies and for profit organizations. Given this trend, it appears that the distinction between social service and other types of organizations will become even more obscure.

Weiner, M.E. (1982). *Human services management: Analysis and applications*. Homewood, IL: Dorsey Press

Although the premise of this work is that there is a distinct field of human service management, the author utilizes traditional theories and concepts from political science, economics, sociology, and psychology to provide a comprehensive view of social service administration. In so doing he demonstrates the underlying similarities between the MSW and other administrative degree programs that draw from the same body of knowledge.

Rejoinder to Professor Rimer   NANCY JOHNSTONE

Dr. Rimer and I are in agreement on several points articulated in his presentation. I do not believe that social service agencies differ drastically from for-profit organizations or that the social services face a more difficult environment. I also agree that good management is generic and is essential to the survival and maintenance of all organizations (although the "business model" may not be universally applicable).

My thesis is that survival and maintenance are insufficient in today's highly complex, competitive, and unpredictable environment. What is required is leaders who can develop innovative, entrepreneurial, cutting edge organizations led by people whose training and experience are consistent with the organization's primary product; in the case of the social service agency, an MSW and social work experience. A striking example of this point from business is the remarkable recovery of Inland Steel under the leadership of Frank Luerssen, a 37-year veteran of the steel industry (Barry, 1989).

My primary areas of disagreement with Dr. Rimer center on three points. The first is his assertion that social work students are at a disadvantage vis-a-vis other administrative degree programs because they are forced to take some courses (clinical) lacking in administrative content. I do not believe that there are any data suggesting that for-profit enterprises, led by people with an MBA or similar degree, are any better managed than social service organizations. In fact, there is mounting evidence that administrators of the top performing corporations are increasingly utilizing skills that social workers learn through their clinical training and experience. These skills fall into the general category of managing people, and they include fostering growth and creativity, unifying staff behind a common purpose, understanding the needs of employees, resolving conflicts, and developing small and effective work groups. With projections of a declining workforce, these skills will become even more critical in the near future. Peters and Waterman (1982), in describing attributes of successful companies, emphasize the importance of "productivity through people . . . these [excellent] companies create environments in which people can blossom, develop self-esteem, and otherwise be excited participants in the business and in society as a whole" (p. 86).

A second point made by Dr. Rimer is that social service administrators believe they are more severely victimized by a turbulent environment and use this to justify crisis management. This view fails to recognize the significant changes occurring in the field, as social service agencies respond to a changing environment, one characterized by decreasing resources, escalating competition (including from the for-profit sector), and increased accountability demands. This is not qualitatively different from changes in business management because it responds to environmental realities such as a global economy, increased government regulations, and a changing workforce. Both the for-profit and nonprofit sectors have been forced to abandon old ways that would be inefficient and ineffective in today's marketplace. Just as process skills and humane values are not the exclusive territory of social workers, the capacity to change and "re-tool" for the future does not reside solely in the business community.

The third issue concerns what Dr. Rimer refers to as "vague goals." I find his point that social service administrators fail to understand the importance of evaluating an organization's performance to be fallacious and a gross oversimplification. Developing experimental designs and scientifically valid data that accurately reflect the essence of what many social workers are trying to accomplish is a very complicated issue. Some services are easier to quantify than others, such as volume of food packages distributed or numbers served in a homeless shelter. Some organizational goals are also readily measured, such as balancing a budget or establishing a management information system. More complex, however, is how one measures subtle changes and quality of service. Rather than hiding behind vague goals, today's social service administrators, working with experts from business and academia, are seeking to better understand what they do in order to improve services, internal planning, and communication to their publics. The problem is not the unwilling social service administrator, but rather a "state-of-the-art" that is evolving but still in its infancy.

Two comments from Dr. Rimer's presentation serve to highlight the major difference in our viewpoints: Rimer describes administration as the art of getting things done, and he defines the planning process as one of allocating resources based on a budget analysis. Emphasis here is on the present. This is in contrast to a concept of administration that extends beyond technical management skills, emphasizing leadership that is visionary, keeps the organization focused on the future, and projects a strong and clear image of the organization to others. James March, in describing leadership, states, "Rather than an analyst looking for specific data, we are inclined to think of a monitor looking for unusual signals" (Peters & Waterman, p. 107). Perhaps the difference in our points of view is best articulated by Bennis and Nanus (1985) who coined the phrase, "Managers are people who do things right and leaders are people who do the right thing"

REFERENCES

Barry, P. (1989). Back from the brink. *Chicago Enterprise, 3*(8), 16–21.
Bennis, W., & Nanus, B. (1985). *Leaders: The strategies for taking charge.* New York: Harper & Row.
Peters, T.J., & Waterman, R.H., Jr. (1982). *In search of excellence.* New York: Warner Books.

Should a Minimum, Mandatory Percentage of Funds Be Set Aside for Prevention in All Social Welfare Program Areas?

EDITOR'S NOTE: There is no more optimistic idea than prevention. It evokes the most satisfying images: of problems that are kept from arising (or at least from arising at a more troublesome level); of potential victims who are spared; of scarce resources that are saved. It seems universally appealing to prevent a problem rather than have to cure it. But is it possible to prevent the serious problems that social workers face every day? For if it is not, then successful advocacy of prevention may end up wasting resources, not saving them; not of sparing victims but doing less for them; and in compromising the credibility of those who go before legislatures and other funders and make promises about prevention that cannot and will not be met. It is because prevention may have negative consequences equal to its brilliant vision that it is important to debate it.

Three members of the faculty of the School of Social Service at Saint Louis University here carry on such a debate. Marie D. Hoff, Ph.D., answers YES to the question. She is Assistant Professor and teaches community-level practice methods and family policy. Her research and writing interests include employment and economic development, the relationship between religion and social welfare, and studies of the welfare state.

The NO response is made by two of her faculty colleagues. William H. Padberg, DSW, holds the rank of Professor and teaches social policy. He also directs a Child Welfare Traineeship Grant and serves as the School's Director of Admissions. His current research interests are in family policy and conservative ideology.

Gary R. Hamilton, Ph.D., is Associate Professor and teaches organizational analysis, human behavior, and social policy. His current research interests are in organizational politics and decision making, alternative human service organizations, and the process of policy formation.

YES

MARIE D. HOFF

For purposes of this discussion, prevention is defined as *primary* prevention: "A social problem . . . is kept from happening, either by doing something to the at-risk client population that strengthens their immunity and resistance . . . or by doing something to diminish the social conditions that breed the problem" (Gilbert, 1982, p. 293). In agreement with the 1978 statement by the President's Commission on Mental Health, this "doing something" is viewed as "seeking to build adaptive strength, coping resources, and health in people" (Nuehring, Abrams, Fike, & Ostrowsky, 1983, p. 12).

Current interest in the concept of prevention dates from the post-World War II effort to respond to the psychological needs of discharged veterans. Studies during the 1950s and 1960s, on mental health and mental illness, which led to development of community mental health and retardation centers, already contained an awareness of the importance of "as much or more, in cutting down the flow of disorder as in developing more effective technologies for undoing damage" (Cowen & Zax, 1967, p. 18, as quoted in Felner, Jason, Moritsugu, & Farber, 1983, p. 4).

Interest in preventive approaches picked up steam with the 1974 studies by both the Canadian and US governments on the health of their citizens. Both studies asserted the link between physical and mental health, as well as the linkages between environment, self-imposed risk, biology, and the logic of preventing rather than treating various forms of distress (Goldston, in Kessler & Goldston, 1968, pp. 363–366; Plaut, 1980, in Price, Ketterer, Bader, & Monahan, p. 195).

"The logic of prevention" can be argued from a variety of perspectives that support the assertion that it is time to require a demonstrable commitment to prevention in all program areas.

The Increasing Magnitude of Social Problems

There is a broadened awareness of the increasing pace and scope of generation of social problems (Albee, Joffee, & Dusenbury, 1988, pp. 17–20). It is increasingly difficult, pragmatically, to treat problems one by one, or even group by group. Thus, a more generalized commitment is needed to uncover and prevent the causes of such broad-based social and personal disorders, e.g., treatment groups for batterers are unlikely to significantly reduce the incidence of spouse or child abuse in our society. However, because research evidence indicates that those who have been abused are those most likely to become abusers, it is logical to argue that prevention of abuse is most likely to reduce the incidence of familial violence.

There is some evidence that researchers and practitioners are more ready than ever to recognize the causal impact of inimical social environments on the manifestation of social problems as well as to acknowledge the intimate and complex interactions among various conditions, e.g., there is probably broad agreement on the relationships between slum conditions and the occurrence of crime, unemployability, and illiteracy; or the impact of homelessness on the physical, psychosocial, and educational development of children. Moreover, experimental approaches to prevention during the past decade have shown some signs of actually transcending the traditionally conceived dichotomy between nature and nurture: a number of early childhood interventions reported by Cowen appear to have succeeded in providing various (nurturing) resources to both parent and child, which fostered the cognitive and psychological development (nature) of children (Kessler & Goldston, 1986). Only a universal program commitment to prevention is likely to generate the resources and cooperation necessary to respond adequately to these broad and complex problems which include elements of "nature and nurture."

Preventive approaches would focus on populations rather than on individuals. Analogous to the public health versus medical model, a prevention model tends to emphasize strategies that reduce risk or improve conditions for an entire population, because individual "victims" are not yet identified for "treatment." This argument certainly does not preclude the possibility of identification of high-risk populations and targeted prevention services toward such specific groups.

Effectiveness

Preventive approaches would eliminate problems at their source (either by removing the causal agents or making the at-risk population invulnerable). A "cure" is usually less strong than if the problem is prevented from occurring. Victims of child abuse are likely to remain more vulnerable to mental or emotional stress throughout their lives than are children raised in a home with a rich offering of positive emotional interactions and mental stimulation.

Cost Efficiency

Prevention is usually agreed to be less expensive than remediation. Given the sheer volume of social problems, it is increasingly apparent that the profession lacks the personnel and material resources for treatment of all of the individuals experiencing various kinds of physical and social deficits. Prevention dollars spent ought to be viewed as a social investment in people who will contribute more resources to society, rather than as a social cost. Persons shielded from problems or handicaps are more likely to be engaged in positive contributions to society (becoming taxpayers and contributing workers instead of tax burdens or requiring the aid or control of other members of society).

Prevention as a Moral and Ethical Imperative

Prevention is more than just stopping something from happening. It entails the provision of concrete community services and insurance of basic resources, which today are increasingly recognized as universal human rights: the right to adequate material resources (food, clothing, shelter, health care) and the right to a positive social environment (freedom from racism and other forms of social discriminatory treatment; actual participation in the educational, employment, and leisure or cultural activities of the community). From this perspective, prevention is viewed as an act of empowerment: enabling people to help and direct themselves through assuring them of adequate resources and education, and control over the conditions of their own lives (Albee, Joffe, & Dusenbury, 1988, pp. 10–11). Assuming that self direction is a feature of mature adult functioning, it can be argued that it may be immoral not to emphasize prevention (i.e., provision of positive resources as a matter of human rights in every program area). In this moral and ethical argument, prevention expresses a commitment to optimizing the quality of life for all person and groups by striving to create conditions in which every person has the freedom and resources to maximize his or her human potential.

Practice Theory Arguments

Funding and requirements to develop preventive approaches in all programs areas would eventually force us to face the connections among social problems and support more wholistic practice methods that respond to persons in a more integrated fashion. Theoretically, this approach is an expression of general systems theory, which seeks to explain complex problems and respond to their interaction, transcending artificial disciplinary barriers (Jason, Hess, Felner, & Moritsugu, 1987, p. 2). Planning for preventive approaches fosters interorganizational coordination and the evolution of common practice and service goals (Swift & Healy, in Kessler & Goldston, 1986, pp. 228–229).

In contemporary research, a strong body of research is developing to demonstrate the linkages between economic fortunes of individuals and communities and various forms of psychosocial dysfunction that have not always been perceived as strongly related to economic factors, such as crime, suicide, schizophrenia, and depression (Seidman & Rapkin, in Felner, Jason, Moritsugu, & Farber, 1983). But without a required commitment to prevention approaches across all program areas, an integrated, wholistic practice response would be unlikely to ensue. A plan to prevent economic decline for a community would not be likely to succeed, for example, without cooperation and common goals from education, housing, employment, and other service systems.

An across-the-board commitment to prevention would gradually lead to a more developmental model of social work practice (Meyer, 1974; Rapoport, 1961), i.e., a focus on the human developmental sequence and on social conditions to support the positive development of all human beings (maximizing human potential), rather than the current focus on remediating social problems of a specific cause. A commitment to prevention might result in a more child-oriented society. Tracing problems and needs to their roots would force more attention to the developmental needs of children, beginning with the prenatal environment (adequate nutrition for the mother and universal prenatal care to prevent or diminish birth defects).

A political corollary to this developmental argument is that prevention is more aligned with a practice emphasis on social reform and improvement of general social conditions rather than with service and ameliorative interventions with troubled individuals and families (Rapoport, 1961). Campbell recommended "an experimental approach to social reform" (1969, p. 409). The innovative problem solving approaches demanded by this developmental model would be responsive to Campbell's suggestion, namely an experimental attitude is a scientific attitude that seeks causal relationships—in this case to demonstrate the relationships between general social conditions and the functioning of individuals. If not all programs are committed to preventive approaches, however, the fragmented, disciplinary responses are likely to continue, rather than the wholistic interventions that respond to persons qua persons rather than as discreet problems, ignoring contributing factors for which the particular programs lack resources or expertise. When all social welfare programs are working on prevention, our social experiments are more likely to be able to account for the influence of a wider range of variables.

Social Planning and Administration Benefits

The necessity to develop preventive programs would lead to more and better planning for provision of the positive material and social resources needed by communities and individuals, rather than the present tendency toward crisis-oriented ad hoc program development (e.g., planning for permanent housing vs. emergency shelters). Planning for a universal guarantee of basic resources, as the sine qua non of prevention, would probably result in a closer alignment of social services with the basic social institutions that have developed over millennia to foster human development, namely family, education, church, and organized recreation, as Rapoport already argued in 1961 (p. 10). Another way of expressing this idea is that social services would move toward becoming institutional, universally available resources rather than residual or remedial interventions with individuals. In terms of social policy and social ethics, such universal provision would reduce stigma and hence enhance personal self esteem and community integration (solidarity among members of the community).

A pragmatic administrative benefit of a planning and experimental approach would be a gradual forcing of more clear conceptualization of program goals, more specificity in description of methods to achieve, and hence more basis on which to evaluate progress or success.

The thrust of my argument is that only a universally mandated commitment to prevention can fully assure the interrelated programming that is necessary to achieve efficiency, effectiveness, and social justice.

REFERENCES

Albee, G.W., Joffe, J.M., & Dusenbury, L.A. (1988). *Prevention, powerlessness and politics: Readings on social change.* Beverly Hills: Sage.

Campbell, D.T. (1969). Reforms as experiments. *American Psychologist* 24(4), 409–429.

Cowen, E.L. (1986). Primary prevention in mental health: Ten years of retrospect and ten years of prospect. In Kessler, M., & Goldston, S.E. (Eds.), *A decade of progress in primary prevention,* pp. 3–45.

Felner, R.D., Jason, L.A., Moritsugu, J.N., et al. (1983). *Preventive psychology: Theory, research and practice.* New York: Pergamon Press.

Gilbert, N. (1982). Policy issues in primary prevention. *Social Work,* 27(4), 293–297.

Jason, L.A., Hess, R.E., Felner, R.D., et al. (1987). Toward a multi-disciplinary approach to prevention. *Prevention in Human Services,* 5(2), 1–10.

Kessler, M., & Goldston, S.E. (Eds.) (1986). *A decade of progress in primary prevention.* Hanover and London: University Press of New England.

Meyer, C.H. (1974). Introduction/preventive intervention: A goal in search of a method. *NASW Reprints,* 1–8.

Nuehring, E.M., Abrams, H.A., Fike, D.F., et al. (1983). Evaluating the impact of prevention programs aimed at children. *Social Work Research and Abstracts,* 19(2), 11–18.

Plaut, T.F.A. (1980). Prevention policy: The federal perspective. In Price, R.H., Ketterer, R.F., Bader, B.C., et al. (Eds.), *Prevention in mental health: Research policy and practice.* Beverly Hills: Sage.

Rapoport, L. (1961). The concept of prevention in Social Work. *Social Work,* 6(1), 3–12.

Seidman, E., & Rapkin, B. (1983). Economics and psychosocial dysfunction: Toward a conceptual framework and prevention strategies. In Kessler, M. & Goldston, S.E. (Eds.), *A decade of progress in primary prevention.* Hanover and London: University Press of New England.

Swift, M.S., & Healey, K.N. (1986). Translating research into practice. In Kessler, M., & Goldston, S.E. (Eds.), *A decade of progress in primary prevention.* Hanover and London: University Press of New England.

ANNOTATED BIBLIOGRAPHY

Albee, G.W., Joffee, J.M., & Dusenbury, L.A. (Eds.) (1988). *Prevention, powerlessness and politics: Readings on social change.* Beverly Hills: Sage

A book of readings that seeks to demonstrate how a wide range of concrete social problems is related to the condition of social powerlessness. The volume includes a section with several chapters debating arguments opposed to or in support of a more general commitment to preventive approaches as means to empower people to be able to meet their own needs.

Bloom, M. (1981). *Primary prevention: The possible science.* Englewood Cliffs, NJ: Prentice-Hall

A spirited introduction, arguing for the feasibility of prevention, combined with a presentation of theoretical frameworks for conceptualizing prevention as a program of practice. Examples of prevention programs for different stages of the life cycle and for different types of problems are included.

Rejoinder to Professor Hoff

WILLIAM PADBERG AND
GARY HAMILTON

We agree with much of Dr. Hoff's "logic of prevention." Prevention can be both effective and highly cost efficient. Sure, we like prevention, but this proposal is about more than whether prevention is a worthy goal or not. It is about whether we should be taking funds from each and every social welfare program area and mounting a preventive effort in that area. Hoff seems unable to see this distinction as she makes a leap of faith from the goodness of the principle to its universal application, and without a pause to reflect on whether it will work everywhere. We also like apple pie, but please do not serve it to us for breakfast, lunch, and supper, nor suggest we use it to fix our broken carburetor.

Hoff supports the proposal as a means of attack on the underlying conditions that generate our thorny assortment of social problems. She fails to tell us, however, how the proposal could possibly effectively attack these conditions. Consider the logic underlying this proposal. It suggests that 1) each program is set up to deal with a certain problem; 2) each problem has a set of causes; and 3) each program should therefore use a part of its funds to attack those causes. This might make sense if indeed each problem had its own discrete bundle of causes. But what if instead, as Hoff contends, many of the problems dealt with by programs are deeply rooted in broad social and economic conditions? If this is correct, why then organize preventive efforts by program? Why attack these conditions with a fragmented aggregation of efforts linked to the large number of existing programs? Program-based preventive efforts would seem to be a contradictory, even futile, way to tackle the very systemic conditions that Hoff insists must be eradicated if prevention is to be effective.

Hoff's position is unassailable at the level of principle but woefully unsupportable at the level of reality. Searching for some convincing argument for her view, Hoff tries the "high ground" by suggesting a moral and ethical imperative for her position. Suddenly her original definition of prevention gives way to an ever enlarging array of universal guarantees that have lost all sense of connectedness to the program-based prevention of the proposal. Like *Alice in the Looking Glass* we wonder how we arrived at this point.

Finally, we do not pretend that one could find moral superiority in our position; we believe the argument is actually quite mundane and should be engaged at that level. But we would question the ethicality of proposing such a massive commitment of funds and reordering of social arrangements without the slightest attention to the questions of whether, where, and how it would work. Acknowledging and at least attempting to grapple with these questions would have made Hoff's position more believable as an ethical concern.

NO

WILLIAM H. PADBERG AND GARY R. HAMILTON

Nothing deceives as effectively as seemingly simple propositions. The inherent sensibility of preventing problems appears so obviously and immediately apparent that few would bother to consider the possibility of an opposite point of view. Perhaps only a reminder that nothing in life is simple pushes one toward a more careful examination of this proposition.

We need to be clear at the start that we do not oppose prevention per se. There are a number of grounds for opposing the call for a minimum mandatory percentage set aside for prevention in all social welfare programs and none of them is founded upon a disagreement with the principle of prevention. Indeed there are many preventive efforts that we could strongly support. Moreover, and perhaps ironically, this proposition is opposed because, as we later demonstrate, it may actually undermine support for preventive efforts. While we can readily support certain preventive efforts, we nevertheless oppose this proposal because it goes far beyond picking and choosing good prevention programs in imposing a preventive focus within or added to all social welfare programs. In order to demonstrate our opposition to this proposition we need to first take a closer look at prevention.

Why Not Prevention?

Who would not fervently wish to prevent child abuse, or homelessness, or mental illness, or any in the long litany of problems that confront our society? How could one oppose adopting a preventive approach for these problems? Is it not better to commit resources to keep problems from developing than to attempt to respond to them when they may be further developed and more costly to correct? Have we not known for all too long that an ounce of prevention is better than a pound of cure?

Yet a careful examination of policy responses to problems over the years would reveal approaches that are typically other than preventive in focus. Most commonly policy makers respond to problems by approaches which are essentially ameliorative in nature; less often they reflect a restorative purpose; only occasionally are the approaches curative. Only rarely do policy makers respond to problems by approaches which are truly preventive in nature.

Why is this so? Are policy makers unique in their failing to have learned this well-worn adage about the ounce of prevention or do they fail to pursue prevention because they are hard hearted or big spenders? Not at all! One major reason that they do not pursue preventive approaches is because they lack what is needed first and foremost in order to pursue a preventive approach. The dilemma, stated in most simple terms, is that prevention demands an agreed upon understanding regarding the nature of problems and their causes. That knowledge and level of agreement often simply do not exist, or, at best, exist only to a modest degree in those areas addressed.

Take the case of child abuse. Most attempts to explain the nature of child abuse and to provide an explanation of the reasons for its occurrence are complex and multifaceted. Experts even struggle to reach agreement on what behaviors will be considered abusive, and when it comes to probing its causes, most theoretical explanations suggest a multiplicity of factors contributing to the existence of this problem including cultural, social, economic, psychologic, and situational (Gelles, 1973). What policy maker, faced with such complexity, would welcome the task of gaining consensus about what needs to be done regarding child abuse?

Agreement upon the nature of problems is but one limitation faced by preventive efforts. Few persons are not moved by the horror stories that all too often tell us of innocent children brutalized by their parents. While the response from some is a vindictive call for harsh punishment to be meted out to the parents, other more enlightened professionals from the field of social welfare recognize the importance of a parent in the life of a child and are chastened by what they know of the perils often associated with removal of the child from his or her home. Their call is for steps to help the parents to be better parents, if that is in any way possible, and to work diligently to avoid the removal of the child from his or her home. But even these efforts would be of a secondary nature, enacted after abuse has occurred rather than constituting a truly preventive approach (Gilbert, 1982). In fact, much of what generally passes for prevention in the matter of child abuse are efforts focused on trying to keep the abuse from happening again. Surely no one with a preventive focus could be satisfied with dealing only with abuse after it has occurred and been reported at least once. But what measures would we adopt if we wanted to prevent this abusive behavior from ever happening in the first place? The answer to this question is exceedingly elusive because there is no real agreement as to what constitutes prevention or what differentiates it from other forms of intervention (Swift & Healey, 1986).

Consider a third major obstacle to prevention. Years ago, Edward Banfield framed the dilemma of pursuing improvement in our inner cities by distinguishing feasible measures from acceptable measures (Banfield, 1968). His message reflected the limits of social policy, limits that are similarly evident in many preventive efforts. Consider the following example. Teenage pregnancy is a major contributing factor to the problem of poverty in single parent families, a problem that we currently address through Aid to Families with Dependent Children. What direction would a preventive program take in responding to teenage pregnancies? Recent experience in this area tells us that would-be preventive approaches are stymied at the very beginning by an inability to obtain consensus on whether the culprit is sexual intercourse in general, or unprotected sexual intercourse, a lack of reproductive knowledge, or a lack of moral values. Distributing free contraceptives to teenagers may be feasible (no constitutional prohibition, having the possibility of reducing pregnancies, and at a cost that would not be prohibitive) but it would not be acceptable (public officials would not be willing to put it into effect). Thus, even when we may have some knowledge of what would work, there is no assurance that this brings agreement on the means to pursue.

No, it is not a matter of hard hearted or big-spender policy makers standing in the way of prevention. Rather, we face serious obstacles regarding a lack of knowledge of causes of problems, a lack of agreement on what constitutes prevention, and a lack of agreement on what preventive means to pursue. These obstacles to preventive measures pose particularly serious problems for the proposal at hand. The proposal suggests an across-the-board preventive response to all social problems. Yet our certainty of knowledge and our agreement about means varies dramatically from one area to another. Ignoring these significant differences may undermine the credibility of preventive efforts in areas where we do have sufficient knowledge and agreement. In fact, there are areas where it is not even clear what is to be prevented.

Consider, for example, the difficulty that Social Security poses for this proposition. What preventive purpose would the funds generated by this proposal address in regard to Social Security? Would we seek to prevent elderly persons from retiring or breadwinners from dying? Would we seek to advise the working population on superior investment possibilities to cushion the financial hardships of retirement? These rather strange options make the point that in many instances there is no agreement on what, if anything, there is to prevent.

A Lack of Discretion

Let us take another look at Social Security to explore another problem posed by this proposal and in particular the matter of the "minimum mandatory percentage." What percentage might we suggest for set-aside that would not generate either an enormous amount, beyond even the most ambitious preventionist's imagination to effectively use, or such a piddling amount as to be not worth the effort to consider spending? We spend approximately eighteen billion dollars each month in cash benefits to retired and disabled workers or their survivors. By contrast we spend approximately seventy-five million dollars per month for victims of black lung disease, a condition for which preventive efforts would seem particularly promising (*Social Security Bulletin*, 1989).

Assuming we could agree what the preventive focus should be relative to Social Security (an assumption that we believe stretches the imagination), the minimum percentage would have to be set exceedingly low, or vast amounts of dollars for prevention would be generated. At a lowly one percent set-aside, Social Security would have $180,000,000 each month to pursue preventive purposes. The same percentage applied to most other programs would generate rather small, even insignificant, amounts.

This problem speaks to the issue of limited discretion. Without available discretion to determine the appropriate amount of prevention dollars in any specific program, we face the prospect of generating grossly excessive amounts for some programs or woefully inadequate amounts in other programs. Although it is possible to argue that the proposition would allow for larger percentages in some programs as long as the minimum were not violated in others, the force of this argument would be to throw the matter back into the political arena where each program fights and scrapes for its prevention dollars. If we were willing to accept this arrangement, what is left of the substance of this proposal? Is this not where we are at the present time without the proposition in operation?

The Politics of Implementation

We have touched on two social welfare areas, child abuse and Social Security, in examining problems surrounding this proposal and have only scratched the surface. Lurking behind every single social welfare program, if this proposal were to be implemented, are not only similar questions to the ones considered for these two areas, but a host of questions of a political nature that serve to thicken the soup of this murky quagmire. Who should decide 1) the minimum mandatory percentage; 2) the prevention programs to pursue; 3) the targets of the preventive efforts; 4) the providers of prevention programs; 5) the measure of success? Would not a program-related organization of prevention efforts move us away from dealing with basic social conditions? Given the lack of understanding about causes alone, do we really want a grand scale, required prevention bonanza where all these questions, and many more, must be answered to the satisfaction of a skeptical and penurious populace?

Conclusion

We repeat that we are in favor of prevention where and when it is clearly appropriate, but we oppose this proposition. Its uniform response creates chaos out of the already troubled area of prevention by requiring action in the face of totally inadequate knowledge about causes by prescribing prevention where no preventive purpose may be called for, by generating vast differentials in prevention funding, and allowing for no discretion as to where preventions funds could best be spent. Let us have good and reasonable proposals for prevention efforts and let us do away with muddled propositions that can only serve to discredit the cause for prevention. A very large price of public goodwill is extracted when we pursue bad policy, a price that friends of prevention can ill afford these days or at anytime.

REFERENCES

Banfield, E.C. (1968). *The unheavenly city*. Boston: Little, Brown and Company.
Gelles, R.J. (1973). Child abuse as psychopathology: A sociocultural critique and reformulation. *American Journal of Orthopsychiatry* 43, 4.
Gilbert, N. (1982). Policy issues in primary prevention. *Social Work*, 2, 4.
Social Security Bulletin (1989), 51, 7, 35–41.
Swift, M.S., & Healey, K.N. (1986). Translating research into practice. In Kessler, M. & Goldston, S.E. (Eds.), *A decade of progress in primary prevention*, Hanover and London: University Press of New England.

ANNOTATED BIBLIOGRAPHY

Gilbert, Neil (1982). Policy issues in primary prevention. *Social Work*, 27, 4, July.

> This article considers policy issues which inhibit the application of primary prevention efforts in social work practice. In doing so, it also makes clear the distinction between primary, secondary, and tertiary prevention.

Kessler, M., & Goldston, S.E., (Eds.) (1986). *A decade of progress in primary prevention*. Hanover, NH: University Press of New England.

> The purpose of this volume is to herald the progress which has been made in the field of primary prevention. Unfortunately what passes for progress often blends with the confusion over what constitutes prevention.

Rejoinder to Professors Hamilton and Padberg

MARIE D. HOFF

Professors Hamilton and Padberg argue that we should not require all programs to expend funds (and by implication, effort) on prevention because 1) we do not know or agree on the nature and causes of social problems; 2) we do not know what prevention is, or how it differs from intervention; 3) even when we know what works we may not agree on what to do, and thus political struggles will continue; and 4) the struggle to achieve consensus on prevention will undermine our credibility in areas where we do agree.

I acknowledge that there is some truth in points one and three. In discussing why we have difficulty agreeing on the nature and causes of social problems, Hamilton and Padberg acknowledge that "most theoretical explanations suggest a multiplicity of factors." At least we know that as human beings, in our actual existence, we are not compartmentalized as are most of our social interventions. Yet the gamut of our programs spans every aspect of human existence—cultural, social, economic, psychological, and biological. If all such programs were required to begin to address the issue of prevention, we would at least be on our way toward approaches that match in complexity the problems they purport to address. This effort, while imperfect, would be more laudable than our current tendency to offer simple answers and limited resources to "clean up" huge gaping social wounds.

With regard to point three, I would simply respond that politics is an inherent feature of social life. Better that we argue over how all programs can contribute to the prevention of child abuse than over how to restrain the violent behavior of adults who were once abused children themselves. Moreover, separating the feasible from the acceptable is part of the "job description" of policy analysts, policy makers, and policy implementers.

I do *not* agree that we do not know what prevention is or how it differs from intervention. The problems we face in our society remain blatant and gross enough that we certainly can distinguish between restorative or ameliorative strategies and measures of problems prevented or measures of positive physical and social functioning. We *do* know the difference between 1) "treating" the victims who suffer from violence, inadequate food and shelter, medical neglect, undiagnosed birth defects, and 2) developing the physical, social, and economic resources that enhance human life. Any prevention program is inevitably going to have to emphasize the latter approach.

Given the fact that the scope and magnitude of social problems seem to be increasing, rather than being cured by our current post-hoc interventive approaches, I question how much credibility we would have to lose by turning to some genuinely new approaches. Hamilton and Padberg's own admission of some "rather strange options" emerging from their argument demonstrates the truth of Moroney's insight that we seem to continue to emphasize process and administrative reforms, to the detriment of ever addressing or trying to come to agreement on what goals and values we are trying to achieve (Moroney, 1981, p. 83).

REFERENCE

Moroney, R.M. (1981). Policy analysis within a value theoretical framework. In Haskins R., & Gallagher, J.J. (Eds.), *Models for analysis of social policy*. Norwood, NJ: Ablex, pp. 78–102.

Should Part of Social Workers' Salaries Be Contingent on the Outcomes They Achieve with Their Clients?

EDITOR'S NOTE: The issue underlying this argument is one that arises in many fields: Should professionals be responsible for the quality of outcomes received by the consumers of their services? Similar questions could (and have been) raised about teachers: should teachers be evaluated in part by knowledge and skills acquired by their students? Notice that the question reads: "Should *part* of social worker's salaries . . . ," not all. Currently, no part of social workers' salaries is contingent on the outcomes achieved with clients. Many would argue that this is how things should be: that part of being a professional is being competent in "state-of-the-art" methods for helping people and that professional standards and ethical codes are sufficient to insure this level of service. Or, the argument could be made that because there is little agreement on what outcomes are desired and how to assess progress, this policy would neither be possible or fair. Both sides of this question are addressed in the following pages. (See also discussion by Bloom and Freud on: Should social workers evaluate their practice based on clearly defined objectives?)

Eileen Gambrill, Ph.D. argues YES. Eileen Gambrill is Professor of Social Welfare at the University of California at Berkeley (see description of editors of *Controversial Issues in Social Work*).

Alex Gitterman, Ed.D and Irving Miller, DSW, argue NO. Alex Gitterman is Professor of social work and director of Maternal and Child Health Training Project, Columbia University School of Social Work. He is the coauthor of: *The Life Model of Social Work Practice* (with Carel

Germain) (1980) New York: Columbia University Press and coeditor of *The Legacy of William Schwartz: Group Practice as Shared Interaction* (with Lawrence Shulman) (1986) New York: Haworth. Irving Miller is Professor Emeritus, Columbia University School of Social Work and special lecturer and consultant to social welfare organizations.

YES

EILEEN GAMBRILL

Social workers' salaries are typically unrelated to the quality of services offered to clients. Is this not odd in a profession that is supposed to be client centered? Performance-based salary systems in which a part of social workers' salaries is based on outcomes achieved with clients provides an alternative to the current state-of-affairs. Advantages of basing a part of social workers' salaries on outcomes achieved with clients include helping staff to enhance practice knowledge and skills, encouraging administrators and supervisors to offer training programs to enhance practice skills, and increasing the likelihood of providing high-quality services to clients. This policy offers a tangible way to give positive feedback to staff. Thus, performance-based salary systems would have benefits both for clients and social workers.

Incentives for meeting individual performance goals could be provided in a variety of ways (Keyworth, 1990). A base salary could be offered and opportunities to increase this could be contingent on meeting specific performance goals agreed on in individual performance contracts. At the Huntsville Community Mental Health Center, appropriate record keeping was encouraged by basing salary increments on such skills (Rinn and Vernon, 1975). Each staff member was evaluated monthly on five client files drawn at random from their caseload (Bolin & Kivens, 1974). Other incentives used to encourage effective counselor behaviors included college credit arranged through local universities and praise and recognition for setting realistic, meaningful, and specific goals and for attaining them.

Required Conditions

Six conditions are required for this policy to be fair and effective. Offering these conditions will address sources of negative reactions to such an arrangement and discourage inappropriate use of such a policy (e.g., selection of trivial outcomes or progress indicators and use of punishing rather than positive contingencies).

Service Outcomes Are Clearly Defined and Relevant to Practice Considerations

Only if outcomes are clearly described can the feasibility of pursuing them or degree of progress in attaining them be clearly discerned. Some would argue that not only is it not possible to clearly describe service goals in social work settings, it is not desirable to do so (see debate by Bloom and Freud in this book). Many argue otherwise (e.g., Rapp & Poertner, 1988). The outcomes desired by clients, significant others, and authorities (such as the court) are often crystal clear and progress indicators are readily available if staff have the required assessment knowledge and related skills to identify these. Service outcomes selected must be relevant to practice concerns; otherwise, trivial outcomes may be selected that are of little value to either clients or social workers.

Relevant, Clear, Agreed-On Progress Indicators Are Tracked

Gathering information about degree of progress on an ongoing basis allows timely clinical decisions about intervention. Should it be continued, altered, or ended? Thus, gathering data about progress is integral to provision of services to clients. Measures selected should be user-focused—of value to social workers and clients (Patton, 1978). Whenever possible, both objective (e.g., observation in real life settings) as well as subjective (self report) measures should be used (Wolfe, 1978; Fuqua & Schwade, 1986). Measures of consumer satisfaction (self report of clients) may not match levels of outcome as assessed by other means; consumer satisfaction is typically very high—ranging from 76 to 83 percent (Lebow, 1983). Service providers tend to report less progress compared to clients (e.g., Garfield, 1983).

Outcomes Are Achievable

We know more about the limits of help that can be offered (Mays & Franks, 1985). For example, one realistic outcome in a child welfare agency may be "25% to 49% of cases entering foster care will have achieved a permanent placement within 6 months" (Carter, 1988). The likelihood of achieving goals should always be considered because this will influence what can be accomplished even by the most competent social worker. Salary incentives in such cases could be contingent on demonstrating that methods that are most likely to be effective were used (on process measures). Incentives could be offered for setting realistic goals and attaining approximations to these.

Performance requirements should be based on each individual's current level of outcomes achieved in relation to a specific outcome (i.e., their baseline levels). (It would be assumed that certain minimal performance levels would be required when staff are hired.) Personalized performance agreements should be drawn up for each social worker. Social workers who are just learning a new intervention method may receive salary incentives for improving their success rate by 10% in relation to a specific outcome. A staff member who already has a high success rate may receive a salary bonus for maintaining this level.

There Is Evidence That Some Interventions and Some Social Workers Are More Effective Than Others

If all interventions were equally effective and all social workers were equally competent, then there would be no need for the policy suggested here. But some social workers are more competent than others. For example, some provide higher levels of relationship qualities known to enhance positive outcomes than do others (Wills, 1982). Individual differences in competency levels are by no means limited to social workers; it is estimated that ten percent of physicians are incompetent (Bok, 1978). We must consider the consequences on quality of service of low competency levels. There is evidence in a number of areas that some interventions are better than others. Examples include family treatment of schizophrenic adults (Falloon, Boyd, & McGill, 1984) and behavioral treatment of agoraphobia (Barlow & Waddell, 1985) to name but two. Although meta-analyses of outcome studies often reveal little difference between methods, this does not mean that there are not any differences (Kazdin, 1989). If some interventions are more effective than others, social workers have a right to learn these and clients have a right to the better ones.

The fidelity with which intervention is carried out is of increasing concern as tested intervention protocols become more available. Although the description of intervention methods with such precision is the exception rather than the rule, it is becoming more common. Lack of appropriate intervention is considered to be one of the main reasons why methods that have been shown to be effective in research studies may not be as effective in everyday practice (Kazdin, 1986). When there is evidence that some methods are better than others in achieving certain outcomes, it would be hoped that clinicians would offer these methods to their clients and that agencies assume some responsibility for insuring that their staff are skilled in providing these interventions. Part of agency-based training programs could consist of occasional review of the treatment fidelity using tested protocols as a criterion as well as degree of success. Individual staff members could assume increasing responsibility for self-review as criterion levels increase.

Staff are Active Participants

Staff should be active participants in selection of performance goals and progress indicators for professional, practical, and ethical reasons. This will prevent the imposition of trivial, unwanted evaluation requirements that have little or no effect on enhancing clinical skills. Each staff person could take responsibility for preparing agreements that would provide a basis for discussions with supervisors. This would involve staff as participants in planning their work and would offer opportunities to enhance skills that are helpful (if not critical) in offering high-quality services to clients such as setting clear objectives and identifying relevant progress indicators.

Constructive Feedback Is Provided

Essential features of constructive feedback include identification and support for use of specific skills and attainment of specific outcomes together with helpful suggestions for improving success (or lowering unrealistic expectations). Increasing attention is being given to how to handle clinical errors (Kottler & Blau, 1989). When staff have experience with the benefits of constructive feedback, it is likely that they will ask for more rather than for less. One performance measure used to assess administrators could be the level of positive feedback offered for use of helpful skills and attainment of outcomes.

Needed Training Is Provided

It would be unfair to have such a policy without providing the training required to ensure that staff at all levels possess knowledge and skills required to attain outcomes that are achievable. This places a responsibility on the administration to provide such training and to ensure that it is successful in developing knowledge and skills that increase the quality of services provided to clients. This training should include skills that staff can use to prompt and support needed competencies "on-the-job." Often, training is provided with little or no effort made to determine whether it makes the slightest bit of difference to clients.

Facilitating Administrative Policies and Practices Are Provided

A well-designed performance management system will require active involvement of supervisors and administrators. Requisite training (e.g., in use of constructive feedback) will have to be provided for these personnel as well as for line staff. Budgeting will have to include allowance for performance based pay.

Obstacles

Different beliefs about the relevance of practice-related research will be an obstacle. That is, some administrators and line staff do not believe that research is available that indicates that some methods are more effective than others. There is little agreement concerning core professional skills that should be mastered in social work training programs, making the problem of transfer of knowledge from such programs to everyday practice even more variable than usual (Freidson, 1986). Incentives could be provided to staff for learning and trying new methods so that staff have a chance to see for themselves. Another obstacle is getting access to empirically-based methods. Who has the time? Agencies could take advantage of people who are knowledgeable in a given area, as well as computer retrieval programs and key review articles. All staff would benefit from monthly clinical conferences at which selected empirically based assessment or intervention methods are described. Each staff person could select a specialty area and keep colleagues up-to-date on developments in this area, including providing copies of helpful material to an agency library.

Other obstacles include a reluctance on the part of staff to have the results of their work carefully reviewed and a reluctance to accept standards of practice that reduce professional discretion. True, social workers are supervised, but typically feedback is not based on degree of progress attained in relation to specific objectives as well as on assessment of treatment fidelity based on a review of video or audiotaped sessions and a comparison of conditions offered with empirically-based assessment and intervention methods. Negative past experiences with the imposition of trivial or punitive evaluation methods understandably creates apprehension. That is, past efforts to evaluate services may not have been user-focused (Patton, 1978). It would be hoped that social workers would learn to identify clear relevant objectives and progress indicators during their social work training. However, this is the exception rather than the norm. Thus, agencies will have to provide instruction in these important skills. Applying new skills to one case at a time would allow for incremental learning of new skills.

Overcoming a reluctance to openly acknowledge that some social workers are more competent than others will be an obstacle. As research increases in terms of what works with what client, having each staff member address a wide range of presenting problems becomes increasingly questionable in terms of offering clients high quality service. It is probably no longer possible, even at this point, for one social worker to be maximally (or perhaps even minimally) effective with a wide range of problem areas. Positive experiences with a performance based salary system would encourage recognition that increased specialization would be a sound policy.

Yet another obstacle is inertia. It is easy to keep doing what has been done. Inertia will encourage one of a variety of reactions that will prevent change: 1) begging the question (simply asserting "it won't work"); 2) appealing to tradition ("that's not the way we do it"); 3) distorting the argument (asserting that it would require selection of trivial objectives or encourage a "police-like" atmosphere in agencies); or 4) saying "we've been doing it all along" (when this is not true).

Benefits of This Policy

Emphasis on clearly describing desired outcomes would help social workers to distinguish between outcomes that are possible to attain, those that will be difficult to attain and those that will be impossible to attain. Without clear description of outcomes, social workers often try to achieve the impossible, with resultant discouragement both for clients and themselves. No doubt this is one of the main causes of "burnout" frequently complained of by social service workers. Offering visible, tangible feedback for success will help to maintain sound practice skills. There are few opportunities in most agencies for formal recognition of clinical competence based on outcomes achieved. Clear descriptions of assessment and intervention programs as well as progress will make it easier for supervisors to carry out both training and administrative responsibilities (given that they have the required knowledge and skills). Benefits of performance-based pay reported by Spectrum (a private, not-for-profit service agency working with children and adults with developmental disabilities) include an increase in hours spent on job-related training, increased reliability in documenting services offered and progress made, creation of innovative curriculum programs, and a decrease in staff turnover (Keyworth, 1990).

I asked a group of second-year masters students whether they would work for an agency in which a part of their salary was based on outcomes achieved with clients under the conditions described in this paper. Most reacted quite positively. They showed particular interest in the opportunities for continued training that would be built into such a system. This group of students may not be typical of all social workers in that they do not have a variety of misconceptions about setting clear objectives and progress indicators (for example, that this requires selection of trivial objectives or progress indicators or that clients are not involved in their selection).

In no way does such a policy imply a speed up of services or an imposition of objectives, intervention methods, or progress indicators on social workers or clients. Quite the opposite. The more people are involved as active participants, the more likely it is that desired changes will occur.

Incentives are offered for achieving client identified goals (within the bounds of legality, practicality, and ethical concerns) and for upgrading the quality of intervention provided to clients. Staff will benefit by working in an agency that is committed to offering relevant training and will have access to higher quality feedback concerning their effectiveness. Clients will receive better services. As evidence accumulates that some methods are better than others in helping clients to attain certain outcomes and that some people are more effective than others in providing these interventions, performance-based salary systems should become increasingly common.

REFERENCES

Barlow, D.H., & Waddell, M.T. (1985). Agoraphobia. In Barlow, D.H., (Ed.), *Clinical handbook of psychological disorders: A step-by-step treatment approach.* New York: Guilford.

Bok, S. (1979). *Lying: Moral choices in public and private life.* New York: Vintage Books.

Bolin, D.C., & Kivens, L. (1974). Evaluation in a community mental health center. *Evaluation, 2,* 26–35.

Carter, R.K. (1988). Measuring client outcomes: The experience of the states. *Administration in Social Work, 11,* 73–88.

Falloon, I.R.H., Boyd, J.L., & McGill, C.W. (1984). *Family care of schizophrenia.* New York: Guilford.

Freidson, E. (1986). *Professional powers: A study of the institutionalization of formal knowledge.* Chicago: University of Chicago Press.

Fuqua, R.W., & Schwade, J. (1986). Social validation of applied behavioral research. In Poling, A. & Fuqua, R.W. (Eds.), *Research methods in applied behavior analysis.* New York: Plenum.

Garfield. S.G. (1983). Some comments on consumer satisfaction in behavior therapy. *Behavior Therapy, 14,* 237–241.

Kazdin, A.E. (1986). Comparative outcome studies in psychotherapy: Methodological issues and strategies. *Journal of Consulting and Clinical Psychology, 54,* 95–105.

Keyworth, R. (1990). Performance pay—an evolving system at Spectrum Center. *Performance Management Magazine, 8,* 6–10.

Kottler, J.A., & Blau, D.S. (1989). *The imperfect therapist: Learning from failure in therapeutic practice.* San Francisco, CA: Jossey-Bass.

Lebow, J. (1983). Research assessing consumer satisfaction with mental health treatment: A review of findings. *Evaluation and Program Planning, 6,* 211–236.

Mays, D.T., & Franks, C.M. (1985). Negative outcome: What to do about it. In Mays, D.T., & Franks, C.M. (Eds.), *Negative outcome in psychotherapy and what to do about it.* New York: Springer.

Patti, R.J. (1988). Managing for service effectiveness in social welfare: Toward a performance model. *Administration in Social Work,* 11, 9–21.

Patton, M.Q. (1978). *Utilization focused evaluation.* Newbury Park, CA: Sage.

Rapp, C.A., & Poertner, J. (1988). Moving center stage through use of client outcomes. *Administration in Social Work,* 11, 23–38.

Rinn, R.C., & Vernon, J.C. (1975). Process evaluation of outpatient treatment in a community mental health center. *Journal of Behavior Therapy and Experimental Psychiatry,* 6, 5–12.

Wills, T.A. (1982). Nonspecific factors in helping relationships. In Wills, T.A. (Ed.), *Basic processes in helping relationships.* New York: Academic.

Wolf, M.M. (1978). Social validity: The case for subjective measurement or how applied behavior analysis is finding its heart. *Journal of Applied Behavior Analysis,* 11, 203–214.

Rejoinder to Professor Gambrill

ALEX GITTERMAN AND
IRVING MILLER

Our major difficulty with the "pro" position, however learned and sophisticated it may be, is that it rests on a set of undemonstrated, "begging the question" assumptions:

- That financial incentives and rewards would mitigate problems in service delivery, allay burnout, enhance motivation for training and augment the service ethic.
- That high-level, creative professional activity without a favorable outcome would not deserve additional financial reward.
- That agency, professional and client interests and goals are congruent and harmonious.
- That the complex, comprehensive, and rational system being proposed can be fairly and effectively administered to reflect and accommodate the interests and needs of the agency, the staff, and the client.

We have serious doubts and questions about the validity of these assumptions.

We see no evidence that financial incentives and rewards based upon successful client outcomes will mitigate problems in service delivery, allay burnout, enhance motivation for training, and augment the service ethic. The assumption, for example, of a favorable impact on staff morale and motivation by this proposed system is highly questionable. There is a vast body of knowledge and experience suggesting that morale and motivation grow out of complex social factors and are not purchased by money alone or primarily. The eponymous "Hawthorne effect" epitomizes the outcome of one of the first and landmark studies showing the great power of the informal systems and social and interpersonal interaction upon worker morale, motivation and productivity (Homans, 1950).

We propose that a system that rewards workers for achieving positive client outcomes and does not reward workers for high-level, creative professional activities that do not result in positive client outcomes would induce or create the very staff conflicts and difficulties it intends to avoid and preclude. Though scholars have identified and specified what good professional practice looks like, they by no means can predict successful outcome. Good practice is one contributing factor inseparable from other factors, such as the politics of the agency, the environmental context, and the amenability of the problems clients present to the help we offer. Indeed, we have observed merely mediocre practice or even occasionally flawed practice followed by successful outcome for the client. Can one imagine the problems created by a system that implicitly assumes the level of worker skill is the only differentiating factor in bringing about successful or unsuccessful outcomes when clients inevitably will bring to the work differing internal, familial, and environmental resources. How would we justify and demonstrate an even-handed application of the system. The struggle and competition for the "easy" case assignments might well dominate the agency climate. The "preferred" client usually defined as an agency intake phenomenon will reach into the daily details of struggle for certain case assignments. Who would get the success prone cases? Would it be the reward given to the worker who has already demonstrated success with such cases or to the worker whose success rate is low and needs a boost in morale, if not income. Who will distribute the patronage of success prone cases? This is quite a kettle of fish and it is inherently encouraged by the system proposed, despite its contrary intentions.

We have already noted the implicit assumption in the "pro" proposal that agency, professional, and client interests are compatible and overlapping. Such an assumption clearly can not withstand the stare of reality. Agency requirements and maintenance imperatives often shape services and professional behaviors. Consequently, a legitimate question becomes: whose outcome will merit reward? To the extent that a compatibility of interests is assumed, it ignores the inherent tensions between what the client wants, what the client needs, and what the client gets (Gitterman & Miller, 1989).

We do not believe that the complex, comprehensive, and rational system being proposed can be fairly and effectively administered to reflect and accommodate the interests and needs of the agency, the staff, and the client. The proposed system sets up performance and outcome norms based upon assessment, characteristics of the clients, and the nature of the problem, the social context, etc. The proposal includes parenthetic caveats and reassuring qualifiers that other matters are also being taken into account. These add to and elaborate the complexity of the system and compromise its feasibility and workability. The very complexity and elaborateness of the system will lead ineluctably to ritualistic compliance and a kind of compliance that subverts the system itself. This would be the case even if the system did not offend, as it probably will, the values, norms, and competing definitions of other groups and actors in the system. Moreover, the "pro" position seeks, in effect, to explain in advance why the system might not work as intended. It does so by attributing it to apathy, inertia, resistance to change even when the proposed change is supposed to be for the better. We do not believe that administrators of complex agencies and departments would be eager to manage and preside over the system as envisioned. And it would not be because of apathy, inertia, and the ordeal of change. They would prefer, we believe, a system of rewards and incentives of retention, promotion, regular increments, and supplementary rewards for noteworthy special achievement and professional contributions.

In conclusion, Professor Gambrill no doubt recognizes and has recognized some of these built-in risks and problems in the system she proposes. Recognition of problems and arguments couched and qualified by what "would," "could," and "should" be done do little to quell or quiet the doubts about the proposal's feasibility and fairness. We would favor a system providing additional rewards for special achievements and urge that such a system take "outcome" into account as only one of several considerations and within a longer and larger perspective than a per capita and "piece work" basis. Other considerations might include persistent, creative, and skillful efforts by the worker on behalf of clients, regardless of outcomes, advanced training and acquisition of new skills; organizational involvement, development of new programs, and contribution to the improvement of delivery of services. In the development of any system, we would applaud staff participation and peer review.

NOTES

1. Gitterman, A., & Miller, I. (1989). "The Influence of the organization on clinical practice." *Clinical Social Work Journal,* 17(2):151–164.

2. Homans, G. (1950). *The human group.* New York: Harcourt Brace Jovanovich, Inc.

NO

ALEX GITTERMAN AND IRVING MILLER

So This Is What We Have Come To!

We assume that the statement means that part of a worker's salary should be contingent on the outcomes achieved with clients. We develop our "con" position from identifying various possible assumptions upon which the pro position might be based.

The Worker's Interventions Are Directly Related to or Are Responsible for the Client's Successes and Failures to Achieve Outcomes

The proponents for the statement implicitly assume that a worker's interventions are directly responsible for the successes or failures achieved, that is to say that effective interventions by the worker lead to successful outcomes and conversely ineffective ones to unsuccessful outcomes.

However plausible this may sound, such an assumption implies a simply unsupportable linearity in the complicated connections between giving and receiving help. In this view, the client becomes an "object" for the worker's treatment interventions. With appropriately selected interventions, the client improves. With inappropriate interventions, the client does not. In this view, the client is a relatively passive "receiver" of the worker's expert professional "inputs."

The statement of the issue bespeaks a view of the helping process that mistakenly places the worker front and center as the maker, shaker, breaker, and doer. The helping process is not a mechanistic procedure or process, but is a disciplined art based and built upon theory, research, and commonly held values. Helping transforms and adapts knowledge into action. It is in the very nature and social reality of helping that the worker does not and cannot alone determine outcomes. The helping effort is in a sense analogous to a joint venture characterized by mutuality, shared goals, and openness about means and ends. The worker needs to gain the client's trust, make the course clear, point out the obstacles and help the client consider options and possibilities. The client essentially does the changing, choosing, and problem solving.

As our profession has assumed a budget-cutting-inspired concern for accountability, one of the side effects has been a mechanistic preoccupation with practice outcomes and a corresponding tendency to evaluate professional competence and skills based upon a priori specified outcomes. The client's progress or lack of progress is attributed to the worker's skills or lack of skills. This ends-means confusion negates the actualities of the process in which a worker tries to be helpful, and a client decides how and whether to use the help from this particular person at this particular time. The worker's behaviors may be skillful, but the client may not progress or may possibly even regress; the worker's behaviors may not be particularly skillful, but the client may progress. Professional skills have to be evaluated in their own terms as well as in relation to specific outcomes. Clients make progress because, despite of, and even without our help. Lawyers who lose their case may be justly praised for their fine work in a lost cause, and doctors do well and act skillfully, but their patient may not necessarily do well because of it. The question or issue is: did the worker do the right thing in the particular circumstances considering the state of the art and available options? And so in social work, the actions of the helper have to be seen in their own terms. Social workers should be evaluated by their behaviors along the way and according to such considerations as: Did they establish the conditions and climate for client trust and acceptance; were they responsive and were their responses relevant to what the client was communicating; were their actions knowledge-based and consistent with the state of the art.

Workers, Clients, and Agencies Usually Have Common or Congruent Definitions about Desired Outcomes

From this it may well be assumed that workers, agencies, and clients have similar or congruent interests that financial incentives for workers will not compromise. Such an assumption also carries the burden of implication that workers are not encumbered by agency and professional imperatives that compromise clients interests.

Although some commonality of interest, even a tenuous one, must exist to provide service, the position seems to assume a self-evident compatibility between agency, professional, and client interests. To the extent that such compatibility is assumed, it negates the inherent tensions between them and what the client wants, needs, and gets. Agency requirements and maintenance imperatives shape services, problem definition, assessment, and a wide range of clinical decisions affecting the "careers" of clients. In health care, for example, "timely" assessment and "timely" discharge planning appear to be the central task for social work. "Timely," however, is an official euphemism in reimbursement regulations. It does not mean the right or the opportune time, but more often it means hurried and inadequate assessment and premature discharge. Because failure to conform with regulations would imperil the already strained financial position of the organization, interventions that are not necessarily in the interest of the client may be accepted and condoned. When we provide additional financial incentives contingent on the achievement of outcomes, the critical question becomes whose outcome do we seek. Will the worker be financially rewarded by the hospital for advocating a lengthier stay for a patient? This is doubtful. More likely, the worker will be rewarded for doing the hospital's business and press for "timely" discharge.

Professionals and agency administrators negotiate accommodations and tradeoffs to satisfy their respective interests. Low salaries, for example, are accepted in exchange for a "preferred" case load or for professional autonomy and perfunctory accountability. Extensive intake procedures and long waiting lists may provide an agency and its professional staff with clients motivated for long-term insight-oriented therapy and screen out those in crisis and those with environmental problems. Such tacit agreements ensure workers with stronger identification with their agencies than with their clients. Providing additional financial incentives may on the surface seem innocent, but, in fact, may further reinforce and assure worker conformity to organizational pressures and practices that are at the expense of client interests and needs.

Most Clients Would Benefit from Such Contingent Incentives

Because the original question (Should part of social workers' salaries be contingent on the outcomes they achieve with their clients?) does not specify conditions or caveats, it suggests a belief in the applicability of such contingent incentives for a wide range of fields of practice and groups of clients with different types of problems.

The logic of this proposition leads inevitably to a scramble for and pressure to be assigned or to assume work assignments with those clients who seem to be most motivated and those with whom we are most likely to achieve a desired outcome. (The joke goes that it takes only one therapist to change an electric bulb but only if the bulb is motivated to change.) It may also mean choosing clients who are most like us and most likely to be congenial to our cognitive styles and predilection. Where does this leave the poor, the most needy, the vulnerable and powerless? Where does it leave those with oppressive environmental problems, those whose problems are "messy," complex, and often quite intractable? Who will want to serve them? Whose outcomes will be rewarded? This kind of choosing of clients is virtually the norm in private practice and is not being impugned. It is questionable if not irreconcilable with the purposes of social agencies.

Salaries Partly Contingent upon Outcomes Will Improve the Quality of Services to Clients

It may be assumed that if workers have greater monetary incentive, they will provide more effective services and clients will be more likely to achieve desired outcomes than if workers do not have a financial stake in the outcome. Thus, financial reinforcements would increase worker motivation and involvement and the ultimate result would be better services to clients.

The N.A.S.W. Code of Ethics states, "The social worker should serve clients with devotion, loyalty, determination, and the maximum application of professional skill and competence." This commitment is not driven by financial incentives. Financial rewards contingent upon outcomes would corrupt and compromise the quality of the helping relationship, the agency's service, and the profession itself.

Conclusion

We have argued against a kind of "piecework" bonus system based upon outcomes. The original question could only have been posed in the last 10 or 15 years, a period in which we have been confronted with an increasing emphasis on accountability, not so much for quality as for quantity of service. Business principles have been misapplied to social agencies. The legitimate purpose of business is to produce profit. Desired outcomes can be specified in advance and their achievement is easily recognized. This lends itself easily to an incentive system for achieving the specified outcomes. But this is clearly not the case in human service organizations.

We think the pro argument may well have similar concerns. The way the issue is posed manifestly acknowledges that there is something inappropriate about the underlying premise by limiting it to "part" of social workers salaries.

To seriously pursue the notion that client outcomes should be used as the basis for judging worker merit and skill is to become involved in a hopeless professional and intellectual thicket.

Rejoinder to Professors Gitterman and Miller
EILEEN GAMBRILL

Any policy can be implemented in a thoughtful or inadequate, even absurd, manner. Professors Gitterman and Miller have noted some of the negative outcomes of poorly designed performance-based systems. These include goal displacement, in which attention is paid to trivial or irrelevant outcomes that are not of concern to clients or staff, and unjust punishment of social workers for not achieving unrealistic performance requirements. These are not inevitable characteristics of performance-based systems but rather reflect ineffective and inappropriate implementation of such a policy—one that diminishes rather than enhances the lives of clients and social workers.

A performance-based system does indeed put the social worker "front and center" in terms of having responsibility for being skilled and knowledgeable about up-to-date clinical methods based on research findings related to clinical practice and offering these methods to their clients. It is assumed that there is a relationship between the decisions made by staff and attainment of outcomes desired by clients and significant others. There is no assumption of linearity of effect. There are many unknowns in clinical practice, and many different kinds of relationships no doubt occur. Clinical practice is an uncertain enterprise and each client, family, and situation is different. In recognition of this, the pro position emphasized the importance of using a system that bases pay on treatment fidelity as well as on outcomes achieved. How well does the worker's performance match what has been found to be effective? Performance-based pay systems are based on the assumption that some interventions are more effective than others in helping clients to attain certain outcomes, as shown in empirical studies and recognizes this both in offering incentives for treatment fidelity as well as outcomes achieved. If research shows that some decisions are better than others (more effective in helping clients and significant others attain desired outcomes), clients are more likely to receive the benefits of these decisions if staff are differentially rewarded for making them. Monetary incentives can enhance outcomes of value to both staff and clients (Keyworth, 1990).

Basing part (or all) of a social worker's salary on the outcomes achieved with clients does not require passive receptivity on the part of clients; quite the opposite, because research indicates that involvement of clients as active collaborators increases the likelihood of positive outcome (Meichenbaum & Turk, 1987). Thus, clients should be active participants in the selection of goals and objectives, both for ethical and practical reasons. Research highlights the interpersonal nature of helping and the many skills that the social worker can and should use to involve clients as responsible participants in the helping process (Wills, 1982). Workers will no longer be able to blame clients for "resistance" or "the system" for inadequacies when a review of their practice procedures reveals that they did not use effective skills to encourage client participation and to overcome system or resource obstacles.

The analogy of "piece work" to a performance-based pay position system is not an accurate one. Clients are not the same; clinical decisions must be tailored to each client and family. Here, too, performance-based pay systems are guided by research findings. A performance-based pay system would offer incentives to staff for individually tailoring assessment and intervention decisions to the unique characteristics and needs of each family or client based on relevant empirical research and available resources. Thus, a well-designed performance-based pay system would be quite the opposite of the alleged mechanistic qualities attributed to it by the authors of the con position.

The authors of the con position contend that there ". . . has been a mechanistic preoccupation on outcomes . . . and a tendency to evaluate professional competence and skills based upon a priori specified outcomes." In fact, evaluation of practice at both individual staff level as well as agency level is often based not on outcome measures, but on process measures such as how many clients are seen. Measures of process are usually indirect, with little or no effort made to review what social workers actually do or what they achieve. Social work practice remains hidden, giving neither staff nor clients opportunities to evaluate the quality of service provided.

A well-designed performance-based pay system will require staff at different levels to come to an agreement on outcomes that benefit clients. Social workers are often encumbered by agency and professional imperatives that compromise clients' interests, as Gitterman and Miller note. This is one of the reasons for having a performance-based pay system in which rewards are offered to staff for achieving goals that are of concern to clients. There is no assumption of self-evident compatibility of goals. Rather it is assumed that staff at different levels should be responsible to their service mandates and conduct the necessary negotiations to hammer out agreements that offer clients the best services possible. There will, of course, be many factors that mitigate against such efforts, such as vested interests in existent systems, inertia, and fears of various kinds, some false, some realistic. (Whoever said change was easy?) Staff satisfaction with their jobs as well as attainment of outcomes of value to clients and society can be used as indicators of a well designed performance based system. Only through monitoring such indicators can the success of these systems be determined. Proper recognition of the difficulty of achieving different kinds of outcomes will avoid a "scramble for easy cases" and will instead encourage workers to take on difficult clients because they are rewarded rather than punished for doing so.

REFERENCES

Keyworth, R. (1990). Performance pay—an evolving system at Spectrum Center. *Performance Management Magazine, 8,* 6–10.

Meichenbaum, D., & Turk, D.C. (1987). *Facilitating treatment adherence: A practitioners handbook.* New York: Plenum.

Wills, T.A. (1982). Nonspecific factors in helping relationships. In Wills, T.A. (Ed.), *Basic processes in helping relationships.* New York: Academic.

Should Community Organization Be Based on a Grassroots Strategy?

EDITOR'S NOTE: The authors of the following debate agreed to go somewhat beyond their own beliefs in the hope of presenting more fully opposed views on the issue. To understand the difference between the next two authors one must be clear about what they believe in common. They agree that:

1) social workers have an important part to play in the life and evolution of a community; and

2) to carry out that part social workers must be ready to pursue a variety of strategies. This includes such things as direct social action, the support of self-help groups, research and demonstration, policy analysis, community education, ongoing coalition building, lobbying, advocacy on a case and systems level, and the development, planning, and coordination of social services.

What they disagree about is the importance of "grassroots organizing"—helping disempowered individuals band together to take action on their own behalf. Wenocur believes that it should, even must, be the primary focus of professional efforts in the community. Weisner just as urgently denies this centrality. He favors a multifaceted "community practice" of which grassroots organizing is one of the elements. The future of community organization by social workers probably depends on how the field resolves the issue debated immediately below.

Stanley Wenocur, DSW, responds to the debate with a vigorous YES. He teaches community organization at the University of Maryland, School of Social Work, in Baltimore. He has a long-standing interest in neighborhood organizing, alternative funds for social change, and dilemmas of practicing in the community as a professional social worker. He is the coauthor, with Michael Reisch, of *From Charity to Enterprise* (University of Illinois Press, 1989), which examines how the professions came to be defined primarily in terms of clinical practice rather than community work and social advocacy.

Stan Weisner, DSW, presents the NO position. He is Associate Director of Coleman Advocates for Children and Youth in San Francisco and has been a Lecturer for the Department of Social Work Education at San Francisco State University and other Bay Area schools. He teaches community practice and research methods. His published work is concerned with community organization and social work in a national and international context.

YES

STANLEY WENOCUR

There are a number of reasons for advocating that community organization practice should be based on grassroots organizing. These can be grouped under three headings—professional, practical, and ideological; each raises significant and interrelated questions. The main professional question is whether social work can honor its fundamental values and its commitment to helping the disadvantaged if it ignores grassroots organizing. The practical question is whether, given changes in the structure of American society, grassroots organizing is an effective way to attack social and economic injustices. The answer to this, however, depends upon how we envision American democracy.

Professional Issues

Social work has gained its legitimacy as a profession from its espoused commitment to alleviating the social problems and accompanying distress that beset the poor and other disadvantaged groups. These problems stem mainly from an inequitable distribution of income and wealth and access to influence. Unfortunately, there is much evidence to suggest that social work has reneged on that commitment because it increasingly supports the growth of private clinical practice and devalues community organizing, especially grassroots organizing. Thus, social work as a profession spends most of its energy applying bandaids to a "sick" system and helping people to cope with it for the short term, rather than change it for the long run.

Although grassroots organizing can have many specific objectives, its general goal is to empower disadvantaged groups to reform the system. Its approach aims to help ordinary people gain sufficient knowledge and skill to make the system respond to their needs. To the extent that social work is concerned with correcting social injustices and creating a more democratic society, it must make grassroots organizing its highest priority. Without this emphasis, all other forms of community organization practice deflect social work from its larger mission. This deflection occurs because even if concessions are gained, say, in the form of better services or fairer policies, the consumers of those services will not have learned how to prevent shifts in their political-economic fortunes for themselves when their professional advocates go on to other interests.

Grassroots organizing thrives on the most fundamental of social work values—self determination and respect for human dignity and worth. Without a practice built around grassroots organizing, social workers can neither learn the meaning of, nor the skills involved in fostering, self-determination. Rather than a professional relationship that embodies power inequalities, as in most professional-client situations, here relations are based much more on reciprocity and power equality. Because the grassroots organizer works with "citizens" rather than "clients," success requires a deep respect for democratic decision making and voluntary action.

Interestingly, social work as a profession suffers from some of the same problems as its espoused constituents, namely a lack of resources to provide effective services and benefits. Social workers in public agencies and many voluntary organizations are grossly underpaid, overworked, and subjected to intolerable working conditions and extraordinary pressures. The conservative political-economic climate of the Reagan years has intensified both the level of social problems and social distress and the pressure on social work and other helping professions to alleviate it, yet without the requisite resources to do the job. Social workers, like their clients, are victims of the system and thereby targets of the "blame the victim" ethos of American capitalism.

The potential exists for social workers to form alliances with their clients and together seek system reforms. Such alliances occurred historically in the 1930s and 1960s. Perhaps if grassroots organizing skills were taught in our professional schools, social workers would be better able to build the kind of mass-based organizations that could address these social inequities. Social work as a profession would do better to attend more to issues of power and less to issues of status both for its own sake as well as to improve the lives of the constituencies it claims to be concerned about.

Practical Issues

In the last 30 years the structure of American society has changed a great deal. We have become a large urban and suburban society in which small local communities and even larger municipalities have lost the ability to control many of the forces that affect their well being. While many have lamented these changes, the reasons for them are complex and unlikely to disappear. Astounding technological advances in communications, information processing, and transportation have decreased the distances across communities and nations. These changes have also increased the power of technical and professional experts and decreased the independence of ordinary citizens. National and international corporations make decisions that affect local and state economies based upon corporate self interest unleavened by community commitment. At the same time, while the cost of alleviating social distress and distributing public benefits has increased beyond the range of local governmental affordability, the federal government has generated a staggering deficit that has hindered social welfare progress. Thus, problems like homelessness, drug abuse, and child abuse have taken on new dimensions, well beyond the potential influence of local grassroots organizations as well as local governments. Why, then, insist on grassroots organizing?

First of all, social welfare services and benefits (in the inclusive sense of health, education, and the like) as well as physical and environmental utilities are delivered locally. This is so whether these are sponsored by governmental, nonprofit, or proprietary organizations and whether they are administratively controlled nationally or locally. The consumers of these services need to organize to keep them accessible and relevant and to generate pressure to develop new programs. In fact, grassroots organizations have frequently done just that, as for example, in keeping utility rates lower, preventing banks from "redlining," making food stamps easier to obtain, improving trash collection, averting or correcting environmental and health hazards, creating day care services, recreational centers, credit unions, and more. Although it is often true that these programs and services do not attack the sources of a problem, they do improve the quality of life for their beneficiaries, not an unsubstantial gain.

In addition, grassroots organizations serve as the building blocks for larger-scale reform efforts through traditional political parties and organizations as well as social movements, city or state-wide coalitions, or other kinds of groups. Power in American society is generally wielded through organizations. Grassroots organizations provide ordinary people with a vehicle for experiencing and exercising political and economic power through collective efforts. The formal political process, in particular, is influenced by constituent votes, and effective constituent organizing requires grassroots organizing skills. A valuable aspect of these "building-block" organizations is their role as a training ground for community leadership and democratic citizen participation. Grassroots leaders frequently go on to positions of great responsibility and influence in other political and organizational arenas where social problems can be attacked more substantively.

Ideological Issues

Questions of ideology center on the kind of democracy we envision for America and how grassroots organizing fits into it. The logic of grassroots organizing leads to a democratic ideal in which all citizens have a reasonably fair chance of influencing the decisions that affect their lives through effective representation in the arenas of public decision making. Whereas the wealthy have many different kinds of opportunities to shape the public agenda, realization of this vision for low- and moderate-income citizens requires effective pressure groups. Without them, low- and moderate-income citizens are at a political disadvantage. Moreover, the high cost of professional and technical expertise is widening that disadvantage.

Grassroots organizing increases the capacity of ordinary citizens to gain access to decision-making bodies, to have their concerns represented fairly by people who share their background and outlook, and to affect the outcomes. Although this form of reconstructed pluralism cannot unmake the inequities inherent in a capitalist economy, it does at least recognize the existence of structural inequalities and create some potential for reform in the future. Social work as a profession is tied to the institutions of privilege and power, to universities, to philanthropists, government. It is difficult, therefore, for social workers to attack systemic problems. Yet, if social workers do not help to build grassroots organizations, then the profession is simply operating to reproduce the social structures that will generate social problems over and over again.

Annotated Bibliography

Ellsworth, S. (Summer, 1981). Organizing the organized: The origins of the Nonpartisan League. *The Organizer,* 9(1), 4–15.

> Unfortunately, this journal is no longer in print and, therefore, the article may be hard to find. It deals with the development of the National Nonpartisan League (NPL) in the 1910s and 1920s, a midwestern, rural-based populist movement for democratic self empowerment. The NPL is an important and exciting chapter in grassroots organizing in this country, and if this article cannot be found, students may want to look for a doctoral dissertation by the author and the book by Robert L. Moran entitled *Political Prairie Fire.* (Minneapolis: University of Minnesota Press, 1955).

Fisher, R. (1984). *Let the people decide: Neighborhood organizing in America.* Boston, MA: Twayne Publishers.

> Fisher describes and analyzes the history of neighborhood movements in America, helping to place grassroots community organizing in a larger perspective.

Kahn, S. (1982). *Organizing: A guide for grassroots leaders*. New York: McGraw-Hill.

> In clear and straightforward language, this longtime organizer (and folksinger) provides a primer for anyone interested in a grassroots approach to organizing.

Perlman, J.E. (1976). Grassrooting the system. *Social Policy*, 7(2), 4–20.

> This article provides an analysis of grassroots organizing in the 1970s.

Reisch, M., & Wenocur, S. (March 1986). The future of community organization in social work: Social activism and the politics of profession building. *Social Service Review* 60(1), 70–93.

> This article reviews the growth of community organizations in social work from a political-economic perspective and proposes ways for community organization practice in social work to prosper in the future.

Staples, L. (1984). *Roots to power: A manual for grassroots organizing*. New York: Praeger.

> This book provides a brilliant introduction to grassroots organizing by a social worker who is both a teacher and an activist.

Rejoinder to Professor Wenocur
STAN WEISNER

Wenocur makes a persuasive case for grassroots organizing, describing it as "an *effective* way to attack social and economic injustices" (italics added). I would agree; it often is.

The point Wenocur misses is that community organizers, to be truly effective, must go beyond a reliance on grassroots strategies every time a community problem is identified and engaged. Constituencies expect community practitioners to use their experience and critical judgment to determine whether a grassroots, or perhaps a less labor- and time-intensive intervention strategy is called for.

Wenocur's vision of American democracy also seems clouded by an overreliance on the role of grassroots organizations in shaping social policy. A more pluralist view, one that takes into account the cultural context and political history of the community being organized, might lead to a broader perspective on what community intervention strategy would be most appropriate at any given time. A community may prefer to use the social worker as a broker of services or outside advocate rather than as a grassroots organizer.

In such circumstances, should a professional organizer refuse to take on such roles or deny the importance of these strategies and assert, as Wenocur does, that grassroots organizing is social work's "highest priority?" Of course not. Creating change in complex social and economic systems and empowering communities require a more flexible and accommodating approach and cannot rely on a strategy aimed primarily at building mass-based organizations.

Wenocur supports the notion that grassroots organizing may not be a necessary and sufficient intervention in the 1990s given the growing influence of the mass media and information processing systems. He then goes on to note that local services delivery issues (e.g., improving trash collection and food stamp policies) are key entry points for grassroots organizers. I could not agree more! However, Wenocur cannot have it both ways, blasting in his opening arguments such efforts as "applying bandaids to a 'sick' system." Community organizers clearly must be able to operate at both the micro and macro levels to be effective in the real world.

Wenocur concludes his comments by asserting that social workers must help build grassroots organizations or they will simply be unable to attack systemic problems and avoid reproducing social structures that generate social problems. Indeed, community organizers must help build grassroots organizations, but if it becomes more than one strategy among many, it will severely limit their impact and credibility as a force for effective and sustained social change well into the twenty-first century.

NO

STAN WEISNER

Community organization must offer the social worker and other professional and nonprofessional organizers the opportunity to choose from the broadest range of community intervention strategies available. This maximizes the chances of success and is in the best tradition of a pluralist political system and effective social work practice.

Community organization can be a powerful tool for creating social change and for realizing collective political and economic goals that cannot be reached by individual initiative alone. It can be used to:

- Create community-based organizations where there are none;
- Coalesce and coordinate the efforts of service providers, pressure groups, and other constituencies to demand changes in the structure or delivery of critical health or social services;

- Develop legislative, research, or media-driven solutions to draw attention to major social and economic inequities in our communities and press for their resolution.

In the field of social welfare, there is a variety of intervention strategies that social workers can draw on to foster individual, family, group, and community-level change. These decisions about strategy have to be shaped by a worker's reasoned assessment of the psychological, social, economic, and political forces at work in a given situation as well as the resources available to respond in a timely and appropriate manner. This is true for professionals in any discipline. It is especially true for social workers who are engaged in community practice where resources are often scarce and social and economic needs are great.

Collective Goals Should Drive Community Practice Decisions, Not the Method of Intervention

Just as the social caseworker determines whether to offer a referral for job training or provide long or short-term family counselling, or both, in response to a plea for assistance, a community practitioner must be equally able to act as an organizer, developer, advocate, broker, or planner (Spergel, 1969). When grassroots organizing, advocacy, or any of the other strategies that emerge from these roles becomes primary and drives the mode of intervention, the community practitioner loses a great deal of flexibility and effectiveness.

Community organization has received much of its passion and legitimacy from "grassroots" victories over the years of the civil rights struggle, the anti-Vietnam war and welfare rights and labor movements. Although social workers only played a peripheral part in many of these struggles, it is essential that these major successes not diminish their desire and willingness to continue to work aggressively on behalf of local constituencies utilizing all modes of community-level intervention. This is especially true for a highly mobile, increasingly complex postindustrial society about to enter the twenty-first century.

Scenarios of Effective Community Practice

Take, for example, the following three illustrations involving a specific target population, geographic area, and social problem.

- You work in a family service agency, and despite a growing incidence of child abuse, there continues to be a shift in public spending away from early intervention and prevention programs in your community. You, several of your staff and clients, and other constituency-based organizations research the problem generate a series of hard-hitting editorials and background stories in the local media, testify at a series of budget hearings on the need to redirect specific funding streams, and positively impact the allocation of resources for the next fiscal year. This is child advocacy at its best, utilizing technical information, the political process, and the media to improve the social conditions of an underrepresented target population—vulnerable children.

, You work in a rural community in an industrialized country (or a small town in a less developed country) and need to develop a strategy to bring in public health services, jobs, or a better transportation system. Instead of spending time organizing and strengthening the already existing "horizontal" ties within the community, you work with existing local leadership and outside organizations to strengthen "vertical" ties to key outside constituencies. This is traditional community development at its best, building on the articulated "felt needs" of existing organizational and social infrastructure.

• You work as a school social worker and recognize the need for a stop sign at the local school intersection or a family outreach worker trained in the substance abuse field to work on the school site twice a week. You work through the local PTA, the school board, and the local traffic (or substance abuse) department to get the job done. This is traditional task-oriented community organization where the goal was clear and the process did not require a long-range and time-consuming grassroots strategy.

In each of these examples, a social worker used analytical and technical skills to select the most effective "winning" community organization strategy. If any one of them had failed, other strategies could have been tried, including a hard-hitting, large-scale grassroots organizing campaign aimed at the neighborhood level—a "geographic" community—or at the most appropriate "functional" community (e.g., impacted ethnic group, age-specific population, etc.). Efforts to do grassroots organizing to empower other frequently disempowered constituencies (public housing tenants, welfare recipients, or farm workers) may be going on simultaneously, but this in no way mitigates the need to engage in more short-term community organization interventions.

Reasons for Going beyond Grassroots Organizing

There are a number of very practical and political reasons for going beyond the grassroots approach to community practice. First, the number of human service agencies that are able to employ community organizers is few. Among those that do, even fewer are likely to employ workers primarily interested in doing grassroots organizing. To a large extent, this stems from a tendency among most agency directors, funding sources, or governing boards of directors to preserve organizational integrity over other competing forces. For organizers on staff, this may require some "changing of the agency from within" (Patti & Resnick, 1972). For the immediate future, however, organizers will remain undervalued and underpaid in the workforce and tend to suffer high turnover rates.

Second, social work, which has long sought recognition as a legitimate, knowledge-based profession, is unlikely to embrace some of the less technical interventions associated with grassroots organizing (e.g., canvassing, leafletting, etc.) and even less likely the more militant, direct action strategies that are often called for when initial interventions fail. To the extent that any profession ventures beyond its conventional boundaries, it runs the risk of alienating its government or private sector sponsors. Frequently, it is the nonprofessional, constituency-based organization that can best wield the political passion and undiluted self interest often necessary to be fully heard. But just as a legal aid attorney will go beyond the class action suit to seek a more immediate remedy for a client, or the public health professional addressing the community and social-epidemiological roots of the AIDS crisis will also be involved in very concrete health education efforts, the social work professional must be open to community organization in all its forms.

Third, the increasing complexity of social policy and public and private financing of social services in the 1990s increases the relative importance of research and media skills as well as legislative experience. The need to influence key policy makers in a timely manner may sometimes outweigh the need to engage in a long-term grassroots campaign. The growing power of the media and the need to capture the public's attention through editorials, talk shows, and other forums may supersede other strategies. A grassroots organizer may manage to compete with other stories of the day to make the evening news, but the media may not follow the story the next day or the day after, without a broader base of information and supporting views from a variety of constituencies.

Finally, there are a number of ideological reasons to reject a grassroots approach as the central underpinning of all community organization practice. The degree of resistance among targets for change varies substantially in each community action sequence, depending on the issue and relative power among the parties involved. Decisions on whether to use consensus or dissensus tactics should be shaped by contingency analysis followed by the selection of appropriate tactics (e.g., collaborative, contest, campaign) (Warren, 1965). This kind of decision-making process may or may not lead to a grassroots organizing response.

Furthermore, community power studies (Hunter, 1953; Dahl, 1961) have long pointed to the need for empirical data to determine the contours, strength, and distribution of local community power configurations before embarking on a change strategy, grassroots in nature or not. Community organizers in the 1990s must be willing to engage in a full and honest assessment of local power structures before shaping an intervention strategy.

Conclusion

In short, social work as a profession must be prepared to go beyond grassroots organizing. How well community organization is able to handle the demands of often competing roles at the macro and grassroots levels may well determine its viability as a method within the social work profession.

Democratization of the American workplace, a more equitable distribution of health and social services, the elimination of discrimination on the basis of ethnicity, gender, sexual orientation, and physical disability—all will call for community intervention strategies in the 1990s specifically tailored to address a wide range of grievances. Social workers bound by a grassroots approach will find themselves unable to respond in the most effective manner.

REFERENCES

Dahl, R. (1961). *Who governs?* New Haven, University Press.
Hunter, F. (1953). *Community power structure.* Chapel Hill: University of North Carolina Press.
Patti, R., & Resnick, R. (1972). Changing the agency from within. *Social Work,* 17(4).
Spergel, I. (1969). *Community problem solving: The delinquency example.* Chicago: University of Chicago Press.
Warren, R. (1965). Types of purposive social change at the community level. Waltham, MA: *Brandeis University Papers in Social Welfare,* No. 11.

Rejoinder to Dr. Weisner   STANLEY WENOCUR

Weisner's arguments and views of grassroots organizing are flawed. They also illustrate some of the dilemmas of community organization practice in social work. I would like to clarify these points with the help of a brief case example.

Several years ago, in Baltimore, many community organizers, most of whom were professionally trained social workers, were involved with tenants across the city in building a campaign to enact rent control legislation. This strategy required extensive grassroots organizing to clarify the issue, place a referendum on the ballot and get out the vote, get media attention, raise funds, develop policy options, and so on. Of course, the issue aroused a strong reaction from the city's power structure. As public sentiment tilted towards rent control, the real estate interests hired professional public relations experts, exploited their media connections, and used a variety of "dirty tricks" to create confusion and fear. The grassroots groups carefully eschewed militant tactics, and in the end, the referendum for rent control passed. The citizens had expressed their will. Unfortunately, this was not enough. The wealthy real estate industry mounted legal challenges and won a judgment that the referendum was unconstitutional. As a result, City Council measures were never enacted. In addition, under pressure from members of the power structure, the social agency whose staff members did much of the tenant organizing reordered its priorities so as to de-emphasize institutional change and re-emphasize social service. The organizers lost their jobs.

First, with respect to the flaws, as can be seen with the rent control campaign, Weisner incorrectly implies that the grassroots organizer does not use a variety of roles—organizer, developer, advocate, broker, planner. In fact, grassroots organizing frequently requires all of these roles and others—enabler, negotiator, researcher, educator, strategizer—a full panoply of analytical, technical, interpersonal, and political roles and accompanying skills. Just as with many other forms of practice, and maybe more so, professional grassroots organizers must use themselves consciously to pursue carefully defined goals and objectives and to continuously evaluate their work.

Weisner also incorrectly associates grassroots organizing with the inflexible utilization of militant, conflict-oriented tactics and strategies, and particularly with the social movements of the 1960s, as if to suggest that the 1960s are over and new approaches are now needed. In the rent control campaign, militant strategies were deliberately avoided, unless one considers peaceful rallies, referendums, voter registration, and media stories—all constitutionally protected democratic rights—to be dissensus tactics. Furthermore, all organizing, no less grassroots efforts, requires a careful assessment of one's organizational strength, the structure of power, strategic information about the target(s) of change, and informed choices about effective strategies and tactics. This assessment may lead to consensus tactics and collaboration just as easily as to dissensus strategies.

Finally, while it is true that every problem does not require a grassroots approach and that community organization practice may take many forms, as Weisner indicates, unless grassroots organizing forms the core of community practice, the goals of empowerment and a more just society will be vitiated if not lost altogether.

It is much too easy for social workers not to stress grassroots organizing and to avoid dealing with issues that challenge the status quo. As Weisner correctly points out, the profession is very status conscious, even while it is resource poor. Because public and private social welfare agencies serving the poor do not have an independent source of funds from client fees and they themselves suffer from the effects of political indifference if not hostility, the profession shies away from protest and from organizing the disempowered, even where it is morally compelling and strategically useful. This reluctance, based upon the aspirations of privilege inherent in the profession, poses a difficult dilemma. The logic of social work's mission demands social action with grassroots organizing at its center, but the logic of professional status demands goals and activities that basically accept the status quo. The dilemma has no simple solutions. If it is faced openly, however, then new alternatives can emerge, such as new forms of funding or new alliances. In the meanwhile, grassroots organizing keeps social workers in touch with citizens who feel disempowered and leads both to confront issues of power and political choice, sometimes even with regard to the most mundane of issues. The political consciousness that this process awakens is crucial to sustaining the vitality of a democratic society.

Should the Right of Mental Patients to Refuse Treatment with Psychotropic Drugs Be Severely Curtailed?

EDITOR'S NOTE: Historically, and even to some degree contemporaneously, institutions for the mentally ill have not been widely thought of as good places to be. They have been popularly identified by terms infused with negative meaning: bedlam, insane asylum, snake pit. Indeed, it probably does not go too far to suggest that they have been thought of as organizations whose main purpose was, like that of prisons, the restraint and isolation of troublesome persons rather than as places of healing or humane treatment. Thus, it was not surprising that many reacted with such enthusiasm and hope when powerful new drugs came along that would enable many inmates to be discharged from mental institutions and that promised fewer physical restraints for those who remained in them. It turned out, however, that these drugs had powerful negative effects as well. Lawyers and others concerned with the civil rights of citizens went to court to severely restrict doctors' legal permission to administer these drugs without first obtaining the patient's informed consent. Here the debate takes place between a social worker and a physician.

Michael Remler, M.D., answers the debate question with an emphatic YES. He is Professor and Acting Chair of Neurology at the School of Medicine of the University of California, Davis. In addition to seeing patients in a number of university-affiliated hospitals, he does research in neurophysiology.

David Cohen, Ph.D., just as emphatically argues NO. He is Assistant Professor at the School of Social Service of the University of Montreal, where he teaches courses on psychopathology and sociolegal aspects of mental health practices. He is currently conducting research in cognitive deficits accompanying neuroleptic drug-induced movement disorders, drug prescription practices with the chronically mentally ill, and legal aspects of iatrogenic illnesses. He is the editor of *Challenging the Therapeutic State: Critical Perspectives on Psychiatry and the Mental Health System.*

YES

MICHAEL REMLER

Why Does the Question Exist?

It is important to begin with the fact that psychotropic medication did not create the problem of mental illness. Rather, it is an attempt to deal with a very real problem for which there have been no easy solutions. Call it what you like, understand it as best you can, mental illness exists. The simple fact is that there are many people in every society who act in ways the society cannot and will not tolerate. In the bad old days those behaviors were attributed to witches or some innate evil in the person and were treated very harshly. As a result of great effort, we now try to explain that behavior as due to brain abnormalities, consider it an illness, and try to be humane. Psychotropic drugs are widely used today because they are thought to be a more humane way to handle people with mental illness than any of the alternatives. If the utilization of such medication is to be restricted, then some alternative, presumably one of those previously rejected, will have to be used.

Pragmatism, Not Theory

The question, "Is it better to expand or restrict the rights of people to refuse psychotropic medication?" can be approached in many ways. I believe the best way is to be totally pragmatic. It is important to be pragmatic because reality is very complex. There is a wide variety of patients in whose lives this question arises. That diversity stretches from those acutely ill who will return to a full life to those who are permanently and severely brain damaged; from those who are passive, silent and immobile to those who are violent, disruptive and aggressive; from those with resources to provide very expensive personalized care to those dependent on public care with strictly limited funding. We should not imagine that such vast diversity can be easily summarized, comprehended, and then "made right." Neither the present arrangements nor any other that may be created in the future will be perfect. The understanding on which they are based will be flawed and the people who carry out the policy will be subject to human flaws. Insofar as no one knows what to do, or some current ideas turn out to be wrong, we are all prisoners of mankind's ignorance. We must be on guard against the law of unintended consequences.

When we consider such a situation we must ask 1) what is the current reality; 2) how will any change alter that reality; 3) would that altered reality be better or worse than the present. The goal of any law, or change in existing law, must be to improve the reality of life. To understand the "current reality" optimally, we should focus on either 1) why previously rejected alternatives are in reality more humane or 2) how we can utilize psychotropic medication better. In fact, no one is in favor of a return to the methods of old: bedlam, lobotomy, and the like. The only serious question is, "Are we giving these medications to the right people?"

There may be many problems in the current pattern of administration of these drugs that are not under discussion here. There are errors in dosage resulting in unwanted side effects. Here we are focused on that situation when the doctor and the patient disagree on the need for this treatment. Our society and our laws favor the autonomy of the individual as one of the highest ethical values. There is, therefore, a great burden of proof on those who take the position defended here that patients be coerced into taking medication that they do not wish to take. We must indeed demonstrate that this is the most humane alternative available.

Consider a Real Case

Perhaps the easiest way to come to grips with reality is to consider a typical case. A 72-year-old man has had a number of small strokes that have left him slightly demented, with some loss of frontal lobe inhibition of behavior, but otherwise able to do most of his own self care. Such a patient may on occasion act out, brandishing a knife, swearing loudly for a long time, or hitting someone. The facts of modern social life are that he must be restrained and typically he does not wish to be restrained. Whatever society may choose to do will be against his will. That socially dictated restraint can be obtained by human methods, e.g., paying someone to follow him around 24 hours a day to stop him; or mechanically, e.g., placing him in a bed with restraints or in a locked room; or chemically, e.g., by giving him medication. Clearly the human restraint is beyond the means of all but the most wealthy. For the overwhelming majority of people it is simply not realistic. Is it more humane to literally, and of necessity, shackle that elderly man to his bed or lock him in a room, both of which are tantamount to being in prison? Or is it more humane to force him to take a medication that will still allow him to move about rather freely and do most of the things human beings like to do?

The same situation exists in the management of many acute schizophrenics, posttraumatic brain damage, and mentally retarded patients. For these and many other conditions, the patients simply cannot be allowed to determine their own behavior. It is not that the patients are offering voluntarily to have their behavior managed by some other means. They do not want their behavior changed. Because society will not acquiesce to them, they must be coerced. That coercion must be applied either to their body, mechanical restraint, or to their minds, chemical restraint. There should be no obfuscation. The whole point of these drugs is that they are "mind altering." They are given to alter the patient's mind. The alternative for all but the rich is a prison of one type or another. Who will say that prison is more humane?

And there should be no misunderstanding of the reality of any such "prison." Society will not lavish its scarce resources on those "warehouses." They may not be bedlam but they will not be a pretty sight. Understaffed, underpaid, with people who often can get no other job, they will be the least the society can do and still face itself.

Restructuring the Question

As with most policy type decisions, the reality is a trade-off, exchanging one type of error for another. If the right of mental patients to refuse psychotropic medication is curtailed (the position defended here) then some patients who would not have gotten the medication will get it. As a result, the number of people who will receive little or no benefit from the medication but were still coerced into taking it will be increased. Also however, more people will be spared from mechanical control who would have suffered its rigors had they remained untreated.

To make the policy choice we must compare the frequency and the significance of each error. If a person's behavior requires restraint and the drugs are insufficiently effective in restraining that behavior, then mechanical restraints will be used also. The alternative is not to release the person into society. Although a person subjected to both chemical and mechanical restraints may be thought to be doubly burdened, the reality is that the chemical restraint makes them at least "more manageable" and therefore the mechanical restraint can be more relaxed. There is nothing good about being both mechanically and chemically restrained. However, given the reality of life with a pattern of behavior that society will not tolerate, the significance of the error of this additional burden is not large.

In contrast, to require that mental patients who refuse medication be in fact managed without those medications is to require their most rigorous imprisonment. They will not be easy prisoners and, sooner or later, they will be in conflict with and at the mercy of their keepers. We may be able to outlaw and even avoid the worse excesses of Bedlam, but we will not avoid all of that horror all of the time.

Who Shall Decide?

There is still the question of on whose authority shall coercion be inflicted on such a person who has committed no crime. Clearly such awesome power over lives of other people cannot be unregulated. When the question is posed in terms of the "right of mental patients," one is naturally drawn to place the decision process in a legal framework. In a society that prides itself as committed to "justice under law" this requires the predominance of lawyers in a court. The only real alternative is to place it in the hands of specially trained, tested, and regulated "experts." If you believe, as almost everyone does, that this kind of abnormal behavior is the result of an alteration in brain function, then the suitable experts are physicians.

Will the legal or the medical system make the fewer mistakes? Is the question better addressed in the legal format, seeking justice and equity from conflict or in the medical format, seeking diagnosis of illness and treatment? Which system and its professionals is better prepared to undertake responsibility for the management of these people?

There is perhaps a concern in the minds of some that there is a variety of normal people who are mistakenly turned over to the medical system and then subjected to ignorant and even malicious therapy. There is no evidence for such errors in modern times. Court proceedings are not without their errors. The legal system has no knowledge of its own to bring to the decision. All it can really do is enforce the patient's wish to refuse. It cannot improve the intelligence of the decision process.

The appropriateness of drug management and its consequences are derived from the relationship of the biology of the brain to behavior. That is intrinsically a medical question. The decision will have to be made by someone, and that someone should be suitably trained, a physician. There simply is no alternative.

ANNOTATED BIBLIOGRAPHY

Meltzer, H. (Ed.) (1987). *Psychopharmacology: The third generation of progress.* New York: Raven Press.

An authoritative encyclopedic book on psychopharmacology. Chapter 117 is on anxiety in the elderly, such as my sample case.

Kesey, K. (1966). *One flew over the cuckoo's nest.* Viking Press.

> This book presents the classic fear that psychiatry is out of control, confining normal people involuntarily. It is fiction! *Henry IV* by Luigi Pirandello is a play that depicts the management of a mentally ill nobleman by his family confining him to a castle attended by servants who humor his delusions. It, too, is fiction, but at least it is possible for the ultra wealthy.

Schatzberg, A.F., & Cole, J.O. (1986). *The manual of clinical psycho-pharmacology.* Washington, D.C.: American Psychiatric Press

> Pages 78 to 104 are most relevant. This is a widely used practical little book directed to treating physicians. I believe readers will find these books' content and tone very pragmatic, trying to make the best of many difficult realities.

Rejoinder to Professor Remler
DAVID COHEN

Remler portrays involuntary drug treatment as the latest, most "humane" effort in the struggle toward "pragmatic" control of the mentally ill. He transforms disturbing and disturbed men and women from moral agents into brain-disordered organisms that deserve neither blame nor praise but restraint and therapy. He concludes this restraint is "intrinsically a medical question," because knowledge of brain-behavior relationships is necessary for drug management. By the same token, the electrocution of convicted criminals is intrinsically an electrical question!

Remler does not tell why it is more humane to use chemical rather than mechanical restraint. I suggest it is because the former is less visible and makes us feel less guilty. How chemical restraint might be experienced by the patient, however, is none of Remler's concern. He just knows that prison is less humane. All of the individuals I met who had experienced both prison as convicted offenders and mental hospitals as involuntary mental patients saw prison as the better alternative. Perhaps they are not typical, but Remler's typical case of forced drugging, that of a slightly demented elderly man, should not make us forget who else gets forced treatment. Persons who have committed violent acts, persons thought to be suicidal or dangerous, persons causing acute discomfort to others in public, persons who feel desperately in need of help for one reason or another, and persons who become violent and unmanageable in response to psychiatric treatment—these categories may be as frequently encountered as the helpless and incompetent.

Remler accepts the notion that mental illness is socially unaccepted behavior, but is unable to follow that insight to its logical conclusion: mental illness is the name we give to particular types of interpersonal and social conflicts. Yet the resolution of these conflicts—these overtly adversary relationships—is not, in Remler's view, to be negotiated through the criminal justice system, typical arbiter of conflicts in a democratic society. No, it is to be decided by "specially trained, tested, and regulated 'experts',", the physicians. But why should physicians, because of their scientific knowledge and technical skills, be the ones with the authority to "inflict coercion on a person who has committed no crime?" Remler is unable to distinguish between possessing the knowledge and the means to deliver treatment from possessing the political power to impose treatment on those who do not want it.

The reader will have noted the fundamental difference between Remler's position and mine. He focuses on whether drug interventions work or not. They are, of course, his interventions, and he decides whether they work or not. If they do, he considers them morally acceptable, regardless of what the recipient thinks about them. Thus, involuntary drugging appears humane and justifiable, because it is for the benefit of the patient. I, on the other hand, focus on whether drug interventions are contracted or coerced. If contracted, I conclude that they benefit both providers and recipients. If coerced, I conclude that they help providers and harm recipients. Thus, involuntary drugging appears inhumane and unjustifiable, because it subverts the ethical mandate of helping professionals.

Our society has given psychiatry the power over treatment. But "the primary lesson of psychiatry's past is that mental patients are better qualified to decide to accept or reject a treatment than are psychiatrists" (Coleman, p. 126). Remler's unabashed endorsement of full medical discretion in involuntary drug treatment damages his case even more than I would want to.

REFERENCES

Coleman, L. (1984). *The reign of error: Psychiatry, authority, and law.* Boston: Beacon.

NO

DAVID COHEN

Before 1970 it was unimaginable that committed mental patients might be able to refuse treatment with psychotropic (in particular, neuroleptic or antipsychotic) drugs. That right has since been won, but it remains sharply limited in theory and practice. This article presents the case as to why that right should be made as broad as possible.

The Constitutional Arguments

Forced drug treatment violates a person's constitutional rights to freedom of speech, protection from cruel and unusual punishment, and privacy. First, because the First Amendment protects an individual's freedom to express ideas (freedom of speech), it follows that it must protect one's freedom to generate ideas (freedom of thought). "Government has no power or right to control men's minds, thoughts and expressions. This is the command of the First Amendment" (Kaimovitz v. Department of Mental Health, 1973). In the 1979 Rogers v. Okin case, the court found it "virtually undisputed" that neuroleptics are "mind-altering," and that

> psychotropic medication has the potential to affect and change a patient's mood, attitude and capacity to think. . . . The right to produce a thought—or to refuse to do so—is as important as the right protected in Roe v. Wade to give birth or abort (pp. 1366–1367).

Second, the Eighth Amendment provides that "excessive bail shall not be required, nor excessive fines imposed, nor cruel and unusual punishment inflicted." Even a cursory review of the literature on adverse effects of neuroleptics (see later discussion) shows that these drugs may cause severe pain, fear, discomfort, and damage. The characterization of an act as "treatment" does not insulate it from Eighth Amendment scrutiny.

Third, the right of persons to control what substances enter their own bodies has long been recognized as a principle of personal autonomy, actualized in Anglo-Saxon law as a right of privacy—"the most comprehensive of rights and the right most valued by civilized men" (*Olmstead v. U.S.*, 1928)—and recently given a constitutional basis in the Fourteenth Amendment's concept of personal liberty. In ruling that this constitutional right extended even to an institutionalized, profoundly retarded man, the Massachusetts Supreme Judicial Court (*Superintendent v. Saickewicz,* 1977) described it as "an expression of the sanctity of individual free choice and self determination as fundamental constituents of life."

In the field of medicine, the privacy right is expressed in the doctrine of informed consent: no matter how much a doctor promotes a treatment and believes that it will be beneficial, a competent patient has the right to know before the start of treatment what the treatment does, what it is expected to accomplish, what dangers it entails. (Adults who have been involuntarily committed to a psychiatric institution are considered legally competent unless they have been judged incompetent by a court). And the patient reserves the right to say no, regardless of the consequences to his life or well being. The law thus entirely disallows nonconsensual treatment. Except in an emergency, an operation without the patient's consent is not treatment but battery. From a legal point of view, there is no reason to regard unconsented psychiatric interventions any differently.

Today, however, the principles of informed consent and of the right to refuse treatment with psychotropic drugs are rarely adhered to. Not only are many patients not informed accurately about common dangers of psychotropic drugs (Brown & Funk, 1986), but they are often incarcerated and treated against their will. In 1980, fifty-one percent of all admissions to state mental hospitals and twenty-six percent of all admissions to private mental hospitals in the United States were involuntary (Special Section, 1989).

Civil rights legislation thus constitutes the cornerstone of efforts to protect mental patients from abuse but does not yet represent an effective barrier to involuntary treatment. One reason is that these rights are balanced against "compelling state interests," such as a state's parens patriae interest (the moral obligation to protect the health and welfare of disabled citizens), or its police power (exercised to protect the health, safety, and morals of all citizens). I believe, however, that no state interest is so compelling that it should outweigh an individual's right to receive unwanted drug treatment. The law requires that the state use any less drastic alternative before it interferes with fundamental rights. Although I do not endorse involuntary confinement in psychiatric facilities of individuals gravely disabled, or posing a danger to themselves or others by reason of mental illness, I believe that confinement by itself is a less drastic alternative to forced drug treatment. Beyond such confinement, such individuals should be let alone.

Another reason is that psychiatry bases its claims for the authority to impose drug treatment in part upon its alleged capacity to reconstruct and maintain individuals as "free," "responsible" subjects (i.e., "mentally healthy"), an allegation accepted by virtually everyone in society, today as in the past. The similarity of this psychiatric argument with the previous theological argument that precisely in order to save souls should freedom of religion be curtailed has already been pointed out by Szasz (1977).

The Historical Evidence

The history of organic treatments for mental illness is the history of the increasing sophistication of methods to assault the mental patient's brain

(Frank, 1978). For nearly 150 years, the efficacy and harmlessness of every such assault has received unqualified support in the psychiatric literature: poisoning with arsenic and cyanide; ice baths; carbon dioxide asphyxiation; barbiturate-induced prolonged sleep; insulin coma; prefrontal lobotomy. Even when these treatments begin to fall in disrepute, reviews will be almost uniformly positive to the bitter end (Valenstein, 1986). The same literature also documents how mental patients consistently and vociferously objected to and resisted these assaults, and, when they were not able to resist, how terrified they were. Ordinarily, professionals involved rationalized these objections and fears by either interpreting their latent psychological meanings or by simply seeing them as "epiphenomena," indicating that the treatment was having its effect on the organism. In either case, patients' objections were dismissed. Only when professionals themselves echoed these complaints did one recognize, belatedly, their validity. Perhaps a right to refuse treatment would have made a large difference.

Today we have replaced these supposedly primitive treatments with modern neuroleptic or antipsychotic drugs, whose efficacy in suppressing psychotic symptoms has made their introduction into psychiatric practice in 1954, that discipline's most widely praised accomplishment. Unfortunately, after 15 years of widespread use, it was recognized that these drugs induced in a substantial proportion of patients a panoply of disabling adverse effects manifesting themselves primarily as abnormalities of movement, cognition, and behavior, some of which appear irreversible. The concern our courts have shown regarding the use of neuroleptics can largely be attributed to the evidence they have heard concerning adverse effects of such medication. Although, once again, patients complained about these effects from the very first psychiatric experiments with neuroleptics, until professionals themselves echoed these complaints they were ignored, minimized, or rationalized away (Cohen, 1988). Today, tardive dyskinesia afflicts, according to a conservative psychiatric estimate, 400,000 to 1,000,000 persons in the United States alone (Lund, 1989) and is recognized as a major iatrogenic disaster with baffling sociolegal implications. I submit that a well-entrenched right to refuse treatment might have greatly limited this problem.

The weight of the historical evidence suggests that organic psychiatric treatments can be very damaging to brain and mind. Recent evidence on the adverse effects of neuroleptics demonstrates the impossibility in many cases to distinguish these effects from the very problems that brought on medication in the first place (Van Putten & Marder, 1987). Individuals on the receiving end of these treatments have usually been quite aware of their toxicity and have often refused them. If only we had listened to them and respected their wishes, much needless suffering could have been, and could still be, avoided.

The Vulnerability of the Hospitalized Mental Patient

In practice, mental patients, especially so-called voluntary patients, are subject to so much intimidation during a psychiatric hospitalization that one may seriously question whether they are able to provide informed consent to drug treatment. Voluntary patients are technically free to leave the hospital whenever they so wish, but in practice they may be told that their decision will be followed by the threat of involuntary commitment. Involuntary confinement in a psychiatric hospital does not automatically imply involuntary treatment with psychotropic drugs, but it does indicate to staff that a person failed to appreciate what is in his best interests.

The vulnerability of the typical mental patient has been described vividly in countless books and articles. The overwhelming weight of the pressure from the institution, the treating professionals, and the patient's family pushes the patient in a single direction: take your medication! It takes a patient with uncommon internal and external resources to resist this pressure. Thus, in fact, the right to refuse drug treatment is already greatly limited by the very structure of the treatment environment. Why limit it even more?

The Empirical Evidence

No single, generic right to refuse drug treatment exists in the United States. From jurisdiction to jurisdiction, rights are premised on different theoretical bases, resulting in large differences in the substantive rights themselves. In addition, various mechanisms are established to enforce the rights (through administrative review of patients' decisions), which often places great limits on these rights. Several studies have shown that regardless of the criteria or procedures applied for review, 70 to 100 percent of refusals that reach the review process are overridden. As Appelbaum (1988) states, "The empirical data are unequivocal: the vast majority of refusing patients who reach review, even under rights-driven models, ultimately get treated" (p. 418). This occurs even when judges, as opposed to doctors or hospital administrators, make the final decision about the use of drugs.

Rather than the anticipated epidemic of refusal after the introduction of the rights under discussion, studies also show that only about 10 percent of patients will maintain their refusal until the review process. This supports my previous point concerning the enormous pressure exerted on the mental patient to conform, but also shows that a right to refuse drug treatment has not had the predicted effect of filling hospital wards with refusers "rotting with their rights on" (Gutheil, 1980). Neither has this right led to a worsening of patient care or clinical practice. On the contrary, it has only sensitized clinical and legal professionals to the premises and constraints guiding their respective endeavors. That such a right is also one of the only ways patients currently have to negotiate treatment-related issues with their clinicians should warn us about the abuses that would follow, should it be further curtailed. Psychiatrists have traditionally defined anything they do in the course of their professional duties as treatment. Although they should be free to promote such definitions, they should not, in a democratic society, be free to impose them on unwilling persons.

The Advantages of Enlarging Patients' Right to Refuse Drug Treatment

Since the advent of the neuroleptics, almost no successful innovations have been developed in psychiatry. Psychiatrists have become completely dependent on the use of psychotropics so that they cannot imagine functioning without them. Drugs are the principal form of intervention in mental health and the technology that provides psychiatrists with their professional identity.

It is obvious to any observer that psychiatry is unable to deal with the problems society insists it should deal with, and that psychiatrists themselves claim to be able to solve. As epidemiologists tirelessly push for a 100 percent incidence of mental illness, 40 million Americans are said to suffer from "DSM-III-diagnosable mental disorders," each one soon to be managed by the appropriate drug treatment. Hospital psychiatry seems to have become a specialty dealing with the psychopharmacological management of young and violent persons, or old and homeless persons. The skill at forming therapeutic relationships is growing rarer by the day among psychiatric practitioners, with drugs used to block precisely that patient-therapist understanding it was once thought they would facilitate. Iatrogenic illnesses are produced at an alarming rate. Yet we continue, as a society, to be intoxicated with psychotechnological "progress," which renders us progressively less and less able to examine rationally the real costs and benefits of widespread drug prescription practices.

Few people realize the extent to which these interlocking ideas and institutions—shaped by vast social and economic forces—rest on the socially and legally sanctioned power of psychiatry to force treatment on mental patients. Deprived of this power, psychiatry would lose its monopoly on mental health just as the church lost its monopoly on faith once it was deprived of its power to enforce religious conformity. Without compulsory drug treatment, psychiatric hospitals would not offer "treatment," just protection and lodging, activities and conversation. Yet, these very services are precisely what many troubled and disturbed persons need desperately (Chamberlin, 1979).

In a noncoercive system of mental health care, more persons would be willing to avail themselves of help because they would not be dehumanized in the process. Psychiatrists would not have to do the impossible: balance patients' and society's interests. Freed of their social control mandate, psychiatrists could devote their considerable talents and energies to devising creative solutions to the problems that beset individuals, families, and communities. Most important, enlarging the right to refuse drug treatment would allow us to give back to mental patients what we have robbed them of for centuries: their authenticity as human beings.

REFERENCES

Applebaum, P.S. (1988). The right to refuse treatment with antipsychotic medications: Retrospect and prospect. *American Journal of Psychiatry,* 145, 413–419.

Brown, P., &Funk, S.C. (1986). Tardive dyskinesia: Barriers to the professional recognition of an iatrogenic disease. *Journal of Health and Social Behavior,* 27, 116–132.

Chamberlin, J. (1979). *On our own: Patient-controlled alternatives to the mental health system.* New York: McGraw-Hill.

Cohen, D. (1988). Social work and psychotropic drug treatments. *Social Service Review,* 63, 66–99.

Frank, L.R. (1978). *The history of shock treatment.* San Francisco: Frank.

Gutheil, T.G. (1980). In search of true freedom: Drug refusal, involuntary medication, and "rotting with your rights on" (editorial). *American Journal of Psychiatry,* 137, 327–328.

Kaimovitz v. Dept. of Mental Health. (1973). Civ. No. 73–19434–AW (Wayne County, Mich., Cir. Ct., July 10).

Olmstead v. United States. (1928). 277 U.S. 438, 478.

Rogers v. Okin. (1979). 478 F. Supp. 1342 (D. Mass.)

Special section: Dangerousness and the civil commitment process. *American Journal of Psychiatry,* 146, 170–193.

Superintendent of Belchertown State School v. Saickewicz. (1977). 370 N.E. 2d 417, 426 (Mass.)

Szasz, T.S. (1977). *The theology of medicine: The political-philosophical foundations of medical ethics.* New York: Harper Colophon.

Valestein, R. (1986). *Great and desperate cures: The history of radical treatments for mental illness.* New York: Basic.

Van Putten, T., & Marder, S.R. (1987). Behavioral toxicity of antipsychotic drugs. *Journal of Clinical Psychiatry,* 48 (suppl.), 13–19.

ANNOTATED BIBLIOGRAPHY

Breggin, P.R. (1983). *Psychiatric drugs: Hazards to the brain.* New York: Springer.

The first book to document the brain-disabling effects of major psychiatric drug therapies and discuss the consequences of abolishing involuntary drug treatment.

Chamberlin, J. (1979). *On our own: Patient-controlled alternatives to the mental health system.* New York: McGraw-Hill.

An ex-mental patient and psychiatric inmates' rights activist details proposals for a humane, pluralistic, and noncoercive system of mental health care.

Szasz, T.S. (1989). *Law, liberty, and psychiatry,* ed 2. Syracuse: Syracuse University Press.

First published in 1963, this remains the classic exposition of the constitutional and libertarian arguments in favor of limiting arbitrary psychiatric power.

Rejoinder to Professor Cohen Michael Remler

The most important sentence in the opposing view is, "Although I do not endorse involuntary confinement in psychiatric facilities of individuals gravely disabled, or posing a danger to themselves or others by reason of mental illness, I believe that confinement by itself is a less drastic alternative to forced drug treatment." He is forced by honesty to acknowledge that there is no way society will allow such people to behave as they wish. Therefore, he wants them in prison. Then he chooses not to face the reality of what that prison will be like. "I believe that confinement by itself is a less drastic alternative to forced drug treatment. Beyond such confinement, such individuals should be left alone." Who is he kidding? There is not enough money in the world, or goodness in its citizens, to play the role of sainted jailer to the severely mentally ill, for the whole of their lives unrestrained by drugs or shackles.

The opposing view has offered a choice between modern psychiatry, warts and all, versus a beatific vision of some idealized free society of mental patients, simply isolated from the rest of us. Offered a choice between imperfect psychiatry and an idealized fiction, everyone would choose the ideal. But that is not the real choice. As they say, "Today, we have replaced [the old] supposedly primitive treatments with modern . . . drugs, whose efficacy in suppressing psychotic symptoms has made their introduction . . . [psychiatry's] most widely praised accomplishment."

They received that praise, not because people thought it was pleasant to receive such treatment but because it was obviously so much better than the alternatives. Judge these drugs and the physicians who administer them against reality, not a sweet fiction.

Should Drug Users
Be Provided with
Free Needles?

EDITOR'S NOTE: AIDS and drug use are recognized as international problems that will get worse before they get better. This debate topic joins the two: a prime cause of the infection that leads to AIDS is the sharing of needles among drug users. Some see an opportunity in this connection: Give addicts free, sterile needles and a major cause of AIDS would be neutralized. Advocates of this position are deeply frustrated because in the United States today the law either forbids or at least makes it very difficult to implement what they see as one of the few effective, inexpensive ways to reduce the AIDS threat. In San Francisco and other places with high-risk populations some have even organized both to distribute needles and invite arrest as a means of bringing about a change in the law. The following debate does make it clear that there are two sides to the argument.

Lorraine T. Midanik, Ph.D., who makes the YES case, is Assistant Professor at the School of Social Welfare of the University of California, Berkeley. She is the author of several articles on the epidemiology of alcohol use and alcohol problems and has focused much of her research on the validity of self reports in alcohol and drug studies.

Lawrence S. Brown, Jr., M.D., M.P.H., makes the NO case. He currently serves in several different capacities: Senior Vice President for Research and Medical Affairs at the Addiction Research and Treatment Corporation; Attending Physician at Harlem Hospital; and Clinical Instructor in Medicine at Columbia University. Dr. Brown's current research and writing interests focus on drug and alcohol abuse and their implications for HIV transmission and disease progression.

YES

LORRAINE T. MIDANIK

We are currently in two very tragic and interrelated epidemics: human immunodeficiency virus (HIV) infection and intravenous (IV) drug use. Each epidemic alone has devastating results: in combination the consequences are even more dire. As of July 1989, over 100,000 cases of acquired immunodeficiency syndrome (AIDS) had been reported to the Centers for Disease Control (CDC) from state and territorial health departments. Of these cases, approximately 19 percent can be attributed to IV drug use by women or heterosexual men; 2 percent attributed to heterosexual IV drug use contact; and an additional 1 percent of the cases are children and sexual partners of IV drug users (MMWR, Aug. 18, 1989). While the exact number of HIV infections is unknown, CDC estimates are between 1.0 and 1.5 million (representing a 0.4 to 0.6 percent infection rate) with the risk of new infection remaining especially high in IV drug users and their sexual partners with incidence rates as high as 19 percent in New York City from 1986 to 1987 (MMWR, May 12, 1989).

The primary mechanism by which HIV infection is spread among IV drug users is by sharing needles and syringes. Thus, one strategy for at least slowing or possibly stopping the spread of HIV infection among IV drug users, their sexual partners, and their unborn children has been to provide IV drug users with clean needles. Yet, despite the growing evidence that serious steps need to be taken to prevent a potential explosion of HIV infection within this high risk group, very few clean needles programs have been fully initiated. Discussion of such programs has generated much controversy and opposition in the United States.

This statement presents the argument for distributing sterile needles and syringes to addicts. It addresses three questions: 1) Why do addicts share needles? 2) What types of clean needles programs currently exist and what success have they had to date? 3) What are the obstacles to the development and implementation of clean needles programs in the United States?

Why Do Addicts Share Needles?

There are two competing explanatory models of needle sharing among IV drug users that have emerged in the research literature: a social context model and a supply and demand model. Those who support the social context model focus on the culture of drug use and argue that the sharing of needles is itself closely associated with a "special" kind of camaraderie and trust that is central to drug experiences. It is within this small group context that, with the help of more experienced drug using friends, new drug users learn the intricacies and rituals of injecting drugs and thus are acculturated and socialized into the group. Further, it is argued that needle sharing among IV drug users decreases the chances for arrest, provides an easier way to obtain relief from withdrawal symptoms, and, in addition, ". . . engenders a social bonding where mistrust and competition prevail" (Brickner, et al, 1989). Proponents of this model claim that even if clean needles were readily available, social forces within addict groups would work against their being adopted by users.

The supply and demand model suggests that addicts share needles and correspondingly use dirty needles for several reasons: they cannot obtain clean needles because of the existing legal sanctions on the sale of needles and syringes; many pharmacists refuse to sell them even under circumstances where they are permitted to do so; and laws prohibit the possession of narcotics equipment for injecting illicit drugs. Moreover, even in those few places where sterile needles and syringes are available, they may not be easily accessible to the addict population (Stimson, 1989).

Recent studies have shown that between 44 and 85 percent of IV drug users report that their primary reason for needle sharing is because they are unable to obtain clean needles (Stimson, 1989). The demand is so high that an illicit market for sterile needles has developed with drug dealers, some of whom were ". . . distributing free needles with drug sales, and some were repackaging old needles as new" (Stimson, 1989). Some dealers are even asking higher prices for sterile equipment (Selwyn, 1988).

Whereas there is little doubt that social norms are important in drug using social groups, most addicts are aware of the dangers of needle sharing (Feldman & Biernacki, 1988; Brickner, et al, 1989). Thus, it is very likely that if the supply of clean needles increased and their accessibility was also significantly increased, a larger proportion of IV drug users would correspondingly decrease the high risk behavior of needle sharing.

What Types of Clean Needle Programs Exist and What Success Have They Had to Date?

Several program strategies have been proposed to provide clean needles and syringes to IV drug users, including vending machines, direct pharmacy supply, and needle exchanges. Of the three, needle exchange is the best known. It consists of an IV drug user anonymously exchanging dirty needles for clean needles. A needles exchange program was originally started in Holland in 1984 by the Junkiebond, a union of drug users, as a public health response to the hepatitis B epidemic. Other countries such as the United Kingdom and Australia also developed needle exchange schemes soon after.

Although most needle exchange programs have not been evaluated primarily because of the confidential and anonymous manner by which they operate, the evidence is growing that needle exchange programs do effectively reach IV drug users who are not involved with treatment agencies. Further, these programs provide this service at a reasonable cost. Moreover, participants in needle exchange programs are more likely to report changes in behavior that lowers their risk of HIV infection (Stimson, 1989), including less sharing of needles (Buning, van Brussel, & van Santen, 1988).

What Are the Obstacles to the Development and Implementation of Clean Needles Programs in the United States?

Aside from the existing laws (mentioned above) that effectively prohibit legally sanctioned clean needles programs within the United States, another way to understand the barriers to the establishment of clean needles programs is to view this as part of a much larger issue concerning the ongoing tension between public health (primary prevention) and treatment (secondary prevention) efforts (Selwyn, 1987).

The public health model focuses on preventive action specifically to groups and individuals who are at risk for a specific disease or condition. Treatment models, on the other hand, address the issue of providing services to individuals who are already affected with a specific disease or condition. Many opponents to clean needles schemes embrace the treatment perspective and point to the need to provide services to addicts instead of undertaking actions that they believe would exacerbate the epidemic of drug abuse. These opponents of clean needles programs also argue that providing clean needles would appear to give a "stamp of approval" to addicts and thus, further encourage drug use. There is no empirical evidence to support these contentions.

Perhaps an approach that combines the best features of these two perspectives is the "harm reduction" model adopted by Holland. It offers programs to care for the addict (which might also include curing) as opposed to programs that have "curing" the addict as their sole purpose. Thus, the Dutch include clean needles programs as an important part of a wider effort to provide an array of social and medical services to addicts and reduce possible harm to them (Buning, van Brussel, & van Santen, 1988). Such a "harm reduction" policy offers a nonjudgmental approach to individual who inject drugs and provides both preventive care and treatment.

Part of the problem of understanding the argument that states that treatment alone is needed (and clean needles are not treatment) is that we are not simply dealing with the "age-old" problem of two competitive programs seeking scarce resources. Rather, we are talking about competing problems within individuals—their high risk of HIV infection and reinfection and their drug abuse.

We are not arguing that drug abuse is not a devastating problem or that drug treatment is not a viable option. Also, we are not arguing that offering clean needles to addicts is the only answer to the problem of the spread of HIV infection among IV drug users; there are multiple answers that include treatment and educational efforts, and we must explore every one.

In an epidemic the magnitude and with the consequences of AIDS, we cannot afford divisive, ideologic turf-protecting inaction that results in thousands of people becoming infected and many of them dying. We do not have the luxury of waiting for additional treatment funds to arrive to solve the HIV infection "problem." Furthermore, we question whether even a substantial allocation of treatment funds would reach a large proportion of addicts who regrettably appear to not be interested in treatment. We do not have the luxury of working only with those addicts who are willing to seek treatment. We do not have the luxury of moralizing about drug abuse while people are dying. Primary prevention, including clean needles programs and treatment efforts, must be offered in combination. The consequences of not doing so are deadly. We simply do not have the time to do otherwise.

REFERENCES

Brickner, P.W., Torres, R.A., Barnes, M., et al. (1989). Recommendations for control and prevention of human immunodeficiency virus (HIV) infection in intravenous drug users. *Annals of Internal Medicine,* 110(10), 833–837.

Buning, E.C., van Brussel, G.H., & van Santen, G. (1988). Amsterdam's drug policy and its implications for needle sharing. *Natl Inst Drug Abuse Res Monogr Ser,* 80, 59–74.

Feldman, H.W., & Biernacki, P. (1988). The ethnography of needle sharing among intravenous drug users and implications for public policies and intervention strategies. *Natl Inst Drug Abuse Res Monogr Ser,* 80, 28–39.

Morbidity and Mortality Weekly Report, 1989, 38(S-4), 1–21.

Morbidity and Mortality Weekly Report, 1989, 38(32), 561–563.

Selwyn, P.A. (1987). Sterile needles and the epidemic of acquired immunodeficiency syndrome: Issues for drug abuse treatment and public health. *Advances in Alcohol and Substance Abuse* 7(2), 99–105.

Stimson, G.V. (1989). Editorial review. Syringe-exchange programmes for injecting drug users. *AIDS,* 3, 253–260.

ANNOTATED BIBLIOGRAPHY

Selwyn, P.A. (1987). Sterile needles and the epidemic of acquired immunodeficiency syndrome: Issues for drug abuse treatment and public health. *Advances in Alcohol and Substance Abuse,* 7(2), 99–105.

This article discusses the conflict between public health and treatment agendas and presents an excellent rationale for developing multilevel strategies for AIDS prevention among drug users.

Stimson, G.V. (1989). Editorial review. Syringe-exchange programmes for injecting drug users. *AIDS,* 3, 253–260.

This is a well-written, up-to-date assessment of current needle exchange programs throughout the world.

Rejoinder to Professor Midanik   LAWRENCE S. BROWN, JR.

The chief difficulties in the arguments advanced by Dr. Midanik lie in the purported theoretical benefits to reduce HIV transmission, the presumed "reasonable cost" of sterile needle programs, and the presentation of drug abuse treatment as "secondary prevention" and as having "curing" as its sole purpose. The theoretical benefits of sterile needle programs in reducing or curtailing HIV transmission have not been verified in practice, using HIV serology or any other laboratory or clinical parameters of HIV infection or disease. For those IV drug users already infected with HIV, the provision of needles or syringes may result in the continued use of disinhibiting substances, setting the stage for unprotected sex, and the potential for furthering sexual HIV transmission.

It is not at all clear that the costs for sterile needle programs would be reasonable. There are the direct costs of personnel, supplies and disposal of the returned, contaminated needle or syringes. There are also the costs of housing the program and of liability insurance. Because parenteral users tend to be a geographically stagnant population, the costs of transporting injectable drug users to the sterile needle programs must be included.

Then, there are the indirect costs. These include the costs of antisocial behavior (criminal activity to procure drugs and law enforcement) and the costs of lost opportunities.

Presenting drug abuse treatment as "secondary prevention" and contrasting it with public health as "primary prevention" is to not really understand the benefits of drug abuse treatment or the intricate relationship between drug abuse and public health. Drug abuse treatment is public health! Reducing drug abuse by expanding the quality and quantity of drug abuse treatment represents primary prevention for persons not currently using IV drugs by reducing the prospects that these potential recruits might be exposed to addicts who are actively injecting drugs. Drug abuse is a chronic disease such that drug abuse treatment is indeed "caring" and not "curing."

I concur with Dr. Midanik that the HIV pandemic warrants a swift and rational response. While drug abuse treatment is a necessary part of this recipe for effective action, it is by no means sufficient. Rather, drug abuse treatment shares an intricate role alongside drug education and prevention as a holistic and comprehensive approach to many of this nation's most troubling public health problems.

REFERENCES

Battjes, R.J., & Pickens, R.W. (Eds.) (1988). *Needle sharing among intravenous drug abusers: National and international perspectives.* NIDA Research Monograph #80, Washington, DC 20402 (ADM) 88–1567.
Turner, C.R., Miller, H.G., & Moses, L.E. (Eds.) (1989). *AIDS sexual behavior and intravenous drug use.* National Research Council, National Academy Press, Washington, DC.

NO

LAWRENCE S. BROWN, JR.

At the threshold of the closing decade of the twentieth century, the worldwide effort to combat AIDS has provided some major advances in many biomedical areas. Nonetheless, in the absence of the still elusive cure or the development of an effective vaccine, prevention remains as the major battle cry. One of the preventable behaviors with a pivotal role in HIV transmission in the United States is IV drug use. While parenteral drug use only accounts for the second largest transmission category associated with United States AIDS case reports, IV drug use is the most crucial behavior related to AIDS case reports among women, children, ethnic and racial minorities, and the heterosexual transmission category of the Centers for Disease Control (Centers for Disease Control, 1989).

A number of approaches have been advanced (and many instituted) to reduce needle-related HIV transmission among IV drug users (Brickner et al., 1989; Des Jarlais et al., 1985). For the sake of discussion, these can be grouped into four categories: 1) education information; 2) the provision of sterilizing solutions (bleach, alcohol, etc.); 3) the provision of sterile needles (with or without the requirement to exchange used or contaminated needles); and 4) the provision of drug abuse treatment.

Although the major focus of this discussion is the issue pertaining to the provision of sterile needles, a brief comment regarding the other approaches is useful. In almost every geographic region where IV drug use makes an appreciable contribution to HIV-related morbidity and mortality, there are variable approaches to inform IV drug users of the consequences of continued sharing of injection paraphernalia. In an increasing number of these same locations, these education and information efforts include instructions on how to sterilize injection equipment or provide the materials (e.g., bottles of bleach) with which to perform these decontaminating procedures. Although there is growing evidence that IV drug users are receiving the information and have increased their HIV-related knowledge (Chaisson et al., 1987; Des Jarlais et al., 1985; Ginzburg et al., Schuster, 1988), it is not at all clear that this information or knowledge is translated into behavior changes that serve to reduce HIV transmission. On the other hand, the approach of providing drug treatment has both theoretical and proven benefits in reducing HIV transmission as a number of investigators have shown (Brown et al., 1988; Hubbard et al., 1988).

It is precisely in the hypothesis of reduced HIV transmission that the idea of sterile needle provision has received its greatest attraction to the supporters of this approach. While there may be suggestive evidence to affirm this hypothesis, this evidence is derived from unverified or unsubstantiated data. The sterile needle approach is embedded in epidemiological evidence that the sharing of HIV-contaminated paraphernalia by drug abusers is a pivotal behavior in HIV transmission. As advocates contend, the provision of sterile needles will discourage the use of needles that may be contaminated with the HIV virus. One problem with this approach is that it focuses, in general, only on the needle or syringe. The cooker, in which injectable drugs are mixed, may also serve as a reservoir for HIV and may continue to be a source of HIV transmission.

A second area of concern is the extent to which these needles serve to continue the practice of needle sharing or to increase drug use among those IV drug users participating in these sterile needle programs. Advocates present claims of data demonstrating no increase in drug use or in needle sharing among sterile needle program participants. However, this evidence is based almost entirely on self reports of program participants. Within drug abuse literature, verification of self reports are notoriously quite variable (Zukerman et al., 1989). There have been no reports that clearly demonstrate that a sterile needle program has been, or is, associated with stabilization or reduction in HIV infection rates among program participants. This is unquestionably the gold standard. Although needle sharing has been associated epidemiologically with HIV transmission among IV drug abusers, self reports regarding needle sharing are not sufficient surrogates for HIV serologic status. Obviously, such an examination would need to provide accompanying data on compliance and dropout rates and the impact of this information on HIV serologic status or clinical progression. Moreover, it is possible that while drug abuse may not have increased among the sterile needle program participants, these same persons may be the source of needle or syringes (possibly contaminated) to nonprogram participants or new recruits to the practice of parenteral drug use. Together, these points suggest that sterile needle programs may be as much a means to further HIV transmission as a mechanism to stem the spread.

Liability has been discussed also as an additional concern with conducting sterile needle programs. Although many sterile needle programs work on an exchange basis (a sterile needle for a contaminated one), up to ten percent of the sterile needles are not returned, based upon available information. The question then remains as to whom does responsibility or liability fall should an untoward event occur as a result of a needle or syringe provided by a sterile needle program. To the extent to which the sponsoring agency of sterile needles programs will be required to shoulder this liability, insurance costs become an important consideration. If the sterile needle program is government sponsored, the use of tax-levy dollars underscores the need for seeking comments and holding discussions of the virtues and limitation of such interventions in public forums. In some portions of the United States this has not been the case, and the absence of opportunity for public comment has been an integral part of the bitter debate.

Finally, sterile needle programs renew discussions of the compatibility of such interventions with public health policy and the goals of drug treatment.

Proponents of sterile needle projects suggest that in the absence of an adequate capacity to accommodate persons who seek treatment, sterile needle programs offer a reasonable alternative to reduce IV drug use-related HIV transmission. Some advocates have even gone as far as to suggest that sterile needle projects may serve as a means to provide access to drug treatment (Joseph, 1989). Admittedly, there is a nationwide inadequate supply of drug treatment resources. However, it should also be clearly stated that in many locations (for example, in New York City) geographic maldistribution is a prominent feature. This is manifested in reports of 6-month waiting lists by some drug treatment programs in the same neighborhoods where other drug treatment programs admit to unfilled capacity.

It is also illogical to believe that establishing a sterile needle program is critical to providing access to drug treatment. To the contrary, what this implies is that the current process to direct individuals seeking treatment to programs with capacity is inadequate.

Supporting a policy of continued drug abuse because of a yet un-proven benefit of reduced HIV transmission deserves further comment. Theory and practice in drug abuse rehabilitation strongly emphasizes the need to discontinue behaviors and avoid circumstances that are associated with continued drug abuse. A policy in support of sterile needles runs counter to this tenet of drug abuse rehabilitation. Although advocates of sterile needle programs suggest that these interventions are not meant to replace or to substitute for efforts to expand drug abuse capacity, they indeed do! In a society where its elected representatives constantly remind us of limited resources and where drug abuse and drug abuse treatment are so stigmatized, incremental approaches are the norm. If there is a sufficient level of belief that sterile needle programs are adequate responses to modify IV drug abuse-associated HIV spread, then society will have truly lost the opportunity to develop a more rational response to the full scope of medi-cal, social, and economic consequences of drug abuse. It is also necessary for us to remember that even with achieving its theoretical aims (which again have not been proven), sterile needle programs do not address the sexual behaviors of parenteral drug users nor the use of noninjectable disinhibiting drugs (e.g., crack) by many parenteral drug users. The sexual behaviors of IV drug users are most responsible for HIV transmission among many women and children.

Because many parenteral drug users consume many types of drugs, the disinhibiting effects of oral psychoactive drugs may result in less efficacious or more inconsistent use of sterile needles.

In summary, sterile needle programs offer many difficulties. For one, their theoretical benefits have not been demonstrated. Secondly, the ab-sence of evidence of increased drug use or needle sharing has not been verified by means other than the self reports of sterile-needle program participants. More importantly, sterile-needle programs violate a major tenet of drug abuse rehabilitation and may send a subliminal message to continue parenteral drug use. Issues of liability also arise in conducting sterile needle projects.

Finally, sterile needle programs may expend invaluable efforts in an alternative of limited, at best, benefits at the expense of developing more socially responsible responses to the full spectrum of consequences of drug abuse. As in many other areas, the HIV epidemic has presented the United States with a "window of opportunity." Developing a more rational drug abuse policy represents one of many of these opportunities.

REFERENCES

Brickner, P.W., Torres, R.A., Barnes, M., et al. (1989). Recommendations for control and prevention of human immuno-deficiency (HIV) infection in intravenous drug users. *Annals of Internal Medicine,* 110, 833–937.

Brown, L.S., Burkett, W., & Primm, B.J. (1988). Drug treatment and HIV seropositivity. *New York State Journal of Medicine,* 88, 156.

Centers for Disease Control (August, 1989). *HIV?AIDS Surveillance.*

Chaisson, R.E., Moss, A.R., Onishi, R., et al. (1987). Human immunodeficiency virus infection in heterosexual intravenous drug users in San Francisco. *American Journal of Public Health,* 77, 169–172.

DesJarlais, D.C., Friedman, S.R., & Hopkins, W. (1985). Risk reduction for the acquired immunodeficiency syndrome among intravenous drug users. *Annals of Internal Medicine,* 103, 755–759.

Ginzburg, H.M., French, J., Jackson, J., et al. (1986). Health education and knowledge assessment of HTLV-III diseases among intravenous drug users. *Health Education Quarterly,* 13, 373–382.

Hubbard, R.L., Marsden, M.E., Cavanaugh, E., et al. (1988). Role of drug-abuse treatment in limiting the spread of AIDS. *Review of Infectious Diseases,* 10, 377–384.

Rejoinder to Dr. Brown LORRAINE T. MIDANIK

Dr. Brown has made a cogent argument against needle exchange programs for IV drug users. He bases his position on the following five points, which I will critically examine.

Benefits of needle exchange programs not proven. While data on needle exchange programs are limited, there is increasing evidence that these programs are effective. Van den Hoek et al. (1989) recently reported the effect of a long-term needle exchange program and found that among program participants there was no increase in IV use and there was a strong decrease in borrowing or lending of drug paraphernalia. They concluded that needle exchange programs are important as a starting point and that such programs should be one part of an overall strategy, which should also include intensive counseling.

Self reports of IV drug users. Dr. Brown objects to the fact that outcome data from these programs are based on self reports and not on HIV status. This presumes that the outcome from these studies should be very narrowly defined. Certainly one goal of the needle exchange programs is to lower the incidence of HIV infection; however, other behavioral measures such as needle sharing and safe sex practices are also important. While multiple sources of data should be encouraged in program evaluations, reliance on self reports should not necessarily lead us to conclude that they are invalid.

"Subliminal" messages to addicts. Concerning the argument that approval of clean needles programs could be perceived as a "subliminal" message indicating that drug use is acceptable, there is no evidence that needle exchange programs increase drug use in the population. This criticism seems to be based more on an ideologic opposition than to any data that would warrant such an assertion.

The "cooker" as transmitter of HIV infection. Dr. Brown is concerned that the "cooker" itself may be a possible transmitter of HIV infection. Once again, there is no evidence for this contention. It is likely that it is the needle that is inserted into the cooker to obtain the drugs that is the transmitter, not the cooker itself.

Liability issues. The contention that there may be liability issues concerning 10 percent of the needles that are not returned appears to be a legal "grasping at straws" for ways to invalidate needle exchange programs. The other side is that 90 percent of the needles are returned (perhaps pointing to the success of the program). If liability were a key issue in this debate, not only would IV drug users be a focus but also other groups who "legally" inject drugs themselves, such as diabetics. Surely the liability issue, if it were a substantial concern, could and should be addressed through the regulatory or legislative processes rather than abandoning this useful approach altogether.

Overall, Dr. Brown's view essentially argues for drug treatment as the only route to combat HIV infection among IV drug users. Such a view is severely limited in scope and renders as unimportant a major aspect of a comprehensive public health approach, namely outreach. Drug treatment as the sole avenue to prevent the spread of HIV infection among addicts might be an ideal *if* all addicts were willing to enter treatment. The reality, however, as we all know, is that most do not appear to seek treatment. This single-focus approach effectively condemns thousands of individuals who continue to be put at risk either because they do not want to enter treatment or cannot enter treatment because of various barriers, not the least of which include inequitable access problems and a paucity of resources for these programs.

Administering our preventive resources to only one select group of addicts is unconscionable programmatically, clinically, epidemiologically, and ethically; a better way must be found. One better way is to combine needle exchange programs with treatment and educational efforts to attempt to reach the entire target population of IV drug users who are at serious risk for HIV infection.

REFERENCE

van den Hoek, J.A.R., van Haastrecht, H.J.A., & Coutinho, R.A. (1989). Risk reduction among intravenous drug users in Amsterdam under the influence of AIDS. *American Journal of Public Health*, 79(10), 1355–1357.

Should Maternal Preference Govern in Child Custody Cases?

EDITOR'S NOTE: Throughout most of the nineteenth century, when a family dissolved the legal presumption was that the child or children ought be placed with the father. Throughout most of the twentieth century the opposite doctrine, maternal preference, prevailed. In the last two decades, however, this changed again. Almost everywhere in the United States maternal preference was put aside by legislatures and replaced by different combinations of other standards, most commonly "the best interest of the child" and presumptions favoring joint physical and/or legal custody. Here two lawyers press the debate anew.

Mary Ann Mason, Ph.D., J.D., argues YES, maternal preference should be the governing doctrine. She is Assistant Professor of Law and Social Welfare in the School of Social Welfare at the University of California, Berkeley. Dr. Mason was a family law practitioner and has written on issues of women and children and the law, including *The Equality Trap* (Simon and Schuster, 1989). She is currently teaching a course on Children, Families and the Law and is preparing to write a book on children and custody.

W. Patrick Resen, J.D., who makes the NO case, is an attorney in private practice in the San Francisco Bay Area. His offices are in San Ramon, California, and he concentrates on family law.

YES

MARY ANN MASON

Who should get custody of a young child after divorce? Until fairly recently it was presumed legally and socially that the mother was the logical choice. Now this most critical choice is governed by a state of legal confusion.

The maternal preference, or tender years doctrine, has been defined as "a blanket judicial finding of fact, a statement by the court that, until proven otherwise by the weight of substantial evidence, mothers are always better suited to care for young children than fathers" (Klaff, 1982, p. 335). What age constitutes "tender years" has been left to judicial discretion, with seven or eight usually considered the upper limit. This presumption was adopted in almost all states by the end of the nineteenth century.

In the 1970s and 1980s, on the heels of no-fault divorce, most states rushed to abolish the legal presumption in favor of mothers. Currently only seven states give mothers an automatic preference. All others consider the parents legally equal. Abolishing a maternal preference and establishing the parents as legal equals met the political need for treating men and women equally, but failed to consider thoroughly the actual needs of the third party, the child.

Best Interest Standard

For most states, the abolition of the presumption in favor of mothers as the best custodian for young children left only the vague "best interest of the child" guideline. Our society lacks any clear-cut consensus on what the "best interests" of the child are, forcing the judge to make a determination, usually based on a confusing legislative laundry list of factors to consider. In no other area of the law do we allow the judge to make a life-determining decision with so few guidelines (Atkinson, 1984, p. 11). Not only is it difficult for a judge to make a decision, it also encourages litigation on the part of the parents because the judge's determination is unpredictable. With the "maternal preference" standard the matter was most often settled without a trial since the outcome was fairly certain. The rate of contested custody determinations has gone up dramatically since the abolition of the maternal preference.

Joint Custody Standard

One way to solve the new problem of choosing between equal parents was pushed by newly formed fathers' rights groups, a presumption in favor of joint custody. California, which had led the nation by introducing no-fault divorce in 1969, again set the trend by creating a legal presumption in favor of joint custody in 1980 (Cal. Civ. Code, Sec. 4600 [1980]). This amendment permitted joint custody to be imposed by the judge even *against* the wish of a parent (In Re Marriage of Wood, 141 Cal. App. 3d64 [1978]).

By 1988, thirty-five states followed the California lead, initiating some form of joint custody law, although not necessarily imposing it on a protesting parent (Freed & Walker, 1988).

The experience of joint custody in California, however, fell short of expectations. Too often it became a bargaining chip where the husband threatened to ask for joint custody unless the wife agreed to drop demands for spousal support or some other property right. Where joint custody was imposed it was found that the children most often live with their mother while the father is paying little or no child support (Weitzman, 1983, p. 144).

In 1989 it was demoted as a presumption in California, becoming just one option with the agreement of both parties (Cal. Civ. Code, Sec. 4600 [1989]). It is not surprising that many divorced parents could not deal with the daily cooperation necessary to make the arrangement work, when in fact they could not agree on the arrangement to make their marriage work. Too often the child became painfully confused in the constant shuttle between two homes.

Primary Caretaker Standard

While joint custody does not appear likely to become a widely accepted substitute for maternal preference in determining joint custody disputes, the concept of the primary caretaker is gaining many followers. The primary caretaker is the parent who has looked after most of the everyday tasks of feeding, clothing, and general maintenance of a child. As David Chambers, noted proponent of this theory has explained, it is the parent who notices when the toes of the child are pushing through the end of his sneaker (Chambers, 1984).

The primary caretaker theory is appealing because it theoretically treats the parents equally, although in fact the mother turns out to be the primary caretaker in most cases. It is so appealing that it has won the status of a legal presumption in at least two states, Minnesota (Pikula v. Pikula, 374 N.W.2d.705 [Minn. 1985]) and West Virginia, where the court declared in Garska v. McCoy:

"Where the primary caretaker parent achieves the minimum, objective standard of behavior which qualifies him or her as a fit parent, the trial court must award the child to the primary caretaker parent." (278 S.E.2d [W.Va. 1981]).

A study of appellate court decisions in 1982 showed that a preference for the primary caretaker was second only to a stable environment in the initial determination of custody. An automatic preference for the mother was a factor far less frequently than a preference for the primary caretaker (Atkinson, 1985, p. 9).

Motherhood versus Fatherhood

A primary caretaker preference appears to be an attractive gender-free alternative to "maternal preference," but parenthood is a situation in which men and women are clearly not biologically or socially equal.

Biologically, the indisputable fact is that mothers carry a child for nearly a year before birth and give birth, but fathers do not. The facts that are in dispute are whether mothers and fathers are "similarly situated" after birth. Until recently, there was little dispute among scientists that the mother-child bond in young children (under 5 years of age) was the focus of the young child's existence and that separation from the mother would cause severe negative effects in the way that separation from the father would not. Margaret Mead expressed the views of a generation of social scientists who looked at mothers and fathers across cultures:

> ". . . we should phrase the matter differently for men and women—that men have to learn to want to provide for others, and this behaviour, being learned, is fragile and can disappear rather easily under social conditions that no longer teach it effectively. Women may be said to be mothers unless they are taught to deny their child-bearing qualities. Society must distort their sense of themselves, pervert their inherent growth-patterns, perpetrate a series of learning-outrages upon them, before they will cease to want to provide, at least for a few years, for the child they have already nourished for nine months within the safe circle of their own bodies." (Mead, 1949, p. 197)

In the spirit of critically examining long-held beliefs regarding differences between men and women, mother and father roles have received a great deal of attention in the past two decades. The thrust of the research that questions gender differences is not that the mother-child bond is the same as the father-child bond in our culture, but that, under different social circumstances, a father could take the role of the mother (Chambers, 1984). This viewpoint posits that human nature is essentially plastic, and cultural training determines our parental behavior as well as other behavior.

This is, however, by no means the opinion of all, or even most researchers, who believe there are biological differences, hormonal and otherwise, that prepare women for giving birth and promote their strong interest in mothering (Klaff, 1982).

This scientific controversy has certainly confused judges and added momentum to the drive to abolish the maternal preference. As the New York Family Court concluded in Watts v. Watts:

> "The simple fact of being a mother does not, by itself, indicate a willingness or capacity to render a quality of care different from that which the father can provide" and that scientific studies show that the "essential experience for the child is that of mothering," regardless of who is performing the mothering function."

But this scientific controversy is based on the supposition, "if men were mothers," when in fact women already are mothers and in most households they perform the mothering function. Even when women work outside the home, as they do in increasing numbers, they still perform far more of the child care functions than do fathers (Mason, 1988, p. 20).

Regardless of the merits of the scientific argument that fathers can, in the right circumstances, be turned into mothers, the social reality is that mothers are already mothers. It is surely in the best interests of children that the law recognizes this social reality and guarantees the continuity of care which will be most protective of young children.

A "primary caretaker" preference has another serious disadvantage over a "maternal preference." In a society where most mothers work because a father's salary cannot support a family, and almost all mothers work after divorce in order to survive, the concept of the "primary caretaker" is not so clear. The actual physical caretaking of children may be, by necessity, largely in the hands of a paid caretaker, either inside or outside the home. Although, according to all studies, the mother still performs most of the caretaking tasks, this may not be immediately obvious to a judge.

There is, in fact, evidence that many judges are critical of working mothers who no longer play the full-time caretaker role (Polikoff, 1982, p. 235). For instance, the father is likely to get more parenting credit for picking up the child each day at childcare after work, because this is not considered a normal father's duty, than the mother is for performing all the other parenting functions, but not spending the day with the child. By traditional standards, the father has performed more caretaking duties and the mother fewer. With a primary caretaker standard this could lean the decision unfairly toward the father. This is ironic, because it is the fact of divorce that forces most women to work full time.

There are, of course, cases where the father is indeed the primary caretaker and the more nurturing parent. However, a maternal preference is a rebuttable presumption that will give way if the father can show that he has indeed been playing the role usually played by mother and it would be in the best interests of the child to continue this relationship. Presumably, only fathers who really function in this way will attempt to rebut the presumption, holding down the number of cases that are actually litigated.

Custody Blackmail

The abolition of the legal presumption in favor of mothers has had serious negative effects that are not immediately apparent. With the application of no-fault standards to property settlements, the resentments that used to be released in property disputes now too often find their vent in disputes regarding the custody of the children. According to family law experts Henry Foster and Doris Freed, "custody blackmail" has become all too common (Foster & Freed, 1984, p. 6).

Under a standard that declares both parents equal and offers the loose "best interest" guideline, the mother can realistically be threatened with the loss of custody of a small child by a father who has no real desire for custody, but uses the threat as a way to bargain away property, spousal support, or child support rights. The frightened mother may agree to an unfair economic arrangement that will result in a lowered standard of living for herself and her children. This is certainly not protective of the rights of children.

The imposition of the fashionable "primary caretaker" preference will not solve this problem. Unlike the "maternal preference," which puts the burden of proof on the father to prove that he is indeed more fit, the "primary caretaker" preference forces the mother (and the father) to compete for the preference. Where judicial discretion is paramount, as it is in deciding between competing parties, the likelihood of litigation increases. Here also, as with a pure "best interest" standard, the threat of litigation can intimidate the mother, leading to custody blackmail, which results in a lowered standard of living for mother and children.

Children First

It is far more protective of the young child to place him or her with the mother, where the strongest bond is most likely to exist. In fact, under both the "best interest standard" and the "primary caretaker" standard the judge most often decides that the mother is in fact the appropriate parent. Too often, however, it is decided after bitter litigation or after the mother is threatened to give up important economic rights that negatively affect both her own life and that of the child in her custody. The standard that is concerned first of all about the welfare of the child is the maternal preference standard.

ANNOTATED BIBLIOGRAPHY

Atkinson, J. (1984). Criteria for deciding custody in the trial and appellate courts. *Family Law Quarterly* 1, 18.

A complete analysis of recent appellate court decisions on factors considered by judges in custody disputes.

Chambers, D. (1984). Rethinking the substantive rules for custody disputes in divorce. *Michigan Law Review,* 83, 477.

The major proponent of the primary caretaker standard.

Freed, J. & Walker, D. (Winter, 1988). Family law in the fifty states: An overview. *Family Law Quarterly,* 21, 417.

An overview of current laws in all states.

Klaff, R.L. (1982). The tender years doctrine: A defense. *California Law Review,* 70, 335.

One of the only commentators who supports a maternal preference standard.

Mason, M.A. (1988). *The equality trap.* New York: Simon & Schuster.

Takes a critical look at changes in law and society and their effect on mothers in the workplace and at home.

Polikoff, N. (1982). Why mothers are losing. *Women's Rts. L. Rep.,* 235.

An examination of why some judges unfairly favor fathers.

Weitzman, L. (1983). *The divorce revolution.*

A comprehensive analysis of the effects of the changes in divorce and custody laws on women and children.

Rejoinder to Professor Mason W. PATRICK RESEN

Dr. Mason, by advocating a maternal preference standard, not only advocates a sexist standard but, and much more importantly, places a parent's (the mother's) rights above the rights of the child.

I readily admit that a best interest standard will most often, in practice, favor the mother, especially where a primary caretaker criterion is added. However, the maternal preference standard applies a prejudice and deals with all custody cases in a gross sense. Each child is entitled to have his or her situation judged on facts favoring his or her individual best interests.

Those who are more concerned with utilizing the divorce process for vengeance, vindication, or "blackmail" will likely engage in bitter litigation regardless of the standard applicable in the jurisdiction. Unnecessary litigation—bitter or not—is best avoided by the use of allied private or public evaluation processes that can provide recommendations to the court, not by a sexist standard that may require a dutiful and concerned father to make any contest as bitter as possible in an unnecessary effort to overcome a prejudicial standard.

NO

W. PATRICK RESEN

Until approximately the last two decades, states routinely utilized, often in practice if not by statute, the maternal preference standard, based on a presumption, both in society and in law, that the mother was the logical choice to care for children, especially young children. This standard must be rejected both on the basis that it is sexist and on the basis that it is not, per se, in the best interest of the children of a marriage.

With the advent of no-fault divorce, many states abolished, at least in theory, a maternal preference and attempted to adopt some sex-neutral standard for awarding custody. This was a truly radical change and caused the involvement of more sociological factors than legal factors.

Historically, four standards for award of custody have been utilized: maternal preference, primary caretaker standard, joint custody standard, and best interest of the child standard. All standards are briefly discussed; however, this article advocates a true "best interest of the child" standard. (It should be noted that in the past, even the best interest of the child standard often included a maternal preference presumption. See, for example, *Messer v. Messer* (1968), 66 Cal. Rptr. 417. For a good example of sex-neutral, nonpresumptive analysis, see *In re Marriage of Carny* (1979) 157 Cal. Rptr. 383).

A primary caretaker standard has been used during the past two decades by various courts. This standard predisposes a court to a determination that the primary caretaker of children, prior to divorce, should continue to be the primary custodial parent. Such constitutes, de facto, a maternal preference in most cases. Such a standard fails to recognize that the postdivorce situation of parents vis-a-vis their children is and must always be significantly different from the predivorce situation of the parents. Whereas our society's traditional norms had indicated that the mother usually provides more quantitative care for children in a nuclear family, such is not necessarily true for a splintered, postdivorce family. Courts are therefore more and more realizing that a "primary caretaker" standard reflects what was as opposed to what is. Such standard, not dealing with the postdivorce situation, is therefore, an inappropriate standard for the care and raising of children after divorce. Nonetheless, the prior primary caretaker is often used as one of the criteria under a best interest standard [e.g., the Supreme Court of West Virginia has interpreted the West Virginia Code to mean that a primary caretaker parent should be preferred. *Garska v. McCoy* (1981) 278 S.E.2d. 357.].

Subsequent to the no-fault "revolution," many states indeed adopted or attempted to adopt a joint custody approach. Many states rejected such an approach as unworkable, although several states, including certain parts of California, attempted to impose such an arbitrarily designed standard under best interest legislation.[1] This was a Solomon-like attempt to divide children on an equal basis. In particular, Marin and Alameda counties in California diligently pursued "equal" custody arrangements. There is, unfortunately, a dearth of research in this area regarding the effects on the children of the marriage, although Wallerstein and Blakeslee (1989)[2] indicate that such attempts seem to have deleterious effect on the children. Because available evidence indicates that such joint custody efforts have been deleterious (or at least not productive) to the children of the marriage, both counties are presently retreating from this approach, acknowledging the consistent enunciation of child development experts that a child should have one clearly recognized "home" for purposes of stability. Such standard, therefore, has been largely rejected or is at least in the process of being rejected by those few jurisdictions that have attempted to enforce such a quantitative and arbitrary standard.

In view of the no-fault revolution as well as other societal imperatives, "the maternal preference" standard has been, at least pro forma, rejected by courts, although such standards often continue to exist in fact if not in law. Despite equal rights amendments as adopted by various states and despite statutory language from legislators directing courts to disregard the sex of either parent[3] in making custody awards, most judges grew up or were elevated to the bench prior to such societal concepts and most judges typically have a natural maternal preference, especially if the child is of "tender years" or the mother has been the "primary caretaker."

The "best interest of the child" standard is, as its name indicates, at least theoretically designed to be in the best interest of the child regardless of the parental situation, the prior parenting roles in the intact family, or sexual prejudices. As even Marianne Takos, a practicing attorney and avowed advocate for mothers, notes: "Officially, in every state, child custody is determined on the basis of the 'best interests of the child.' That is as it should be" (Takos, 1987, p. 1).

As a practical matter, given the societal values that judges bring to bear, while such is a truly neutral standard there is often a de facto maternal preference, especially when a primary caretaker overlay is used. However, assuming that any particular judge can be neutral in this regard, such standard is the appropriate standard because it is the most neutral standard that the court can bring to bear and will allow all appropriate evidence to be considered and an award made without placing an unequal burden on the father.

It may well be in any particular case that the mother is the better person to have primary custody of the child or children of the marriage. Under a "best interest of the child" standard a mother would not be harmed by such a standard. However, such standard allows the child to receive the most favorable developmental environment regardless of the primary custodial parent's sex. In addition, such standard allows for award or change of custody, which recognizes the development needs of the individual child who may be better served by being in the primary custody of one parent while young and with the other parent when reaching adolescence. The child's rights must be paramount and not subordinated to the parents' rights. As the authors noted in *Before the Best Interests of the Child*, "The child's well-being—not the parents', the family's or the child care agency's—must be determinative once justification for state intervention has been established" (Goldstein, Freud, Solssit, & Goldstein, 1973, pp. 4–5).

A quick hypothetical situation can illustrate the result of applying a maternal preference as opposed to a best interest standard. Suppose both parents were more or less equally involved as a "primary caretaker" of the child. Both parents are loving, concerned, and "fit" to have custody. Father plans to remain in the geographical area where child has lived thus far, and his parents and his siblings also reside in the same area. The child's established peers reside there as well, of course. Mother plans to move to another state because of career requirements, a location where she has not had prior residence and is not near any relatives. What result? Under a maternal preference standard, mother gets custody because the presumption is in her favor; under a best interest standard, father probably gets custody. Under maternal preference the mother's rights are recognized ahead of the child's; under best interest the child's rights are primary.

There should be no logical presumption in favor of the mother in raising young children. Are mothers more successful in rearing young children than fathers? T. Barry Brazelton of the Child Development Unit at Boston Children's Hospital has addressed this issue squarely. His results, together with that of his colleagues, have indicated that fathers are as competent as mothers in raising young children (Brazelton, 1989). For example, their studies indicated that fathers fed their babies as successfully as did mothers and were as sensitive to their small babies' cries. Their research further indicated that fathers touched and played with sons more but that fathers showed more quick affection for daughters, whereas mothers touched and talked more to daughters and held their sons more closely, and that this is especially important to consider in view of the fact that a boy's intellectual development depends more on a father's presence than does a girl's. Their studies indicated that a father's absence affects achievement-test scores, IQ scores, and grade point averages. Finally, their studies indicated that a father's involvement in child rearing does not alter sex-role identification, except in regard to housework. In summary, then, a father's role in child rearing is as important as a mother's role in child rearing. As Wallerstein and Blakeslee noted: "Women are not ordained to be better parents than men, just as men are not ordained to be better career professionals than women" (Wallerstein & Blakeslee, p. 257).

Can there be any other standard but that of the best interest of the child?[4] Family law courts should not be designed to "reward" one parent over the other; certainly no court should "reward" one parent over the other because of his or her sex. Rather the award must be designed to benefit the unrepresented parties of any divorce, i.e., the children. If such is true, then the only appropriate standard is the best interest of the child. As a practical matter this standard may more often reward the mother over the father, but, if this is in the best interest of the child, so be it. There is no demonstrable evidence that a mother, by virtue of being a female, has greater assets to bring for the raising of the children of the marriage than the father does.

NOTES

1. Cal. Civ. Code section 4600(d), which expresses that the court has "the widest possible discretion to choose a parenting plan which is in the best interests of the child or children" and section 4608 which also acknowledges a "best interest" standard.

2. See also individual studies by Center for the Family in Transition, Marin County, California, J. Wallerstein, Director. Findings include the fact that where divorce disputes were severe, children who had greater access to both parents, as in a joint physical custody arrangement, were more emotionally troubled and emotionally disturbed.

3. See, e.g., Cal. Civ. Code section 4600(b)(1) that custody awards "shall not prefer a parent as custodian because of that parent's sex," and W.Va. Code section 48-2-15 which abolishes "all gender (sic) based presumptions."

4. A variant of the "best interest" standard is the "least detriment available alternative" as enunciated by Goldstein, Freud, and Solssit (1973),

Beyond the best interests of the child. New York: The Free Press. The standard was specifically utilized by the court in *Adoption of Michelle T.* (1975) 44 CA 3d. 699, 117 CR 856.

REFERENCES

Brazelton, T.B. (1989). *San Francisco Chronicle*, August 1.
Goldstein, J., Freud, A., Solssit, A.J., et al. (1973). *Before the best interests of the child.* New York: The Free Press.
Takos, M. (1987). *Child custody: A complete guide for concerned mothers.* New York: Harper & Row.
Wallerstein, J.S., & Blakeslee, S. (1989). *Second chances.* New York: Ticknow & Fields.

ANNOTATED BIBLIOGRAPHY

Goldstein, J., Freud, A., Solssit, A.J., et al. (1973). *Before the best interests of the child.* New York: The Free Press.

See also *Beyond the Best Interests of the Child* and *In the Best Interests of the Child* by the same authors, who include attorneys as well as psychologists. An excellent guide to not only custody issues per se but also to the role of various professionals—attorneys, judges, psychologists, and social workers—in the process.

Takos, M. (1987). *Child custody: A complete guide for concerned mothers.* New York: Harper & Row.

Avowedly takes an advocacy position advising mothers regarding custody disputes. Despite some errors, it is a good basic guide to custody issues from the mother's perspective.

Wallerstein, J., & Blakeslee, S. (1989). *Second chances.* New York: Ticknor & Fields.

Anecdotal approach based on authors' cases as psychologists. Dr. Wallerstein is one of the few evaluators of joint custody effects on children.

Rejoinder to W. Patrick Resen, Esq. MARY ANN MASON

Mr. Resen's confidence that a judge can determine the best interests of a child by choosing between two parents he or she has never met before is remarkable. When faced by parents with equal legal rights and a legislative laundry list that is supposed to give him or her clues for making a decision, a judge may as well flip a coin. What the judge does is reach into the grab bag of his or her own personal experiences and pull out a decision that feels right. This is not good enough. This does not serve the best interests of children.

A judicial presumption in favor of the mother will produce the correct decision in most cases. In those cases where the mother is clearly not the appropriate choice, the father may provide evidence that will turn the decision toward him. A presumption in favor of the mother is based on this culture's collective experience that small children need to be with their mother, not on the arbitrary individual experience of a single judge.

Mr. Resen does not confront the very real possibility of custody blackmail with the loose best interest standard. When a judge's decision is "up for grabs," the father may, and too often does, use the threat of litigation to intimidate the mother into giving up legitimate property or support rights. This also does not favor the best interests of the child, who must live with a poorer mother.

Finally, Mr. Resen argues for equal rights between mother and father. He forgets that custody is not about equality between men and women, it is about the rights of three parties, and it is the third party, the child, whose rights are paramount. No one comes out a winner in custody disputes, but the battle must be handicapped in favor of the child. A "best interest" standard favors fathers. It denies the reality that small children need the continuity and care of their primary caregiving parent, who is almost always the mother.

Is Tarasoff Relevant to AIDS-Related Cases?

EDITOR'S NOTE: Is there a duty to warn in AIDS-related cases in which people who may have been exposed to the AIDS virus have not been informed by clients and social workers who are privy to this information? Does the value of insuring confidentiality to clients override a duty to warn? Is the *Tarasoff* decision relevant to such cases? This case involved a student who told his counselor that he intended to kill a particular woman and in fact did so. In Tarasoff versus the Regents of the University of California, it was argued that the counselor had a duty to warn the threatened person. Since that time there have been further refinements concerning the duty to warn (related, for example, to whether a particular individual is named in a threat). A case example is first presented and two different positions are described concerning confidentiality and the duty to warn.

Frederic G. Reamer, Ph.D., argues YES. He is Professor in the School of Social Work, Rhode Island College. His research and teaching interests include mental health, public welfare, criminal justice, and professional ethics. Reamer is the author of numerous publications, including *Ethical Dilemmas in Social Service* (Columbia University Press, ed 2, 1990), *Rehabilitating Juvenile Justice* (with Charles Shireman, Columbia University Press, 1986), and *The Teaching of Social Work Ethics* (with Marcia Abramson, the Hastings Center, 1982). He is also the author of the chapter on professional ethics in the *Encyclopedia of Social Work*.

Sheldon R. Gelman, Ph.D., argues NO. He is Professor of Social Work and director of the social work program at Penn State. He has published numerous articles dealing with the impact of legislation and policies on the delivery of social services. Recent publications have appeared in *Social Work, Social Casework, Health and Social Work, Encyclopedia of Social Work, Mental Retardation,* and the *Prison Journal.*

YES

FREDERIC G. REAMER

Case Presentation

Frank S. has been a client at the Ocean State Community Mental Health Center for 3 months. He was originally referred to the center by emergency room staff at a local hospital, after treatment for an overdose of drugs. Mr. S. later admitted to his Ocean State social worker, Maria W., that he tried to kill himself after having been fired from his job at a prominent insurance agency.

Mr. S., age 33, explained to Ms. W. that he has been depressed for some time, and that his performance at work had been declining. At first he insisted that he could not put his finger on any particular reason for his depression. After some probing by Ms. W., however, Mr. S. began to cry and told Ms. W. that he could barely bring himself to tell her what he was crying about. Mr. S. eventually told Ms. W. that several months ago, after a number of consultations with physicians about a variety of physical symptoms, he was diagnosed as having acquired immune deficiency syndrome (AIDS).

Mr. S. explained that shortly after his thirtieth birthday he had become involved in two homosexual relationships that together lasted for a period of about 18 months. Mr. S. said that at the time he considered himself to be bisexual. Mr. S. assumes that he contracted AIDS as a result of one of these relationships.

During an earlier session, Mr. S. had told Ms. W. about a woman with whom he is currently involved sexually. Ms. W. is not aware of the woman's identity. Mr. S. claims to be in love with her and plans to marry her.

After spending considerable time talking with Mr. S. about the tragic news of his AIDS diagnosis, Ms. W. asked him whether he has informed his current lover about his disease. Mr. S. again began to cry and explained that he cannot possibly share this news with her. He said he cannot tell his lover about his diagnosis because of his fear that she would abandon him. Mr. S. explained that his lover does not know about his bisexual history. Mr. S. reminded Ms. W. that for some time he has had difficulty maintaining intimate relationships, and that he is terrified that his lover would leave him if she knew about his diagnosis. He assures Ms. W. that he loves his partner deeply and would do nothing to harm her. Although Mr. S. says that he is skeptical of all of the publicity about risks associated with AIDS, he promises to practice "safe sex."

Ms. W. tried to persuade Mr. S. that he has a responsibility to inform his lover about his AIDS diagnosis. However, Mr. S. refused to concede that he should inform his lover. Ms. W. explained that she might be obligated to take steps to protect Mr. S.'s lover if he continues to refuse to disclose the news himself. At this point, Mr. S. became indignant and insisted that Ms. W. not violate the confidentiality she had promised him during their first session.

Although Ms. W. is not aware of the identity of Mr. S.'s lover, she feels confident she could discover her name by contacting one or more of Mr. S.'s relatives whose names appear in Mr. S.'s record.

Is Ms. W. obligated to warn Mr. S.'s lover, despite his explicit wish for confidentiality? Would it be permissible for Ms. W. to contact Mr. S.'s relatives for information without his permission?

Commentary

There is no question that the AIDS pandemic is forcing social workers to face a broad range of ethical issues that could not have been imagined when the profession got its formal start in the late nineteenth century. Since the first AIDS case was identified in the United States in 1981, social workers and other professionals have begun to grapple with complex issues related to mandatory testing, confidentiality, the allocation of scarce resources, and the protection of civil liberties. Both the questions and the answers are complicated.

Among the most difficult dilemmas facing social workers is the one concerning the duty to protect third parties from a threat posed by a client who has HIV or AIDS. The case involving Frank S. is prototypical. In asserting his right to confidentiality, Mr. S. has forced the social worker, Ms. W., to choose between two unappealing options: breaching her client's right to privacy and risking harm to a third party.

This troubling choice is characteristic of what ethicists typically call "hard cases." Hard cases are those where there is no clear choice, no obviously right answer. Hard cases force us to choose among professional duties we would ordinarily fulfill (such as protecting clients' right to confidentiality and protecting third parties from harm). Sometimes such sensible duties conflict, as in the case of Mr. S.

What makes this case particularly difficult is that social workers have historically placed the principle of confidentiality on an exalted pedestal. It is among the most sacred of social work values, and for good reason. Yet we know that sometimes, in extreme cases, confidentiality may have to be breached in order to protect third parties. The clearest examples involve instances when a social worker is privy to confidential information about abuse or neglect of a child, elderly individual, or some other vulnerable third party. As the NASW code of ethics states: "The social worker should share with others confidences revealed by clients, without their consent, *only for compelling professional reasons* (emphasis added).

Cases that are less clear involve clients who threaten to harm a third party, such as an estranged lover. Such threats are often vague and ambiguous. By now, however, there is considerable consensus that when a client poses a serious threat to a third party, the social worker may have to divulge confidential information to protect this individual. This consensus has emerged as a result of a critically important case known as Tarasoff v. Regents of the University of California (1976).

The Relevance of Tarasoff

In the Tarasoff case, Prosenjit Poddar, a graduate student at the University of California at Berkeley, sought counseling at the student health center. Poddar revealed to his therapist that he was having thoughts about killing his exgirlfriend, Tatiana Tarasoff. The therapist decided to alert campus police and considered civil commitment to a psychiatric hospital. After questioning him at length, the police concluded that Poddar did not pose a genuine threat to Tarasoff and, after receiving a promise from Poddar that he would stay away from Tarasoff, released him. Poddar never returned for additional counseling, and after about 2 months he murdered Tarasoff.

Tarasoff's parents filed suit against the University of California Regents, the psychotherapists at the student health clinic, and the campus police, claiming that each party had a duty to warn Tarasoff of the danger posed by Poddar. The case was initially dismissed in the original court, was appealed, and was heard again in the California Supreme Court. The Supreme Court's final decision, in 1976, concluded that "the public policy favoring protection of the confidential character of patient-psychotherapist communications must yield to the extent to which disclosure is essential to avert danger to others. The protective privilege ends where the public peril begins."

Since *Tarasoff*, a number of courts have ruled similarly, concluding that in extreme cases professionals have a duty to breach confidentiality when necessary to protect third parties (Lewis, 1986). In general, courts have found that professionals must disclose confidential information when a client presents an imminent, foreseeable, and serious danger of violence to another identifiable individual.

When the *Tarasoff* decision was handed down by the California Supreme Court, no one anticipated that it would be applied to AIDS cases. In fact, the 1976 *Tarasoff* decision predated by five years the first known case of AIDS in the U.S. Nonetheless, the Tarasoff case is now the center of attention in every serious debate about social workers' duty to protect potential victims of clients with AIDS.

Although the circumstances surrounding the Tarasoff case differ some from those surrounding the case involving Frank S. (for instance, Mr. S. has not actually threatened to harm his lover and, at this point, Mr. S.'s lover has not been identified), they are sufficiently similar to warrant using *Tarasoff* as a precedent. As far as we can tell, Mr. S. presents a serious threat of harm to his lover, despite his promise to practice "safe sex." The threat is foreseeable and may be imminent, given their sexual contact. We would be splitting too many hairs if we concluded that the profile in the Tarasoff case is too different from that in the Frank S. case to justify using it as a precedent.

Is the Tarasoff case relevant to AIDS-related cases? Certainly. As Gray and Harding (1988, p. 221) conclude, "a sexually active, seropositive individual places an uninformed sexual partner (or partners) at peril, and the situation therefore falls under the legal spirit of the *Tarasoff* case and the ethical tenets of 'clear and imminent danger.'" Does this mean that the social worker, Ms. W., should necessarily violate Mr. S.'s right to confidentiality in order to protect his lover? No. Before reaching such a conclusion, Ms. W. should do everything in her power to protect Mr. S.'s lover through other means. She should use her best clinical skills to get Mr. S. to share this information with his lover. She should offer substantive information, consultation, and support in her effort to move Mr. S. to a point where he is willing to share the information with his lover or is willing to have Ms. W. assist him in sharing this information. Social workers believe strongly in the value and strength of the therapeutic relationship, and Ms. W. should as well (also see Gostin & Curran, 1987; Lamb, Clark, Drumheller, et al., 1989; and Winston, 1988).

It is possible, however, that despite Ms. W.'s best efforts, Mr. S. would refuse to share information about his diagnosis with his lover and would not give Ms. W. permission to disclose this information. If every reasonable effort fails—and if Ms. W. has grounds to believe that Mr. S. and his lover may engage in high-risk sexual behavior—Ms. W. would be obligated to take steps to protect Mr. S.'s lover, and this may entail disclosing confidential information against Mr. S.'s wishes. This would be an unfortunate outcome and a last resort, but under these circumstances it would be an essential one. Current research suggests that each unprotected sexual encounter confers a one in 500 risk of contracting the virus that causes AIDS. Over the course of 5 years of average sexual activity in a relationship, the likelihood jumps to 66 percent; there is a 9 percent chance of contracting the virus even with the use of condoms (Eth, 1988).

Such disclosure of confidential information against a client's wishes certainly comes with strings attached. It may undermine the trust that the general public has in social workers and other professionals. Disclosure may discourage individuals who have tested positive for HIV or who have AIDS from seeking social workers' services. Pressure to disclose may lead to overreporting and may exacerbate discrimination against individuals with HIV or AIDS.

These would be regrettable consequences, and social workers should do their best to minimize their likelihood and to advocate for policies that would prevent them as much as possible. In the end, however, social workers have a duty to protect third parties when clients present a serious threat of harm. This is as much a part of professional responsibility as is the delivery of competent services to clients.

The Duty to Protect

Given Ms. W.'s obligation to take steps to protect Mr. S.'s lover, what actions would be appropriate? Assuming Ms. W. is not able to convince Mr. S. that the sensitive information should be shared with his lover, what exactly should Ms. W. do?

The original appellate court decision in *Tarasoff* held that psychotherapists have a duty to warn the potential victim in order to prevent danger. However, upon hearing the final appeal, the California court altered this language and concluded that psychotherapists have a duty to protect, a much broader expectation. That is, the court concluded that it is not reasonable to expect practitioners to literally warn the potential victim in every instance; rather, the court determined that the obligation to protect potential victims could be fulfilled in several ways, including actual warning, notifying appropriate law enforcement authorities, seeking civil commitment, or other reasonable steps.

Under the circumstances, it seems most appropriate for Ms. W. to notify public health authorities, rather than taking matters into her own hands. The public health field has a long history of involvement in cases where third parties are at risk because of possible exposure to a communicable disease. Given this experience and the public health departments' mission, it would be best for Ms. W. to turn the matter over to them. Shifting this responsibility to public health officials may also help to defuse the tension in the relationship between Ms. W. and Mr. S.

And what about contacting Mr. S.'s relatives without his permission in order to identify his lover? Such an action by the social worker would be inappropriate. It is one thing, in the spirit of *Tarasoff*, to take steps to protect a third party at risk because of the behavior of one's client. It is quite another for a client's social worker to begin playing detective in a way that clashes with her client's wishes. It is best to leave such sleuthing, if it is necessary, to appropriate public health authorities who are better equipped to trace Mr. S.'s sexual partner(s). This sort of reconnaissance work is also more consistent with the public health field's mission than it is with social work's.

This case points up a chronic challenge in social work: the occasional need for practitioners to make difficult choices between conflicting professional duties. When we face such choices, our obligation is to think as systematically as possible about competing obligations and the rights of the parties involved. In the final analysis, reasonable people may disagree about the best course of action. This is to be expected, and it is one of the enduring features of professional practice. Our ultimate obligation is to be thoughtful and circumspect, and to be able to justify our conclusions.

REFERENCES

Eth, S. (1988). The sexually active, HIV infected patient: Confidentiality versus the duty to protect. *Psychiatric Annals*, 18(10), 571–576.

Gostin, L., & Curran, W.J. (1987). AIDS screening, confidentiality, and the duty to warn. *American Journal of Public Health*, 77(3), 361–365.

Gray, L.A., & Harding, A.K. (1988). Confidentiality limits with clients who have the AIDS virus. *Journal of Counseling and Development*, 66(5), 219–223.

Lamb, D.H., Clark, C., Drumheller, P., et al. (1989). Applying *Tarasoff* to AIDS-related psychotherapy issues. *Professional Psychology, Research and Practice*, 20(1), 37–43.

Lewis, M.B. (1986). Duty to warn versus duty to maintain confidentiality: Conflicting demands on mental health professionals. *Suffolk Law Review*, 20(3), 579–615.

Melton, G.B. (1988). Ethical and legal issues in AIDS-related practice. *American Psychologist*, 43, 941–947.

Reamer, F.G. (1988). AIDS and ethics: The agenda for social workers. *Social Work*, 33(5), 460–464.

Tarasoff v. Regents of the University of California. (1976). 17 Cal. 3d 425, 551 P.2D 334, 131 Cal. Rptr. 14.

Winston, M.E. (1988). AIDS, confidentiality, and the right to know. *Public Affairs Quarterly*, 2(2), 91–104.

ANNOTATED BIBLIOGRAPHY

Eth, S. (1988). The sexually active, HIV infected patient: Confidentiality versus the duty to protect. *Psychiatric Annals*, 18(10), 571–576.

This article provides a succinct summary of the clash between professionals' duty to maintain confidentiality and to protect third parties from contracting AIDS.

Lewis, M.B. (1986). Duty to warn versus duty to maintain confidentiality: Conflicting demands on mental health professionals. *Suffolk Law Review*, 20(3), 579–615.

This article provides an unusually comprehensive and detailed overview of case law and legal concepts related to the general subjects of confidentiality and the duty to warn.

Melton, G.B. (1988). Ethical and legal issues in AIDS-related practice. *American Psychologist*, 1988, 43(November), 941–947.

This article provides a valuable summary of the Tarasoff decision and its relevance to AIDS-related cases.

Rejoinder to Professor Reamer
SHELDON R. GELMAN

Although Professor Reamer analyzes Ms. W.'s dilemma from a different perspective, the points he raises and the suggestions he offers are remarkably similar to those that I have previously raised. The exercise illustrates the difficulty in choosing between "competing goods" and the delicate line that a social worker must tread in meeting professional and societal obligations.

The workers' course of action must be guided by applicable state and federal laws, their professional code of ethics, and the operating procedures of their employing agency. This case, or any other, must be viewed in its individualized context. If in doubt, clarification should be sought from supervisory personnel, agency legal counsel, and, if necessary, from the court regarding specific reporting responsibilities relating to AIDS and HIV-seropositive individuals. Even after careful analysis and consultation there is no guarantee that the worker will be comfortable or at ease with his or her decision or resultant actions.

The worker must utilize the relationship that has been established and all of his or her clinical skills to assist Mr. S. in setting appropriate goals and in pursuing a reasoned and responsible course of action. The worker should be prepared to set and communicate to Mr. S. a realistic time limit after which she must act on obligations that may supersede the traditional doctrine of confidentiality. The workers actions need to be reasoned and reasonable. She must avoid an emotional or panic reaction in order to resolve her dilemma.

She should be aware of the consequences of unnecessary, unwarranted, or inappropriate disclosure to herself, her client, and to other at-risk individuals. She must be prepared to live with a degree of doubt or uncertainty as to whether she has acted correctly in this most difficult situation. Although maintaining confidentiality is critical in encouraging individuals to avail themselves of available testing programs and to minimize discrimination, reasonable behavior may include notification of the appropriate authorities in order to prevent harm to others.

NO

SHELDON R. GELMAN

Ms. W., an employee of the Ocean State Community Mental Health Center, has been presented by Mr. S. with a dilemma that exists on three levels: moral, professional, and legal. Ms. W. now possesses information about potential risk to an unidentified person. She is knowledgeable about AIDS and its transmission and the consequences of her client being sexually involved with this unnamed individual. As a counselor, she has committed herself to maintaining the confidentiality of information shared with her by Mr. S. Because Mr. S. is presently unwilling to release her from her promise of confidentiality, she must carefully analyze both her obligations and responsibilities.

Whereas she may have a moral responsibility to alert the person at risk, she may have no professional or legal obligation to do so. Social workers are often placed in situations in which they must confront difficult if not unresolvable ethical dilemmas. Calabresi and Bobbit (1978) refer to such encounters as "tragic choices" between competing societal values. Whereas some state laws require that professionals either notify persons in imminent danger of harm by one of their clients or risk personal liability, other laws prohibit disclosure of health information, particularly information related to AIDS and HIV, yet other states leave disclosure to professional discretion, with no attendant liability. Some states classify AIDS as a communicable, as opposed to a venereal, disease with minimal protection of confidentiality. At this point in time, actions to warn potential victims must be considered in light of laws that are applicable in the geographic locale where service is being provided.

As a social worker, the code of ethics of the National Association of Social Workers addresses Ms. W.'s responsibilities and obligations in two ways. First, a social worker's primary responsibility is to his or her client. Second, the social worker should respect the privacy of clients and hold in confidence all information obtained in the course of their professional service. Ms. W.'s obligation is therefore to Mr. S. and not to an unidentified third party. Because Mr. S. shared the information about his diagnosis of AIDS with her in confidence, she is bound by the code to hold that information in confidence. Unlike situations in which child abuse occurs, social workers are not bound by mandatory reporting statutes to breach confidentiality and to make known the nature of the risk presented to either the authorities or to particular individuals who may be at risk.

Additionally, the social worker providing services within a mental health clinic is neither an investigator nor a detective. In order to learn the identity of the party at risk, Ms. W. has to assume the role of detective, and in so doing breeches the confidence of her client with more than the party at risk. Using information within the record to contact Mr. S.'s relatives without his consent would be a clear breech of confidentiality. While the code of ethics does permit social workers to share with others confidential information revealed by clients without their consent for compelling professional reasons, this situation may not warrant such immediate action. Her responsibility in this instance is to maintain the trusting therapeutic relationship that has been established with Mr. S. and to use that relationship as a means of assisting Mr. S. in sharing the information relating to his medical condition with his lover. The need for educational and counseling services before and after AIDS testing is clearly recognized. Bringing about such a change in Mr. S.'s attitude may take time and will require nonjudgemental support and strong clinical skills. Working through this dilemma and enabling him to do the right thing will be critical to his future functioning. Ms. W. should offer to be available when this information is shared and to support both individuals in dealing with the psychosocial aspects of their treatment.

Federal and state legislators have been very clear in their desire to maintain the privacy of the individuals infected with AIDS and HIV. In order to encourage individuals infected with the virus to seek treatment, strict regulations for preserving the confidentiality of health records have been issued. The Surgeon General's report on AIDS (1986) notes that "current public health practice is to protect the privacy of the individual infected with the AIDS virus and to maintain the strictest confidentiality concerning his/her health records." This approach to encouraging treatment is identical to that currently in use with clients who are drug or alcohol dependent. Adequate statutory protection of confidentiality and privacy is essential to assure the cooperation of high-risk groups with public health objectives. Because testing for AIDS is voluntary, no adverse consequences should occur to the individual who requests this service.

Individuals with AIDS or related conditions have received special protection against discrimination under Section 504 under the Rehabilitation Act of 1973 and the Americans with Disabilities Act of 1989. The inclusion of individuals with AIDS under this legislation has been necessary because of both the stigma and the resultant discrimination that occurs against such individuals. Many states have followed by adopting policies that recognize AIDS as a handicap or disability that is subject to the jurisdiction of their Human Relations Commission. These commissions will entertain complaints brought by individuals with AIDS who believe that they have been discriminated against because of violations of their personal privacy or the confidentiality of their health records. Legislation currently being discussed in the Commonwealth of Pennsylvania (SB 1163 and HB 1864) guarantees the confidentiality of HIV-related medical records. "No person who obtains confidential HIV related information in the course of providing any health or social service or pursuant to a release of confidential HIV related information . . . may disclose or be compelled to disclosed the information . . . and that no court may issue an order to allow access to confidential HIV related information unless specified, narrowly drawn conditions exist." The only professional group that has permission to disclose information relating to AIDS or HIV is physicians, and again that disclosure is limited to very narrowly drawn situations. The proposed legislation concludes that "physicians shall have no duty to identify, locate or notify any contact, and no cause of action shall arise for non-disclosure, or for disclosure in conformity with this section." This legislation and the approach it takes to confidentiality is supported by a variety of interested groups and individuals (i.e., ACLU, Pennsylvania Bar Association Task Force on AIDS, the Pennsylvania Medical Society, the Department of Health, the Human Relations Commission). For a social worker to disclose confidential information to a third party could leave that social worker at risk. If disclosure is to take place in an effort to warn or protect individuals at risk it must be done by a physician and not another service provider.

Does the social worker have a duty to warn under the Tarasoff decision? The language of *Tarasoff* is as follows: "when a therapist determines, or pursuant to the standards of his profession should determine, that his patient presents a serious danger of violence to another, he incurs an obligation to use reasonable care to protect the intended victim against such danger." It is interesting to note, in the only study done of social workers' response to *Tarasoff*, that although social workers believed that they had a professional obligation to warn or protect potential victims, "their responses about confidentiality and actions in particular cases belied this sense of responsibility" (Weil & Sanchez, 1983, p. 118).

Whereas AIDS is clearly a life-threatening manifestation of infection with HIV, it may or may not be an act of violence in the sense of the Tarasoff definition. The duty to warn and protect may not be applicable given the special provisions proposed to assure the confidentiality of individuals infected with AIDS and HIV. In all probability, Mr. S.'s lover has already been placed at risk. Immediate testing of Mr. S.'s lover and her knowledge about HIV antibody presence, without available or effective treatment, does not reduce, limit, or prevent the risk of transmission. The social worker's actions should be reasonable (Yorker, 1988). Efforts to identify that individual and to provide a warning or protection need not be handled in a crisis-like manner. Before a duty to warn exists, a helping person must be aware of specific risks to specific persons (Dickens, 1988). The worker must challenge the client both through educating him about AIDS and the risk of transmission to both his partner and to potential offspring.

Another goal for both the worker and Mr. S. would focus on the basis of relationships that must include trust, mutuality, sharing, and openness. She must also make clear to the client that promises of confidentiality, except where specifically limited or restricted by law, means that information will be used in a responsible manner. Responsibilities exist for both the worker and for the client and the failure to share information with their partner is a demonstration of lack of responsibility that may necessitate breaching confidentiality and alerting public health authorities. As indicated previously, the worker may offer to assist Mr. S. in revealing his diagnosis to his lover and to provide supportive counseling to both individuals. The danger to the client or to the third party, although real, is not imminent, and therefore the worker has time to assist the client in reaching a responsible decision that will enable the warning to take place.

The social worker should base his or her actions on an ethical analysis of the competing values (Joseph, 1982) and reasoned clinical judgements that are least restrictive or intrusive of the privacy of their client. Social workers must be fully cognizant of their ethical and professional responsibilities, the laws in their state that apply to AIDS and HIV, and their obligations relating to confidentiality.

REFERENCES

Calabresi, G., & Babbit, P. (1978). *Tragic choices.* New York: W.W. Norton and Company.

Dickens, B.M. (1988). *Legal limits of AIDS confidentiality. JAMA*, 259 (23), 3449–3451.

Joseph, V.M. (1982). A Model for ethical decision making in clinical practice. In Germain, C.B. (Ed.), *Advances In Clinical Social Work Practice.* Silver Spring, MD: National Association of Social Workers.

Koop, C.E. (1986). *Surgeon General's report on acquired immune deficiency syndrome.* Washington, DC: U.S. Department of Health and Human Services.

Weil, M., & Sanchez, E. (1983). The impact of the Tarasoff decision on clinical social work practice. *Social Service Review*, 57, 112–124.

Yorker, B.C. (1988). Confidentiality—An ethical dilemma, balancing the "duty to warn" against the right to privacy. *American Association of Occupation Health Nurses Journal*, 36, 346–347.

Rejoinder to Professor Gelman
Frederic G. Reamer

Professor Gelman has made a number of useful points about the intersection in this case of moral, professional, and legal considerations. He is right to point out that a social worker's obligation may vary depending on whether one is viewing the case through a moral, professional, or legal lens. Certainly there are instances when a specific law may clash with one's moral beliefs. For example, a social worker who believes that competent homeless people have the right to be left alone and should not be forced into a shelter against their wishes may place his or her moral beliefs above a local law that mandates shelter care when the temperature drops below a certain level. In the face of such conflict, the worker must choose which duty will take precedence.

It is not the case, however, that moral, legal, and professional considerations always clash. In particular, it is not clear that the legal guidelines in this case are inconsistent with professional responsibility and moral duty. What we seem to have here is a significant difference of interpretation. It is true, as Gelman suggests, that local law may prohibit disclosure of information about a client with AIDS without the client's permission. However, most jurisdictions have been silent on this particular issue, at least with respect to social workers. In the absence of a statute that clearly spells out a social worker's duty to disclose, case law—drawn in particular from the Tarasoff case and its descendants—would likely serve as the basis for judicial guidance. This is based on the legal doctrine of stare decisis, where principles laid down in previous judicial decisions are followed unless they contravene ordinary principles of justice.

Professor Gelman argues that the social worker may not be justified in disclosing confidential information because of the absence of "compelling professional reasons." More specifically, Gelman argues that *Tarasoff* may not apply because the danger to a third party is not imminent and there is no clear threat of violence. He argues further that in all probability, Mr. S.'s lover already has been placed at risk.

I see the matter differently. We cannot be certain that Mr. S.'s lover already has been placed at risk. In fact, the risk to her *may* be imminent, and we should act accordingly. And although we might debate whether the threat Mr. S. poses technically constitutes a violent threat, I am willing to conclude that at the very least it comes close enough to what we generally mean by a serious threat of harm to satisfy the criteria ordinarily applied in "duty to protect" cases.

Gelman and I generally agree on the principal issues that need to be examined in this complex case. We even agree that the social worker should not play detective. Despite this agreement, however, we differ significantly in our interpretation of legal, moral, and professional obligations. In this sense, this debate typifies what is characteristic of hard cases.

DEBATE 24

Should Welfare Clients Be Required to Work?

EDITOR'S NOTE: Most historical accounts trace the origin of national legislation to provide for the poor to the enactment in England of the Statute of Laborers in 1348. Ever since then a central consideration has been the relationship between welfare—programs that provide the poor with income—and work. Although Congress in 1988 passed the Family Security Act, which includes a national workfare program, it will not settle the issue. Requiring welfare recipients to work in exchange for their grants will remain deeply controversial for many years to come.

The debate of this issue was prepared differently from all others in this book. First, it is more fully pursued. Divided evenly on the yes and no sides of the question, four academics were asked to take sides. Because there was no attempt to coordinate their arguments, one thing to observe is what the two authors on each side say in common and where they follow different lines of argument. Second, instead of rejoinders among the debaters, all of their statements were turned over to someone who played a key role in the evolution and passage of the Family Security Act. In the light of her participation in the congressional debate, she was asked to comment on what the academics had come up with.

The YES arguments were prepared by Ailee Moon, Ph.D. and Robert Pruger, DSW. Dr. Moon is Assistant Professor in the School of Social Welfare at the University of California at Los Angeles, where she teaches social policy and research methods. Her interests include the political economy of welfare states, fiscal welfare systems and tax expenditures, and ethnic minority older populations. Her current research activities include

356

studies of the determinants of individual charitable contributions to voluntary human service organizations and the politics of Catastrophic Health Insurance.

Robert Pruger is Professor in the School of Social Welfare at the University of California, Berkeley. His courses and publications are in the area of social policy and administration. Most of his recent work applies the microeconomic concept of efficiency to the production and distribution of social services.

The first NO argument is jointly authored by Ann Nichols-Casebolt and Jesse McClure, the second, by David Stoesz. Ann Nichols-Casebolt, Ph.D., is Assistant Professor of Social Work at Arizona State University. Her areas of interest are in poverty of single-parent families, income support policy, and child support reform. She has recently coauthored an article with Jesse McClure entitled, "Social Work Support for Welfare Reform: The Latest Surrender in the War on Poverty." Jesse McClure, Ph.D., has been Dean of the School of Social Work of Arizona State University since 1983. He previously served as Dean of the School of Social Work of Sacramento State University.

David Stoez, DSW is Associate Professor in the School of Social Work, San Diego State University and Director of policyAmerica. He has written about social welfare theory, the role of think tanks in the policy process, and for-profit provision of social welfare. His *American Social Welfare Policy* (with Howard Karger) was published by Longman in 1990.

Rikki Baum, DSW, prepared the comment on the debate. She was Senior Legislative Assistant for Social Policy for Senator Daniel Moynihan. She staffed him in his capacity as Chairman of the Subcommittee on Social Security and Family Policy of the Senate Finance Committee. Senator Moynihan was the chief author of the Family Support Act of 1988, the legislation that creates a national workfare requirement; Dr. Baum played a major role in the process leading its enactment.

YES

AILEE MOON

Whereas the popular usage of the term "workfare" is a relatively recent phenomenon, the notion that "employable" public assistance recipients be required to work or participate in a work-related activity in exchange for their benefits is neither a new nor radical departure. If one defines workfare as encompassing any form of mandatory work-related obligation, workfare was already at work when participation in the Work Incentive (WIN) program became mandatory in 1971. That is, in order to receive AFDC benefits, all ablebodied adults without preschool children or special circumstances that prevented them from participating would have to be engaged in job search or job training activities. They would have to seek and accept employment offers. Similarly, the Carter and Reagan administrations had included in their welfare reform proposals some form of mandatory work requirements, although there were important differences in their designs of workfare. Nine states already operate statewide mandatory workfare programs.

The Family Security Act of 1988 enacts a new nationwide workfare scheme in the name of a Job Opportunities and Basic Skills (JOBS) program. Most long-term AFDC recipients with children under age 3 (or, at state option, age 1) or those at highest risk of becoming long-term recipients, such as teenage mothers, are required to "work off" their benefits by participating in the JOBS program. The nature of work activities includes job search, community work experience (CWEP) or other unpaid work, subsidized employment, or on-the-job training. Child care, transportation, and other work-related expenses needed for a recipient to participate in the program are assured.

Whether welfare recipients should be required to work is a question of pragmatism, values, and politics. Workfare in theory and workfare in practice may not be identical. Thus, it is important to be pragmatic and judge the merit of workfare in the light of the practical feasibility of making workfare work. Can workfare be constructed in a way that helps break the cycle of welfare dependency, restores individuals to self-sufficiency, and leads to welfare savings? What are the preconditions for workfare to work? The answers to these questions provide a strong rationale for or against workfare.

Although the pragmatic approach is essential, it is nevertheless insufficient to determine the appropriateness of workfare. In fact, the issue of workfare cannot be dealt with in isolation of prevailing social values and political reality. Even in the absence of a strong economic rationale, workfare may be preferred if it better fits with the nation's social values and improves equity or perceived fairness of the welfare system. Furthermore, any proposals that claim to serve the best interest of welfare recipients but ignore political reality are doomed to failure. Thus, before saying "yes" or "no" to workfare, one must further consider the following questions: "What are the likely consequences of opposing workfare on recipients themselves?" "What are the trade-offs involved in workfare?" In short, "Workfare in exchange for what?"

Facing Economic and Social Realities

When the Aid to Dependent Children (now AFDC) was enacted as part of the original Social Security Act of 1935, the initial assumption was that only a small number of poor families with children would receive benefits, and that enabling mothers to stay home and care for their children was better than compelling them to go to work. It was also expected that the need for the program would diminish as more and more of the typical ADC beneficiaries—widows and wives of disabled workers with children—would become eligible for social security benefits. Strong support for the program prevailed. Issues of possible work disincentives and long-term dependency did not arise. The focus was on the welfare of financially needy children.

Fifty years later, the AFDC program has become the least popular and the most problematic social welfare program. Political controversy has focused on the able-bodied adult beneficiaries. In fact, every major welfare reform proposal since the mid-1960s has called for a redefinition of welfare entitlement and restoration of the work ethic by weaving work incentives together with financial assistance. What happened?

Clearly, the modern reality of AFDC is quite different from what the advocates of its original ADC program could imagine. At the same time, other social, economic, and political realities of the country have undergone considerable changes. Conceived during the New Deal as a program for children of widows, today the children in most AFDC families have fathers who are absent through divorce or desertion, many of them were born out of wedlock, and many of their parents never married. The program did not diminish as expected, but instead had evolved over time into a major welfare program. Both the number of AFDC families and the program's total costs have risen rapidly, especially during the 1960s and 1970s. The number increased from about 490,000 in 1940 to over 3.7 million in 1987 and the costs from $133 million in 1940 to 42.5 billion in 1987.

The continued rise in the number of nontraditional AFDC cases has weakened public support and sympathy towards AFDC recipients. It also has provoked public suspicions that the program sends wrong signals. AFDC has come to be regarded by some as a cause, not a cure, of many social problems—erosion of the very foundations of sexual morality and parental responsibility, family breakdowns, teenage pregnancy, illegitimate birth, poverty, and dependency. The consensus is reached that something must be done to reverse the trends and to restore a strong sense of personal responsibility among AFDC recipients. In this context, workfare emerges as an expression of public insistence upon fulfillment of parental obligations by all parents, including the poor, in one way or another.

It is also important to assess the appropriateness of workfare in a broader context of social and economic realities of contemporary American families. At a time when few mothers worked outside the home, forcing mothers on welfare to work would be considered punitive and inappropriate as it would be inconsistent with the prevailing norms of family life. This would have been the case in the 1940s, 1950s, and even 1960s.

In the last two decades, however, the situation has changed dramatically. For many two-parent families, one income is no longer adequate to maintain their previous standard of living and most mothers, including single parents with very young children, work outside the home to make ends meet. Today, less than 10 percent of all families are families with the father at work and the mother at home taking care of the children. Almost two thirds of all mothers with children younger than 14 are in the workforce. The percentage of working women with children under the age of 14 rose sharply from 12 percent in 1950 to 56 percent in 1988. Most strikingly, more than 50 percent of working mothers have children under age 1!

The trend of increasing employment rate of all women may be comforting or disturbing, depending on one's point of view. What is evident, however, is that the trend is irreversible. From the previously mentioned figures it is also evident that most women with children, including single parents, take their financial responsibility seriously. Of course, financial responsibility is only one of many parental responsibilities. Nonetheless, it is a critical one. Thus, at a time like today when most women with young children work outside the home, the idea of asking welfare recipients to work is in itself neither inhumane nor inconsistent with social norms. Rather, it is only fair to expect welfare recipients to contribute to their own support by working or participating in training to help them become self-sufficient. This is the reality of the 1980s. Being on the welfare rolls is no shame. It is not a privilege, either.

Long-Term Dependency Is the Target

Whereas receiving AFDC is a short-term, transitional phenomenon for most recipients, it is also a long-term source of income support for some. Approximately 25 percent of recipients are on welfare for a period of less than 6 months, almost one third for less than 1 year, and almost half of the total for less than 2 years. But 15 percent of the total—a small percentage but a large number—remain on welfare for some 10 years.

In fact, the 15 percent of 3.7 million families dependent on AFDC, approximately 555,000, is a large enough number to lead to "the new consensus" that "the problem of the late 1980s is no longer poverty but rather dependency and that the problem of dependency is primarily a moral problem" (Novak, 1987, p. 26). Consistent with this diagnosis, the target of welfare reform efforts of the 1980s has been long-term welfare dependency.

The shift in focus of the problem further raises a new set of AFDC policy questions. Who are the long-term recipients? What causes and perpetuates their condition? Does the AFDC promote a "culture of poverty," for example, intergenerational dependency, teenage pregnancy, and social isolation among the poor? What are the barriers to independence? Finally, what is to be done to break the cycle of welfare dependency and to facilitate work and independence?

As people persistently disagree on the causes of poverty and dependency, there is no agreed upon single cure for the problem. Is the lack of jobs the only cause of dependency? If so, workfare will not be fruitful. Is the inability of AFDC recipients to afford medical care and day care for their children after they leave welfare rolls the barrier to work and independence? If so, the government ought to remove the barrier by providing or subsidizing these services for needy families. What about the lack of incentives to work, social isolation, and the lack of education, skills, and work experience? Are they not part of the cause of dependency and barriers to self-sufficiency? The point is that there is no single cause of dependency that explains it all. It is undeniable that workfare, as a solution to welfare dependency, is far from perfect. However, considering the components of workfare and a variety of services attached to it, is it not worth pursuing?

Can Workfare Work?

Many argue that workfare does not work, sometimes with reference to the unsuccessful story of the WIN program—its failure to establish "meaningful" work-related obligations for recipients. Because WIN was never fully funded or properly implemented, however, it still leaves much room for imagination. What would have been the outcome if it had been adequately funded and properly implemented? Some argue further that workfare does not work simply because there are no jobs. No one disagrees that the lack of jobs is the primary barrier to self-sufficiency and that even workfare, to be successful, must rely on the existing market for the supply of jobs. The "jobs-only" explanation is an oversimplification of the complexity involved in the problem of poverty and dependency, however. For example, between 1960 and 1985, the number of AFDC grew constantly and at a fast rate regardless of the unemployment rate, so that it continued to grow even when the unemployment rate fell. Between 1968 and 1978, the number of AFDC families doubled. Although the increase was attributed in part to changes in eligibility criteria and the increases in the number of children who do not receive financial support from their absent parents, the labor market condition alone seems to leave a substantial portion of the increase unexplained. After all, it must be remembered that workfare targets long-term recipients who tend to remain on welfare regardless of the labor market condition.

Now focusing on the findings from experiments with workfare in five states, using control groups, a study indicates that:

1. The programs led to increases, though relatively modest, in employment, except in West Virginia.

2. The programs had a stronger impact on recipients who had some obstacles to employment, as opposed to the more job-ready recipients.
3. Within a relatively short time, program savings offset costs.
4. Most of the participants regarded a work requirement as fair and responded positively to the work assignments (Gueron, 1987).

Although the workfare programs did not move substantial numbers of people out of poverty, and although in a state (West Virginia) with the nation's highest unemployment rate then, the program did not lead to employment gains, it suggests that workfare had its intended impacts in four states, that is, cost-effective employment gains, not to mention possibly greater welfare savings in the long run and intangible gains such as felt sense of dignity and responsibility among the participants. Thus, although it remains unclear whether the gains come from the services provided or the mandatory aspect of the programs and whether a comprehensive universal workfare would lead to more or less employment gains, the outlook for the feasibility and effectiveness of the program is not quite as bleak as some believe. Rather, the overall findings are encouraging.

Facing Political Realities

Considering that workfare was only one of several major components of the 1988 welfare reform bill, it raises a question as to whether a strong opponent of workfare would still oppose the entire bill on behalf of welfare recipients because of the workfare component (Congressional Digest, 1988). How would social workers have voted? When the political reality dictates that to kill workfare would also be to kill some or all other provisions in the bill, including establishment of AFDC-UP and child support enforcement in all states and extended child care and medical benefits for AFDC recipients who leave the rolls which will lead to significant improvement in the lives of poor families with children, the question becomes, is workfare not worth a price of passing such a bill? Those who still insist not remind us of those liberals who opposed Family Assistance Plan (FAP) almost three decades ago.

Those who oppose workfare call it "slavefare." Those who support it call it "workfare." Whatever terminology one prefers, workfare is not a bad idea for what it reflects and for what it brings in exchange in the context of political, social, and economic realities of the late 1980s.

REFERENCES

(1988). Should the "family welfare reform act of 1987" be enacted? *Congressional Digest*, pp. 40–64.

Danziger, S., & Weinberg, D. (1986). *Fighting poverty: What works and what doesn't.* Cambridge, MA: Oxford University Press.

Executive Office of the President. Intragency Low Income Opportunity Advisory Board (April). *Up from dependency: A new national public assistance strategy.* Supplement 4 Research Studies and Bibliography. Washington, DC: U.S. Government Printing Office.

Gueron, J. (1987). Reforming welfare with work. *Public Welfare,* 45, 13–25.

Novak, M. (1987). Sending the right signal. *The Public Interest.* No. 89, 26–50.

Novak, M. (Ed.). (1987). *The new consensus on family and welfare.* Washington, DC: American Enterprise Institute for Public Policy Research.

Training Research Corporation. (1988). *Training for change: An analysis of the outcomes of California employment training panel programs.* Santa Monica: Training Research Corporation.

Weidman, J., White, R., & Swartz, B. (1988). Training women on welfare for "high-tech" jobs: Results from a demonstration program. *Evaluation and Program Planning,* 11, 105–114.

Wilcox, L. (1988). Reworking welfare: Creating jobs in Maine. *Public Welfare,* 46, 13–18.

NO

ANN M. NICHOLS-CASEBOLT AND JESSE MCCLURE

The current AFDC program is a philosophical offspring of Mothers' Aid Laws enacted by several states in the early part of this century. State sponsored Mothers' Aid programs and the subsequent federal Aid to Dependent Children program launched in 1935 were specifically designed to permit and encourage mothers to eschew the world of work in order to provide the caring and nurturing that children with only one parent were presumed to need. In contrast to this, there is a growing consensus that the receipt of welfare benefits should be linked with a clear and mandatory obligation to work. Although in the past two decades the federal government has supported a variety of employment programs in an effort to reduce welfare dependence, the notion that work and welfare, especially AFDC, should be related is relatively new.

For social workers, improving and reforming the welfare system has historically been a matter of significant concern. Social work as a profession has been in the forefront of advocacy for the development of a more meaningful and humane income transfer system. As the support grows for requiring welfare recipients to work, it is incumbent upon the profession to examine the many issues that, in our view, make mandatory work requirements an ineffective and inappropriate welfare reform strategy.

Welfare Mothers Are Already Working Mothers

Most people would argue that raising children is one of the most important jobs in our society, yet the current emphasis on welfare-to-work strategies does not view caretaking of one's own children as legitimate employment. What is even more ironic is that a mother who obtains a job caring for someone else's children is considered to be gainfully employed. In addition, adequate child care represents a major unmet need in this nation. Thus, rather than expend resources to force these women to work at jobs that do not exist, a more appropriate choice might be to use resources to assist these women in their role as parents. Mandatory work requirements for welfare recipients also imply that it is appropriate and desirable for mothers to work outside the home—a view that is still vigorously debated when applied to non-AFDC mothers.

Similarly, the goal of the women's movement over the past 20 years is to promote the concept of choice in the lives of all people. Mandatory work requirements are antithetical to this concept of choice when they force individuals to alter their lives and the lives of their children because they are recipients of assistance. For those women who would like to work, a more appropriate strategy would be to help them develop their academic and vocational skills to a point where a job can be a meaningful choice. Mandatory work requirements thus have the potential for both negatively effecting the ability of mothers to play significant roles in the rearing of their children and also in undermining the efforts to allow women to make choices in their lives.

Mandatory Work Requirement Lacks Economic Incentives to Work

After 4 months of employment, AFDC benefits are cut one dollar for every dollar earned. And once earnings exceed benefits, not only does the family lose their AFDC check, but they also must often lose eligibility for child and health care benefits. Thus, unless a recipient can earn considerably more than their welfare payment they will potentially be worse off with earnings. It has been estimated that in California a family of three would need a wage of $10.26 an hour to have an income that exceeds AFDC cash and in-kind benefits (McFate, 1988). However, because of limited education and job skills among many of the long-term dependent (the stated target of most welfare-to-work programs), the type of job many recipients will be able to obtain is not likely to be enough to compensate for lost benefits or move the family out of poverty. A full-time job at the minimum $3.35 an hour will pay less than $7000.00 a year, not enough to raise a mother and her child above the poverty line. In addition, most low-wage jobs do not provide job security, much less health care benefits or enough money for the single mother to purchase quality day care for her children.

Employment Programs Do Little to Reduce Poverty and Welfare Dependency

In 1967 the Work Incentive Program (WIN) was established to provide AFDC recipients with incentives for working their way off welfare. At the same time a variety of Great Society programs were targeting welfare recipients as one of the hard-to-employ groups that should be offered special employment and training assistance. However, neither the WIN program or other employment and training programs have achieved much success in reducing welfare dependence (Bassi & Ashenfelter, 1986). And those few that did show some success, such as the Supported Work Demonstration, were very expensive and often the net benefits to recipients kept many of them squarely in the ranks of the poor (Gottschalk, 1983). In addition, a review of the effectiveness of experimental mandatory work programs during the Reagan administration (often called "workfare") concluded that these programs did not deter dependency or assist many people off the welfare rolls (Gueron, 1987).

In Many Sections of the Country Jobs Are Not Available

Although national unemployment rates have dropped in recent years, the national rate masks significant variation among and within states. For example, in 1988 the national unemployment rate was 5.5 percent, whereas Louisiana's was 9.6 percent, and while California's unemployment rate was 5.1 percent, in the Modesto area 11.7 percent of the population was unemployed (Committee on Ways and Means, 1989). In addition, industries have been moving out of the central cities where many of the poor and welfare-dependent reside. Coercing people to find employment when jobs are scarce will do little to reduce welfare dependency and will likely demoralize recipients and entrench them more firmly into the welfare system.

Bureau of Labor projections do indicate, however, that there will be an increase in the number of job opportunities available over the next decade. But the data suggest that most of these jobs will be in the low-wage, low-skill sector of the economy. These low-level jobs not only pay low wages but are often tedious and expose workers to potential occupational health hazards. This type of labor market offers little hope for entrance into a job that pays adequate wages or "career advancement" to a better paying job (Applebaum, 1984). Thus, even if one finds employment, the chances of a single mother with limited education escaping poverty in the paid labor force, even in the long-term, are slim at best.

Requiring Women to Take Any Job at Any Pay Perpetuates Labor Market Discrimination

Sexual and racial discrimination in the labor force continue to hamper economic opportunities available to women, particularly minority women (who comprise over 50 percent of the AFDC caseload). A variety of studies have shown that, even after controlling for education, training, and family background, women and minorities are more likely to be unemployed and have lower wages if employed. Data on the weekly earnings of workers who usually worked full time in 1983 indicate that the ratio of female to male earnings were, on average, less than 67 percent of the wages of male workers (Mellor, 1985). And for minority women, labor market disparities are even greater. Occupational segregation is a major source of the earnings disparity. Women and minorities are more likely to be restricted to a limited number of occupations and jobs within each occupation. In addition, discrimination in employment often forces women to work less often, for fewer hours, and ultimately for less income.

The Link between Work and Self Sufficiency Is Tenuous

Exiting welfare through employment does not mean that the individual is able to obtain or maintain economic self sufficiency. Of the roughly 21 percent of all persons who left welfare between 1968 and 1981 through earnings, only 30 percent had earnings of over $8000.00, just enough to push a family of three above the poverty line. In addition, "fully 40 percent of all women who leave with an earnings increase eventually return for a later spell of AFDC" (Bane & Ellwood, 1983).

In 1985 almost one of every ten workers did not earn enough to move a family of three out of poverty (Levitan & Shapiro, 1987). When work brings few economic rewards and upward mobility is unachievable, commitment to work is easily eroded and individuals become alienated from the social mainstream.

Mandatory Work Programs Promote the Concept of "Blaming the Victim"

By focusing attention on changing welfare recipients so that they can enter the world of work, we place the blame for the individual's dependency squarely on the victim. Proponents of mandatory work for welfare mothers appear to be assuming that AFDC recipients just need to be socialized to the concept that in our society you cannot get "something for nothing" (of course, this also gives a clear message that caring for your children is "nothing"). This view portrays AFDC mothers as lacking effort, ambition, or motivation for work. It does not focus on such important issues as economic and social inequality, lack of decent paying jobs, or discrimination against women and minorities in the workplace.

As a profession we may laud efforts that promote "client self-sufficiency," but are we supporting programs that require work when jobs are not available or those that pay below poverty level wages? In addition, even for those who are able to find employment and escape welfare, the current economic situation will relegate many of them to the ranks of the working poor. Mandatory work requirements place a high moral value on work, without recognizing the low economic value of the jobs that may be available to recipients. Should social work be a party to increasing the numbers of working poor? What will happen to individuals who must continually struggle to achieve economic security?

Similarly, many of the current reform ideas seem to have lost all sight of the fact that AFDC was designed primarily as a child welfare strategy. Many of the new reform initiatives include mothers with children over the age of 3 in their mandatory work requirements. What impact might this have on children? Will the mother's full-time employment create other family problems? From a perspective of professional social workers, any reform of the current system that does not attempt to address the needs of children in these efforts is at best incomplete.

A final and more fundamental challenge involves the value commitments of the social work profession itself. It is apparent that the prevailing political climate has indeed changed the stated perspectives of the social work profession. This shift toward burdening the poor with the responsibility for their own economic improvement is a radical shift in philosophy. Although reforming the "welfare system" is a noble and worthy goal, it should not be done at the expense of the basic values of the social work profession. Social work throughout history has been an advocate for the disenfranchised, the downtrodden, and those for whom the nation's economic system has not worked. Today it appears that advocacy is being replaced by acquiescence. Clearly, a reexamination of new approaches to reforming income maintenance in this nation is required by social workers and others who are genuinely committed to the concepts of equality and humanity.

REFERENCES

Appelbaum, E. (1984). High tech and the structural employment problems of the 1980s. In Collins, E.L., & Tanner, L.D. (Eds.), *American jobs* and the changing industrial base. Cambridge, MA: Ballinger Publishing Co.

Bane, M.J., & Ellwood, D.T. (1983). The dynamics of dependence: The routes to self-sufficiency. (Contract No. HHS-100-82-0038). Cambridge, MA: Harvard University, John F. Kennedy School of Government.

Bassi, L.J., & Ashenfelter, O. (1986). The effect of direct job creation and training programs on low-skilled workers. In Danziger, S.H. & Weinberg, D.H. (Eds.), *Fighting poverty: What works and what doesn't.* Cambridge, MA: Harvard University Press, 133–151.

Committee on Ways and Means. (1989). *Background material and data on programs within the jurisdiction of the Committee on Ways and Means.* Washington, DC: U.S. Government Printing Office.

Gottschalk, P. (1983). *U.S. labor market policies since the 1960s: A survey of programs and their effectiveness.* (IRP Discussion Paper #730-83). Madison, WI: University of Wisconsin, Institute for Research on Poverty.

Gueron, J.M. (1987). Reforming welfare with work. *Public Welfare*, 45(4), 13–25.

Levitan, S.A., & Shapiro, I. (1987). *Working but poor.* Baltimore, MD: Johns Hopkins University Press.

McFate, K. (1988). Welfare: Dependency vs. reform. *Focus: The Monthly Magazine of the Joint Center for Political Studies*, 16(7), 3–4.

Mellor, E.F. (1985). Weekly earnings in 1983: A look at more that 200 occupations. *Monthly Labor Review*, 108(1), 54–59.

ANNOTATED BIBLIOGRAPHY

Bassi, L.J., & Ashenfelter, O. (1986). The effect of direct job creation and training programs on low-skilled workers. In Danzinger, S.H., & Weinberg, D.H. (Eds.), *Fighting poverty: What works and what doesn't.* Cambridge, MA: Harvard University Press, 133–151.

A review and analysis of various social programs and policies initiated since the 1960s, thus making the book an excellent resource for those interested antipoverty policy.

Committee on Ways and Means. (1989). *Background material and data on programs within the jurisdiction of the Committee on Ways and Means.* Washington, DC: US Government Printing Office.

This report is published yearly and is one of the best sources for up-to-date information on social welfare programs. It includes brief discussions of the most recent legislative changes in each of the programs as well as national and state data on recipients, benefits, and expenditures.

YES

Robert Pruger

The Social Security Act of 1935 created both the social security system and the family welfare program (originally named Aid to Dependent Children, later Aid to Families with Dependent Children). The contrasts between the two are stunning. The former is widely regarded as the crowning accomplishment of our welfare state; the latter, its greatest failure. Every expansion of the social insurances is celebrated; every increase in the welfare rolls is taken to mean that something is very wrong, including antagonistic donor suspicions of exploitation by recipients. One builds the social bond, the other weakens it. When poll takers ask, "Should we help the poor?" every segment of the American public answers in the affirmative. When asked, "Should 'welfare' be increased?" the response is equally strong—in the negative.

These evaluations, arising from deep within our culture, are potent and durable. Reforms of welfare that ignore them and the popular values they bespeak can no longer be considered serious proposals. Workfare, the requirement that welfare recipients work in exchange for their grants, is responsive to these concerns. It is an idea whose time has come.

Historical Background

Prior to the twentieth century, dependent women and their children were not ordinarily supported in their own homes. Institutional relief was the norm. The 1909 White House Conference on Children ushered in a new era. Soon thereafter the States came to agree that:

> . . . the contribution of the unskilled or semi-skilled mothers in their own homes exceeded their earnings outside of the home and that it was in the public interest to conserve their child caring functions (Bell, 1965, p. 16).

By 1935 this idea was the prevailing dogma. It was so dominant that ADC, whose whole intent was to enable poor mothers to stay at home, was virtually ignored in the debate preceding passage of the Social Security Act. One congressman, when asked about this, responded, "How can you be against mommies and babies?'' Thus, the welfare program that today evokes so much divisive hostility and complaint once inspired nothing worse than tolerant indifference.

This lasted about 20 years. Beginning in 1956 the proper relationship between work and welfare was redrawn. In that year, and again in 1962, Congress strengthened the expectation that welfare recipients work. By 1967 the legislative language was getting quite insistent. It required a plan for each recipient household that would assure ''to the maximum extent possible that each relative, child and individual will enter the labor force and accept employment so that they become self-sufficient'' (House of Representatives, 1967). Loss of benefits was specified for refusal to cooperate.

Also instructive is the content of the congressional opposition to the compulsory work requirement. Most of it was concerned not with the abandonment of the original purpose of the AFDC program, but rather with doubts that the requirement could be administered. One senator tried to stem the tide but his argument already sounded musty. There no longer was effective political support for his plea on the Senate floor that:

> . . . for the mother with a nine-year-old child, there is a higher purpose (than work), and let us make sure that the Congress does not make it more difficult for her to achieve that highest of all purposes, to be home with the child (Congressional Record, 1967, p. 36924).

The Nixon, Carter, and Reagan presidencies put new welfare reform proposals on the table, each another attempt to better integrate welfare and work. The argument was over things like how to provide day care for working welfare mothers, not whether or not they should be able to stay at home. By the time the states received permission in 1981 to experiment with workfare, even liberals were getting on board. As one writer pungently characterized their traditional posture, ''Workfare drove liberals berserk'' (Kaus, 1986); they called it ''slave labor.'' The most salient political fact about welfare today has been their large shift to support such programs. By the time federal legislation required all states to go this route, the most liberal ones had already put their own versions in place.

The Family Security Act of 1988 creates the ''New Workfare.'' Long-term dependents, including mothers with children 3 years old or older who have received payments for over 2.5 years, are required to participate. The states are also given the option of lowering the minimum age of the child to *1!*

Given this almost total reversal of the norm that governed the program in 1935, the obvious question is . . .

What Happened?

The definitive analysis has yet to be done, but the following developments, presented in crude approximation of their temporal occurrence, clearly had substantial impact:

The Characteristics of the Recipients Changed Dramatically—Favored Clients Were Replaced by Unfavored Ones

In the early years the major reason for dependency was widowhood. To state it with its proper coloration, a woman and her "orphans" were on ADC because her husband had died prematurely, or even more pathetically, because he had been killed in an industrial accident in the noble course of working to support his family. Also of import, the typical recipient was thought of as being white.

By the 1960s the modern character of the welfare rolls was becoming apparent. The new causes of dependency were much less wholesome: desertion, never having been married, illegitimacy, and intergenerational dependency. It would be difficult to think of a list less likely to evoke a sympathetic response from the American public. The fact that blacks were disproportionately represented on the rolls did not increase popular patience with the program.

The Rolls Got Much Bigger and More Expensive Than Anyone Had Expected

In its original conception, welfare was supposed to "wither away" (Steiner, 1966). Instead, it "exploded." For example, during the 1960s the number of families on AFDC "almost tripled—from 800,000 to 2.2 million," and "total payments increased from $1 billion to almost $5 billion (an almost fourfold increase after adjusting for inflation)" (Congressional Budget Office, 1985). In California in the last 2 years of the decade the number of recipients increased by 70 percent!

In a different world this might be taken as a measure of society's expanded effort to meet increased human needs, and thus something the nation as a whole could take pride in. That is precisely the reaction that attends every social insurance increase. But as anyone with the least grasp of our civilization must intuitively understand, social security and welfare are judged according to cultural values about growth that is good and growth that is bad: social security gets better by getting bigger; welfare gets better by getting smaller. A rapid rise in the AFDC rolls is a "crisis," and a crisis establishes the psychological and political urgency that demands a reevaluation of what we are doing and strong, new ways to make things right.

Women, Particularly Those with Young Children, Massively Increased Their Participation in the Paid Labor Force

The statistics can be dizzying, and they are subject to qualification. But the general character of the phenomenon is beyond dispute. Of particular relevance here is how the percentage of married women with children younger than 6 who were in the work force grew: 1948, 11 percent; 1960, 18.6 percent; 1965, 23 percent; 1970, 30.3 percent; 1980, 45.1 percent; 1985, 53.4 percent; 1988, 57.1 percent. (For separated women, the proportions are approximately the same; for divorced women, the figures are appreciably higher, rising, for example, to 70.1 percent in 1988.)

Demographic changes of this magnitude affect everything and it can take decades to understand the forces released. One change, however, is unmistakable: it has become untenable to exempt welfare mothers from effective work expectations. Whatever the barriers to reorienting the system, there can be no turning back.

New Ideas about Poverty and Welfare Have Emerged

Two things here should prove influential over time. First, scholars, journalists, and other careful observers of the scene have confirmed what every layman knows from the omnipresent portrayals of the homeless—that for many enmeshed in poverty and welfare, much more is wrong than simple income deficiency. Merely sending checks out, as was done in ADC, or was called for in the various negative income tax proposals, just will not do. The problem of the "underclass" requires more.

Second, the ideological debate among elites has become much livelier. There was a time when a leading welfare scholar, referring to the broad array of those active at the federal level regarding these programs, could state: "Given the composition of the various committees, consultant staffs, and advisory groups there was never any danger of honest differences of opinion" (Steiner, p. 37). This condition, too, seems permanently in the past. The ideas and followers of writers such as Charles Murray, Lawrence Mead, and William Julius Wilson have forced elites to deal with concepts, such as the obligation to work, that previously they would not touch.

The net effect of the above developments was to erode the legitimacy of AFDC. Put more directly, a program that is widely perceived as being bad for the taxpayer, injurious to its clientele, and offensive to prevailing civic values, is vulnerable. This was clearly demonstrated in California in 1964.

Proposition 41

In 1970 California's AFDC payment ranked twenty-sixth among the states. By 1984 it paid the most. Moreover, over those years its benefit went up 16 percent in real terms, while the nationwide median declined by a quarter (Wiseman, 1985). Maintaining the purchasing power of the AFDC payment was the legislature's top priority regarding the poor.

The shock came in 1984. A draconian ballot initiative, Proposition 41, attacked the two largest state assistance programs, AFDC and Medi-Cal (in all other states called Medicaid). If enacted, California would have been thrown back almost to its 1970 standing, for family welfare payments would have been reduced from the highest in the nation to 110% of the national average. AFDC benefits would have been cut 60 percent; Medi-Cal expenditures, 36 percent.

Although the initiative failed by a substantial margin, it was not the crowd of AFDC defenders that did it; they cannot finance a modern statewide campaign. But the defenders of Medi-Cal can and did. With doctor and hospital income seriously threatened, the medical community essentially paid for the effort to defeat the proposition. Wisely, that campaign featured the consequences of much reduced medical care for children and the elderly, rather than the effects of the even larger reductions in welfare cash benefits.

But even the Medi-Cal constituency does not get primary credit for the outcome. As many observed, it was not the good guys who had won it, but the bad guys who had lost it. If Proposition 41 had gone after only AFDC and left Medi-Cal alone, the outcome could have been very different. As one liberal assemblyman put it, "As long as they can claim people are getting something for nothing, those folks are going to come back again, and next time they may win."

He forged a bipartisan coalition in support of a more defensible program. Complaints that mandatory unpaid work was unfair were dismissed as "the kind of attitude that brought us Prop. 41." One year later, in a party-like mood that AFDC rarely evokes in politicians, California enacted its version of workfare:

> At the bill-signing ceremony, praise was being ladled out like whipped cream on a hot fudge sundae. Republicans were saying such nice things about Democrats and Democrats were saying such nice things about Republicans that you could imagine—at least for the moment—that partisan politics had become as passé as the hula hoop (Kirp, 1985).

Every other state is now somewhere along in this same process. The question, then, is . . .

Can Workfare Secure Welfare?

Workfare is associated with different objectives. However, when most of these effects occur at all, their magnitude is insignificant: a small percentage of clients end up with permanent jobs, fewer still at good wages; the rolls may decline or rise less rapidly because some are discouraged from applying for aid. Costs, on the other hand, rise rather than fall.

Enthusiasts make much of this unexceptional mix of outcomes, but over time that strategy will wear thin. More importantly, none of this is relevant to AFDC's fundamental problem, which is its lack of legitimacy. Until that is addressed the program and its clients will be vulnerable to mean-spirited, devastating attacks like Proposition 41. No gain or improvement that might be won could ever be treated as secure.

AFDC needs a new moral and political foundation. Its traditional basis—unilateral transfers ought go to poor households because they needed them—has to be replaced with a comprehensive reciprocal obligation between beneficiaries and the state.

To satisfy the requisites of legitimacy, two conditions have to be met. First, the new terms have to implicate a large majority of the clients. Anything that leaves out most recipients, as most programs do, ultimately will fail to win popular acceptance of the program, no matter what grounds are offered to explain those exemptions. To put it crudely but pointedly, it is a matter of not being able to fool all of the people all of the time. Second, the agreement has to be based on work. Nothing else will do.

The remaining question is, what specifically should be required? "Soft" workfare, which essentially is what has been tried so far, requires prework activities such as registration, remedial education, skills training, and job search, but not work itself, at least not on a meaningful scale. The alternative, "hard" workfare, would require work and would do so virtually across the board.

Soft workfare can be responsibly endorsed only if one believes one of two things. First, that the required services will result in substantial numbers of recipients becoming employed. The workfare record accumulated thus far does not support this possibility. Second, that client participation in pre-employment services will satisfy public expectations, even if no substantial increases in employment occur. Maybe. More likely, this underestimates what it would take to rehabilitate AFDC.

To be sure, the effort to successfully require work would meet formidable obstacles. The federal government has been trying to do this for more than 20 years; each effort failed. The costs would be high. Public service positions would have to be created on a very large scale. Unions would oppose it. For different reasons, many conservatives and liberals would be uneasy about it. Nevertheless, these are the relevant barriers to struggle with because:

Welfare doesn't work. Work "incentives" don't work. Training doesn't work. Work "requirements" don't work. "Work experience" doesn't work and even workfare doesn't quite work. Only work works (Kaus, p. 33).

REFERENCES

Bell, W. (1965). *Aid to dependent children*. New York: Columbia University Press.
Congressional Budget Office. (1985). *Work-related programs for welfare recipients*. Washington, DC: The Congress of the United States.
Congressional Record December 15, 1967.
House of Representatives. (1967). *House Bills*, Vol. 61, part one, H.R. 12080, Title II, Part 1, Section 201.
Kaus, M. (1986). The work ethic state. *The New Republic*, July 7.
Kirp, D. (1985). How workfare became law—an amazing compromise. *The Sacramento Bee* October 13.
Steiner, G. (1966). *Social insecurity: the politics of welfare*. Chicago: Rand McNally, 18–47.
Wiseman, M. (1985). From statement prepared for roundtable on Poverty and Poverty Policy in California convened by the Assembly Committee on Human Services of the California Legislature, March 12 (unpublished).

ANNOTATED BIBLIOGRAPHY

Steiner, G. (1986). *Social Insecurity: The politics of welfare*. Chicago: Rand McNally.

An oldie but a very goodie. No other work offers such an insightful, well told portrayal of how AFDC evolved from its beginnings to the mid 1960s.

Mead, L. (1986). *Beyond Entitlement: The social obligations of citizenship*. Free Press.

This book and subsequent articles written by this author make the fullest case for obligating welfare clients to work. A particularly interesting follow up piece is his "The Hidden Jobs Debate," *The Public Interest*, No. 91, Spring 1988. This article makes the case that there is more than an ample supply of work available to absorb the AFDC caseload. His work has its critics, but it clearly is one of the things opponents of mandatory work have to address.

NO

DAVID STOESZ

The relationship between welfare and work—perhaps the most tantalizing of questions for welfare moralists—is often reduced to moronic simplification. "Should welfare clients be required to work?" "Of course!" comes the response—out of some assumption that *we* all work, but with little appreciation for the demographic and economic complexities of the question. Yet if we are serious about understanding the relationship between work and welfare, we must clarify what we mean by "welfare client" and "work."

Consistent with the conservative times that give rise to this question most recently, "welfare client" has come to mean a recipient of the Aid to Families with Dependent Children (AFDC) program. But is an AFDC mother who gets a modest public assistance grant for the year between the departure of her husband and her getting a job any more a "welfare client" than Donald Trump, who claims annually millions of dollars in tax deductions in order to finance future acquisitions? Consider for a moment a report by Citizens for Tax Justice: between 1981 and 1983 a majority of large corporations studied paid no federal income taxes or less (i.e., they received rebates of taxes in earlier years or sold "excess" tax benefits in at least one of the three years, while earning profits of $57.1 billion). In limiting the welfare question to public assistance programs, like AFDC, the practices of wealthy individuals and corporations are conveniently excused, although by any logical standard they should be included since they are also recipients of welfare.

What, then, do we mean by "work"? Is not raising children a productive activity that requires effort? If so, many welfare clients are already "working." If child rearing is not considered work, is it reasonable to require good mothers to leave their children for paid employment? Considering the future decline in number of younger workers in the population, a cogent argument can be made that some of the most productive work to be done at the moment is for mothers to stay home, have more children, and raise them well—not force mothers to take jobs outside the home. Then, of curse, many welfare clients already "work," although this is notoriously underreported in public welfare documents.

In introducing welfare reform legislation, Senator Daniel Patrick Moynihan claimed that no more than 5 percent of AFDC heads-of-households were employed, a gross underestimation to anyone familiar with the economic history of the AFDC program and the economic reality of AFDC families. In 1988, the median state AFDC grant was only 46 percent of the poverty level. Not only do current AFDC grants fail to provide enough income to poor families, but the amount received has been declining. From 1970 to 1989, the median state AFDC grant dropped 37 percent in value. What this means for AFDC heads-of-households is that supplementing the meager public assistance grant is simply a necessity. But because a portion of earned income is deducted from the AFDC grant, there are powerful incentives not to report outside income. "The public assistance system discourages full-time work," observed one labor market analyst, "and forces those on welfare into jobs that are either part-time or which pay cash which will not be reported to the social worker or can be quickly dropped or delayed when the social worker discovers them or seems in danger of doing so." Because of the pathetically low level of AFDC payments and the high deduction from these payments when outside income is reported, the incidence of employment among AFDC heads-of-households is much, much higher than that acknowledged by public welfare officials. In actuality, probably over one half of AFDC heads-of-households are employed—if part time and irregularly—although income from this is not reported.

To return to the question: "Should welfare clients be required to work?" If by welfare client we mean AFDC head-of-household, most of them probably *already are.*

The work and welfare issue would be little more than semantic argument were it not for the Family Support Act of 1988, the most recent example of welfare reform. Budgeted at $3.34 billion over a 5-year period, the act emphasizes workfare, essentially changing AFDC from an income support to a mandatory work-and-training program. The stated objective of the act is to encourage self-sufficiency among welfare recipients; to carry out this goal, the bill requires states to develop workfare programs that compel women on welfare who have children under age 3 (at state option, age 1) to participate in a work-and-training program. By 1990, each state will be required to enroll at least 7 percent of its AFDC recipients (by 1995, 20 percent) in a state basic education program, or in job training or work experience. Among the more progressive provisions of the bill are transitional benefits, the extension of eligibility for day care and Medicaid for 1 year after leaving AFDC for private employment.

Yet for all the flap about the Family Support Act—the chair of the House Subcommittee on Public Assistance claimed it was "the most significant change in the welfare system since its inception"—this legislation of workfare is seriously flawed. First, it restores to the AFDC program only 57 percent of the income lost to inflation since 1970, and then diverts it, not directly to beneficiaries, but through workfare programs. Second, it limits transitional benefits to a 1-year period after gaining employment, disregarding the fact that 44 percent of new, service sector jobs are part time and pay less than $7400.00 per year, meaning that many welfare clients really need a continuous wage supplement. Third, the prospect of welfare recipients becoming economically self-sufficient through workfare is overrated.

Through workfare, "annual earnings are raised $200.00 to $750.00 and welfare savings are more modest," concluded Harvard researcher David Ellwood. "Most work-welfare programs look like decent investments, but no carefully evaluated work-welfare programs have done more than put a tiny dent in the welfare caseloads, even though they have been received with enthusiasm."

Why, then, the infatuation with workfare? Certainly the inclusion of workfare in the Family Support Act is one way of accomplishing the illusion of welfare reform while doing little more than making AFDC more punitive. By focusing on the experience of the welfare beneficiary in dealing with the work and welfare issue, proponents of workfare have achieved with smoke and mirrors that which would not have been possible in earlier discussions of welfare reform. Previous welfare reform addresses systemic problems, and the programs of the New Deal and the War on Poverty were accordingly more ambitious and expensive than the Family Support Act. By contrast, the Family Support Act puts the lash to low-income mothers, driving them into the labor market, while offering little in the way of income and benefit supplements.

The result is predictable. Poor mothers will bounce back and forth between public assistance and marginal employment, seeking to comply with workfare requirements, yet never quite becoming financially independent of the welfare dole. Because the public welfare bureaucracy is notoriously incapable of making the kind of benefit adjustments associated with such frequent transitions between welfare and work, each shift will result in delays and errors in benefit provision. Clients will either be left without benefits for a time or obliged to reimburse the welfare department for overpayments. Except for the rare client able to find the "good job"—full-time work with sufficient income and benefits to vault her family out of poverty—workfare for AFDC families will be an exercise in frustration. Most AFDC clients will find minimal compliance with workfare to be the safest strategy; if forced, they will find minimum wage, part-time jobs at convenience stores or fast food restaurants to avoid the harassment of workfare bureaucrats. Workfare officials will find that such marginal employment does not lead to the enhanced job skills required for the type of work that could take beneficiaries off of welfare altogether. Instead, workfare officials will find themselves operating increasingly costly programs trying to keep track of the erratic employment experience of workfare participants. Too late, workfare managers will have learned an important lesson: McJobs will not solve the welfare problem.

To fully appreciate the work and welfare issue, it is useful to consider the employment opportunities actually available to poor workers. Dual labor market theory posits that work opportunities exist bimodally; that is, there are two sectors in the job market. The primary labor market consists of full-time, salaried positions with health, vacation, and pension benefits and that which have a career ladder through which employees can advance. The primary labor market, then, includes those well-paying jobs with which most professionals are familiar. The secondary labor market, by contrast, includes part-time or seasonal work, hourly (often "minimum") wages, without any benefits or a career ladder; unable to move up occupationally, workers in the secondary labor market move laterally from job to job. Clearly, the secondary labor market is populated by most low-income workers, including those on welfare. Without addressing the characteristics of the secondary labor market, any workfare approach to welfare is doomed to recycle poor workers from welfare to marginal work and back again.

The key to the work and welfare issue, then, is to identify ways in which the secondary labor market can be a more adequate base of employment for poor workers. From a stable base, the more ambitious of poorer workers would be more inclined to take on the type of education and training which could launch themselves into the primary labor market and out of poverty altogether. A first step in this direction would be a minimum benefit package to complement the minimum wage. Such a benefit would include health insurance, a child care benefit, vacation leave, and a portable pension plan that would increase as the worker moved from job to job. If mandated by law, a minimum benefit package would take much of the obligation for the working poor off of welfare and place it with employers where it belongs.

With adequate support, workers in the secondary labor market are more likely to take advantage of education and training programs in order to get better jobs. To enhance advancement to the primary labor market, legislation should entitle workers who successfully completed high school and military service to a full-time job at a wage that assures economic self-sufficiency. For purposes of continuity, individual training accounts should be created through which workers are reimbursed for periodically upgrading their skills.

A labor market approach to the work and welfare problem is not cheap. An Employment Incentives Act of 1988, proposed by Representative Thomas Downey and Senator Albert Gore to augment the Family Support Act, provided a wage supplement and health benefits for poor workers but was budgeted at an unacceptable $34 billion. Rather than a deterrent, the price tag of adequate employment should be recognized as an indicator of the degree to which work has eroded as a guarantee of economic self sufficiency. For a nation as wedded to the work ethic as the United States, welfare advocates would be wise to exploit this fact in order to advance social welfare. But the key to the strategy is not to emphasize the right to welfare per se, rather the right to an adequate wage with benefits is the best way to enhance the circumstances of the welfare and working poor.

During the last decade, welfare advocates have become more accustomed to the idea that a standard of conduct can be expected of welfare clients in exchange for benefits. The simplest, most direct expression of this is to require those on welfare to work. While it is to the credit of welfare advocates that they no longer treat "work" as if it were a four-letter word, they have yet to address the systemic problems relating to the work and welfare issue. It is unrealistic and self-defeating to expect those on AFDC, many of whom are earning income (reported and otherwise), to get off welfare without substantial improvement in employment opportunity. Indeed, this is one of those unusual situations where a classic social work issue is being played out—change the client or the system? Until now, efforts to resolve the work and welfare problem have focused on the individual; it is time to turn our attention to the system, in this case the labor market.

REFERENCES

Danziger, S., & Weinberg, D. (1986). *Fighting poverty: What works and what doesn't.* Cambridge, MA.: Oxford University.

Ellwood, D. (1988). *Poor support: Poverty and the American family.* New York: Basic Books.

Karger, H., & Stoesz, D. (1989). When welfare reform fails. *Tikkun,* 4, 23–25, 118–122.

Novak, M. (Ed.) (1987). *The new consensus on family and welfare.* Washington, DC: American Enterprise Institute.

A Comment on the Workfare Debate from the Legislative Perspective

Rikki Baum

After 20 years of failed attempts, Congress finally passed a major overhaul to the Aid to Families with Dependent Children (AFDC) program, the Family Support Act of 1988 (FSA). The process did not lack for controversy. But the issue that most captured the classic liberal-conservative rift over how to reform welfare was the question of obligatory work. The papers presented here reflect part of the debate over the workfare component, the Job Opportunities and Basic Skills (JOBS) training program. The NO arguments by Casebolt-Nichols, McClure, and Stoesz reflect most of the liberal objections to mandatory work. The YES articles by Moon and Pruger more closely resemble the arguments we made in favor of the JOBS program than the case actually made by conservatives for mandatory work.

Academics may overlook the need for compromise. Legislative sponsors of controversial bills cannot. The JOBS program was the common ground eked out during the pitched battle over CWEP, The Community Work Experience Program. Under CWEP, a state option since 1981, an AFDC adult could be required to work in a public or private nonprofit job in exchange for the family's AFDC grant.

Generally the left wanted to increase benefits, repeal CWEP, and block the imposition of a work requirement. The right (particularly the Reagan White House) wanted to spend no new federal money, return more of the program to the states, and make CWEP a mandatory requirement for all AFDC households. The arguments waged on both sides during the FSA debate are summarized below. Reviewing some of the truths and fallacies of the reasoning on both sides helps to illustrate how we came to craft the JOBS program.

The Anti-Workfare Case

The liberal argument against mandatory work goes something like this:

1. Poor mothers are already working; they are raising children. Taxpayers should recognize the importance of this and pay higher AFDC benefits. David Stoesz adds a new twist to this theme: AFDC mothers are actually working outside of the home to supplement their meager benefits, but do not report their income. Unreported earned income is a double-edged sword. On one hand, it taints the AFDC program with pervasive fraud. Congress does not usually throw money at tainted programs. On the other hand, if AFDC families are "getting by" somehow, combining unreported earnings (and perhaps illegal income from drugs) with their AFDC benefits, then why raise benefits? For these reasons, this is an argument that liberals did not raise during the FSA debate. Conservatives might have liked to make this case but they could not prove it.
2. Requiring poor mothers to take or prepare for tedious jobs that do not offer career advancement or benefits, such as health insurance or vacations, is mean.
3. These jobs pay so little that many would remain on the welfare rolls.
4. Where good jobs are offered, employers are displacing regular salaried employees with a cheaper, "second class" workforce.
5. Previous work-training programs have not worked. Why throw good money after bad?

Liberals conclude that federal policy makers should quit "blaming the victim." Instead, reform the terrible education system. Banish racism. Pay a living wage. Provide decent housing, adequate nutrition, health care, and child care. While working on these reforms, substantially raise AFDC benefits, which are totally inadequate. Allow welfare mothers to choose whether they will work or not. By all means, offer them incentives to go to work and provide whatever training and support services they need.

The Pro-Workfare Case

The conservatives' argument can be summarized as follows:

1. Work is inherently good. The work ethic is a central value of life in this country.
2. Most parents today, even those with young children, are in the labor force.
3. AFDC recipients who do not work are drains on the economy and are exploiting the taxpayers. Those who do work help save welfare expenditures, thereby freeing public revenues for other public purposes (pick your favorite "unmet need").
4. Providing benefits to those who can but do not work mires them in dependency and perpetuates the "cycle of poverty." The same for raising benefits.
5. Adults who work to support their families have greater self-esteem and are, therefore, better role models for children than are those who only collect welfare checks.

Conservatives would happily replace welfare with "workfare." Those who are able should at least be required to work at "real" (i.e., private sector) jobs or, if none are available, at public service jobs that are created to keep welfare parents gainfully employed.

Where liberals would reform social institutions, conservatives want to reform personal behavior. They argue that if one would take their income supports away they would be a lot more likely to pull themselves up by their proverbial bootstraps. They would start behaving like the rest of us because they would have no real alternative.

Sure they will have to start at the bottom. They may have to work hard at tedious, low-paying jobs, but there are millions of Americans who started that way and went on to live the American dream. Moreover, illegal aliens are taking those same jobs because welfare parents are too lazy or too dependent on welfare to be bothered.

Truths and Fallacies

On the left: Liberals are right to draw attention to all the conditions that contribute to poverty. The plain fact, however, is that no single piece of federal legislation is going to solve all of these problems or even a few of them in one fell swoop. In the case of FSA, the House, the Senate, and the President had serious disagreements. A more comprehensive bill would certainly have been doomed. And even if that were not true, the sorry state of the federal budget meant that the congress would not finance huge, comprehensive social programs like it did in the 1960s. Only a more modest, incremental approach had the least chance of success.

Liberals usually want to begin the incremental reform process by raising AFDC benefits. Their reasons are sound. Between 1970 and 1989 the real purchasing power of AFDC benefits declined by 37 percent, a decline that helps to explain why children are the poorest citizens in the United States, with a poverty rate of 20 percent. A great country cannot remain great when its most precious resource, its children, are ill-fed, ill-housed, and ill-educated.

The problem lies with the liberals' proposed solution. For 20 years they have rallied behind welfare bills that would raise AFDC benefits "with no strings attached." In short, more money, no requirements. (Do not be mean.) This strategy failed throughout the 1970s and 1980s, no matter which party occupied the White House or controlled the Congress. And it certainly would have failed in the Congress that sat in 1988. Moon has this point dead to rights. The "more money/don't be mean" formula has been a disaster for AFDC recipients. While liberals have busily opposed any work requirements, AFDC families have gotten a lot poorer.

On the right: Conservatives start with a serious nugget of truth: Most Americans believe that work is a dignified, desirable thing. Taxpayers and their congressional representatives will not support more generous benefits for people who do not even try to support themselves. As the labor force participation rates of mothers make all too clear, this is more true today than ever.

Conservatives are wrong, however, in thinking that requiring work is going to save much money. The evidence says otherwise. But this may change. The American economy has been producing record numbers of jobs. In addition, between 1985 and 2000 the population of young adults entering the labor force will decline by a whopping 23 percent (U.S. Census Bureau, May, 1984, p. 8).

This demographic trend, the so-called "birth dearth," has helped create a tight labor market. As employers struggle to find workers, able-bodied AFDC adults ought to be drawn into the labor force. Because of the labor shortage, many of these jobs are paying more than the minimum wage.

Conservatives claim that AFDC recipients do not take such jobs because welfare fosters dependency. The far right would overcome this by abolishing all welfare benefits. This draconian solution is expected to force people to work and to reduce the behaviors that lead to the need for AFDC, such as youngsters dropping out of school, or young girls having babies out of wedlock that they cannot support (Murray, 1984).

This sort of thinking fails to recognize two things. First, the real value of AFDC benefits has declined sharply. According to conservative reasoning this should have lead to a decline in dependency, increased work effort, and fewer births to unmarried women. The opposite has occurred. Second, many recipients are too unskilled to qualify for even minimum wage jobs.

Abolishing AFDC would create cruel hardship for most poor families and make no headway against the underlying causes of poverty. Most welfare parents want to work. The training and support they need to do so cannot be done on the cheap. Merely requiring work will not make much of a dent in the AFDC caseload.

Forging Consensus

In developing the JOBS program, we tried to acknowledge the truth on both sides of the workfare debate. The compromise was obvious: obligate AFDC adults to take bona fide jobs when they were available and make sure that they were no worse off for working. Moreover, provide some additional benefits that may actually make welfare families with a working parent better off (such as increased earned income disregards and continued help with medical care and child care). That is what the FSA does. The benefit increases we include are not nearly enough to satisfy the liberal quest for the sun, the moon, and the stars. But they are real, incremental improvements over the old law.

For those AFDC adults who cannot work because they lack skills, we challenged the orthodoxy of the left and the right. We rejected the liberal claim that it is kinder to leave such AFDC families to stew in their own juices, just as we rejected the conservative claim that mandated work is the magic bullet.

The JOBS program in every state must include a broad array of education, training, and work experience options (one of which is mandated work). No less than 7 percent of the nonexempt caseload must be served in fiscal year 1991, rising to 20 percent by fiscal year 1995.

The FSA will spend about $3.3 billion in net new federal dollars over 5 years. In roughly equal thirds, it is spent on the JOBS program; on the transitional Medicaid and child care assistance provided to families who work their way off welfare; and on the mandated extension of the AFDC-Unemployed Parent program.

In this time of budget cutting it is nothing short of amazing that we secured over $3 billion in new federal spending for AFDC families. Still, what we failed to do is just as revealing. The FSA did not raise cash benefits. We could not do it. There was insufficient support, even among Democrats. Two thirds of the bill's total cost goes to expanded benefits, but not the sort of grant increase that liberals have long sought.

The FSA brought moderate liberals and conservatives together by asserting that obligation is a two-way street. The government is obligated to care for AFDC families. Able-bodied welfare parents are equally obligated to try to become self-sufficient. Specifically, absent parents (usually fathers) must try to pay child support and custodial parents (usually mothers) must try to prepare for and take jobs.

The child support and JOBS provisions of the FSA were drafted with these objectives in mind. Will the new law work? Will we collect more child support for children and help more poor mothers learn to speak English, learn to read, graduate from high school, and even go to college? Will more poor parents earn income to help defray the costs of welfare or, best of all, earn enough to leave welfare behind for good? Let us hope the new law does some measurable amount of good. Our ability to raise AFDC benefits in the future may depend on it.

REFERENCES

Murray, C. (1984). *Losing ground: American social policy, 1950–1980.* New York: Basic Books.

U.S. Census Bureau. (May 1984). Projections of the population of the United States, by age, sex and race: 1983–2080. *Current Population Reports, Series P-25*, No. 952.

SOURCES OF FALLACY
Dishonest Tricks
Commonly Used
in Argument

1. *Use of emotional or "buzz" words.*

Remedy: Translate emotionally toned words into neutral statements.

2. *A statement in which "all" is implied but "some" is true.*

Remedy: Put the word "all" into the statement and show that it is then false. If someone tries to misrepresent an argument by saying someone meant "All _____" rather than "Some _____," restate the position.

3. *Attempted proof by selected instances, testimonials.*

Remedy: Dealt with dishonestly by selecting instances opposing a position or honestly by pointing out the true form of the proof as a statistical problem in association and either supplying the required facts or pointing out that your opponent does not have them.

4. *Extension of a proposition by contradiction or misrepresentation.*

Example: If you disapprove of X (e.g., allowing teams in from countries in which discrimination against blacks is accepted), you would have to refuse entry to teams from Russia, Portugal, etc. This would be true only if a reason applied equally well to these other countries. Otherwise, this is an inaccurate extension of an argument.

Remedy: Refer back to the more moderate position being defended.

Source: Adapted from Thouless, R.H. (1974). *Straight and crooked thinking.* London: Pan, 192–199. Additions have been made based on MacLean, E. (1981). *Between the lines: How to detect bias and propaganda in the news and everyday life.* Montreal: Black Rose Books; and Kahane, H. (1971). *Logic and contemporary rhetoric: The use of reason in everyday life.* Belmont, CA: Wadsworth.

5. *Use of a sophistical (plausible but false) formula.*

Example: Arguing that an exception proves a rule.

Remedy: Show the unsoundness of the assumption that exceptions prove a general rule.

6. *Diversion to another question, to a side issue, irrelevant objection.*

Remedy: Refuse to be diverted from the original question; restate the real question at issue.

7. *Proof by inconsequent argument.*

Remedy: Ask that the connection between the proposition and the alleged proof be explained.

8. *Arguing that we should not make efforts against X, which is admittedly evil because there is a worse evil, Y, against which efforts should be directed.*

Remedy: Note that this is a reason for making efforts to abolish Y, but no reason for not also making efforts to get rid of X.

9. *Recommending a position because it is a mean between two extremes.*

Remedy: Deny the usefulness of this principle as a method of discovering the best option. Show that your view also can be represented as a mean between two extremes.

10. *Pointing out the logical correctness of the form of an argument whose premises contain doubtful or untrue statements of fact.*

Remedy: Point out the defects of the argument's presentation of alleged facts. These may be just opinions presented as facts.

11. *Use of a logically unsound argument.*

Remedy: The unsoundness of arguments can be seen when the form of the argument is clearly displayed; make a simple diagram of an argument so revealing its unsoundness.

12. *Argument in a circle (pseudoexplanations).*

Example: This child throws rocks at other children, therefore he is aggressive. We know he is aggressive because he throws rocks.

Remedy: Show the circularity of the argument.

13. *Begging the question.*

This refers to assuming the truth or falsity of what you are trying to prove. An example is: "The disgraceful practice of strikes must be put to an end." It is assumed that strikes are disgraceful; no evidence is presented supporting this claim.

Remedy: Restate the argument clearly so that the lack of evidence is revealed.

14. *Discussing a verbal proposition as if it were a factual one: confusing verbal and factual elements in a proposition.*

Remedy: Point out how much of the question at issue is a difference in the use of words and how much (if at all) it is a difference as to fact or values.

15. *Use of tautology (e.g., too much of the thing attacked is bad) as if it were a factual judgment.*

Remedy: Point out that the verbal form of the statement makes it necessarily true.

16. *Misuse of speculative argument.*

Remedy: Note that what *is* cannot be inferred from what *ought to be* or from what the speaker feels must be.

17. *Change in the meaning of a term during a discussion.*

Remedy: Define the term or substitute equivalent words at points where the term is used and see whether use of these words will make true other statements in which the term is used.

18. *False dilemma (use of a dilemma that ignores a continuous series of possibilities between two extremes).*

Remedy: Refuse to accept either alternative, but point to the continuity that has been ignored. Note that this argument is the same as asking "Is this paper black or white?" when it is, in fact, gray.

19. *The use of the fact of continuity to throw doubt on a real difference.*

Remedy: Note that the difference is real; that use of the same argument would deny the difference between "black" and "white" or "hot" and "cold."

20. *Illegitimate use of or demand for definition.*

Remedy: If someone uses definitions to produce clear-cut views of facts that are not clear-cut, point out how complicated the facts really are. Refuse formal definition but adopt some other method of making your meaning clear if a person tries to force you to define terms for the same purpose.

21. *Suggestions by repeated affirmation, use of a confident manner ("bold assertions") or by prestige.*

Remedy: The best safeguard against all three of these tricks of suggestion is a knowledge of suggestion, so that their use may be detected. Merely pointing out that the speaker is trying to create conviction by repeated assertion in a confident manner may be enough to neutralize this device.

22. *Prestige by false credentials.*

Remedy: Expose the falsity of titles, degree, etc. that are used.

23. *Prestige by the use of pseudotechnical jargon.*

Remedy: Seek clear explanations.

24. *Pretending to fail to understand backed by prestige.*

Remedy: Offer clear explanations of your concerns/positions.

25. *Appeal to mere authority.*

Remedy: Consider whether the individuals alleged to have authority have a sound reason for making their assertions. For example, is a famous athlete really an authority on cereals?

26. *Overcoming resistance to a doubtful proposition by initial statement of a few easily accepted ones.*

Remedy: Knowledge of this strategy and preparedness for it are the best safeguards against its effects.

27. *Statement of a doubtful position so that it fits in with the thought-habits or prejudices of the audience.*

Remedy: A habit of questioning what appears obvious is the best safeguard. Restate the proposition in a new context in which beliefs do not lead to ready acceptance.

28. *Use of generally accepted predigested thought as premises in arguments.*

Remedy: Point out, with a backing of evidence, that matters are more complicated than someone supposes.

29. *An attitude of detachment such as saying, ''There is much to be said on both sides, so no decision can be made.''*

Remedy: Note that taking no action has practical consequences no less real than those that result from acting on options in dispute, and that this is not more likely than any other to be the right solution.

30. *Argument by mere analogy.*

Remedy: Examine the alleged analogy and point out where it breaks down.

31. *Argument by forced analogy.*

Remedy: Show how other analogies supporting different conclusions could be used.

32. *Angering an opponent so that he will argue badly.*

Remedy: Do not get angry however annoying or provoking an opponent may be.

33. *Special pleading.*

Remedy: Apply special arguments to other propositions that people are not willing to accept.

34. *Commending or condemning a proposition because of its practical consequences to the hearer.*

Remedy: Cultivate a habit of recognizing tendencies to be guided by prejudices and self-interest and of distrusting your judgment on questions in which you are practically concerned.

35. *Argument by attributing prejudices or motives to an opponent; attacking the person not the argument (ad hominem).*

Remedy: Note that other prejudices may equally well determine the opposite view and that, in any case, the question of why a person holds an opinion is an entirely different question from whether the opinion is or is not true.

36. *Incomplete quotation.*

Remedy: Request or seek out complete quotation.

37. *Quoting out of context.*

Remedy: Ask for the context of the quote.

38. *Innuendo and baseless speculation.*

Innuendo is a remark with an implied criticism or accusation. Such statements subtly question the credibility of individuals, groups, or causes.

Remedy: Seek clarification of the innuendo and request evidence supporting it.

39. *Ignoring the question.*

Remedy: This common strategy works surprisingly often. Restate the question at issue. A common ploy for ignoring real issues is to make a joke instead of dealing with the argument seriously. This can distract listeners or make the other person look stupid or pedantic for sticking to the point.

40. *Misuse of statistics.*

Examples include referring to correlations to support causal assumptions, use of selected instances (see No. 3), and use of selected portions of graphs.

Remedy: The remedy depends on the kind of misuse. Point out that correlations do not yield information about causal relationships. When confronted with attempted proof by selected instances note that data are needed about all four cells of a four-cell contingency table to determine the relationship between two variables; one cannot simply point to the one cell supporting a favored position (usually this is the positive-positive cell).

41. *Selective omission or suppression of critical facts.*

This refers to presenting just facts that support a favored position while ignoring other significant data. This is an especially insidious one because listeners might not be aware of important related facts.

Remedy: Talk to people holding other views, explore all possible effects of a decision, and ask a speaker if there are any important consequences of a proposed option that have not been mentioned. He or she may not be willing to lie and so reveal the suppressed evidence or be unwilling to appear uninformed at a later date by not mentioning other important effects under direct questioning.

42. *Snob appeal.*

This refers to appeals based on elitism.

Remedy: Point out that this appeal provides no support for a position.

43. *"Plain folks" appeal.*

Also known as provincialism: Assuming that the familiar is better or more important (Kahane, p. 71). This is the opposite of snob appeal.

Remedy: Point out that this appeal provides no evidence for a position.

44. *Ridicule of a position.*

Remedy: Restate your position clearly, noting again why you think it should be taken seriously. If the ridicule is offered by a person in authority, you could also point out that this is a common (but not very sophisticated) trick of attempting to undermine a position.

45. *Hasty generalization.*

Arguing that what is true for some cases is true for all cases.

Remedy: Show that the generalization does not apply to all cases by giving examples.

46. *Bandwagon appeal* (appeals to consensus).

An example is "Everybody is behind _____ ."

Remedy: Note that because many people believe or support something does not mean it is accurate. Also, there may not even be a consensus; that is, "Everybody may indeed *not* be behind _____ ."

47. *Glittering generalizations.*

Use of abstract "buzz" words, such as "brotherhood."

Remedy: Seek clarification as to what exactly they refer to.

48. *Name calling.*

Use of negative labels to refer to a disliked person or position such as "mechanistic" or "officious." This common ploy is often increased in effectiveness by being paired with behaviors that attempt to show that the person using the negative labels does so only because he has been forced to by the "supposed facts" related to the names used. Or a joking manner is used so that the label will leave its mark but the name caller can deny that he meant it in "that way."

Remedy: Point out that name calling is just that—without convincing evidence to substantiate such claims.

49. *Use of stereotypes.*

A stereotype is an oversimplified belief that all people in a particular group share the same characteristics. There may be some elements of accuracy in a stereotype but not enough to accurately represent the broad array of characteristics and situations to which the stereotype refers. Examples of stereotypes are "old lady" and "welfare cheat." Stereotypes are often used for the same purposes as name calling.

Remedy: Show that the stereotype is not accurate through examples.

50. *Two wrongs make a right.*

This fallacy argues that if he does it, then it is OK if I do it. Appealing to common practice is a variant of this strategy.

Remedy: Note that this provides no evidence for a position.

51. *Inconsistency.*

Arguing from contradictory premises.

Remedy: Point out the contradictory nature of premises, that both cannot be accurate.

52. *False charge of inconsistency.*

This refers to alleging an inconsistency when in fact none exists, as when someone has changed his or her belief.

Remedy: Describe why the charge of inconsistency is not accurate.

53. *Use of doubtful evidence* (see also number 10).

This includes the fallacy of the *unknown fact* (some facts cannot be known by anyone) and *doubtful evaluation* (use of an unsupported value judgment in an argument) (Kahane, 1971, p. 9).

Remedy: In case of unknown facts, point out that these facts cannot be known (e.g., exactly how many gay or lesbian people there are in the United States). In cases of doubtful evaluation, note that value judgments are being used to support a position rather than evidence being provided.

54. *Tokenism.*

Inaccurate perception of an ineffective gesture as an adequate effort.

Remedy: Point out the minimal effort extended using comparative data.

55. *Ambiguity.*

Use of vague terms to mislead.

Remedy: Seek clarification of terms.

56. *Associating oneself or a preferred option with positive symbols.*

Remedy: Note that this provides no evidence for a position.

57. *Using empty, hackneyed phrases that are vague, such as "on target," "a window on."*

Remedy: Seek clarification of terms.

58. *Newsspeak.*

This refers to "language that distorts, confuses or hides reality" (MacLean, 1981, p. 43). Examples include "neutralized" (meaning killed) and community care (referring to the release of mental patients from mental hospitals with no follow-up care).

Remedy: Seek clarification of the exact meaning of such terms.

59. *Strawman.*

Attacking (or defending) a position similar to, but different from, one presented; an argument is distorted and this distorted version is then attacked.

Remedy: Reaffirm the true position asserted.

60. *Hasty conclusion (use of relevant but insufficient evidence to reach a conclusion).*

Remedy: Seek additional evidence for a position.

61. *Questionable classification.*
The incorrect classification of something or some person.
Remedy: Describe why the classification is inaccurate.